The Ritual of May Day in Western Europe

T0384969

Eric Hobsbawm claimed that the international May Day, which dates back to a proclamation in 1889 by the Second International, 'is perhaps the most ambitious of labour rituals'. The first international May Day demonstrations in 1890 were widely celebrated across Europe and became the one day each year when organized labour could present its goals to the public, an eight-hour workday was the first concrete demand, shortly followed by those for improved working conditions, universal suffrage, peace among nations, and international solidarity. The May Day ritual celebration was the self-assertion and self-definition of the new labour class through class organization. Thus, it was trade unions and social democratic and socialist parties throughout Europe which took the initiative and have sustained May Day as a labour ritual to this day. Part I of this theoretically-informed volume explores how May Day demonstrations have evolved and taken different trajectories in different political contexts. Part II focuses on May Day rituals today. By comparing demonstration level data of over 2000 questionnaires from six countries, including Belgium, Italy, Spain, Sweden, Switzerland, and the UK, the reader is able to gain a thorough understanding of how participants are bestowing meaning on May Day rituals. By concluding with reflections on the future of the May Day ritual in Western Europe, this ground-breaking book provides a detailed analysis of its evolution as a protest event.

Abby Peterson, University of Gothenburg, Sweden.

Herbert Reiter, European University Institute, Florence, Italy.

The Mobilization Series on Social Movements, Protest, and Culture
Edited by Hank Johnston
San Diego State University, USA

Published in conjunction with *Mobilization: An International Quarterly*, the premier research journal in the field, this series disseminates high quality new research and scholarship in the fields of social movements, protest, and contentious politics. The series is interdisciplinary in focus and publishes monographs and collections of essays by new and established scholars.

Performing Political Opposition in Russia
The Case of the Youth Group Oborona
Laura Lyytikäinen

Economic Crisis and Mass Protest
The Pots and Pans Revolution in Iceland
Jón Gunnar Bernburg

Crisis and Social Mobilization in Contemporary Spain
The M15 Movement
Edited by Benjamín Tejerina Montaña and Ignacia Perugorría

The Brazilian Landless Movement
Critical Dialogues on History, Experiences and Trajectories of a Radical Social Movement
Edited by Alex Flynn and Elena Calvo-González

Austerity and Protest
Popular Contention in Times of Economic Crisis
Edited by Marco Giugni and Maria T. Grasso

Social Movement Dynamics
New Perspectives on Theory and Research from Latin America
Edited by Federico M. Rossi and Marisa von Bülow

The Ritual of May Day in Western Europe

Past, Present and Future

Edited by

Abby Peterson

Department of Sociology and Work Science, University of Gothenburg

Herbert Reiter

European University Institute, Florence

Routledge
Taylor & Francis Group

LONDON AND NEW YORK

First published 2016 by Routledge

2 Park Square, Milton Park, Abingdon, Oxfordshire OX14 4RN

52 vanderbilt Avenue, New York, NY 10017

Routledge is an imprint of the Taylor & Francis Group, an informa business

First issued in paperback 2020

British Library Cataloguing in Publication Data
A catalogue record for this book is available from the British Library

Library of Congress Cataloguing in Publication Data
Names: Peterson, Abby, author. | Reiter, Herbert, author.
Title: The ritual of May Day in Western Europe : past, present and future / by Abby Peterson and Herbert Reiter. Description: [2016] |
Series: The mobilization series on social movements, protest, and culture |
Includes bibliographical references and index.
Identifiers: LCCN 2015043215 (print) | LCCN 2015047182 (ebook) |
ISBN 9781472415271 (hardback : alk. paper) | ISBN 9781315553344 (ebook) |
Subjects: LCSH: May Day (Labor holiday)–Europe, Western. |
Labor–Europe, Western–History.
Classification: LCC HD7791.P459 2016 (print) | LCC HD7791 (ebook) |
DDC 394.2627094–dc23
LC record available at http://lccn.loc.gov/2015043215

ISBN: 978-1-4724-1527-1 (hbk)
ISBN: 978-0-367-59650-7 (pbk)

Typeset in Times New Roman
by Out of House Publishing

Contents

List of Figures   vii
List of Tables   viii
Notes on Contributors   x
Foreword: The Myth of May Day   xii
RICK FANTASIA
Acknowledgements   xvii
List of Abbreviations   xviii

1   **Introduction**
     Western European May Day Rituals: Past,
     Present and Future   1
     ABBY PETERSON AND HERBERT REITER

2   **The Origins of May Day: History and Memory**   14
     HERBERT REITER

3   **The First of May in Germany and Italy**   31
     HERBERT REITER

4   **The May Day Tradition in Finland and Sweden**   75
     CHRISTER THÖRNQVIST, TAPIO BERGHOLM AND
     MARGARETHA MELLBERG

5   **May Day in Spain: Socialist and Anarchist Traditions** 106
     EDUARDO ROMANOS AND JOSÉ LUIS LEDESMA

6   **May Day in Britain**   133
     CHRIS WRIGLEY

7   **The Context of Contemporary May Day Demonstrations**
     in Six European Countries   160
     ABBY PETERSON

8   Who Takes Part in May Day Marches?   187
    MAGNUS WENNERHAG

9   Why Do People Demonstrate on May Day?   217
    MATTIAS WAHLSTRÖM

10 The Future of May Day   245
    ABBY PETERSON AND HERBERT REITER

    Appendix
    Methods for Studying May Day Demonstrators: Sampling,
    Estimating Non-Response Bias and Pooling Data with
    General Population Surveys
    MATTIAS WAHLSTRÖM AND MAGNUS WENNERHAG   262

    Index   279

List of Figures

5.1 May Day contention, Spain, 1900–1930 116
9.1 Percentage of participants citing broader motive types 234
9.2 Demonstration residuals for external influence
(controlling for country clustering) 237
A.1 Example of how an ideal-typical demonstration
can be sampled 268

List of Tables

8.1 Oesch class scheme, 9-class version   192

8.2 Socio-demographic characteristics for participants in May Day demonstrations surveyed within the CCC project   194

8.3 Socio-demographics: participants in May Day and other CCC-surveyed demonstrations and general population (ESS5 data)   197

8.4 Class composition (Oesch-9) in May Day demonstrations surveyed within the CCC project   200

8.5 Class composition (Oesch-9): participants in May Day and other CCC-surveyed demonstrations and general population (ESS5 data)   202

8.6 Class identification among participants in May Day demonstrations surveyed within the CCC project   204

8.7 Class identification: participants in May Day and other CCC-surveyed demonstrations   206

8.8 Binary logistic regression for determinants of working-class and middle-class identification (CCC data)   207

8.9 Binary logistic regression: factors contributing to May Day participation (CCC and SOM institute data), part 1   210

8.10 Binary logistic regression: factors contributing to May Day participation (CCC and SOM institute data), part 2   211

9.1 Types of motives   231

9.2 Percentage within each category of demonstrations citing different types of motives, weighted according to relative demonstration size in country   232

9.3 Binary logistic regressions with external motives as dependent variable   238

9.4 Binary logistic regressions with external motives as
      dependent variable   240
A.1 Overview of surveyed demonstrations   264
A.2 Surveyed demonstrations, distributed questionnaires and
      response rates   266
A.3 Cases of significant non-response bias in the dataset   270
A.4 Survey question wordings and response alternatives   274

Notes on Contributors

Tapio Bergholm is Associate Professor at the University of Helsinki, Finland, and the University of Eastern Finland. His research interests are the history of industrial relations and transport. He is presently engaged in a three-volume history of the Confederation of Finnish Trade Unions covering the years 1944–1977, 2005, 2007 and 2012.

Rick Fantasia is the Barbara Richmond 1940 Professor in the Social Sciences at Smith College, in Northampton, Massachusetts, USA. His research and writing have concerned labour and culture, and their interpenetration, in the US and in France. His book *Cultures of Solidarity* (1988) received three awards from the ASA. Fantasia's book (with K. Voss), *Des syndicats domestiqués: Répression patronale et résistance syndicale aux États Unis*, was commissioned by Pierre Bourdieu for his Raisons d'Agir book series (2003) and an expanded English edition was published in 2004 as *Hard Work: Remaking the American Labor Movement*.

José Luis Ledesma is a Juan de la Cierva Fellow in the Department of History of Political Thought and Social and Political Movements at the Complutense University of Madrid, Spain, where he teaches contemporary history. He previously taught at the University of Saragossa (2008–2013). He has a PhD in History and Civilization from the European University Institute (Florence, Italy) and his work mainly deals with the Spanish Civil War, violence and anarchism.

Margaretha Mellberg has a PhD in History from the University of Gothenburg, Sweden. She has been a lecturer and researcher at the University of Gothenburg and the University College of Gotland, Sweden. Mellberg's field of research is educational history with a focus on literacy and compulsory education in Sweden. In addition she has researched Finland's modern political history.

Abby Peterson is Professor of Sociology at the Department of Sociology and Work Science, University of Gothenburg, Sweden. Peterson is currently directing a research programme on 'policing ethnicity' and a research project on Pride parades in seven European countries and Mexico. She has published extensively within the fields of social movement research, cultural sociology and criminology.

Herbert Reiter is a research assistant at the European University Institute (Florence, Italy) for the ERC project 'Mobilizing for Democracy' directed by Donatella della Porta. He has a PhD in History and Civilization from the European University Institute. Among his publications are: *Policing Protest: The Control of Mass Demonstrations in Western Democracies* (1998, ed. with D. della Porta); *Polizia e protesta. L'ordine pubblico dalla liberazione ai 'no global'* (2003, with D. della Porta); *Policing Transnational Protest* (2006, ed. with D. della Porta and A. Peterson).

Eduardo Romanos is a Ramón y Cajal Fellow in the Department of Sociology I at the Complutense University of Madrid, Spain. He has a PhD in Political and Social Sciences from the European University Institute, Italy, and a European Doctorate Certificate in Social History from Ca' Foscari University of Venice, Italy. Recent publications include articles in *Contemporary European History*, *Social Movement Studies* and the *Journal of Historical Sociology*.

Christer Thörnqvist is Associate Professor in Work Science and Senior Lecturer in Business Administration at the University of Skövde, Sweden. His research interests lie within the field of industrial relations and HRM. He has published extensively on collective bargaining, industrial conflict, workers' representation and influence, labour legislation, labour migration and precarious work.

Mattias Wahlström is Associate Professor at the Department of Sociology and Work Science, University of Gothenburg, Sweden. He has a PhD in sociology from the University of Gothenburg. His research mainly concerns social movements, protest and the policing of social protest, and his recent publications include articles in *Global Environmental Politics*, *International Sociology*, *Mobilization*, *Social Movement Studies* and *Environment and Planning D: Society and Space*.

Magnus Wennerhag is a researcher at the Department of Sociology and Work Science, University of Gothenburg and is Senior Lecturer at Södertörn University, Sweden. He has a PhD in Sociology from Lund University. His research mainly concerns social movements, political participation, social stratification and theories of modernity.

Chris Wrigley is Emeritus Professor of Modern British History at the University of Nottingham. His books include *David Lloyd George and the British Labour Movement* (1976); *Arthur Henderson* (1990); *Lloyd George and the Challenges of Labour: The Post-War Coalition 1918–1922* (1990) and the edited volumes *A History of British Industrial Relations 1875–1979* (1982–1997, 3 vols) and *Challenges of Labour: Central and Western Europe, 1917–1920* (1993).

Foreword
The Myth of May Day

Rick Fantasia

Like an epic poem, May Day has told an enduring story, one that has annually recounted the life of a social group. Replete with legendary figures, heroic deeds and transcendent acts, May Day has played a central role in the social process and collective formation that has been known as 'The Working Class'. Indeed, May Day has performed a vital ritual of 'group-ness' that has given form to the working class. Like all social classes, and all social groups, the working class can be seen as being partly real and partly mythic. Real in its corporeal dimensions; in its organizational forms; in the dull drudgery of routinized labour; in its material deprivations and powerlessness; as well as in its periodic acts of refusal. But the working class is also real as a mythic construction; in its evocative forms, its symbolic vocabulary and in its capacity to transcend itself in the imagination of its members and its followers.

May Day has been a central ritual site in which the working class, normally invisible, is visualized in its mobilization and assembly, thus demonstrating its social presence in practice. It is a ritual assembly that also serves as a barometer of its potential strength. That means that May Day has also been a symbolic (but very real!) site of struggle over the jurisdictional claims made by competing social and political groups; each seeking to represent the working class, to itself and to others, and to act as its organizational embodiment, against competing organizations, competing groups. Where labour organizations and working classes must operate in a hostile social universe, where the market, for example, is becoming the supreme arbiter of all that is good and valuable, they must constantly 'demonstrate' their potential to advance the position of the group. 'Demonstrations' are, after all, just that. They 'demonstrate', to participants and potential participants, to both friends and foe, not what a group 'is' at any given time, but what it is *potentially*, with respect to mobilization, commitment and solidarity. Whether they have effectively demonstrated their potential tends to be what is at stake in the frequent disparities and disputes between the activists and the authorities, over the 'actual' or 'true' numbers of participants in demonstrations (Bourdieu 1993, p. 175). Not only are the numbers objects of contention, but so is the collective bodily pose of the demonstrators. Are they militant or peaceful, disruptive or orderly? Are their slogans and symbols reassuring or threatening? In other words, group formation and collective actions are social representations and, as such, are never fully formed, are in flux, in contention, and are thus also partly allegorical. For well over a century May Day has served as just such a crucial social representation.

Or at least I think so, since throughout my lifetime, and as an American, I have only really been able to experience May Day as a kind of chimera. The images of May Day that I carried around in my head were those drawn from newspaper clippings and the television news, to be sure, but were also furnished by sympathetic elders, and especially by my grandfather. Usually in response to my begging him: 'Grandpa, please tell me again about when you were in the war.' He would recount the stories of his experience in World War I, and about how he and his fellow soldiers of the Austro-Hungarian army, defeated on the Italian front, had dropped their weapons and returned to Budapest to participate in the revolutionary uprising of Hungarian workers. His exciting depiction of May Day in Budapest in 1919 was of a world being suddenly turned upside down, as the streets overflowed with joy and celebration for a new world being birthed. As a young boy, I was mesmerized by such tales and, along with the photos and drawings from books that he shared, a vivid picture of May Day was created for me. In this mental tableau, a veritable sea of workers filled the broad boulevards for as far as the eye could see, with placards and red banners dancing above the crowd, accompanied by the music of marching bands and the chants of the multitudes echoing off of the buildings. It was a story recounted as a kind of sacred narrative of internationalism, of solidarity and, ultimately, of human potential. While I suppose these images were initially associated with Grandpa's Budapest, they were gradually blended together with images of Barcelona, and Paris and Bologna and Hamburg, and any number of other European cities.

From the standpoint of an American, May Day was regarded as a European celebration, a foreign thing, and for the typical American citizen, of both my and my parents' generation, May Day was not only a foreign, but a Soviet thing. Featured prominently by a US media fully engaged by the Cold War, Soviet May Day was presented in images decidedly different from those my grandfather had inscribed in me. For most Americans, May Day was presented as a 'Communist holiday'; as a military spectacle, designed to showcase the Soviet Union's latest military hardware. Interspersed with brigades of uniformed troops, the fearsome weaponry was ritually marched in front of a gaggle of greying party apparatchiks, huddled together approvingly on a viewing platform in Red Square. For most Americans, this was the only May Day that existed, represented as a direct threat to our putative freedom and to the security and well being of our families. May Day was presented as the terrifying battle cry of The Enemy, and is the version that is still very likely etched into the psyches of most Americans of a certain age.

The supreme irony, of course, is that May Day has been celebrated virtually everywhere but in the place of its birth. Although its true provenance has been somewhat uncertain, whether the roots of May Day can be accurately traced back, directly or indirectly, to Chicago and the Haymarket massacre of 1886, as has often been asserted (and as is fruitfully and judiciously examined in the present volume), it is indisputable that May Day as a workers' day was established in the context of the struggle to secure the eight-hour working day. This struggle had been an ongoing one, in both Europe and the United States, but a series of explosive and bloody events in Chicago in early May of 1886, culminating in the execution of the Haymarket martyrs, provided the labour movement in Europe (and in the US) with a bracingly dramatic narrative. In other words, Haymarket presented May Day with a kind of militant 'creation myth', and thereby made it available for use by certain social and political perspectives, against others, in the struggle to assert the 'true' meaning of May Day.

For as we learn from so many of the chapters in this wonderfully rich volume, very different inflections of meaning have been attached to May Day, in different societies, in different historical contexts, as well as in the different political or ideological factions within a labour movement. So it would not be surprising to find that the story of the genesis of May Day (the 'legend of the origins' as it is termed in the book) is shaded differently by competing groups (i.e. by groups of moderates and of radicals) within a labour movement, with each stressing different elements of the story to advance their positions against others in the movement. Indeed, in a related way, one senses in the debates over the origins of May Day a certain resistance, or hesitation, from some European analysts to the possibility of a May Day spawned by American events. In other words, there can seem to be an almost proprietary posture in questions about the role of Haymarket in the origins of May Day. This would be understandable, for May Day in Europe has been so firmly established for so long, and has been consecrated to such an extent that it serves as a national holiday in many European nation states. On the other hand, claims for the American roots of May Day can appear like the affectations of an *arriviste* or an amateur. Moreover, such misgivings may be compounded by resentment toward the hegemonic pretensions of the US in the world. That is, resistance may not just rest in different interpretations of historical facts, but in a certain predisposition against American cultural and economic 'impositions' (in Europe and elsewhere). At the same time, we might do well to remember that, of the eight Haymarket martyrs falsely convicted of a crime that they did not commit, six were European immigrants themselves (five Germans and one Englishman), thereby complicating attempts to determine May Day's origins as truly 'American' or 'European'.

Whether such latent interpretive nuances can be discerned in the analysis of its origins, the fact is that May Day was subsequently, and quite effectively, outlawed in American society. Moreover, there is another irony that resides in the fact that the same configuration of social and institutional forces that conspired to legally murder the Haymarket martyrs, along with several striking workers on the picket line at the nearby McCormick Reaper factory (whose killings precipitated the Haymarket rally in the first place), were able to mobilize once again, some 65 years later, to essentially ban May Day, along with those political movements seeking to promote it. As World War II came to an end and with President Roosevelt gone, the largest corporations in the US launched a new offensive against labour. Even though the US had emerged from the war in a dominant position in the world, with foreign competition all but eliminated by the war's devastation, and with the heavy debt incurred by foreign governments creating a 'useful dependency' on American bankers and industrialists, two problems were seen to remain. These were summarized by Charles E. Wilson, head of the General Electric Corporation, upon his entry into the administration of President Truman as: 'Russia abroad, Labor at home' (cited in Boyer & Morais 1955, p. 345). The Cold War fever of anti-communism would provide a solution to both problems, personified in the signing of the Taft–Hartley Act. This was a law enacted to outlaw militant labour practices by workers, to drive out left-wing union leaders and to domesticate the system of labour relations (cf. Fantasia & Voss 2004, ch. 2). Anti-communist purges of artists, journalists, teachers and union leaders were designed to constrict political discourse by isolating groups likely to promote May Day in the labour movement and in the society at large. As the historian Haverty-Stacke (2009) has written: 'The story of how Americans abandoned this radical holiday – then came to forget its history in the United States – became a part of the process through which political discourse in America dramatically narrowed in the two decades after World War II' (p. 193).

Further, she makes the point that in the context of the anti-communist purges, May Day proponents in the US were forced to defend their position by stressing the distinctly *American* roots of May Day, in order to ward off any accusations of 'foreign' influence or association (pp. 207–208). Thus the claims, only partially true, but apparently necessary for political survival in the Cold War context, that May Day had American roots and that it was an American tradition. This would seem to complicate, and add another irony to, my earlier suggestion about resistance by Europeans to American assertions about the origins of May Day! An added paradox is the fact that, since the US was only at the early stages of its hegemonic reign in the immediate post-war years, its economic and cultural will had not yet been fully imposed on Europe.

To this day, if asked, most Americans would know very little, if anything, about the Haymarket Massacre or about May Day itself. However, Europeans have been asked about May Day, thanks to this very book. That is, this remarkable study includes not only the historical analyses of May Day demonstrations in six European countries, examining the changing dynamics and meanings of ritualized May Day demonstrations and celebrations through wars and dictatorships and liberations, but also includes a fascinating, theoretically informed survey of the demonstrators themselves, illustrating their social characteristics and explaining the reasons for their participation. Thus, we have a historically grounded analysis that is also especially timely, for it is intended to help us to grasp the social logic of collective action, across Europe, through the recent wave of anti-austerity protests and in the context of the neoliberal onslaught. Whether a scholar of social movements or an interested, informed citizen, the fortunate reader of this book will come to see May Day through a new lens, as a vividly drawn, yet changing picture under which various, and even competing, captions are written.

References

Bourdieu, P. (1993). *Sociology in Question*. Thousand Oaks, CA: Sage Publications.

Boyer, R.O., and Morais, H.M. (1955). *Labor's Untold Story*. New York: United Electrical, Radio, and Machine Workers of America.

Fantasia, R., and Voss, K. (2004). *Hard Work: Remaking the American Labor Movement*. Berkeley: University of California Press.

Haverty-Stacke, D.T. (2009). *America's Forgotten Holiday: May Day and Nationalism, 1867–1960*. New York: New York University Press.

Acknowledgements

The research for chapters 7, 8 and 9 was conducted with support from the Swedish Council for Working Life and Social Research (FAS 2008-1799) and the European Science Foundation, EUROSCORES Programme and is part of the collaborative research project 'Caught in the Act of Protest: Contextualizing Contestation' (CCC) led by Professor Bert Klandermans. Herbert Reiter acknowledges the support of the European Research Council advanced scholars' grant 'Mobilizing for Democracy' (GA 2691) awarded to Donatella della Porta.

List of Abbreviations

ABVV/FGTB	*Algemeen Belgisch Vakverbond and Fédération Générale du Travail de Belgique*, Belgian Socialist Union Confederation
ACLI	*Associazioni cristiane lavoratori italiani*, Italian Catholic Workers' Associations
ACV/CSC	*Algemeen Christelijk Vakverbond and Confédération des Syndicats Chrétiens*, Confederation of Christian Trade Unions of Belgium
ACLVB/CGSLB	*Algemene Centrale der Liberale Vakbonden van België and Centrale Générale des Syndicats Libéraux de Belgique*, Belgian Liberal Union Confederation
ADGB	*Allgemeiner Deutscher Gewerkschaftsbund*, Social democratic German trade union federation of the Weimar Republic
AFL	American Federation of Labor
CCC	European Science Foundation Euroscores Programme 'Caught in the Act of Protest: Contextualizing Contestation' (database)
CCOO	*Comisiones Obreras*, The Workers' Commissions (Spain)
CDU	*Christlich Demokratische Union Deuschlands*, German Christian Democratic Party
CGIL	*Confederazione Generale Italiana del Lavoro*, Communist-socialist Italian trade union federation
CGT	*Confederación General del Trabajo*, General Confederation of Labour (Spain)
CIG	*Confederación Intersindical Galega*, Galician Union Confederacy
CISAL	*Confederazione Italiana Sindacati Autonomi Lavoratori*, Italian Confederation of Autonomous Workers' Unions
CISL	*Confederazione Italiana Sindacati Lavoratori*, Catholic Italian trade union federation
CISNAL	*Confederazione Italiana Sindacati Nazionali dei Lavoratori*, Neo-fascist Italian trade union federation
CNT	*Confederación Nacional del Trabajo*, National Confederation of Labour (Spain)
Cobas	*Confederazione dei Comitati di base*, Italian grassroots trade union federation

CONFSAL	*Confederazione Generale dei Sindacati Autonomi dei Lavoratori*, The Workers' Autonomous Trade Union Confederation (Italy)
CPGB	Communist Party of Great Britain
CUB	*Confederazione Unitaria di Base*, Italian grassroots trade union federation
DGB	*Deutscher Gewerkschaftsbund*, Trade Union Federation of the German Federal Republic
EGP	Eriksson–Goldthorpe–Portocarero class scheme
ESS	European Social Survey
ESS5	2010 European Social Survey Round 5
FCOs	*Fackliga Centralorganisationer*, Swedish Central Trade Union Associations
GLATUC	Greater London Association of Trade Union Councils
IKL	*Isänmaallinen Kansanliike*, The People's Movement of the Fatherland (Finland)
ILP	Independent Labour Party (UK)
KPD	*Kommunistische Partei Deutschlands*, German Communist Party
LCC	London County Council
LO	*Landsorganisationen*, Swedish Trade Union Confederation (blue-collar)
MSI	*Movimento Sociale Italiano*, Italian Social Movement (neo-fascist party)
N-VA	*Nieuw-Vlaamse Alliantie*, New Flemish Alliance
NUWM	National Unemployed Workers' Movement (UK)
OECD	Organisation for Economic Cooperation and Development
PCE	*Partido Comunista de España*, Communist Party of Spain
PCI	*Partito Comunista Italiano*, Italian Communist Party
PD	*Partito Democratico*, Italian Democratic Party
PS	*Parti Socialiste*, Francophone Socialist Party (Belgium)
PSI	*Partito Socialista Italiano*, Italian Socialist Party
PSOE	*Partido Socialista Obrero Español*, Socialist Workers Party of Spain
SAC	*Sveriges Arbetares Centralorganisation*, The Central Organization of Sweden's Workers (syndicalist)
SAK	*Suomen Ammattiliittojen Keskusjärjestö*, Confederation of Finnish Trade Unions
SAP	*Socialdemokratiska Arbetarepartiet*, Swedish Social Democratic Party
SDF	Social Democratic Federation (UK)
SDP	*Suomen Sosialidemokraatti*, Finnish Social Democratic Party
SED	*Sozialistische Einheitspartei Deutschlands*, East German Socialist Union Party
SKP	*Sveriges Kommunistiska Parti*, Swedish Communist Party
SOM	Swedish public opinion research institute
SPD	*Sozialdemokratische Partei Deutschlands*, German Social Democratic Party
SSV	*Sveriges Socialdemokratiska Vänsterparti*, Swedish Social Democratic Left Party

TCO	*Tjänstemännens Centralorganisation*, The Swedish Confederation for Professional Employees
TUC	UK Trades Union Congress
UGL	*Unione Generale del Lavoro, General Labour Union* (Italy, post-fascist trade union federation)
UGT	*Unión General de Trabajadores, General Union of Workers* (Spain)
UIL	*Unione Italiana del lavoro, Italian Labour Union* (secular centre-left trade union federation)
USPD	*Unabhängige Sozialdemokratische Partei Deutschlands*, German Independent Social Democratic Party
WFTU	World Federation of Trade Unions

1 Introduction

Western European May Day Rituals Past, Present and Future

Abby Peterson and Herbert Reiter

Eric Hobsbawm (1984, p. 76) claimed that the international May Day 'is perhaps the most ambitious of labour rituals'. It dates back to a resolution passed at the founding congress of the Second International in Paris in 1889, which called for an international demonstration to be organized on 1 May 1890 demanding the eight-hour workday and other measures for the protection of workers (see Chapter 2). The first international May Day demonstrations in 1890 were widely celebrated across Europe and were held in Stockholm, Madrid, London, Brussels, Geneva and other capitals and cities (Foner 1986, p. 45). The remarkable and often unexpected success of these demonstrations led to the rapid rise and institutionalization of May Day in Western Europe. At least to a certain extent this evolution was the result of popular enthusiasm and pressure from below overcoming the cautious stance of working-class parties and unions, and can be described as unintended and unplanned (Hobsbawm 1991, p. 106).

After 1890 May Day became the one day each year when organized labour presented its concrete 'class demands of the proletariat' to the public, with the eight-hour workday and improved working conditions to be joined by the struggle against war, international solidarity and (in countries with franchise limitations) universal suffrage. Of equal importance for the success of the May Day liturgy was the evocation of the new (socialist) society to come. Outside the range of anarchist influence (see Chapter 2), in fact, May Day did not commemorate anything, 'it was about nothing but the future' (Hobsbawm 1991, p. 118). It was labour organizations – social democratic and socialist trade unions and political parties – throughout Western Europe which took the initiative in shaping May Day as a labour ritual and which have sustained it to this day.

According to Eric Hobsbawm (1984, p. 80), May Day rituals were essentially self-assertions and self-definitions of the new labour class through class organization. As the German social democratic daily *Vorwärts* (1 May 1902) stressed, May Day in addition became a day for organized labour to politically engage with the issues currently dominating public life. As a political ritual, therefore, May Day in Western Europe took on the form of a protest demonstration, and as Mattias Wahlström shows (see Chapter 9) this remains true today. Ideally May Day connected 'class demands' and general political claims with the evocation of a specific vision of a future society, and the intended effects of the staged events were as much internal as external. May Day rituals were (and are) for organized labour, at least potentially, eventful protests in the sense of having relevant cognitive, affective and relational transformative impacts on the very movement that carried them out (cf. della Porta 2008).

May Day Demonstrations as Political Ritual Performances

A number of social and cultural theorists departing from a neo-Durkheimian approach have focused on political rituals. Steven Lukes (1975) has defined ritual as 'rule-governed activity of a symbolic character which draws the attention of its participants to objects of thought and feeling which they hold to be of special significance' (p. 291). Lukes (1975) further develops his definition of political ritual as a political performance which reinforces, recreates and organizes *representation collectives*, in that the symbolism of political ritual 'represents, *inter alia*, particular models or political paradigms of society and how it functions' (p. 301).

This extended definition highlighting both *internal and external* functions of mass demonstrations as political rituals dovetails well with, for example, the early May Day demonstrations in Sweden. In these mass demonstrations of labour, organized by the trade unions and the Social Democratic Party, the demonstrators forcefully dramatized the power they still lacked but struggled to attain. Political rituals can be perceived as such as modes of exercising, or seeking to exercise, power along the cognitive dimension, both externally and internally (cf. Alexander 2004). Citing a classic quote from Murray Edelman, Lukes argues that political ritual is a mechanism through which 'politics influences what they [demonstrators] want, what they fear, what they regard as possible, and even who they are' – that is, the exercise of power along the cognitive dimension (Lukes 1975, p. 302). May Day rituals are collective practices in themselves in which in their expressive dramatizations, the values, images and desires of the labour movement are revealed and membership solidified.

The cognitive dimension of political rituals also builds upon what we designate as memory work. The past is brought to play upon the present and future aspirations of a social movement. May Day demonstrations in Western European countries

> link the political past to an imagined future. They evoke, generate, and communicate the important sense of collective memory that sustains movement participation .... They help to marshal the past in support of present and future goals.
>
> (Pfaff and Yang 2001, pp. 579–580)

As mentioned above, being about 'nothing but the future', early May Day rituals did not commemorate anything, but their symbolic representations were filled with references to past movements of emancipation, in particular with reference to the (Jacobean) French revolution, and also to the Paris Commune (cf. Chapter 6). The memory of conflicting versions of the origins of May Day was used to argue for specific aims and forms of action (Chapter 2, Chapter 3 and Chapter 5). Yet even today May Day demonstrators evoke tradition/celebration as a motive for their participation. Wahlström found that tradition and celebration of the achievements of the labour movement are still today ubiquitous motives for May Day participation (Chapter 9). In the rituality of annual demonstrations, from the 1890s up to the new millennium the past was brought to bear on the present and helped shape also diverging visions for the future of a sometimes deeply divided labour movement. In Jeffrey Alexander's (2004, p. 530) terms, during the demonstrations the labour movement 'walks and talks' its collective representations.

The symbolically constructed events of May Day celebrations, marches and rallies were (and are) communicating to the wider public and political authorities their political demands and visions for society, 'walking and talking' and even singing their political messages, but perhaps most importantly, the demonstrations communicated internally to their participants and sympathetic audiences, instilling a sense of solidarity within the working class and forging a sense of community with a common political cause. The mechanism through which the sense of 'we' is temporarily constructed can be captured with Durkheim's notion of 'collective effervescence' (Peterson 2001). In moments of collective effervescence psychological identification and cultural extension is achieved, that is, cultural meanings are temporarily forged with the identifications of the ritual participants and their (sympathetic) audience. According to Alexander (2004, p. 547), the elements of the ritual performance are *fused*, or rather, temporarily *re-fused*. Ritual performances

> try to recover a momentary experience of ritual, to eliminate or to negate the effects of social and cultural de-fusion [*sic*, fragmentation in complex societies]. Speaking epigrammatically, one might say that successful performances re-fuse history.

What is important to stress here is that while political rituals endeavour to negate the effects of complex societies' social and cultural de-fusion, their endeavours are necessarily limited to specific groups or communities. Paradoxically, political rituals are both inclusive and exclusive. As Casquete (2006) argues, political rituals aim at 'expanding group solidarity and, often at the same time, also at contracting solidarity when looked at from the perspective of wider society' (pp. 46–47; cf. Alexander 1989, p. 180). Solidarity acquired through political ritual is exclusive along the social scale of the political community it celebrates. For example, rituals of national commemoration attempt to consolidate the national community; organized labour's May Day rituals aspire to reinforce the collective identity of the labour movement. But in times of crisis May Day organizers can seek to include broader society. The May Day demonstrations staged in Stockholm during the early war years in 1940 and 1941 sought to consolidate the national community in the face of the threat posed by the war in Europe. The Social Democratic leadership invited the centre and right-wing parties to join them in a 'civic march'. However, in 1942, concerned that the symbolic value of 1 May could be lost for the labour movement, May Day was again declared 'the workers day' (see Chapter 4).

May Day has traditionally celebrated 'the working class', but this characteristic faced repeated challenges that left their impact on the ritual of May Day – its traditions, symbols, form and content. In the early days May Day rituals were shaped not only by pressure from below and the strategic and tactical decisions of organized labour, but also by state repression and the hostility of employers. After World War I internal division contradicted the image of one working class united behind the banners of socialism. Fascism attempted to eradicate the socialist May Day tradition by usurpation (in Germany) or by the creation of a fascist labour day (in Italy and Spain). The increasing recognition of May Day as an official state holiday in Western Europe (and around the world) after World War II reflected the need to come to terms with the tradition of the unofficial May Day and has been defined as an attempt to detach it from labour movements, class consciousness and class struggle (Hobsbawm 1991, p. 106). Similar objectives stood behind the decision of the Catholic Church to 'baptize' May Day by declaring it St Joseph's day in 1955, a move that permitted even the Spanish dictator Franco to celebrate 1 May (see Chapter 5). Finally, in societies in transition the organized labour movement with its working-class base has evolved during its long history. In many countries social democratic/socialist parties and labour unions now organize a broader class spectrum, subsequently widening its social scale to include middle-class participants and supporters. Magnus Wennerhag (Chapter 8) finds that contemporary May Day demonstrations are not just a working-class affair. Outnumbering traditional working-class participants are middle-class demonstrators, particularly socio-cultural professionals and semi-professionals.

Ritual Performances: Actors and Directors, Choreography, Scripts and Props

Rituals *may* fulfil the latent function of reinforcing group identity, reminding us that the question of rituals forging a sense of collective identity is empirical. Rituals do not necessarily reinforce identity, and the degree to which they act upon the emotive sentiments of collective belonging can vary in time and place. As Alexander (2004) points out, ritual performances can be more or less successful in achieving their intended function of fusing cultural texts with the psychological identifications of its participants and audience. The meanings and relevancies of ritual can shift with the environments of its occurrence, which emphasizes the situated, dynamic features of the ritual process (cf. Roth 1995). The study of political rituals is an empirical undertaking and this challenge is taken on in the contributions to this volume.

Linking concretely to the performative aspect of ritual, Ron Eyerman (2006, pp. 199–200) succinctly describes the ritual performance of a May Day demonstration.

> Here there are actors and directors, symbols and scripts. There are also designated places, which may have symbolic value themselves, a certain city square and parade route may have historical reference. The event is also staged and choreographed, placards are printed in advance and laid out in designated places in the staging area, so that demonstrators can fall in line behind them as they prepare to march. Time-tested slogans may be called out and responded to during the march, as it follows its designated route. After moving to the final destination, a historical square, for example, speakers and speeches make use also of formats and phrases which represent the traditions of the group, recalling its history and linking the present event to those of the past. Depending on the context, May Day can represent, perform, power or protest, and opposition.

According to Eyerman, 'collective actors must find ways to express that they are worthy, united, numerous and committed' (p. 196). An underlying choreography for social democratic and socialist May Day demonstrations was their peaceful and orderly performance. The organizers of these May Day rituals sought to stage demonstrations that would communicate to the general public the worthiness of organized labour to shoulder the responsibility of government. Reiter writes that SPD leader Philipp Scheidemann, who from February to June 1919 led the German government, admonished workers at the open-air rally on 1 May 1919 'to strive onward to socialism "on the path of an ordered democracy"' (Chapter 3, p. 42). To express their worthiness and at the same time their commitment workers were marshalled onto the streets to march in an orderly fashion, and march stewards kept order among the ranks. We can observe in photographic records of early May Day celebrations that demonstrators wore their best 'Sunday suits and dresses'. Reflecting the close ties between the temperance movements and labour movements in Scandinavia, sobriety was prescribed for organized labour's May Day ritual to ensure the dignity of the celebration. Thörnqvist, Bergholm and Mellberg write about how socialist activists and the temperance movement joined forces in 1898 to declare a 'drinking strike' in Finland during May Day in an attempt to wrench May Day away from inebriated upper-class student Vappu celebrations (Chapter 4, pp, 84–85). Sobriety was rigorously enforced in Sweden's early May Day demonstrations: marching on stage were what Ambjörnsson (1993) called the 'conscientious workers' – worthy (and committed) to enter the larger political community.

The May Day ritual opens for a variety of potential actors and directors, for example, trade unions, socialist/social democratic parties, communist parties, anarchist groups, new left parties, etc., together with scripts and props, for example, badges and buttons, flags, banners and placards, slogans and songs, which reinforce the sense of 'we'. Throughout the book the May Day rituals' colourful iconography and scripts are brought in focus. For example, during May Day each year the red flags and banners were (and are) paraded on the streets and squares. In the historical chapters in this volume the colour red appears as a common symbol for labour movements' struggle for recognition. Thörnqvist, Bergholm and Mellberg (Chapter 4) write how the colour red was so infused in the May Day iconography that it was officially banned by the Finnish authorities with the so-called flag decree in 1934, which was first lifted in 1940 in recognition of workers' patriotic participation in the 1939 'Winter War'. Chris Wrigley points out in Chapter 6 that 'The Internationale' was an important element in Britain's early May Day events and still today its use is widespread in Western Europe for buttressing participants' sense of group solidarity, their sense of 'we' and their connection to the past achievements of the labour movement.

In addition to what Alexander, Giesen and Mast (2006) call foreground scripts, e.g. the specific demands raised in the demonstration, the ritual of the May Day demonstration has a deep background script with its underlying memories, narratives and collections of symbols which together form its collective representation of the labour movement. One of the more persistent 'origin myths' is the connection between the Haymarket tragedy in Chicago 1886 and European May Day – 'the dual origin of May Day' – which Herbert Reiter traces in Chapter 2. Eduardo Romanos and José Luis Ledesma argue that the 'dual origin', the two rival background scripts for the origin of May Day, exemplified the twofold nature of the Spanish organized labour movement (Chapter 5). The anarchists connected their May Day ritual to the tragedy in Chicago, celebrating May Day as a day of mourning for the Haymarket martyrs and staging their May Day events as dress rehearsals for the general strike bound to bring down the system. In contrast, the socialists looked to Paris and the congress of the Second International's call to keep demonstrations peaceful and to present the workers' demands in an orderly fashion. For the Spanish socialists, according to Romanos and Ledesma, the May Day ritual had a joyful meaning. These two distinctively different background scripts provided the Spanish May Days with two distinctively different May Day ritual performances. So while the Haymarket tragedy was not mentioned in the Paris resolution, and had played no role in the discussion on the international workers' May Day (see Chapter 2), the narrative of the tragic events in Chicago were nevertheless appropriated by the Spanish anarchists to lend their May Day performances their radical meaning and format.

Ultimately the success and longevity of May Day in Western Europe are directly linked not with a radical agenda referring to Haymarket but with the Paris congress of 1889 and with the organizations represented in or linked to the Second International (see Chapter 2). This success was based also on the specific conception of May Day and on the content and form of May Day ritual events developed by the socialist organizations. Within this tradition, May Day was both a day of struggle and a day of celebration, and demonstrations and strikes were combined with festive and entertaining events. In particular in periods with declining participation, the exact mix between elements of protest and of celebration, i.e. the concrete form of May Day rituals, was and continues to be the object of sometimes heated debates.

May Day as Eventful Protest

In both the more radical and the more moderate conceptions, the intended effects of May Day rituals, as mentioned above, were as much internal as external. It was the labour movement's annual trooping of the colours and a protest event for the claims on the movement's current agenda. At the same time the organizers of May Day events strove to strengthen the emotional, intellectual and organizational cohesion of the workers' movement. In present times this finds its reflection in the importance, on the one hand, of organizational affiliation with a political party, party sympathies and general ideological orientation for participation (Chapter 8), and on the other hand, in the weight that motives of solidarity/loyalty and the tradition to celebrate the workers' day have for individuals' decision to demonstrate on May Day (Chapter 9).

These characteristics make May Day an early example of the 'eventful protest' conceptualized by Donatella della Porta (2008). Della Porta proposes to treat protest as an independent variable, and to focus not on what produces protest but on the by-products of protest itself, e.g. a sense of collectivity promoted by protest, which is a precondition for collective action. Protests are understood as being eventful in the sense of having relevant cognitive, affective and relational transformative impacts on the very movements that carry them out. Such impacts were the declared aim of socialist organizers in the early constitutive period of May Day (see Chapter 2, p. 23). Similarly applicable to May Day are the general elements singled out by della Porta (2008) as making eventful protest more likely: long-lasting events (or chains of events) and the connection with a protest cycle; a plurality of participants and a transnational nature of protest bringing with it a particular need for communication; an ongoing process of identity building; interaction between the state and the movement.

If not a transnational, certainly its international character was fundamental for the emotional hold that May Day took on the early workers' movement in Western Europe. Not only its constitution but also fundamental characteristics of May Day rituals can be traced back to congresses of the Second

International. The first decades of the existence of May Day coincided with the period of identity building of the socialist movement in Western Europe and in certain countries with the founding period of the socialist parties. Finally, all of our historical chapters chronicle the interaction between the state and the movement provoked by the staging of May Day rituals. The May Day rituals of organized labour were met with varying degrees of repression, which inexorably shaped their performances in historically situated socio-political contexts.

It can hardly be surprising, however, that a political ritual (and in particular a demonstration ritual) cannot be successful as an eventful protest year after year for more than a century. In one sense the history of May Day demonstrations stands out as a compelling success story. Labour demonstrations' tumultuous journey, from in some national contexts brutally suppressed political rituals to more or less routinized political rituals that were first sanctioned and later officialized, is investigated in this volume. By the time of its centennial in 1990, May Day was an official holiday in 107 countries – making May Day perhaps unique in the social movement histories of Western democracies. But what was lost in this transition? Already in the 1890s some argued that May Day had lost its novelty and zest. 'The first demonstration here [in London] was very nice', Engels wrote to Friedrich A. Sorge on 17 May 1893, 'but it is already becoming somewhat of an everyday or rather annual matter; the first bloom is gone' (cited in Foner 1986, p. 65). However, others emphasized the continued strength and vigour of the ritual. The social democratic *Hamburger Echo* (1 May 1912) underlined the vitality of the May Day idea, which although time and again challenged by employers, the state and the cold and calculating reason within the labour movement's own ranks, 'Twenty times already it has been accounted finished, and twenty-one times it has been seen resurging.'

In actual fact, May Day depended for its long-term success on repeated processes of reappropriation and revitalization. For such processes the combination with a protest cycle or with moments of 'collective effervescence' seems of fundamental importance. The very institution of May Day by the Paris congress in 1889 was inseparably linked with the European strike waves of those years (Boll 1992, p. 430). In Germany and Italy, the revolutionary period after World War I witnessed the most massive May Day demonstrations, and in the post-World War II years reappropriation processes were favoured by the movements of the 1960s (see Chapter 3 and Chapter 10). In Spain, the most euphorically remembered May Days coincided with the introduction of the republic in the 1930s and the fall of the Franco dictatorship in the 1970s (see Chapter 5).

The literature, however, has traced a slow decline and loss of significance of May Day celebrations. In particular in the second half of the twentieth century, along with the weakening of working-class culture and the 'loss of "proletarity"' (Mooser 1983), May Day increasingly lost its character as the day of struggle of the workers' movement. Since 1968 within the public arenas opened by the annual ritual of May Day, growing competition posed by new social movements, new left parties and, more recently, grassroots trade unions has led to the situation that May Day less and less 'belongs' to the traditional workers' movement and its organizations. Abby Peterson writes that the current financial crisis has unleashed a wave of anti-austerity protests across Europe and May Day demonstrations are today mobilizing labour movements within this climate of economic grievances and increase of mistrust in institutions of representative democracy – including (although to a lesser degree) a growing mistrust in their own traditional institutions, both unions and left parties (Chapter 7). This situation has led in some countries to new actors attempting to wrest control over the May Day rituals from the traditional labour movements.

In particular the loss of utopia that has been observed for the socialist workers' movement (Eley 1995) inevitably had a deep impact on a political ritual that at its conception was 'about nothing but the future' (Hobsbawm 1991, p. 118; see Chapter 10). However, also up to the most recent times, alongside a tenacious insistence on the significance of May Day celebrations, repeated attempts to reappropriate and revitalize May Day can be observed, albeit not always leading to greater public and political resonance.

According to Eyerman (2006, p. 199):

> [S]ocial movement is a form of acting in public, a political performance which involves representation in dramatic form, as movements engage emotions inside and outside their bounds attempting to communicate their message. Such performance is always public, as it requires an audience which is addressed and must be moved.

The May Day ritual for the labour movement was eventful, both historically and today, when it could 'move' its participants emotionally, cognitively, morally and even physically; when it could make possible cathexis between participants and their causes and roused empathy and identification in the ritual's audiences.

The Contributions to the Volume

The more-than-120-year history of May Day offers scholars a unique opportunity to follow the labour movement through the lens of its most important ritual event. The volume provides a comparative and theoretically informed overview of the celebration of international May Day by organized labour in Western Europe. The book brings together scholars in the fields of history and of social movement studies to reflect on the evolution of May Day as a political ritual both historically and today.

In the first part of the book the authors comparatively trace the transitions of the May Day rituals in the selected Western European countries included in our volume. From the very beginning of May Day celebrations, in all the countries covered in this volume conflicting (radical and moderate) May Day narratives coexisted within the workers' movement. These internal divisions had a significant impact on the development of May Day in Western Europe. Equally important, however, was the impact of external factors, of cataclysmic events like World War I and the Russian October revolution as well as of long-term societal changes like the 'loss of proletarity'.

In Chapter 2, Herbert Reiter discusses the (not always coinciding) history and memory of the origins of May Day. The use made of the two main scripts – May Day as a commemoration of Haymarket or as the socialist international holiday of the proletariat instituted by the Paris congress of 1889 – in arguing for specific forms and objectives of May Day rituals shows that, and how, history and/or memory matter. These debates and conflicts were always also debates and conflicts about the general strategies and tactics of the workers' movement. More than a sign of unity, the increasing tendency to weave both scripts together into one legend of the origins appears as one more sign of the weakening of the traditional labour movement and its May Day rituals in Western Europe.

Using a comparative approach, in Chapter 3 Reiter follows the *longue durée* history of May Day in Germany and Italy from 1890 up to the new millennium. Without ignoring the impact of the important differences in the development of the workers' movement in Germany and Italy of the May Day rituals in the two countries, this chapter aims above all at underlining similar and parallel developments, concentrating in particular on state reactions, May Day memories and narratives, event formats, dominant themes and levels of participation.

Christer Thörnqvist, Tapio Bergholm and Margaretha Mellberg compare the historical development of the May Day rituals in Sweden and Finland (Chapter 4). In international comparisons, industrial relations systems and labour movements in the five Nordic countries are often lumped together as 'the Nordic model'. One could therefore expect that labour movement rituals would also look rather similar. At this political cultural level, however, the differences between the countries become apparent. The celebration of May Day had been more or less accepted in Sweden ever since the first manifestation in 1890, with comparatively limited repression. In Finland, on the other hand, in a much more authoritarian context the labour movement developed in strong conflict with bourgeois society in combination with serious frictions within the movement. The civil war (1918) left its mark on Finnish society and on May Day rituals for decades.

In Chapter 5 Eduardo Romanos and José Luis Ledesma analyse the anarcho-syndicalist May Day rituals in contrast with the socialist May Day traditions in Spain. Here a particularly strong anarchist movement impacted on the evolution of May Day since 1890 and, differently from other countries (like Italy), it remained in continued strength also after World War I. The authors highlight the profound differences between anarchists and socialists regarding May Day scripts, objectives and forms of action. Interrupted by the Franco dictatorship, the Spanish May Day tradition revived as an oppositional protest ritual in the last phase of the regime, but in the forms that it took after the re-establishment of democracy converged with the models dominant in the rest of Western Europe.

In Chapter 6 Chris Wrigley describes the long history of May Day and the traditions that evolved in Britain, tracing the uneven support that the ritual evoked during its history and its pendulation between protest processions and cultural festivities. He writes that in 1890 May Day banners with, for example, 'Workers of the World We Hail You As Brothers', in English, French and German, were carried by the demonstrators. London was home to a large number of socialist and anarchist refugees and they made their presence felt in the demonstration and on the speakers' platform. According to Wrigley, the international character of British May Day rituals has more or less continued throughout its history.

The historical chapters also show how May Day organizers, in particular in more recent times, have sought new performance strategies to instil what was believed to have been lost – not only the numbers of participating demonstrators, but also the revolutionary fervour of the event. In short the authors examine how organizers have time and again sought to renew and revitalize the official and routinized ritual demonstrations that in many Western European countries May Day had become. In doing so, we argue, May Day organizers were attempting to recreate the emotive power – the eventfulness – of political ritual for strengthening the collective identity of organized labour.

While we recognize that May Day's most militant manifestations of class struggle and protest fervour have indeed declined during the more than 120 years of May Day history, they continue to rally participant demonstrators and audiences of onlookers. The second part of the book brings our comparative approach to May Day rituals today.[1] Here we look at the 'who' and 'why'. What are the meanings inscribed in contemporary May Day demonstrations? First, however, in Chapter 7 Abby Peterson presents an overview of today's May Day demonstrations in Belgium, Italy, Spain, Sweden, Switzerland and the United Kingdom, outlining the dominant organizational actors, their major claims, as well as the general socio-economic and political contexts – the current crisis of neoliberalism – within which May Day rituals in Western Europe are played out today. The chapter summarizes how organized labour – the principal protagonists for European May Day demonstrations – has been institutionalized in these countries, which also sets its imprint on how the rituals of May Day are enacted today.

In Chapter 8 Magnus Wennerhag investigates who demonstrates on May Day today. In a comparative perspective Wennerhag conducts a socio-demographic analysis of May Day demonstrators in the respective countries. Here he looks closely at how class, both subjectively experienced and objectively assigned class positions, together with the organizational composition of the marchers, influences the propensity to demonstrate in different political contexts.

While Chapter 7 reviews how organizers are bestowing meaning on contemporary May Day rituals, we argue that our knowledge of large protests and ritual events are typically biased in favour of the meanings conferred to them by organizers, movement intellectuals and media commentators, whereby the variation among participants is lost. Not only the organizers of May Day events, but also the demonstrators give meaning to their participation. In the third and concluding chapter in this part of the volume Mattias Wahlström uses the same sample of countries to shed light on the 'why', that is, the motives for participation in the six countries (Chapter 9). The individual motives for demonstration participation help reveal the meaning that is brought to the ritual events. In operationalizing the ritual character of demonstrations in terms of individual motives, he agrees with Roth's (1995) expansion upon a neo-Parsonian conception of ritual, which emphasizes the importance of humans' active roles in determining and conducting their courses of action. Roth argues that ritual 'served both to "stimulate the will" of *actors* engaging in action and, thereby, to clarify for *analysts* the role of will in social action more generally' (p. 319; emphasis in original). Therefore, Wahlström argues, we must turn to the participants' own orientations, motivations and aspirations as the basis for analytic insight into ritual action. Consequently, variations in the dominant sets of motives among individual participants reveal the type of ritual processes that can be found in the countries in question. An analysis based on the perspectives of contemporary protest participants, according to Wahlström, has the potential to simultaneously link the past to the present, relate the characteristics of individual demonstrators to their contexts and help identify differences between contemporary May Day rituals in different countries.

The volume concludes with a discussion concerning the future of May Day. In Chapter 10 we reflect upon May Day's utopian dimension – its erosion and the prospects for its resurrection – arguing that the rituals' various utopias have provided labour movements with their challenges to the prevailing order and their emotive power. We find contemporary May Day rituals ambiguous. On the one hand, we have those mobilized by traditional workers' movement organizations clinging to celebrations of the past achievements of organized labour. On the other hand, we find May Day rituals mobilized by radical left organizations invoking a utopian strategy to challenge the present, which potentially brings a creative dynamics to the ritual of May Day. However, these creative utopian attempts by new political actors for a new beginning have still to prove their robustness and their capacity to connect with the efforts within the traditional workers' movement to incorporate new elements into their May Day conception and to revitalize the May Day celebrations.

Note

1 The data for this part of the volume is a unique dataset that has been gathered in the collaborative research project CCC: 'Caught in the Act of Protest: Contextualizing Contestation' (principal investigator Professor Bert Klandermans) (see Appendix).

References

Alexander, J.C. (1989). Culture and political crisis: Watergate and Durkheimian sociology. In J.C. Alexander (Ed.), *Structure and Meaning* (pp. 174–216). New York: Columbia University Press.

Alexander, J.C. (2004). Cultural pragmatics: Social performance between ritual and strategy. *Sociological Theory*, 22(4), 527–573.

Alexander, J.C., Giesen, B., and Mast, J.L. (Eds). (2006). *Social Performance, Symbolic Action, Cultural Pragmatics, and Ritual*. Cambridge: Cambridge University Press.

Ambjörnsson, R. (1993). Den skötsamme arbetaren or the conscientious worker. *Libraries and Culture*, 28(1), 4–12.

Boll, F. (1992). *Arbeitskämpfe und Gewerkschaften in Deutschland, England und Frankreich. Ihre Entwicklung vom 19. zum 20. Jahrhundert*. Bonn: J.H.W. Dietz.

Casquete, J. (2006). The power of demonstrations. *Social Movement Studies*, 5(1), 45–60.

della Porta, D. (2008). Eventful protest, global conflicts. *Distinktion: Scandinavian Journal of Social Theory*, 17, 27–56.

Eley, G. (1995). What's left of utopia? Oder: Vom 'Neuen Jerusalem' zur Zeit der Wünsche. *Werkstatt Geschichte*, 11, 5–18.

Eyerman, R. (2006). Performing opposition or, how social movements move. In J.C. Alexander, B. Giesen and J.L. Mast (Eds), *Social Performance, Symbolic Action, Cultural Pragmatics, and Ritual* (pp. 193–217). Cambridge: Cambridge University Press.

Foner, P.S. (1986). *May Day: A Short History of the International Workers' Holiday 1886–1986*. New York: International Publishers.

Hobsbawm, E.J. (1984). The transformation of labour rituals. In *Worlds of Labour: Further Studies in the History of Labour* (pp. 66–82). London: Weidenfeld and Nicolson.

Hobsbawm, E.J. (1991). Birth of a holiday: The first of May. In C. Wrigley and J. Shepherd (Eds), *On the Move: Essays in Labour and Transport History* (pp. 104–122). London and Rio Grande: Hambledon Press.

Lukes, S. (1975). Political ritual and social integration. *Sociology*, 9, 289–308.

Mooser, J. (1983). Abschied von der Proletarität. Sozialstruktur und Lage der Arbeiterschaft in der Bundesrepublik in historischer Perspektive. In W. Conze and M. Rainer Lepsius (Eds), *Sozialgeschichte der Bundesrepublik Deutschland. Beiträge zum Kontinuitätsproblem* (pp. 143–186). Stuttgart: Klett-Cotta.

Peterson, A. (2001). *Contemporary Political Protest: Essays on Political Militancy*. Aldershot, UK: Ashgate.

Peterson, A., Wahlström, M., Wennerhag, M., Christancho, C., and Sabucedo, J. M. (2012). May Day demonstrations in five European countries. *Mobilization: An International Quarterly*, 17(3), 282–300.

Pfaff, S., and Yang, G. (2001). Double-edged rituals and the symbolic resources of collective action: Political commemorations and the mobilization of protest in 1989. *Theory and Society*, 30(4), 539–589.

Roth, A.L. (1995). 'Men wearing masks': Issues of description in the analysis of ritual. *Sociological Theory*, 13(3), 301–327.

2 The Origins of May Day

History and Memory

Herbert Reiter

The difficulties in writing the history of May Day have been repeatedly underlined: researchers are confronted with the conflicting alternatives of privileging certain actors, of covering local, national or international aspects and of concentrating on single years or on the long-term developments of the 'world-holiday of the international proletariat'. Not infrequently, in addition, they are confronted with different memories of key moments of May Day history within the various wings of the workers' movement, in conflict among each other, but also with the historical reality as it can be reconstructed on the basis of primary sources. These difficulties emerge in an exemplary way in the different narratives of when, how and where May Day originated and what were its intended forms and objectives.

Singling out the rank-and-file input (which went far beyond the expectations of socialist leaders) as decisive for the success of the first May Day celebrations, Eric Hobsbawm (1991, p. 106) argues that May Day 'was not so much an "invented tradition" as a suddenly erupting one'. What was so suddenly erupting, however, was not one tradition but a contested field offering various opportunities for the invention of different and potentially conflicting traditions. In 1890 Western European workers' movements were still weakly defined, both ideologically and organizationally. In the months leading up to May Day 1890, in a largely spontaneous way, numerous well-attended meetings and assemblies developed different ideas about 'what should happen on 1 May'.[1] The spectrum of these ideas, ranging from festive events on the first Sunday in May to mass strikes and street demonstrations on 1 May, reveals how undefined the form and content of May Day presented itself at that point. Before long, however, the various wings within the workers' movement developed their distinct narratives of the origins of May Day and of its intended form and content.[2]

In what follows, a historiographical reconstruction of the origins of May Day is contrasted with the collective memories of the event that were developed within a social movement, the workers' movement, or more precisely within the different wings of this movement.[3] If memory is collective in so far as it is produced in 'social frameworks', in the context of social groups structured by social relationships, then a society – or a social movement, as in our case – produces a plural, and often contested and contentious memory of the past (Zamponi 2015, p. 258). The collective memory, in fact, is promoted within groups, and it is 'as much a result of conscious manipulation as unconscious absorption and it is always mediated' (Kansteiner 2002, p. 180). Diverging memories of the origins of May Day were employed by entrepreneurs within the different wings of the workers' movements in recurrent contentious debates as an argument for specific forms, contents and objectives of May Day rituals. These debates served as a proxy for disputes between the more moderate and the more radical wings of the workers' movements on the overall strategies and tactics to be followed, with different intensity and extension in time in the various countries.[4]

Like the workers' movement in general, so also the memories of the origins of May Day promoted by entrepreneurs of its different wings were shaped by the specific conditions in the countries covered in this volume, changing over time. For reasons of space, the following discussion will concentrate on ideal types based on examples from the most clear-cut country traditions in the formative phase of the respective May Day narratives. The grey zones, the overlaps and blurred borders between the different narratives that evidently did exist, are not discussed.

The Origins of May Day: A Historiographical Reconstruction

Depending in particular on the political and ideological position of the authors and on specific national traditions, the different memories of the origins of May Day left their imprint also on historiography. Historians in fact have advanced different interpretations as to which event is to be privileged as the origin of May Day – the Chicago Haymarket tragedy in 1886 *or* the 1889 founding congress of the Second International in Paris. For Eric Hobsbawm (1991, p. 106), 'the immediate origin of May Day is not in dispute' and is located in the Paris congress. From a Spanish perspective Lucía Rivas (2010) speaks of a 'dual origin' located on the one hand in the Chicago incidents and on the other hand in the Paris congress. Indicating 1986 as the centennial of the international workers' holiday, Philip Foner (1986) clearly privileged Haymarket as the originating event. More recently Donna Haverty-Stacke (2009) took a similar position, describing May Day as 'America's forgotten holiday'. To the contrary, research on the specific question of an American origin of May Day has affirmed: '[i]t is safe to say that there was no explicit link between the Haymarket affair and the decision to institute an international First of May' (Perrier and Cordillot 1992, p. 174). What then was the connection between the Chicago events of 1886 and the international workers' day, in particular in the Western European countries covered in this volume?

The history of the Haymarket tragedy has been extensively studied (Avrich 1984; Green 2006). For our purposes it is sufficient to recall that on 1 May 1886 a broad coalition of labour organizations in the United States, led by the Federation of Organized Trades and Labor Unions, the predecessor of the American Federation of Labor (AFL), and reaching from the Knights of Labor to the anarchists, attempted a general strike in order to gain the eight-hour workday. The date was chosen for practical reasons: as 'moving day' 1 May for many trades was traditionally also the day for renewing contracts between workers and employers. A general strike was only partially realized, and the gains made also remained partial. In Chicago the anarchists – who were initially sceptical towards the objective of the eight-hour workday, but who nevertheless joined the coalition for mainly tactical reasons (Haverty-Stacke 2009, p. 28) – were particularly strong within the labour movement. On 3 May heavy police intervention against a rally in front of the McCormack plant protesting against strike breakers resulted in two deaths. In protest against police violence a rally on Haymarket Square was called for the following day. Towards the end of the until then peaceful rally, when a considerable number of the *c.* 4,000 participants had already left, the police arrived and ordered the crowd to disperse. At this moment a bomb exploded, killing seven policemen and wounding about 60. The police opened fire on the fleeing crowd killing at least four workers, wounding as many as 70. The bombing was blamed on the Chicago anarchists; in a subsequent trial, several of their leaders, who were not tied to the actual bombing, were nonetheless sentenced to death on the grounds of being the 'spiritual instigators' of the attack; they were executed on 11 November 1887.

In 1887 voices from within the anarchist movement called for 1 May (because of Haymarket) to be considered the anniversary of the modern labour movement and the modern struggle for freedom (Haverty-Stacke 2009, p. 35). In the climate of the 'red scare' following the Chicago events, however, these voices remained isolated and without a following. For the 1887 Labor Day (in September), the Chicago labour organizations banned all red flags: only the American flag and the flags of the organizations were allowed. On the national level the AFL immediately distanced itself from the Haymarket incidents and the socialist and anarchist agenda. According to AFL leader Samuel Gompers, Haymarket was a 'catastrophe' for the eight-hour programme. The national organization for the eight-hour day was suspended in 1887 and in the following years the efforts of the organization in favour of the eight-hour day were restructured into a 'patriotic' campaign (Haverty-Stacke 2009, pp. 37–39).

In July 1889, for the centennial of the storming of the Bastille, an international workers' congress was convened in Paris that became the founding congress of the Second International. One of the resolutions voted on by this congress called for a great international demonstration to be organized for the coming year in such a manner that the workers in all countries and in all cities on a specific day simultaneously addressed to the public authorities a demand to fix the working day at eight hours and to put into effect the other resolutions of the congress. These other resolutions centred on measures for the protection of workers, but also included the political demands for unrestricted freedom of coalition and of association. The resolutions also declared it a duty of workers to consider women as their equal comrades and to push through the principle of 'same pay for same work'.

It can be assumed that the American events served as a catalyst for the demand for the eight-hour workday. However, this demand also had a long history in Europe (see e.g. Chapter 5), including the 1866 congress of the First International in Geneva, which had proposed eight hours as the legal limit of the workday. In fact, whereas the American actions in 1886 and 1890 were directed at employers, in Europe the demand for the eight-hour day was principally addressed to the state: the 1889 Paris congress called for securing the measures demanded by law and international treaties.

The Paris resolution was brought to the floor by a French delegate, the Guesdiste (socialist) Raymond Lavigne. The proposed modalities of action – to address to the public authorities a demand to fix the working day at eight hours – followed those of a campaign for the eight-hour day conducted in France by the Fédération Nationale des Syndicats in February 1889 (Dommanget 1972, pp. 56–85). Following a proposal by Lavigne, the national council of the Fédération Nationale des Syndicats subsequently decided to present the project of an analogous international manifestation at the Paris congress (Giovanoli 1925, pp. 10f., 13). In fact, an article on the origin of May Day in the German social democratic daily *Vorwärts* (30 April 1899) refers only to this French campaign without mentioning the American events (cf. also Giovanoli 1925, p. 9).

The Haymarket tragedy is not mentioned in the Paris resolution, and according to the (official and unofficial) surviving accounts, the event played no role in the discussion on May Day (Perrier and Cordillot 1992, pp. 159, 174). The material evidence that American events played a role in the decision taken rests on the second paragraph of the resolution, which states that 1 May 1890 was accepted as the day for the international demonstration as the AFL at its St Louis convention in December 1888 had already decided to conduct a campaign for the eight-hour workday on that day. Official AFL delegates were not present in Paris, but AFL leader Samuel Gompers had addressed a letter to the congress that was read out to the delegates by his personal envoy, Hugh McGregor. The letter itself did not survive. Most likely, however, it contained an appeal for action showing solidarity with the AFL's campaign for the eight-hour day. There was a five-day delay between the reading of Gompers's letter and the debate on Lavigne's resolution, with nothing to indicate that McGregor was present at the session (Perrier and Cordillot 1992, p. 186 n. 62).

Considering that Lavigne would still have proposed his resolution in the absence of Gompers's letter (Foner 1986, p. 40) and that the project of an international manifestation was a French initiative, does the American influence on the Paris decisions therefore boil down to the suggestion of a date, as Giovanoli (1925, p. 9) has submitted? Radical voices would certainly disagree. For them the reference to America indicated not only a call for direct action and a general strike as on 1 May 1886, but also Haymarket as the dominant point of reference.[5] However, the decisions of the AFL's St Louis convention in 1888 – and it is to these decisions that the Paris resolution refers – do not lend themselves to such an interpretation. Instead these decisions designed a moderate and patriotic campaign for the eight-hour day avoiding any reference to Haymarket. The AFL's special committee on the eight-hour day had in fact decided on periods of agitation to take place on Washington's Birthday, 4 July and the first Monday in September 1889 (already at that time celebrated as Labor Day by the AFL).[6] The meetings were to continue on Washington's Birthday in 1890, and to culminate in strikes on 1 May 1890. As far as these strikes are concerned, the AFL shifted away from the tactic of the general strike that had been attempted in 1886; representatives of only one trade per year would make the demand for the eight-hour day, in 1890 the carpenters (Haverty-Stacke 2009, pp. 38–40).

As an additional argument for the influence of the American events on the decision of the Paris congress, Philip Foner (1986, p. 41), among others, underlines that everybody present knew about the Haymarket incidents. In fact, this can be assumed as certain. In particular the subsequent trial reached great notoriety far beyond the United States. Within the workers' movements (among moderates as well as radicals) the execution of the Chicago anarchists was widely seen as judicial murder. However, neither the knowledge of Haymarket, nor the denunciation of the death penalties, should be equated with a willingness to closely associate a planned socialist initiative with an event notoriously associated with anarchism. The position on Haymarket of Wilhelm Liebknecht, together with August Bebel, one of the leaders of the German social democrats, has been seen as characteristic of the more moderate socialists dominating the Paris congress: as a matter of principle, solidarity against repression but condemnation of anarchist strategies and tactics (Cordillot 1988, p. 184).

In this context it has to be underlined that for Liebknecht and his comrades the controversy with anarchism predated Haymarket by years. After the promulgation of the anti-socialist law in Germany in 1878, for which two assassination attempts against Emperor Wilhelm I served as a pretext, differences about the tactics to be followed by the social democrats under the new conditions led to increasing hostility between Liebknecht and Johann Most, later advocate of 'propaganda by deed' but at that time still a prominent member of the German Social Democratic Party. Because of increasingly anarchist leanings, in 1880 Most was expelled from the party and subsequently emigrated to the United States. He was one of the organizers of the Pittsburgh congress of 1883 in which August Spies and Albert Parsons, also two of the later Chicago martyrs, participated. The Chicago *Arbeiterzeitung*, the organ edited by Spies, was associated with the International Working People's Association founded on this occasion.[7]

From mid-September to the end of November 1886, Wilhelm Liebknecht, together with Karl Marx's daughter Eleanor and her husband Edward Aveling, conducted an agitation tour throughout the United States in which the relationship between socialism and anarchism was an important theme (Obermann 1966; Becker 1967). Liebknecht consistently condemned anarchist tactics and strategies but also, at the same time, the Chicago verdict. Already the party newspaper *Der Sozialdemokrat* (25 August 1886) had defined this verdict as 'sevenfold statutory murder' and as an 'emanation of the most brutal class justice, of wildest vindictiveness' (Becker 1967, p. 845). On 4 November 1886, in an assembly in Chicago, Liebknecht affirmed that although in principle he disagreed with the convicted anarchists, he saw them as people who wanted the same ends as his party and that differences existed only concerning the means to be employed. The following day, after visiting Spies and the others in prison, Liebknecht said: 'Today I visited men who were my enemies and who were convicted not because they were anarchists but because they were representatives of the proletariat' (Becker 1967, p. 860).

Although these positions went beyond solidarity as a mere matter of principle – and also had the tactical aspect of reaching out to anarchist activists and sympathizers – they did not mean that Liebknecht advocated a direct action approach to May Day. On the contrary, together with August Bebel he convinced Lavigne to add a third paragraph to his resolution, specifying that the workers of the various nations should organize the demonstration in a manner suited to conditions in their country, thereby leaving complete freedom as to what kind of May Day events to organize.

In the face of this vagueness of the Paris resolution a debate about 'what should happen on 1 May' developed, whose strength and enthusiasm took party and union leaders by surprise, and in which also ideas were advanced that went far beyond the intentions of the Paris congress. It is important to underline that this debate was set off not by Haymarket or in its aftermath, but by the founding congress of the Second International. In particular for Western Europe, in fact, 'there was no explicit link between the Haymarket affair and the decision to institute an international First of May' (Perrier and Cordillot 1992, p. 174).

The Origins of May Day: Conflicting Memories

As Danielle Tartakowski, a well-known French expert on the history of May Day, has stated, references to Chicago were largely, at least in Europe, an a posteriori reconstruction (*Nouvelle Observateur*, 30 April 2012). Through the narratives developed in this process, Haymarket exerted its influence on May Day also in Western Europe. In the anarchists' and anarco-syndicalists' narrative of the origins of May Day, the Chicago events became a central element, and in certain countries, particularly in Southern Europe, played an important role in the establishment of May Day traditions (see chapters 3 and 5). To a considerable extent, the prominence and strength of this narrative depended on the windows of opportunity for a proletarian revolution (or what were perceived as such) opening up. It did receive for instance a boost with the Russian revolution of 1905.

In Western Europe the narrative connecting the origins of May Day with the Chicago events of 1886 was advanced most forcefully by Spanish anarchism (see Chapter 5). In Spain the anarchist May Day celebration focused on mourning the Chicago martyrs. Their fate served as a lesson that the working classes had nothing to expect from the state, irretrievably in the service of the bourgeoisie, also in the form of a democratic republic as in the USA. Like their American (Haverty-Stacke 2009, p. 28) and French comrades (Tartakowsky 2005, p. 21), the Spanish anarchists remained sceptical if not hostile *vis-à-vis* the objective of the eight-hour workday, which was seen as unrealistic in the bourgeois regime. Instead of a demand to be realized in the existing society, it became a symbol of open warfare between the working class and the state. Polemicizing with 'peaceful demonstrations' and 'slavish petitions', i.e. the forms of action most clearly in line with the spirit of the Paris resolution, Spanish anarchists promoted the general strike and staged May Day as a dress rehearsal of social revolution (Chapter 5, p. 107). The basic script of this narrative of the origins of May Day located in the Haymarket incidents and its use as an argument for direct action on May Day, and in general for the revolutionary general strike as the principle weapon in the fight for the liberation of the working classes, remained unchanged when Spanish anarchism came under the influence of French syndicalism.[8]

In the countries covered in this volume, only in Italy did the anarchist narrative of the origins of May Day have a similar influence, albeit to a lesser extent and for a shorter time period. In Germany, with a weak if not marginal anarchist movement and an overpowering social democracy, references to Haymarket in pre-1914 anarchist May Day rituals and publications are not absent.[9] but it was not unusual for the event to go unmentioned. In this case German anarchists presented a narrative very similar to that of the radical wing of the Social Democratic Party. According to this narrative it was the Paris resolution that called for direct action in the form of a general abstention from work that in its final consequence would grow into a revolutionary general strike.[10] At the same time the Paris congress was defined as a concoction of the international Marxist clique, and its authoritarian conduct at the congress and its intolerance towards the (actually exceedingly few) anarchist delegates were criticized.[11] This narrative was later taken up by the minority of the so-called locally organized trade unions, expelled in 1908 from the Social Democratic Party for their anarco-syndicalist tendencies (see Chapter 3, p. 39).

Common to all anarchist and syndicalist May Day narratives were heavy attacks on the socialists as the betrayers of the original significance of May Day as a day of international direct action. The socialists were accused of reigning in and frustrating the revolutionary enthusiasm of the masses; of having worked, since the first May Day celebrations in 1890, or already at the Paris congress of 1889, for a docile and emaciated May Day, harmless for capitalism and the bourgeois state. Heroicized accounts of early May Days were contrasted with an anaemic socialist May Day emptied of its real significance. In particular the socialist festive May Day events were presented as nothing but a generalized blue Monday, 'a welcome occasion for binge drinking and dancing in [social democratic] party pubs'.[12] It did not prove easy, however, to translate a radical May Day narrative into radically different May Day events.[13]

Yet it was not the radical anarchist and/or syndicalist narrative of the origins of May Day that emerged as dominant in Western Europe, but the more moderate socialist narrative. According to this narrative – compared to the anarchist narrative more directly connected with structured organizations of the workers' movement – it was the Paris congress of 1889 that had established May Day as the 'international holiday of the world proletariat'. The accounts in May Day speeches and in the May Day editions of the socialist press usually glossed over the fact that in Paris the delegates had decided for a single mobilization on 1 May 1890 and not for an international holiday of labour. Only the massive response of the rank and file had led subsequent international and national socialist congresses to commit the movement to a May Day to be celebrated yearly (e.g. in Germany the Halle party congress in 1890) and on 1 May (the Second International's Brussels congress of 1891).

For the socialist narrative, references to Haymarket were of little importance.[14] As an exemplary episode of repression of the workers' movements' mobilizations for the eight-hour workday, the Chicago events remained connected also with the general socialist May Day tradition. By and large, however, socialists did not keep up the memory of the martyrs, at least not as part of their militant culture. A country like Italy, where the radical wing of the socialist movement was particularly strong and May Day events saw the common participation of socialists and anarchists, was an exception in this respect. In general, for socialist theory and policies only negative lessons were drawn: the American tragedy made most socialist strategists even more determined to steer clear of all dangerous connections with violence and what were perceived as reckless expressions of revolutionism. Haymarket has been defined as one factor (among many others) in the process through which most European socialist parties changed from marginal, vocally revolutionary organizations, into social democratic parties rooted in the life of the nation-states (Perrier *et al.* 1986, pp. 46–49).

One could argue that among socialists the legacy of the Chicago events was felt in the growing importance of the suspension of work on May Day. Although this form of action was not endorsed by the Paris resolution – on the contrary, a resolution calling for a general strike was presented in Paris but voted down by the congress – it rapidly came to be regarded (as was repeatedly stressed by national and international socialist congresses) as 'the most dignified' way of celebrating the 'world holiday of the proletariat'.[15] However, socialist calls for a suspension of work on May Day always made its realization dependent, in varying degrees, on the conditions in the various countries. Moreover, in the mainstream socialist narrative this form of action was not associated with the American events of 1886 and the general strike idea propagated by anarchists and syndicalists.

In fact, more than the legacy of Haymarket, this development mirrored the influence of the general example of coordinated mass strikes for the eight-hour day in the United States. In addition this example could find its echo in Europe because it connected to similar events on the Old Continent. When launching the French campaign for shorter working hours in February 1889, Raymond Lavigne referred to the American, but also to the English example of simultaneously resorting, on the same day, to a similar form of action (Perrier *et al.* 1986, p. 47). As Friedhelm Boll (1992, p. 430) has underlined, May Day did not come into existence sometime and somehow; it is inseparably connected not only with the American mass strikes but also with the European strike waves developing in the same years. The different forms that the European strike wave of 1889/90 assumed under the diverging conditions in the various European countries had a formative influence on the shape of early May Days (Boll 1992, pp. 429–467).

Ultimately, the success and longevity of May Day in Western Europe are directly linked not with the radical narrative referring to Haymarket but with the moderate narrative referring to the Paris congress of 1889 and with the vitality, strength and international connectedness of the organizations represented in or linked to the Second International. This success was based also on the specific narrative of May Day and the connected content and form of May Day events developed by the socialist organizations – up to the present, in fact, other conceptions of May Day to a considerable extent are constructed in contrast to this dominant one. For (European) socialists, May Day from its beginnings was more than a demonstration or a strike for a single (if symbolic) measure. Already the Paris resolutions, containing both economic and political demands, can be defined as a minimum socialist programme presented to the political authorities. Moreover socialists staged May Day as both a day of struggle *and* a day of celebration: May Day publications from as early as 1890 defined it as 'Maifeier', 'festa del lavoro', 'fêtes du travail', and so on. This narrative of May Day not only as a political activity but as a festival was made official by the Brussels Congress of the Second International already in 1891. The idea of a universal public festival or holiday of labour was presented as in itself filled with political meaning (Hobsbawm 1991, pp. 111–115). According to an editorial in *Vorwärts* (1 May 1891), the newspaper of the German social democrats, a world festival, instituted by the workers and made a reality by the workers, notwithstanding all the hostility of the united enemies, was in itself a triumph for international social democracy.

Not being rooted in an exemplary conflict between the workers and the state but in a resolution calling for the presentation of the immediate demands of the proletariat to the authorities, the mainstream socialist narrative certainly did not have the same revolutionary immediacy as the anarchist one. For socialists the political significance of May Day, however, went far beyond the mere institution of a universal public festival or holiday of labour. According to *Vorwärts*, May Day was not only the world holiday of labour but also the day on which the organized workers counted themselves and their adversaries.

> To show us our goal in flaming radiance, to present the immediate demands of the working people to the authorities, to bring us to fullest and clearest conscience the community of interests, of feeling and of thinking with our comrades in the fatherland and in all other countries of the world, and to burn deep into our hearts the duties that the common struggle for emancipation imposes on us – that is the purpose and the destiny of the May labour holiday.
>
> (1 May 1892; author's translation)

In other words, May Day was the one day on which the socialist workers' movement presented its strength to the external world and strove to reinforce the movement internally. In the May Day events the organizers attempted to connect the 'small utopias' (the immediate demands of the working people) with the 'great utopia' (the final goal of socialism) (see Chapter 10). Beyond the awareness of common material interests, they worked at strengthening an emotional and intellectual community of the workers' movement beyond national boundaries. Finally they strove to reinforce the commitment of their members, reminding them of their duties, and also (as e.g. the reports on agitation tours and on new members won in the May Day coverage of the workers' press show) to broaden their organizational base. At all events, the socialists attempted to stage the May Day ritual as an occasion for eventful protest (della Porta 2008; Chapter 1, p. 7–8).

The mainstream socialist narrative, however, did not remain uncontested within the socialists' own ranks. Radical socialists located the origins of May Day in the Paris resolution but they interpreted it in a more radical way. The Berlin resolution from March 1890 mentioned above (see note 1) called for making the suspension of work dependent on the organizational strength of the workers' movement, and not on general conditions. Describing May Day as the 'flaming emissary of revolutionary class struggle', Rosa Luxemburg defined the idea of the mass strike as the spirit from which May Day was born and that more and more had to dominate the strategy of the international proletariat (*Breslauer Volkswacht*, 30 April 1914). Favoured forms of action of radical socialists for May Day were the strike and street demonstrations. They accused moderate and cautious leaderships of watering down the original spirit of the Paris decision and warned against the degeneration of purely festive events.[16] References to the Chicago events remained more typical for the radical socialists in Latin countries, which in Italy became majoritarian within the party. Radical socialists in general integrated Haymarket into a series of key events for the movement for the eight-hour workday contributing to the establishment of May Day.

This radical socialist narrative of the origins of May Day formed the basis of the communist script that developed with the October revolution and the end of World War I. According to the *Rote Fahne* (1 May 1919), the newspaper of the German communists, the first May Day in 1890 was not meant as a joyous day of the proletariat but as a day of struggle against the bourgeoisie. From year to year more and more limited by trade union and party bigwigs, according to the communists, now May Day should be marked not only as a day of struggle, but also as a day of judgement over class traitors. An appeal of the Communist International published by the Italian communist newspaper *L'Unità* (1 May 1924) argued that the spirit of May Day had been betrayed by the social democratic leaders, but that now May Day had returned to being a day of revolutionary preparation. With a specific reference to Haymarket, the same appeal underlined that May Day had its story of martyrdom and sacrifice. The communist narrative of the origins of May Day did in fact integrate the Chicago events into a script of the 'world holiday of the proletariat' as characterized from its beginnings, on the one hand, by clashes between the workers and the state and, on the other hand, by the struggle between reformists and revolutionaries within the workers' movement (*Rote Fahne*, 14 April 1929).

German communists made massive use of a memory of May Day based on this narrative in the weeks leading up to the Berlin 'Blutmai', i.e. the bloody May Day of 1929, when clashes with the police in the wake of demonstration attempts disregarding a ban on street demonstrations led to at least 30 deaths (see Chapter 3, p. 46). Pre-1914 quotations from the social democratic press, venerated leaders like August Bebel and present party leaders served as proof for the betrayal of the original May Day spirit by the Weimar Republic social democrats. The *Rote Fahne* (13 March 1929; 14 April 1929) connected the Haymarket events with references to national martyrs, from Rosa Luxemburg and Karl Liebknecht to the activists of the Munich soviet republic, suppressed on May Day 1919. Subsequently, the Berlin 'Blutmai' became an event of May Day history characterized by the same tension between history and memory as the narratives about the origins of 1 May, and used in a similar way in contentious debates between moderates and radicals about the form and content of May Day.

In its further development, the communist narrative about the origins of May Day tended to connect the Chicago events directly with the Paris congress of 1889 in a script difficult to correlate with the historical reality as it can be reconstructed on the basis of primary sources. According to the *Great Soviet Encyclopaedia* (English translation of the 3rd edition, vol. 19, Macmillan, 1979), the Paris congress made 1 May a day of annual demonstrations to commemorate an action by the workers of Chicago who organized a strike for 1 May 1886 demanding an eight-hour workday and held a demonstration that ended in a bloody confrontation with the police. Underlining the frequent disagreements about the form and content of May Day between the revolutionary and reformist tendencies in the working-class movement, the Soviet encyclopaedia ascribes the clearly revolutionary, anti-capitalist tendency of May Day celebrations to the enormous revolutionizing effect of the October revolution.

***

The narrative of a May Day instituted in 1889 by the Paris congress as a commemoration of the Haymarket tragedy is hardly compatible with the accounts of historians, according to which references to Chicago in May Day narratives were reconstructed a posteriori and no explicit link existed between the Haymarket affair and the decision to institute an international 1 May. Especially in the last decades, however, this narrative became more and more widespread. It is not only shared by many left-wing activists, but in synthesis also contained in the articles on May Day in the *Encyclopedia Britannica* (2014 online edition) and the English, German, Italian, Spanish and Swedish Wikipedia editions (accessed 24 August 2015).

A first explanation for the success of this narrative can be found in the direct and indirect influence of Soviet communism that integrated Haymarket into its May Day tradition and allowed for the spread of a tradition directly linking May Day with Haymarket far beyond anarchist and syndicalist circles. The direct and indirect influence of Soviet communism, however, seems insufficient to explain the extent of the success of this narrative in countries with a workers' movement dominated and profoundly shaped by social democrats. To a certain extent, this success could be a consequence of the movements of the 1960s/1970s that largely referred to the radical socialist and/ or communist May Day narrative, and a reflection of the cultural climate of these years, e.g. in the encyclopaedia entries of the following decades. A more general factor that may come into play is the increasing loss of the socialist movement's capacity to determine the definition of May Day that went hand in hand with the incorporation of the date into the official calendar, with general processes of secularization and with the weakening of socialist organizations. Increasingly May Day appeared not as 'a manifestation of the workers for the class demands of the proletariat and world peace' but as a holiday like other holidays. As such, it was more and more understood as commemorating a distant event, and Haymarket with its tragic and heroic content lent itself more easily to that purpose than the Paris congress and the May Day celebrations of 1890.

As far as the traditional workers' movement itself is concerned, the developments of the last decades could be interpreted as a sign of the abating of the harsh ideological contrast between the radical (anarchist, communist, etc.) and the moderate (socialist, social democratic) wings within the traditional workers' movement, at least as far as its history is concerned. It seems however more to the point to read them as a temporary stage in a still ongoing contentious debate about both the memory and the essence of May Day.

Memory is not only inherently plural and contentious (Olick and Robbins 1998, p. 126), but also rooted in the present. The reading of the past depends on the present, including its potential use by contemporary actors that work as agents of memory (Maines, Sugrue and Katovich 1983).

The recent prominent use of the memory of Haymarket by an organization dominated for so long and to such an extent by social democrats like the German trade unions can be read along these lines. According to the section on the history of May Day on the website of the union federation DGB, 'today' the Haymarket riots are considered to mark the birth of May Day and the decision of the Paris congress occurred 'following the American example'.[17] This reference to Haymarket by an organization with the characteristics and the history of the DGB can be interpreted as a sign of crisis – both of the socialist/social democratic May Day tradition and its actual politics – and as an attempt to revitalize its own May Day rituals by incorporating elements of a more radical May Day memory (see Chapter 10).

Reactions to the recent tendency of moderate mainstream trade unions to incorporate Haymarket into their narratives confirm the interpretation of an ongoing struggle over the memory of May Day. One example is the debate concerning the prominent involvement of unions in the USA in memory work directly targeting Haymarket. In Chicago radicals denounced the dedication of the Haymarket Martyrs Monument as a US National Park Service Historic Landmark as an attempt to domesticate the radical May Day memory. Similar reactions were provoked by a new Haymarket monument (dedicated in 2004) focusing on free speech instead of the struggle for the eight-hour workday or the anarchist martyrs (Doebler 1999; Shackel 2011; Lampert 2013, pp. 71–85).[18] After more than 120 years the contentious debate about both the memory and the essence of May Day continues.

This chapter has concentrated on presenting ideal types of memories of the origins of May Day and its intended forms and objectives in the formative phase of the respective narratives. The last examples show, however, that these memories are not only plural but also transform over time. The actual conditions within the workers' movement and society at large in the various countries that shape – as the following chapters demonstrate – the staging of May Day rituals also shape May Day memories, favouring at times the presentation of a more radical narrative, or of a more moderate one or leading to moments of synthesis.

Notes

1 With a resolution on 'What should happen on 1 May' a group of Berlin trade unionists and social democrats proposed a far more radical May Day ritual than was the intention of the party leadership. On this specific case and for Germany in general see Müller 1990; for Italy see Renda 2009, p. 75ff.
2 The older literature speaks of legends of the origins of May Day (Antonioli 1988, pp. 39ff., 69). Critics of a collective memory concept have argued that it has nothing to add to older formulations like myth, tradition, custom and historical consciousness (Olick and Robbins 1998, p. 112; Gedi and Elam 1996).

3 On social movements and memory as well as for a review of the relevant literature see Zamponi 2015; della Porta 2015. In the wake of Pierre Nora's work, Fincardi (1997) has treated May Day as a 'lieu de mémoire', a memory site understood as 'any significant entity, whether material or non-material in nature, which by dint of human will or the work of time has become a symbolic element of the memorial heritage of any community' (Nora 1996, p. xvii), in this case the Italian national community.

4 In this necessarily brief presentation, the different ways in which memory influences, both as a resource and as a constraint, the strategic choices of a movement cannot be discussed in any detail. For an interpretative approach see Zamponi 2015, pp. 218–256.

5 For Eric Hobsbawm (1983, p. 283), 'the choice of this date was certainly quite pragmatic in Europe. It probably had no ritual significance in the USA, where "Labour Day" had already been established at the end of summer.'

6 At its 1884 convention the AFL's predecessor, the Federation of Organized Trades and Labor Unions, had adopted a resolution which established the first Monday in September as a 'laborers' national holiday' (Fine 1954, p. 134). In order to fix this holiday in fact as well as in law, workers in the United States had to engage employers and the state in direct confrontations (Kazin and Ross 1992, p. 1303).

7 On the Pittsburgh congress and differences between Most and the Chicago group see Avrich 1984, pp. 68–78; Green 2006, p. 129f.

8 On the prominent use of Haymarket in the French May Day campaigns in 1905 and 1906 see Perrier *et al.* 1986, p. 48; on the connection between the general strike idea and French May Days and the debate about the origins of May Day between the socialists and the syndicalist trade union CGT see Tartakowski 2005, p. 69ff.

9 According to a police report dated 4 May 1914, the speaker at the anarchist May Day celebration underlined that the social democrats were in the wrong, celebrating that year the twenty-fifth anniversary of May Day, as May Day had been celebrated by comrades for the first time in 1886 in Chicago and later had been consecrated with their blood (Landesarchiv (LA) Berlin, A Pr. Br. Rep. 030 Nr. 8694, f. 64).

10 Cf. the 1897 May Day numbers of *Der arme Konrad* and *Der Sozialist*, Geheimes Staatsarchiv Preußischer Kulturbesitz (GStAPK), Berlin, I HA Rep. 77 CB S Nr. 604, ff. 109, 110.

11 In 1893 the Zürich congress formally excluded anarchist delegates from the Second International. Some German anarchists even denied that May Day – having been dominated for years by the social democrats – in the future could become the day for a massive international demonstration through a general strike. 'And what should it import us? Any day is the appropriate one'. *Der arme Konrad*, 29 April 1899, GStAPK Berlin, I HA Rep. 77 CB S Nr. 677a, f. 82.

12 *Der arme Konrad*, 29 April 1899, GStAPK Berlin, I HA Rep. 77 CB S Nr.677a, f. 82; see also Chapter 5, p. 119.

13 See Chapter 3, p. 40; Chapter 5, p. 115. For similar problems for the communists in the 1920s and 1930s see Chapter 3, p. 45 and Chapter 6, p. 147–148.

14 Haymarket is not even mentioned in an article with the title 'The Labour Day in the United States' published in the 1892 *Mai-Festzeitung*, the special newspaper edition published yearly by the German Social Democratic Party on the occasion of the May Day celebrations (Achten 1980, p. 32). Paradoxically, in the yearly May Day coverage of the party newspaper *Vorwärts*, i.e. all articles dedicated to the event published between 27 April and 4 May, the first article discussing Haymarket at any length appeared on 30 April 1929, i.e. the day before the Berlin 'Blutmai' (see Chapter 3).

15 According to the account of August Bebel (1893, p. 438), the idea of a general strike was ventilated but met with so little response that it was not even formulated. On the reluctance among trade union leaders to commit organizational and

financial resources to an event perceived as having symbolic but little practical relevance see Chapter 3, p. 64 n.8; Chapter 6, p. 139.

16 On the particularly strong criticism of May Day as a mere festival among Italian socialists see Antonioli 1988, p. 69; on the rejection of May Day as a mere celebration of work by radical Spanish socialists see Chapter 5, p. 113.

17 See www.dgb.de/themen/++co++4b259ae4-759a-11e0-7c08-00188b4dc422 (accessed 9 December 2014); earlier versions of this section did not contain such an explicit reference to Haymarket. Together with the Spanish Confederación General del Trabajo (CGT) and the Swedish Landsorganisationen (LO), the DGB is one of the European trade union confederations that affixed a commemorative plaque on the Haymarket monument. The DGB's plaque carries the inscription: 'If the workers are united, they will never be defeated. In memory of the victims of the Haymarket massacre in May 1886. Dedicated on May 1, 2015 by Deutscher Gewerkschaftsbund, remembering 125 years of Labor Day.'

18 According to the inscription on the monument, over the years 'the site of the Haymarket bombing has become a powerful symbol for a diverse cross-section of people, ideals and movements. Its significance touches on the issues of free speech, the right of public assembly, organized labor, the fight for the eight-hour workday, law enforcement, justice, anarchy, and the right of every human being to pursue an equitable and prosperous life. For all, it is a poignant lesson in the rewards and consequences inherent in such human pursuits.'

References

Achten, U. (Ed.). (1980). *Zum Lichte empor. Mai-Festzeitungen der Sozialdemokratie 1891–1914*. Berlin and Bonn: J.H.W. Dietz.

Antonioli, M. (1988). *Vieni o maggio. Aspetti del Primo Maggio in Italia tra otto e novecento*. Milan: Angeli.

Avrich, P. (1984). *The Haymarket Tragedy*. Princeton, NJ: Princeton University Press.

Bebel, A. (1893). Die Maifeier und ihre Bedeutung. *Die Neue Zeit*, 11(14), 437–444.

Becker, G. (1967). Die Agitationsreise Wilhelm Liebknechts durch die USA 1886. Ergänzendes zu einer Dokumentation von Karl Obermann. *Zeitschrift für Geschichtswissenschaft*, 15(5), 843–862.

Boll, F. (1992). *Arbeitskämpfe und Gewerkschaften in Deutschland, England und Frankreich. Ihre Entwicklung vom 19. zum 20. Jahrhundert*. Bonn: J.H.W. Dietz.

Cordillot, M. (1988). Les réactions européennes aux événements de Haymarket. In M. Debouzy (Ed.), *A l'ombre de la Statue de la Liberté. Immigrants et ouvriers dans la République américaine 1880–1920* (pp. 181–190). Saint-Denis: Presses Universitaires de Vincennes.

della Porta, D. (2008). Eventful protest, global conflicts. *Distinktion: Scandinavian Journal of Social Theory*, 17, 27–56.

della Porta, D. (2015). Past and present: History as resource and constraint for social movements. Lecture on the occasion of the conferral of an honorary doctorate of the University of Gothenburg, 15 October 2015.

Doebler, G.L. (1999). The contest for memory: Haymarket through a revisionist looking glass, http://theanarchistlibrary.org/library/g-l-doebler-the-contest-for-memory-haymarket-through-a-revisionist-looking-glass.

Dommanget, M. (1972). *Histoire du premier mai*. Paris: Éditions de la tête de feuilles.

Fincardi, M. (1997). Il 1° Maggio. In M. Isnenghi (Ed.), *I luoghi della memoria*, vol. 2: *Personaggi e date dell'Italia unita* (pp. 130–137). Rome: Laterza.

Fine, S. (1954). Is May Day American in origin? *The Historian*, 16(2), 121–134.

Foner, P.S. (1986). *May Day: A Short History of the International Workers' Holiday 1886–1986*. New York: International Publishers.

Gedi, N., and Elan, Y. (1996). Collective memory: What is it? *History and Memory*, 8(1), 30–50.

Giovanoli, F. (1925). *Die Maifeierbewegung. Ihre wirtschaftlichen und soziologischen Ursprünge und Wirkungen*. Karlsruhe: G. Braun.

Green, J. (2006). *Death in the Haymarket. A Story of Chicago, the First Labor Movement and the Bombing that Divided Gilded Age America*. New York: Anchor Books.

Haverty-Stacke, D.T. (2009). *America's Forgotten Holiday. May Day and Nationalism, 1867–1960*. New York and London: New York University Press.

Hobsbawm, E. (1983). Mass-producing traditions: Europe, 1870–1914. In E. Hobsbawm and T. Ranger (Eds), *The Invention of Tradition* (pp. 263–307). Cambridge: Cambridge University Press.

Hobsbawm, E. (1991). Birth of a holiday: The first of May. In C. Wrigley and J. Shepherd (Eds), *On the Move: Essays in Labour and Transport History* (pp. 104–122). London and Rio Grande: Hambledon Press.

Kansteiner, W. (2002). Finding meaning in memory: A methodological critique of collective memory studies. *History and Theory*, 41, 179–197.

Kazin, M., and Ross, S.J. (1992). America's Labor Day: The dilemma of a workers' celebration. *Journal of American History*, 78(4), 1294–1323.

Lampert, N. (2013). *A People's Art History of the United States: 250 Years of Activist Art and Artists Working in Social Justice Movements*. New York: The New Press.

Maines, D.R., Sugrue, N.M., and Katovich, M.A. (1983). The sociological import of G.H. Mead's theory of the past. *American Sociological Review*, 48(2), 161–173.

Müller, Dirk-H. (1990). Was soll am 1. Mai geschehen? In I. Marßolek (Ed.), *100 Jahre Zukunft. Zur Geschichte des 1. Mai* (pp. 77–101). Frankfurt a.M. and Vienna: Büchergilde Gutenberg.

Nora, P. (1996). From *Lieux de mémoire* to *Realms of Memory* [preface to the English-language edition of *Lieux de mémoire*]. In P. Nora (Ed.), *Realms of Memory. The Construction of the French Past*, vol. 1: *Conflicts and Divisions* (pp. xv–xxiv). New York: Columbia University Press.

Obermann, K. (1966). Die Amerikareise Wilhelm Liebknechts im Jahre 1886. *Zeitschrift für Geschichtswissenschaft*, 14(4), 611–617.

Olick, J.K., and Robbins, J. (1998). Social memory studies: From "collective memory" to the historical sociology of mnemonic practices. *Annual Review of Sociology*, 24, 105–140.

Perrier, H., and Cordillot, M. (1992). The origins of May Day: The American connection. In M. Debouzy (Ed.), *In the Shadow of the Statue of Liberty: Immigrant Workers and Citizens in the American Republic 1880–1920* (pp. 157–187). Urbana and Chicago: University of Illinois Press.

Perrier, H., Collomp, C., Cordillot, M., and Debouzy, M. (1986). The 'social revolution' in America? European reactions to the 'great upheaval' and to the Haymarket affair. *International Labor and Working-Class History*, 29, 38–52.

Renda, F. (2009) *Storia del Primo Maggio dalle origini ai giorni nostri*. Rome: Ediesse.

Rivas, L. (2010). El doble origen del 1° de Mayo: La celebración del primer 1° de Mayo en España. In L. Rivas (Ed.), *1890–2010. El 1° de Mayo en España: 120 aniversario* (pp. 19–42). Madrid: Fundación 1° de Mayo.

Shackel, P.A. (2011). Remembering Haymarket and the control for public memory. In L. Smith, P.A. Shackel and G. Campbell (Eds), *Heritage, Labour and the Working Classes* (pp. 34–51). New York: Routledge.

Tartakowsky, D. (2005). *La part du rêve. Histoire du 1ᵉʳ mai en France*. Paris: Hachette.
Zamponi, L. (2015). Memory in action: Mediatised public memory and the symbolic construction of conflict in student movements. PhD thesis, European University Institute, Florence.

3 The First of May in Germany and Italy

Herbert Reiter

From its very beginning, 1 May has been characterized by the dialectic national–international. Aspects beyond the national framework have been repeatedly treated in the scientific literature, and more than one study has been presented specifically as an international history of 1 May (Foner 1986; Panaccione 1990). Almost completely lacking, however, are studies explicitly following a comparative approach.[1] In the following, it is not possible to bridge this gap, but only to give some indications for a comparison of the history of 1 May in Germany and Italy, on a limited documentary basis and restricted to certain aspects of May Day – in particular, state reactions, May Day narratives (see Chapter 2), event formats and levels of participation.[2]

A comparison between Germany and Italy seems to suggest itself because of numerous parallel developments in the two countries: late national unity, late industrialization, late democratization and a fascist experience. With regard to our particular topic, however, important differences must also be underlined. Nineteenth-century industrialization was stronger and more dynamic in Germany than in Italy. Correspondingly, particularly in the earlier periods under study, the German workers' movement was stronger than the Italian. The latter showed a more plural development and, unlike in Germany, the more radical wing constituted the majority for long periods. Without ignoring the impact of these differences on May Day celebrations in the two countries, this chapter aims above all at underlining similar and parallel developments.

The first part of the chapter will be dedicated to the birth of May Day, the reaction of the German and Italian states to the phenomenon and the characteristics of May Day narratives and rituals in Germany and Italy up to and including World War I. The second part will highlight the developments in the turbulent interwar period, in particular the divisions within the left, the rise of the fascist movements and the different reactions of the fascist regimes in both countries towards May Day – i.e. prohibition in Italy and usurpation in Germany. A final part will discuss the development of May Day after World War II as a history not only of decline, but also of repeated periods of reappropriation by the labour movements and also increasingly by the new social movements in Germany and Italy.

May Day Rituals in Germany and Italy from the International Congress in Paris (1889) to 1918

Regarding the early development of the labour movement in Germany and Italy, several differences must be underlined. Compared to its German counterpart, the Italian socialist labour movement was a late starter. Concentrated in the north of the country, until World War I it remained considerably smaller in terms of both the number of party and trade union members, and the number of votes polled in general elections.[3] Unlike the German social democrats, the Italian socialists collaborated closely in parliament with other 'extreme' parties, and the local 'Camere del lavoro' ideally brought together trade union organizations with different ideological outlooks. Finally, within the Italian Socialist Party, the left 'maximalist' wing was stronger than within the German Social Democratic Party; it held the party leadership from 1912 until the establishment of the fascist regime.

The Birth of May Day and Bourgeois State and Society

For the German workers' movement, dominated by social democrats, May Day was based on the resolution of the founding congress of the Second International in Paris in July 1889 (see Chapter 2). For the first May Day celebrations in Germany, the Haymarket affair was of little or no importance and remained so in the coming years.[4] Initially even the Italian anarchists referred to May Day as the 'festa del Primo Maggio' (Antonioli 1988, p. 28) but from early on integrated Haymarket into their May Day narrative as proof that the call for direct action had been an integral part of 1 May from its very beginning. In this way they created a 'legend of the origins' of May Day – partly shared by radical socialists in Germany and Italy – that also connected an action-orientated and potentially revolutionary interpretation with the Paris congress of 1889.[5]

The Paris resolution, however, in consideration of the specific national conditions, had left the decision about forms of action to the workers' organizations of the individual countries. In particular, delegates from Germany, where the anti-socialist law was still in force, had spoken against declaring a mass strike the only form of May Day demonstration, arguing that it should not be dictated as compulsory if action was to be international. Subsequently the German party leadership continued to take a cautious stance, and calls for more radical forms of action rose above all from the grassroots level. In fact, the May Day narratives promoted within parts of the labour movement went beyond the intentions expressed in the resolution passed by the Paris congress (Braun and Schwarz 1989, p. 15). If the many assemblies discussing the preparation of the first May Day celebrations proved the success of the May Day idea, the spectrum of the scripts advanced – from mass strike and demonstrative action to festive celebrations – reveals how undefined the form and content of May Day presented itself in both countries in 1890 (Müller 1990, pp. 79, 82ff.; Renda 2009, p. 75ff.). But as Antonioli (1988, p. 27) underlines, the scripts' 'day of celebration' and 'day of struggle' did not initially constitute a contradiction: Both types of action were used complementarily by the workers in order to appropriate the day for themselves.

Against the background of the major North American and European strike wave with which the birth of May Day is closely connected (Boll 1992, p. 430), fears about the dimension of the action planned for 1 May 1890 were nevertheless rampant in the bourgeois press. The *Hamburger Nachrichten* (27 April 1890) defined it as the 'dress rehearsal for the social world revolution' and, according to the liberal Berlin *Volks-Zeitung*, the enthusiasm of certain classes of workers had been ignited to a flame by unscrupulous and dishonest demagogues.[6] The Turin newspaper *La Stampa* (30 April 1890) argued that this widespread fear justified restrictive government measures.

In fact, governments in both countries took severe restrictive measures against the first May Day celebrations (see also chapters 4 and 5). The Italian government prohibited all public demonstrations and assemblies, allowing only closed meetings of associations. The Prussian government ordered full use of all legal measures, including the anti-socialist law, against calls to suspend work, against public assemblies and demonstrations in the open, but also against indoor meetings and closed meetings of associations (Saul 1972, p. 298). Similarly in the parts of Germany (such as the city-state of Hamburg) that allowed closed meetings of trade unions and evening celebrations, May Day preparations and activities remained under strict surveillance, especially the excursions organized in order to evade the ban on demonstrations (Hund 1990; Lerch 1988, p. 366ff.). In Italy police and military intervened against all attempts to form street demonstrations or to persuade fellow workers at the factory gates to suspend work and participate (*La Stampa*, 2 May 1890). Trespassers were immediately sentenced to prison terms ranging from several months to up to four years (*La Stampa*, 3 May 1890).

Decisive resistance against the May Day celebrations came also from public and private employers, who threatened workers with immediate dismissal or several days or weeks of lockout if they suspended work. Employers that consented to the day off remained a clear minority. In Hamburg, where the calls to suspend work for 1 May were particularly successful (and the workers' movement particularly well organized), the reaction of employers was particularly violent. Approximately 20,000 workers were locked out and the ensuing conflict, which dragged on until late summer, ended with a clear defeat for the workers and their organizations.[7] A direct consequence of these experiences was a centralization process within the German trade unions, a process which the employers had already concluded in April 1890 in anticipation of the conflicts expected for 1 May (Saul 1990).

The Format of May Day Events and State Response

Considering the format of May Day events in the period before World War I in a comparative perspective, some differences emerge. According to all national and international decisions of the socialist workers' movement, abstention from work was to be considered the most important and 'dignified' form of action for May Day. Particularly in the 1890s, in both countries this form of action faced the opposition of both government and employers – in Italy to the extent that socialist leader Filippo Turati spoke of a 'privilege of a few better-organized workers' (Antonioli 1988, p. 55). Judging from the accounts in *Vorwärts* and *L'Avanti!*, the 'Arbeitsruhe' saw a continuous expansion in the years leading up to World War I, reaching massive proportions especially in the larger Italian cities. It must be considered, however, that abstention from work did not necessarily mean going on strike. In Florence (*L'Avanti!*, 3 May 1900) and Brescia, for example, agreements were sought and reached with employers to give the day off, a practice that parts of the workers' movement criticized as a loss of the class character of May Day (Bertozzi 2009, p. 117f.). Increasingly – as in Turin (*L'Avanti!*, 3 May 1907) – 1 May was also officialized as a holiday in collective bargaining contracts. Under these circumstances, a high degree of abstention from work did not necessarily translate into high numbers of participants in rallies and demonstrations. In Milan in 1901, of the *c.* 80,000 blue-collar workers, 60,000 were said to have abstained from work – but the May Day rally saw only 3,500 participants (Renda 2009, p. 133). Agreements similar to the Italian ones were also reached in Germany, but employers seem to have remained more hostile to May Day, regularly resorting to the lockout of participating workers.[8]

Especially in the 1890s, in a central component of the Italian May Day ritual, a delegation of the workers presented their demands to the mayors of the respective cities. This format was lacking in Germany, where city mayors were far more public officials than the expression of popular will.[9] The demands presented to the mayors were predominantly practical and concrete, aiming at local taxes, schools, housing and public transport, but in individual cases also called for democratic improvements: the 1901 petition of the Turin workers proposed the introduction of local referenda for important questions concerning all citizens.[10] Later, with the gaining of the mayorship by the Socialist Party, in certain Italian cities May Day celebrations took on an official form.[11]

In both countries the most popular formats, both in terms of the number of events and the number of participants, were organized mostly by the political parties and had a predominantly festive and entertaining character. In Italy the dominant form consisted of garden celebrations outside the city gates, in Germany of evening indoor celebrations that extended (weather permitting) to the gardens of the various establishments. It has to be underlined that, considering the hostility of the state and employers towards May Day, any May Day event had a political character. In addition, even the events with a predominantly festive character contained clearly political elements. The May Day speech was part of both the Italian and the German festive celebrations. Party newspapers characterized the pieces performed by workers' choral societies as 'songs of freedom and struggle'. Consequently, all elements of the predominantly festive May Day events were also scrutinized by the state censorship.[12]

In line with their May Day narratives, different parts of the workers' movement in the two countries promoted different formats of May Day events with a clearly political character (see Chapter 2). The actual realization of the different formats, however, was determined above all by the level of state repression. In Italy, the rise of Antonio Giolitti as the dominant statesman, usually in the double function of prime minister and interior minister, at the beginning of the twentieth century led to a liberal turn, resulting in 1913 in the first Italian national elections with universal male suffrage. Especially in the northern cities, street demonstrations and outdoor rallies (in the 1890s an exception) became increasingly possible, although closely watched by police and military (Antonioli 1988, pp. 95ff., 121ff.). This surveillance extended to the speeches held, which were interrupted by police officers in the case of violent language or attacks on the crown or the military. It also has to be underlined that Giolitti always gave free rein to the prefects, the *longa manus* of the government in the periphery, to prohibit demonstrations and rallies as they saw fit.[13]

In Germany in the 1890s a tradition of May Day street demonstrations also hardly existed outside the city-state of Hamburg.[14] A development similar to Italy can be observed in the smaller German states, in particular in the south, where universal male suffrage was introduced in 1906 for regional elections – a right that existed in the rest of Germany only for national votes. In by far the largest German state, Prussia, however, authorities fought a strenuous rearguard action against permitting street demonstrations, in particular on May Day. In doing so, they acted against the spirit of the new 1908 national law on associations, according to which the prohibition of open-air rallies and street demonstrations was possible only for reasons of public security (no longer for public order and security). As the highest Prussian administrative court repeatedly stressed, arguments for a possible danger to public security had to be grounded in concrete facts in the specific context of time and place. The same court, however, lowered safeguards specifically for May Day demonstrations, pronouncing such demonstrations as per se a provocation of bourgeois society.[15]

This situation made indoor morning assemblies organized by the trade unions the main format for predominantly political May Day events in Germany, with attempts to form demonstrations before or after the assembly regularly prevented by the police. The assembly did have the advantage of allowing greater organizational control over attendance, as participants had to buy a May Day stamp to be glued into their membership book. In comparing attendance reported by the workers' press for the Hamburg demonstration and for the Berlin assemblies, we find far greater variation in Hamburg (705,738 inhabitants in 1900), with participation reaching 100,000 and more, but also dropping to 7,000 in 1897; in Berlin (1,888,848 inhabitants in 1900) the morning assemblies saw a fairly steady increase from just below 20,000 in the early years to more than 90,000 in 1910. In addition, May Day demonstrations in Germany (but also in Italy) had to cope with police restrictions concerning the venue, the flags to be carried (the colour red but even more so the black of the anarchists being a continuous cause of friction), the music to be played by the bands, singing and shouting, the carrying of sticks, and so on (see also chapters 4 and 5). In particular, the practice by police authorities in cities like Hamburg of confining demonstrations to the periphery provoked disaffection with this form of action.[16] After the success of the huge demonstrations in favour of universal suffrage in 1910, however, May Day participants were also increasingly unwilling to respect the ban on street demonstrations in Prussia.[17]

Even in the early years of May Day, a higher level of conflict and of violent coercion emerges as an important difference between Italy and Germany, especially in connection with street demonstrations and open-air rallies. In Italy, a first serious incident happened as early as 1891. Police had consented to an open-air rally in Rome, allowing workers' associations to walk with their banners (taking the shortest route) from their offices to the site of the rally (*La Stampa*, 29 April 1891). At the rally, incidents between demonstrators and police broke out, for which the anarchists were held responsible; one policeman and one demonstrator were killed, an estimated 100 people were wounded and 300 arrested. In the same year, the police and army intervened in Florence (with two wounded demonstrators and 70 arrests), Milan, Bologna and Naples (Renda 2009, p. 101f.). In Germany incidents were more contained; legal battles over police prohibitions and intervention were more common than violence.

The Level of Participation in May Day Events

The level of participation in the first May Day celebrations in 1890 is difficult to determine. In the whole of Germany, *c.* 100, 000 workers are said to have suspended work for the day, 20,000–30,000 in Hamburg alone (Müller 1990, p. 85). May Day events were also well attended in other cities like Berlin (*c.* 20,000) and Dresden (*c.* 12,000) (Schuster 1991, p. 12). According to the associations of employers and the police, however, the percentage of striking workers was generally low (*Berliner Tageblatt*, 2 May 1890). The same holds true for Italy, where for most cities police reported the number of participants in May Day events in the hundreds and not thousands (*La Stampa*, 2 May 1890).[18] In general, for both countries strong local differences have to be underlined, regarding both the number of participants and the format of the events (street demonstrations, assemblies during and after working hours, excursions, popular fairs, events on 1 May or on the first Sunday in May, and so on). In any case, the success of the first May Day celebrations was of such a dimension that it persuaded workers' movement organizations to transform them from a single experience – the decision of the Paris congress had referred only to the year 1890 – into a permanent feature.

For the following years prior to World War I, even the participation numbers reported by *Vorwärts* – those given by the police often stayed significantly lower – indicate that, notwithstanding a general increase at least up to 1910, May Day in Germany was not the demonstration day of 'the proletariat' but of the organized workers' movement, that is, a minority within the workers' population. Police reports repeatedly even argued that the number of participants was lower than the number of workers organized in the trade unions and the Social Democratic Party. In years of low attendance the same argument was made by workers' movement newspapers, for instance in 1914 by the Stettin *Volksbote*. The same seems to hold true for Italy. According to *L'Avanti!*, in the years before World War I, participation in the capital Rome (with a population of 519,000 in 1911) exceeded 10,000 only in 1906 and 1911. In the cities of the so-called 'industrial triangle', as well, the considerable peaks reached in particular years remained exceptions – for example, the 1908 demonstration in Turin (with a population of 416,000 in 1911), in which 90,000 are reported to have participated. In Milan (with a population of 701,000 in 1911), for instance, participation peaked in 1910 with 25,000 participants, but typical attendance stayed below 10,000. Above all it has to be underlined that after the suppression of the 'Fasci siciliani' in 1894, May Day celebrations in the southern part of Italy were rare occasions.[19]

The level of mobilization for May Day events, however, consistently surpassed those of the other political movements. In addition, May Day actions radiated beyond the circle of participants, with demonstrations and the display of flags and symbols reaching onlookers and neighbours. As a result, we must qualify the evaluation of a part of the secondary literature which claimed that, before World War I, with the May Day celebrations the workers' movement hardly succeeded in occupying a significant part of the public space (Seeger 1995, p. 161). On the occasion of May Day, workers' protests reverberated beyond the subcultural ghetto, through the state's massive civil war preparations and the coverage in the bourgeois press. This coverage did not exist exclusively in the extremes of panic-mongering and minimization. Liberal-democratic newspapers like the *Frankfurter Zeitung* criticized the overreaction of conservative organs, defended the workers' right of assembly and reported in a fairly objective way on May Day events and the demands raised by the workers. In Italy, since the early 1890s, certain sectors of the liberal bourgeoisie and socially advanced Catholic circles saw 1 May as the symptom of a problem that had to be confronted in an innovative way, in contrast with the repressive course of the government (Antonioli 1988, p. 33).

Dominant Themes and Conflicting May Day Narratives

The indisputable success of the May Day rituals – despite the obstacles – was closely connected with the fact that their events were emotionally and mythologically charged. For the *Hamburger Echo* (4 May 1909), every May Day was a stage on the way to victory. The *Maizeitung* of 1907 defined 1 May as a 'pre-celebration of socialism, the day on which to everything which is oppressed and miserable the vision of a free and harmonic society appears that unfolds all developmental seeds of mankind' (Achten 1980, p. 152). According to a May Day manifesto of the Italian Socialist Party, for the proletariat 1 May was the 'inaugural day of its own redemption' (*giorno augurale della propria redenzione*) (*L'Avanti!*, 1 May 1905). These sentiments were less the expression of an ideology of revolutionary class struggle than of socialism as an 'ideology of hope' that also dominated in the iconography of May Day publications (Bouvier 1993; Marßolek 1990b; Panaccione 1989).

From the very beginning of May Day, this 'ideology of hope' was connected with concrete demands. In 1891 the international workers' congress in Brussels added peace and anti-militarism to the calls for an eight-hour workday and workers' protection. In addition, as *Vorwärts* (1 May 1902) stressed, May Day became a day to demonstrate for the demands currently dominating public life. In both Germany and Italy, protests were repeatedly directed against the tariff on grain. At the Hamburg demonstration in 1912, the worker teetotallers agitated and on banners single groups demanded the repeal of the servants' regulations or the abolition of the rules forcing workers to take board and lodging with their employers (*Hamburger Echo*, 3 May 1912). Above all, on May Day the workers consistently protested against infringements of democratic rights – in Germany in 1894 and 1899 against proposed repressive laws, in Italy in 1899 and 1900 against the reactionary government. Demonstrators asked for the full and unrestricted concession of those rights, in particular for the free, equal, secret and direct right to vote at all levels, regardless of gender.[20] Voting rights were the central demand on May Day 1910 in Germany and Italy, and in Germany the connection with the voting rights campaign for Prussia conducted by the Social Democratic Party led to the biggest mobilization success on May Day for the period prior to World War I (for Sweden see Chapter 4).

A specifically Italian theme remained the protest against 'eccidi' (massacres), i.e., the killing of workers by police forces and the military during demonstrations and strikes. The 1906 May Day manifesto of the Italian Socialist Party lamented that it was not strong enough to secure for Italian workers the most elementary of rights, the respect for their lives, on the part of the government and its coercive arm (*L'Avanti!*, 1 May 1906). While moderate social democratic politicians in Germany increasingly considered (but generally rejected) the idea of a general strike in order to win equal voting rights for Prussia, their comrades in Italy considered it as a defensive weapon against 'eccidi'.[21]

Probably one of the most important achievements of May Day, however, lay not in the realization of demands, but in the strengthening of the workers' movement. According to the *Maizeitung* of 1907, May Day united the proletariat, made it conscious of its power and strengthened its trust in itself (Achten 1980, p. 152), constituting an early example of eventful protest (della Porta 2008; see Chapter 1). Unlike Germany, however, counter-celebrations in Italy of Catholics and even liberals and monarchists openly contested the socialist May Day idea.[22] In addition, reflecting the pluralist development of the Italian workers' movement, May Day was far less a demonstration of organizational unity than it was in Germany. In the Italian street demonstrations (organized by the trade unions), various groups and parties – the Republican Party, various factions of the Socialist Party, the syndicalists, the anarchists – all participated, usually providing speakers at the rally. At times, this led to conflicting opinions being voiced at rallies and even to physical clashes. At the Rome rally in 1910, the syndicalist speaker openly criticized the Socialist Party and the anarchist speaker pronounced himself against universal suffrage – the central demand of the socialist manifesto in that year – and in favour of direct revolutionary action. At the same rally, a fistfight broke out between republicans and workers whose strike that party had criticized (*L'Avanti!*, 3 May 1910).

For Germany the image of complete organizational unity before World War I is largely but not completely accurate. Repeated debates at SPD party congresses on how to stage May Day testify to the presence of diverging May Day narratives within the party (see Chapter 2). Unlike in Italy, however, there were no events in which organizations with potentially conflicting ideological outlooks participated. The anarchists were so weak that they did not manage to organize their own event every year. In this case they attended the trade union assemblies and SPD events and attempted to agitate, but apparently without success and in the face of considerable hostility.[23] Throughout the pre-war years, the so-called 'locally organized' trade unions (far smaller than the main 'centrally organized' unions) held their own May Day events. Although part of the SPD, they stood for a more political role for the unions, and their May Day resolutions were more radical. When they moved increasingly in a syndicalist direction, the locally organized unions in 1908 were expelled from the SPD. From 1906 on their May Day resolutions had defined the general strike as the most important tool for the liberation of the proletariat.[24]

In both Germany and Italy, more radical groups put forward a May Day narrative geared to direct action (see also Chapter 5); they accused reformist socialists and moderate trade unions of smothering the original May Day spirit and their events of being nothing but festive occasions.[25] In Italy, where the maximalist faction gained the party leadership in July 1912, a similar May Day narrative is visible in the May Day manifestos of the Socialist Party and in the coverage of the party newspaper *L'Avanti!* from 1913 on. Starting with the 'legend of the origins' in the early years of May Day celebrations, in both

Germany and Italy conflicting moderate and radical May Day narratives therefore coexisted, the latter featuring more prominently in Italy. Prior to World War I and to the Bolshevik revolution in Russia, however, the impression of cohesion and (national and international) unity of the working class transmitted by the May Day celebrations was strong enough to mask these differences.

Radicals however had difficulties translating their May Day narratives into corresponding event formats. The format of the more radical groups' May Day events was in fact largely similar to that of the main actors. The same songs were sung at the morning assemblies of the locally and the centrally organized unions in Berlin; only the content of the speeches and resolutions was different. The locally organized unions held the same sort of festive event in the afternoon/evening as the Social Democratic Party did, with singing, dancing and various performances (in addition to the May Day speech). Furthermore, the same argument for organizing such an event – that it strengthened the sense of unity and solidarity – was used by both the locally organized unions and the SPD (*Die Einigkeit*, 9 May 1914; *Vorwärts*, 2 May 1911). Similarly, for the events of Italian radical groups, we find documented the same festive and ludic elements, such as concerts or lotteries, for which they criticized the moderates. Accusations of betraying the original significance of May Day by organizing predominantly festive events have to be read as a rhetorical element used in putting forward a radical May Day narrative and not as an indication of radically different formats.

The Divisive Impact of World War I

In particular in Germany, the divisive forces within the workers' movement became uncontrollable, not because of the contrast between moderates and radicals but as a result of the outbreak of war. The new dividing line, however, did not coincide with, respectively, the moderate and radical wings of the SPD. In the camp opposing the social democratic vote in favour of war credits, we find both the moderate Eduard Bernstein and the radical Rosa Luxemburg. During the war years, the party and trade union leadership opposed abstention from work on 1 May, and police enforced government restrictions allowing only closed meetings of trade unions and/or the Social Democratic Party.[26] The growing opposition to the official line of the main workers' movement organizations became visible in Berlin on 1 May 1916, when according to some accounts up to 10,000 people responded to Karl Liebknecht's appeal for the first public May Day demonstration since the outbreak of the war. From 1917 on, the newly formed USPD organized its own May Day events in opposition to the majority party's 'internal truce' politics sustaining Germany's war effort. The twofold division (moderates vs radicals and internal truce vs peace) complicated the realignment of the workers' parties in the early years of the Weimar Republic.

In Italy the colonial adventure in Libya had already added a new dividing line to the existing rift between radicals and moderates within the Socialist Party. During World War I the Socialist Party and trade unions continued to call for abstention from work and for the organization of May Day events against the war. In 1915, with Italy still remaining neutral, some of the largest May Day demonstrations up to that point took place – including in Turin (according to *L'Avanti!*), with 100,000 participants; but the following years saw growing police restrictions on street demonstrations and public rallies as well as censorship of May Day publications. In addition, the compromise formula to neither adhere to nor to sabotage ('nè aderire, nè sabotare') Italy's war effort veiled internal divisions concerning the war issue – which in the expulsion of Mussolini and his followers found only their most visible expression – that became apparent on 1 May with events organized separately by interventionists and neutralists (Giagnotti 1988; Renda 2009, p. 165ff.). As in Germany, the first peacetime May Day in Italy was celebrated by a variously divided workers' movement.

The First of May in the Interwar Period

The history of 1 May in Italy between the end of World War I and the advent of fascism is short and marked by various conflicts, in particular increasing fascist violence leading up to the outlawing of May Day celebrations in 1923. This violence overshadowed the internal divisions of the workers' movement that, except for a few years in the beginning of the 1920s, were the dominant theme of May Day in the Germany of the Weimar Republic (see also chapters 4 and 6). In both countries the optimism of the pre-war May Days gave way to a gloomier atmosphere against the background of the disenchanted hopes of both reformists and radicals connected with the revolutionary period of 1918–1920, and a subsequent retreat to defensive positions against reactionary and fascist counter-revolution.[27]

Disenchanted Revolutionary Hopes

In Italy only in 1919 did 1 May see large and peaceful demonstrations and rallies with few restrictions by the authorities, albeit under massive police surveillance and only a few weeks after a first serious episode of fascist violence: the destruction of the central offices of the party newspaper *L'Avanti!* on 15 April. The socialists' manifesto combined concrete demands with the uncompromising (verbal) revolutionism that has been underlined as characteristic of the party in those years (Eley 2002, p. 171). Within the Socialist Party the conviction was widespread that the final victory was just around the corner and would come inevitably, almost automatically. As an editorial in *L'Avanti!* (1 May 1919) explained, demands such as universal suffrage, a proportional election system or a constitutional assembly with the aim of introducing the republic, once assumed to necessitate years of political activity, were now revealed to be 'riformette' (small reforms) to be conquered on the double, the last fast steps for reaching the supreme destination of socialism.[28]

In many German cities, the 1919 divisions within the workers' movement found their expression in three separate demonstrations and/or rallies. The social democrats and the free trade unions celebrated as a victory the introduction of the democratic republic and the recognition of the eight-hour workday. But like the Italian socialists, for the Independent Social Democrats and the communists the revolution could come to an end only with the advent of socialism. This objective was called into question on 1 May 1919 by the suppression of the Munich soviet republic.

Social democrats and communists were further divided on the question of democracy and, together with the alignment with the Third International, it was this question that in the early 1920s brought about the disintegration of the USPD. In fact, the credo of the leading revisionist theorist Eduard Bernstein that democracy was a means and an end at the same time – both the means for fighting for socialism and the form of its realization – was shared beyond the rump SPD of 1919. Philipp Scheidemann, who from February to June 1919 led the German government, in an editorial for *Vorwärts* (30 April 1919), defended the position to strive onward to socialism 'on the path of an ordered democracy' and included the same concept in his speech at one of the SPD open-air rallies on 1 May (*Vorwärts*, 3 May 1919).[29]

Further signs of the divisions within the workers' movement were the contrasting opinions on the declaration of May Day as a public holiday by the German constituent assembly. The Italian *L'Avanti!* (29 April 1919) denounced this decision as an attempt to turn 1 May into a holiday for all parties and classes, envisioning a May Day stripped of its significance as a celebration of the proletariat. The final decision of the national assembly in 1919 had considerably changed the original social democratic proposal by adding to the reasons for the holiday calls for a just and fair peace and for the immediate liberation of all German prisoners of war.[30] Under the headline 'Farce – Komödie – Burleske', the *Rote Fahne* (29 April 1919) accused the SPD and trade union functionaries – who according to the Communist Party newspaper had strangled the original May Day, transforming it into a beer fest and a dancing party – of calling on the proletariat to demonstrate for national interests instead of promoting its own objectives and the proletarian world revolution. At the rallies in Berlin, held by the communists together with the independent social democrats, one of the speakers called it a disparagement of the revolutionary workers that the national assembly with its bourgeois majority had declared 1 May a public holiday (*Vorwärts*, 3 May 1919). For Philipp Scheidemann, instead, the destiny of 1 May revealed the essence of the revolution: May Day as a public holiday was a symbol for the increased power of the socialist workers (*Vorwärts*, 30 April 1919).

Throughout the German national territory, however, 1 May remained a public holiday only in 1919.[31] In 1920 the same parliament – the only legislature in which the republican parties of the so-called Weimar coalition between the social democrats, the Catholic Centre Party and the Democratic Party held a majority at the national level – voted down the renewed proposal to declare 1 May a national holiday. In the Prussian parliament, the Centre Party and the democrats opposed a similar proposal. An editorial in *Vorwärts* (28 April 1920) characterized this position of the SPD's bourgeois partners – along with their contemporaneous vote against the payment of wages for the days of the general strike that had brought down the reactionary Kapp Putsch – 'two slaps in the face' of the people. These decisions were in fact a sign that the policy pointed out by Scheidemann – to strive onward to socialism 'on the path of an ordered democracy' – might face different but equally insurmountable difficulties as a maximum programme of socialist revolution or insurrectional attempts.[32]

In Italy, where the Socialist Party never backed a reformist programme of parliamentary stabilization, the hopes for the immediate institution of a socialist republic did indeed prove fragile (Eley 2002, p. 169ff.). The 1920 May Day manifesto of the Socialist Party continued to point at the dictatorship of the proletariat as the supreme end to which all other ends were to be subordinated. However, now this supreme end appeared reachable only after hard battles, and not as easily as it had seemed in 1919.[33] In 1921 the climate had definitely changed. If in 1920 May Day for *L'Avanti!* (4 May) had been a 'marvellous class conscious and internationalist demonstration', in 1921 it had become a 'holy 1 May of struggle, martyrdom and faith' (*L'Avanti!*, 1 May 1921). Faced with fascist violence, the workers' movement found itself increasingly on the defensive (Renda 2009, p. 194). A few days before May Day, after the killing of one of their comrades, the Turin fascists conducted a 'spedizione punitiva', devastating and setting fire to the trade union building. In reaction, factories were occupied and a general strike was called, leading to arrests and further clashes between fascists and activists of the workers' parties. The police issued a ban on the May Day demonstration and on the central rally, allowing only three smaller rallies in the periphery of the city. As *La Stampa* remarked (2 May 1921), since the beginning of May Day celebrations in Turin no one recalled such a quiet and colourless 1 May. In other cities as well, police restrictions and fascist aggression marked the celebrations.

In a climax of fascist violence, in 1922 May Day was marred in 26 cities by various aggressions, shootings and clashes, with six people killed and 25 wounded (Renda 2009, p. 194). Although a government decree declared May Day an official holiday (but not a bank holiday) for that year, the government's giving a free hand to the prefects to prohibit May Day events in the provinces led to numerous restrictions.[34] In this respect, *L'Avanti!* (28 April 1922) spoke of a new record for Italy in comparison with the other countries of the world.

44 *Herbert Reiter*

Conflicting May Days and May Day Narratives in a Divided Workers' Movement

With the foundation of the Italian Communist Party (PCI) in January 1921, the divisions within the socialist workers' movement that had been visible in Germany since 1916/17 became apparent in Italy as well, with evident repercussions on May Day celebrations. At the indoor rally in Milan – where socialist leader Turati lamented that this day should have imposed reciprocal respect – and at the Rome rally, communist speakers polemicized with the socialists, provoking the reaction of the majority of the participants; *L'Avanti!* (3 May 1921) spoke of 'the usual vulgar insults against the Socialist Party'. In the months leading up to May Day 1922, attempts to bring the different parties and organizations of the socialist workers' movement together in a common effort against fascism proved unsuccessful (Renda 2009, p. 192f.). Again, May Day rallies were disturbed by bickering between ideologically dissenting groups.[35]

The 1923 outlawing of May Day celebrations by the fascists discussed below did not change this situation: editorials in the communist daily *L'Unità* (1 May 1924; 3 May 1924) affirmed that those who once had spoken in the name of the proletariat had betrayed it and that the socialists were sabotaging unitarian May Day activities. Under the title 'the proletarian unity is realized within the Socialist Party, purified from conciliatory illusions and extremist infantilism', *L'Avanti!* (26 April) underlined instead the profound contradiction between the policy of alliance continuously proclaimed by the communists and the campaign they conducted among their members for the elimination of the Socialist Party from Italian politics.

In Germany, as we have seen, separate May Day events had become the norm since 1916/17. Only in the years 1922 and 1923 were unitarian May Day celebrations held throughout the national territory, with the trade unions as the official organizers (Andersen 1990, p. 132ff.). As the example of Berlin shows, up to 1933 these were the May Day celebrations with by far the highest level of participation. According to *Vorwärts* (2 May 1922; 2 May 1923), almost half a million people participated in the rally in the Lustgarten in 1922, and more than half a million in 1923, along with a well-attended second rally for the western districts of the city in the hippodrome at the zoo.

Although these unitarian rallies stressed the unity of the working class, the underlying conflictual positions of the different parties remained. During or at the end of the unitarian rallies the communists conducted their own activities, for instance in Frankfurt in 1923, where they distributed leaflets calling for a general strike and world revolution. Running against the agreement to abstain from party politics at the May Day demonstration and rally, this attitude – especially if it tinged the speeches, whose content had been previously arranged – was taken badly by the trade unions and other parties and was one of the reasons for the discontinuation of the unitarian rallies. In certain local contexts, however, unitarian May Day celebrations continued throughout the Weimar Republic (Mallmann 1996, p. 222).

The different May Day narratives remained a dividing issue between the main parties of the socialist workers' movement. Even more forcefully than in 1919 (see Chapter 2), in its May Day manifesto of 1920 the German Communist Party (KPD) had defined 1 May exclusively as a day of struggle and not (also) a day of celebration (Andersen 1990, p. 130). The KPD insisted on this script in 1922, the year in which all three Internationals (Socialist, Independent Socialist and Communist) published a common call for May Day demonstrations (Andersen 1990, p. 134). In the following years the KPD polemicized against the events organized by the SPD and the German trade union federation (ADGB), defining them as fun-fairs and sad spring walks (Lischber and Algermissen 1983, pp. 13f., 28). It did not prove easy, however, to translate the narrative of 1 May as exclusively a day of struggle into a corresponding practice of communist May Day events. In fact, the internal guidelines on how to organize May Day events were widely and consequently ignored by the rank and file (Mallmann 1996, p. 222f.; Dyck and Joost-Krüger 1990, p. 215ff.).

The SPD dismissed the KPD's critiques that it organized only harmless walks and fun-fairs and insisted on 'the old characteristic of struggle' of their May Day events (Lischber and Algermissen 1983, p. 13), which alongside the festive elements continued to form an integral part of social democratic May Day rituals. The literature underlines, however, the loss of the social democratic confidence in victory that had dominated the atmosphere of the May Day celebrations of imperial Germany and an increasing erosion of utopian perspectives (see Chapter 10).[36] The SPD found itself in the dilemma, on the one hand, of understanding itself (and quite rightly so) as the true (and maybe only) prop of the democratic republic – the development of which, on the other hand, betrayed the hopes that it would lead to socialism. The May Day events of the party were also the expression of a retreat into the subcultural milieu and of an increasing 'camp mentality', feigning a strength that did not correspond with reality (Dyck and Joost-Krüger 1990, p. 212ff.; Marßolek 1990b, p. 167).

In particular in the first half of the 1920s, the social democratic press underlined the lesser mobilization successes of the communists, whose May Day demonstrations in general saw significantly fewer participants than those of the SPD and the ADGB. Reciprocal attacks against the form and content of the May Day events of the other camp – including the belittling of the respective numbers of participants – remained rampant in the social democratic and the communist press and only in 1932 receded behind the warning of the Nazi threat.

The polemic centred also on the memory of May Day. For communists, as earlier for anarchists and syndicalists, May Day from its very beginning had been a day of direct action (see Chapter 2). In repeated articles throughout April 1929, the Communist Party newspaper *Rote Fahne* presented images of a heroic past difficult to correlate with the historical reality as it can be reconstructed on the basis of primary sources. According to this version, proletarian masses led by an August Bebel, who had always advocated street demonstrations, had already conquered the 'right to the street' under the empire. This heroicized past was contrasted with a present in which the social democrats were not only betraying their original aspirations but emerged as the worst enemy of the working class. The social democrats tried to counter this campaign by stressing that for leaders like August Bebel it had been inconceivable to risk human lives for some kind of revolutionary gymnastics; that street demonstrations had been first advocated by the revisionists in the campaign for equal voting rights; that social democracy had finally conquered the 'right to the street' in 1918; and that it was the communists who were endangering this right by their 'shameless misuse' of it (*Vorwärts*, 30 April 1929).

As the characteristic elements of 1 May during the Weimar Republic, the division of the workers' movement and the conflicting May Day memories were definitely cemented by the Berlin 'Blutmai' of 1929 (Bowlby 1986; Kurz 1988; Schirmann 1991; Schwarz 1990). KPD attempts to demonstrate, notwithstanding a ban on street demonstrations that had been promulgated on 13 December 1928 and had not been lifted for 1 May, led to serious clashes with police. The KPD could hardly expect that demonstrations would be tolerated, as the *Rote Fahne* repeatedly suggested. In a similar situation in 1924, massive police intervention had prevented any demonstration, but without serious consequences. In 1929, however, the political atmosphere was far more explosive, with the KPD having abandoned its more moderate political line from the mid-1920s, with the SPD – a government party on the local, regional and national level – openly accusing the communists of speculating on people getting killed for propaganda reasons and with repeated previous violent clashes between communist demonstrators and the police. Not during the attempts to demonstrate in the city centre, but in the aftermath, between 1 and 3 May 1929, more than 30 civilians were killed by police, most of them completely uninvolved in demonstration attempts.

What happened in May 1929 seems to have been neither the communist uprising conjured up by the right-wing press, nor the barricade fighting of the police reports (and of a part of the communist literature). The editions of the more neutral democratic newspaper *Frankfurter Zeitung* from 1 to 5 May contain sufficient elements to classify the events as a particularly serious case of a 'police riot'.[37] The Berlin police headquarters and the Prussian interior ministry, both led by social democrats, had direct responsibility not only for failing to lift the ban on street demonstrations for 1 May (for which they were also criticized by parts of the bourgeois press), but for factors internal to the police forces that contributed to the escalation, in particular militaristic training, equipment and tactics, along with the well-founded conviction of being protected from above even in the case of over-reaction. The following year showed that, with corresponding instructions, the Berlin police were capable of different behaviour; at the KPD May Day demonstration they remained in the background and collaborated without any problems with the communist marshals (*Frankfurter Zeitung*, 2 May 1930).

The events of May 1929 were taken up with enthusiasm by the right-wing press. The newspapers of Hugenberg (the nationalist press baron) called for the resignation of the responsible politicians because the police had not intervened with sufficient force against an attempted communist uprising. The national socialist *Völkischer Beobachter* (3 May 1929) came out with the headline 'Der Bankrott des Gesamtmarxismus' (the bankruptcy of entire Marxism). The Berlin 'Blutmai' not only deepened the division of the workers' movement but also discredited the SPD leadership and the republican institutions. These incidents and the different memories developed remain a divisive element between the moderate and the radical left today.

The division of the workers' movement seems to have had a clear impact on the level of participation. In 1919 both the social democratic *Vorwärts* (3 May 1919) and the communist *Rote Fahne* (3 May 1919) agreed that participation had not been exceptional. The all-time high for the unitarian May Day demonstrations of the early 1920s was followed by a significant drop. We then see a period of stabilization and apparent (partial) recovery up to 1928 – the May Day shortly before the national election that gave the SPD its second-best result during the Weimar Republic – followed by further decline. It was in this last period that the Communist Party, within a shrinking overall reservoir of supporters, managed to mobilize more participants than did the SPD and the ADGB – both in Berlin (although only in the year 1932) and in certain other parts of Germany. This partial trend, however, should not be misinterpreted. The literature has underlined that participation figures for communist May Day events in general never again reached the high point of 1920, stabilized on a significantly lower level in the mid-1920s and, contrary to the KPD gains in political or trade union elections, saw a further decline after 1929 (Mallmann 1996, p. 223).

The Fascist Challenge to May Day

During the Weimar Republic, the division of the workers' movement was not the only factor that challenged 1 May as a day of struggle and celebration for the international proletariat. The (albeit partial) recognition as a legal holiday favoured the development of conceptions competing with socialist understandings of May Day. At least in 1919, the Democratic Party also organized May Day events, stressing in particular a just peace treaty and victory over the enemies of internal freedom (*Frankfurter Zeitung*, 2 May 1919). Openly directed against the 'May celebration forced upon people with other convictions' were the assemblies organized by associations of white-collar workers and the Christian trade unions.[38]

Beginning in the early 1920s, socialist May Day celebrations were also openly challenged by the extreme right (Cahill 1973). Towards the end of the 1920s, NSDAP (Nazi) May Day rallies became more and more visible, competing directly with socialist May Day events. According to police figures, in 1932 the NSDAP demonstration in Hanover with 4,000 participants surpassed the KPD demonstration with 2,500.[39] Already before 1933, therefore, NSDAP's intention to usurp May Day became evident, promoting a national socialist narrative, e.g. in the party press.[40] Equally clearly expressed were threats against the socialist 1 May. In 1932 Joseph Goebbels prophesied in the local NSDAP paper *Angriff* that Berlin had seen the last socialist May Day celebrations.[41]

On 13 April 1933 the national socialists declared 1 May the public 'holiday of national labour', on which the overcoming of class struggle and the 'Volksgemeinschaft' were to be celebrated.[42] The mass staging of 1 May 1933 has to be considered together with the occupation of all ADGB buildings the following day and the taking over by force of the free trade unions. With the aim of integrating the workers into the 'Volksgemeinschaft', in the following years the 'holiday of national labour' of the regime continued to move between a hegemonic staging of events and the violent oppression of the workers' movement (Elfferding 1989, p. 57). This oppression was also directed against the personal actors of the Weimar Republic's social democratic May Day celebrations. Of the May Day speakers mentioned in *Vorwärts* from 1919 to 1932, 55.6 per cent were dismissed from their job by the Nazis, lost their pension or had it cut; 53.4 per cent were incarcerated in prisons or concentration camps; 28 per cent went into exile; and 13.8 per cent were executed or killed, or died as a consequence of incarceration and mistreatment.[43]

An important element in the national socialist staging of 1 May was the use and reinterpretation of socialist May Day traditions (Marßolek 1990c, p. 20f.; Korff 1989, p. 96ff.; Dyck and Joost-Krüger 1990, p. 226). However, the NSDAP May Day script also incorporated new elements, especially a centralization without precedent and a militarization that was visible as early as in 1933 and continuously increased in the years leading up to World War II (Marßolek 1990c, p. 20f.; Kehm 1986, p. 83). In addition, an increasing recourse to folkloristic and pagan symbols and traditions could be observed (Kehm 1986, p. 80). The ideology of the 'Volksgemeinschaft' was fanned out further: the symbol of the May tree and spring metaphors were supposed to express the new 'we-feeling' of the people, in contrast to class identity (Marßolek 1990c, p. 21).

Without any doubt, the 1933 staging of 1 May was a big success for the regime, reinforced by the massive coverage in the press. Participation was also consistently high for the following years, for instance in the city of Bremen (Dyck and Joost-Krüger 1990, p. 232). The workers' high level of participation was not only due to the pressure exerted by the regime but also resulted from a certain level of approval, for instance of the fact that on 1 May the managers had to march in one column with the workers (Dyck and Joost-Krüger 1990, p. 229). At the same time, the repressive measures that the regime employed in order to ensure high levels of participation should not be underestimated (Ruck 1990). Furthermore, according to the official registration lists, a considerable number of participants were provided by nationalist and bourgeois associations, public employees, guilds and national socialist organizations.[44] For the longer period it can be observed that the official and militaristic elements of the events were brought more and more to the foreground. With the outbreak of the war, the May Day celebrations were moved indoors and, in 1943, discontinued (Elfferding 1989, p. 58; Ruck 1990, p. 184ff.).

In Italy the fascist regime had taken a different attitude towards 1 May. In 1923 the government of Mussolini – who in 1922 had already pronounced the funeral of May Day (*L'Avanti!*, 3 May 1922) – declared the civic recurrence of 1 May abolished (see also Chapter 5). It issued a ban on all demonstrations, rallies or conferences intended to remember May Day as the 'festa dei lavoratori'. In addition, issuing posters and leaflets recalling the significance of 1 May was prohibited, and the special edition of the Socialist Party newspaper was confiscated (*La Stampa*, 1 May 1923). According to a communiqué of the Socialist Party, with its repressive policy the fascist government had restored the purity of the class-conscious and revolutionary origins of May Day (*L'Avanti!*, 24 April 1923).

In order to prevent or limit May Day celebrations and abstention from work, numerous preventive arrests were made of anarchists and communists, and police and fascist militia were deployed at factory gates. Nonetheless, even *La Stampa* (2 May 1923) reported that the appeal of the socialist organizations to suspend work for 1 May found a certain echo.[45] In Milan, according to *L'Avanti!* (2 May 1923), approximately 70 per cent abstained from work, although employers had declared null and void the provision of collective bargaining contracts that acknowledged 1 May as a holiday. Up to the promulgation of the special laws in 1926 and the suppression of *L'Avanti!* and similar organs, the workers' movement organizations could agitate in semi-legality for 1 May. However, the number of workers abstaining from work on May Day seems to have diminished fairly rapidly. In Milan in 1924, according to *L'Avanti!* (3 May 1924), the abstention rate had decreased to 40 per cent. From 1926 to 1945, any agitation for and celebration of May Day had to be conducted clandestinely.

Fascism declared 21 April – the traditional holiday recalling the foundation of Rome – the national celebration of work. This idea had been formulated in 1921, with the intention of ideally connecting a national labour day with the Great War (Riosa 1990, p. 74). The following year, *L'Avanti!* (2 May 1922) had to comment on the first attempts to celebrate a labour day according to a fascist script. At the official celebrations since 1923, speakers of the fascist unions contrasted the new spirit of collaboration between the classes with the strife brought about by May Day, and celebrated the integration of the workers into the nation (*L'Unità*, 23 April 1924). As in Germany, parades of the army and the fascist militia gave the day a strong militaristic imprint (Riosa 1990, p. 76). Festive and ludic events, however, enjoyed a certain popularity, and with a stronger emphasis on work the fascist holiday seems to have experienced a certain success (Riosa 1990, pp. 79, 82). As the bellicose aims of the regime became more apparent, attempts emerged to construct an imagery identifying the worker, in particular the rural worker, with the soldier (Riosa 1990, pp. 83, 85).

For a small minority in Germany and in Italy, 1 May under the respective fascist regimes was an occasion for oppositional activities. Police reports of illegal graffiti and leaflets, of the tearing down of fascist flags and hissing of red flags testify to resistance against the usurpation of the world-holiday of the proletariat by the NSDAP in Germany and its outlawing in fascist Italy – as do eyewitness accounts of illegal May Day celebrations (Wahlich and Willmer 1990, p. 99; Dyck and Joost-Krüger 1990, p. 237; Ulrich 1985; Neri Serneri 1990; Casali 1990; Sobrero 1990, p. 305ff.).

Doubts exist about the lasting effects of, above all, the national socialist 'ideological transformation work' (Bosch 1980). Most of the literature assumes that only a minority identified with a May Day narrative celebrating the 'Volksgemeinschaft' and that the overall effects of the national socialist usurpation attempt were negative. According to this interpretation, with the destruction of the workers' movement by the Nazis, the roots of the socialist May Day tradition, already weakened in the Weimar Republic, were definitively cut off (Ruck 1990; Marßolek 1990c, p. 21). However, the history of May Day in the decades after World War II in Germany (and also in Italy) appears to be characterized above all by repeated attempts at reappropriation or appropriation of 1 May by organizations of the workers' movement and newly emerging actors, in particular new social movements. But as far as the old left is concerned, these attempts were increasingly marked by the disintegration of a social, cultural and political milieu.

The First of May after World War II

After World War II, both Germany and Italy were in a very exposed position at the front line of the Cold War. However, in Italy defences were mounted against an internal enemy, in the Federal Republic of Germany against an external one.[46] In both countries one party had a predominant position within the traditional left – in Germany the Social Democratic Party (with an electoral high of 45.8 per cent in 1972), while in Italy the largest communist party in the Western world (with an electoral high of 34.4 per cent in 1976). In both countries one of the lessons drawn from the fascist experience was the formation of a unitarian trade union federation, which in West Germany proved durable but in Italy foundered because of Cold War tensions (Pepe 1999). In Italy, with the post-World War II period the history of May Day finally became part of national history, even if subjective and objective differences between the north and the south remained (Renda 2009, p. 339).

The Resurrection of May Day and Cold War Tension

With May Day a public holiday in both countries, mobilization for 1 May 1946 in Germany and Italy maintained or exceeded the average participation of earlier periods. *L'Unità* (3 May 1946) reported 100,000 participants for the demonstration in Rome and 200,000 in Milan. In Berlin, 500,000 people were said to have participated in the May Day celebrations, 80,000 in the rally in Hamburg, 60,000 in Munich and 20,000 in Bremen. The following years saw a further increase. For Rome, *L'Unità* reported all-time highs for 1952 and 1956 with 120,000 and for 1955 with 150,000 participants. In Bremen – where during the Weimar Republic up to 15,000 people participated in the SPD demonstrations and (according to the newspapers of the workers' movement) 40,000–50,000 in the joint demonstration of SPD and KPD in 1922 – participation in the 1950s ranged between 70,000 and 100,000 (Dyck and Joost-Krüger 1990, pp. 210, 213, 254).

In the first post-war decades in both Germany and in Italy, we find the same traditional organizers as before the advent of the fascist regimes. In both countries the literature has concentrated almost exclusively on trade union demonstrations and rallies as the main political events of the day. In fact, the unions increasingly emerge as the principal organizers of May Day events. This was a conscious policy in Italy since 1945, pursuing the objective of preserving or obtaining trade union unity: political parties (in particular the communist but also the socialist and Christian democratic parties) participated with their own blocs in the street demonstrations; but in contrast to the earlier periods discussed, they did not supply speakers for the rally. Formally, therefore, a clearer division existed between party and union in Italy than in Germany, where prominent social democratic politicians regularly spoke at the trade union rallies.[47] In Germany, the growing predominance of the trade unions as organizers of May Day events seems above all a consequence of the efforts to concentrate resources in order to counter dwindling participation in the 1960s, discussed below.

Initially, however, in both countries other organizations of the workers' movement also continued to organize May Day events. In particular, political parties continued their tradition of staging events of a more festive character in the afternoon and evening of 1 May, although, as in the past, the May Day speech remained a central part. In 1946 the programme in Rome, Florence and Milan included football matches, concerts, popular fairs and dancing (*L'Unità*, 1 May 1946). In the same year in Frankfurt, the SPD organized 24 and the KPD 14 events in different parts of the city (*Frankfurter Rundschau*, 30 April 1946).[48] Notwithstanding a stronger emphasis on May Day as a day of struggle in the KPD manifestos, the communist events also had a clearly festive character.[49]

In Germany the May Day celebrations in Berlin were an exceptional case. In 1946 and 1947 the dominance of the East German SED at the central May Day celebrations in the Lustgarten had already led to separate SPD events being organized in the western sectors of the divided city. With the 'May battle' of 1948 this conflict was brought into the open, with a rally in the eastern sector of Berlin incorporating 600,000 to 800,000 participants and a separate rally in the western sectors with 50,000 to 150,000. In the following years, the

May Day rally in West Berlin took on a particular characteristic. It retained a strong trade union component; but together with the trade union federation DGB, all political parties represented in the West Berlin parliament called on citizens to participate in the 'freedom rallies', which attracted up to 750,000 participants.[50] The division of the workers' movement, which in the Weimar Republic had found its expression in separate social democratic and communist May Day events, now became visible at the border as the division of a city, of a country, of a continent. Only in exceptional cases did tension deteriorate into physical clashes; but it found its outlet in agitation attempts across the border, with loudspeakers and propaganda rockets.[51]

In Italy as well, the Cold War tensions exploded on May Day 1948, signalling the beginning of the end of the CGIL as a unitarian trade union confederation. A few weeks before, on 18 April, the Christian Democratic Party had won an impressive victory in the general elections, gaining the absolute majority of seats in parliament. In the aftermath of the election, the right-wing press had called for 'adjusting' the board of the CGIL to reflect the election results. For the May Day demonstrations and rallies, the Christian democratic wing of the CGIL posed a number of conditions: only trade unionists in the strict sense as speakers; an agreement in advance on the content of the speeches; no offence to political and religious feelings; no banners of political parties or placards that could offend the government or other organizations; no uniforms or red handkerchiefs;[52] and an official warning to political parties that their intervention could be the cause for a break-up of trade union unity. If most of these conditions were clearly unacceptable for the communist and socialist wing of the CGIL, for the Christian democratic trade unionists it was equally unacceptable to share the podium with a trade union representative of the Soviet Union, as was planned for the rally in Rome (Renda 2009, p. 234f.). These unionists boycotted the May Day rallies of 1948; their leader Giulio Pastore (who had been scheduled to speak at the rally in Rome) commented that he had seen too many red flags and heard too many communist hymns (*L'Unità*, 4 May 1948). The final end of trade union unity in Italy came with the general strike proclaimed by the CGIL in reaction to the assassination attempt against communist leader Palmiro Togliatti in July 1948.

In the following years, the public image of May Day in Italy was dominated by the demonstrations and rallies of the CGIL, reduced to its communist and socialist components. The 'free' trade unions – which in 1950 would develop into the Catholic CISL and the secular UIL – did not renounce street demonstrations and open-air rallies. However, their events remained significantly smaller than those of the CGIL. According to *L'Unità* (3 May), in 1949 the CGIL rally in Rome saw 100,000 participants, the rally of the 'free' unions only 3–4,000. Significantly, the communist daily drew a line between this poor performance and the (according to this report) equally poor showing at the rally in the western sectors of Berlin. For the following years, a telling example of the differences among the May Day events of the three Italian trade union confederations is provided by *La Stampa* (1 May 1956) for Turin: the CGIL held its traditional demonstration and rally, the members of the CISL gathered in various halls in the city for the showing of films celebrating the history and the successes of the union and the most important event of the UIL consisted in a boat excursion.

The Catholic trade unionists, however, were very conscious of the importance of May Day for the workers' movement, as testified by the date of the founding congress of the CISL, 1 May 1950. At this congress Giulio Pastore accused the CGIL of celebrating May Day with purely political and pro-Soviet speeches (Renda 2009, p. 244). More 'ideological transformation work', however, was necessary to strip May Day of those aspects that the Catholic workers' movement found unacceptable, in particular Marxism and a repudiated atmosphere of violence and hate.[53] In 1955 the Catholic workers' associations (ACLI) celebrated their tenth anniversary and – as a leaflet distributed by them for the occasion pronounced – the old ambition of the Catholic workers' movement to 'baptize' May Day was finally realized before 150,000 people in St Peter's square by Pope Pius XII, who proclaimed 1 May the day of St Joseph the worker (see also Chapter 5).

Although the CGIL had been forced to renounce the traditional site of its May Day rally on Piazza del Popolo in favour of the ACLI, *L'Unità*'s editorial (3 May 1955) trod a cautious line, defining the Catholic celebration of 1 May, regardless of the original intentions, as proof of the exceptional advancement of workers throughout the world. About the intentions of the Catholic operation, the bourgeois press had no doubts: according to *La Stampa* (1 May 1955), the Catholic Church had understood the mistake committed by the fascists when they had pretended to substitute May Day with 21 April: on the basis of its hundred-year tradition the Church had understood that it was better to annex the existing celebration than to substitute it, resurrecting a policy pursued in the case of numerous pagan festivities in the past.

In West Germany the Communist Party was already politically marginalized and subject to state repression before it was declared illegal by the constitutional court in 1956. At the end of the 1940s, even a newspaper like the *Frankfurter Rundschau* had ceased to report on communist May Day events. In the days around 1 May, as 'subversive' elements the communists were the object of targeted police measures (Brackmann 1990, p. 140). In the 1950s they appeared in the press only as disturbers of trade union rallies. In general, these disturbances were limited to attempts at agitation or counter-propaganda, prevented by the police. The DGB called upon its local chapters to decisively oppose such attempts (*Frankfurter Allgemeine Zeitung*, 30 April 1952).

May Day and the Integration of the Workers' Movement into the State

In contrast to Italy, in Germany the anti-communist line of the DGB (and the SPD) facilitated the preservation of the unitarian trade union federation. If the trade unions addressed controversial social or political issues on May

Day, the conservative press, the employers and the bourgeois parties tended to accuse the DGB of resurrecting the old (Marxist) 'day of struggle'. This was the case in years in which more strictly trade union themes stood at the centre of May Day activities (in 1963 the strike of the metal workers, in 1978 the 'Mitbestimmung' (worker participation) or in 1986 a new law restricting trade union freedom) and in years dominated by more political themes (in 1958 the campaign against nuclear war or in 1972 the defence of 'Ostpolitik'). Themes having strong potential for conflict with governments led by Christian democrats also led to disputes within the union, although without ever endangering trade union unity. As a consequence, May Day in Germany led to comparatively few conflicts with state authorities, and on 1 May a higher degree of institutional integration of the workers' movement than in Italy became visible.

In fact, there were hardly any noteworthy clashes between the police and May Day participants in the first decades of the Federal Republic. An exception was incidents like those in Munich, where in the early 1950s police interpreted the groups of participants leaving the site of the May Day rally as an unannounced demonstration that had to be dissolved (Achten 1990, p. 236; Alto 1990, p. 54f.). In Italy, to the contrary, state intervention against the May Day activities of the CGIL was fairly frequent. In some cases the placarding of its May Day manifesto was prohibited, as in 1949 in Rome and Turin, because of criticism of Italy's adherence to NATO (*La Stampa*, 30 April 1949). In the 1950s *L'Unità* reported fairly frequently on incidents and clashes with police, caused by alleged noncompliance with the restrictions placed on May Day activities.[54] These restrictions included the prohibition of non-trade-union slogans on banners – calls for peace and the protest against atomic weapons were interpreted as such[55] – or the provision against organizing street demonstrations on the way to or from the site of the Rome May Day rally. Italian state authorities also strove to enforce moral values. For the Bologna May Day demonstration of 1955, groups of women in 'revealing' (gymnastic) dress were strictly forbidden (Arbizzani 1990, p. 176). As late as 1960, the executive committee of the CGIL lamented the massive police presence at May Day demonstrations (*Rassegna sindacale* 1960, p. 1399). In Southern Italy, in addition, a particular problem was posed by organized crime, responsible for the most violent May Day incident in Italy's post-war history, with 11 people killed and 27 wounded at Portella della Ginestra in 1947 (Renda 2009, p. 221ff.).

The comparatively higher degree of institutional integration of the workers' movement in Germany became visible on May Day by the early 1950s, with the president of the republic participating as a speaker in May Day events of the DGB (*Frankfurter Rundschau*, 4 May 1953). This development reached its climax in 1970, when in Dortmund the first social democratic chancellor of the Federal Republic, Willy Brandt, walked at the head of the demonstration of the Hoesch workers from the factory gate to the site of the May Day rally, at which he was the main speaker (*Die Zeit*, 8 May

1970). In Italy, a high-ranking national politician officially participated for the first time in a trade union May Day event in 1990, when the president of the Italian Republic, Francesco Cossiga, intervened at the centenary celebration of May Day.

Similar differences also become apparent for the echo of May Day in the press and the public media up to the 1970s. In Germany, not only the centre-left *Frankfurter Rundschau* but also the conservative *Frankfurter Allgemeine Zeitung* published, besides editorials and reports on the May Day events, the full text of the DGB manifesto. Since the early years of the Federal Republic there had been radio broadcasts of May Day celebrations and union rallies. In the first decades of the Italian Republic, in contrast, labour day was relatively absent in the public media.[56] Unlike its German equivalent the *Frankfurter Allgemeine*, the Italian *Corriere della sera* conceded very little space to May Day and considered it of insufficient importance to warrant an editorial, as was underlined by the official CGIL journal (Livi 1964, p. 4).

Institutional integration in Germany, however, led to a particularly strong challenge to 1 May as the specific day of struggle and celebration of the international workers' movement.[57] In repeated editorials, the *Frankfurter Allgemeine Zeitung* (e.g. 1 May 1951; 1/2 May 1952) argued that May Day had lost its class characteristic and become a national holiday and a day honouring any kind of work. Similarly, statements by employers (Achten 1990, p. 241), by the Christian Democratic Party (*Frankfurter Rundschau*, 1 May 1957) and by members of the federal government can be interpreted as attempts to influence or change the memory of May Day as the holiday of the workers' movement.[58]

The 'Farewell to "Proletarity"' and the Crisis of May Day

Confronted with similar statements, the DGB insisted on its traditional narrative of 1 May, and the characteristic of May Day as a day of struggle was underlined also in more recent times in manifestos and rally speeches (Schuster 1991, p. 106). Such affirmations have been judged to be more significant for the DGB's understanding of 'struggle' than for the characteristics of May Day in West Germany (Braun, Reinhold and Schwarz 1990, p. 12). However, the transformation of May Day should not be reduced to a reflection of the political positions of the DGB leadership. These developments were above all an expression of the slow process of dissolution of working class culture and of the 'farewell to "proletarity"' (Mooser 1983) that had comparable effects on 1 May in Italy, forcing a communist-dominated workers' movement to adjust its understanding of May Day. These processes were the background for internal discussions in the unions of both countries, which, under different circumstances and with diverging ideological positions, had to come to terms with the fact that in the immediate post-war period they had substantially failed to realize their ideas for reorganization of their respective countries.

In Germany, after the disastrous results of its campaign 'for a better parliament' in 1953 – in that election, with a stagnating SPD Adenauer's CDU jumped from 31 per cent to 45 per cent, just missing the absolute majority it would gain in the subsequent election of 1957 – the DGB decided to concentrate on concrete trade union demands. At the centre of its action programme, published on 1 May 1955, stood the demand for the five-day, 40-hour working week without cuts in retribution. Hand in hand with this repositioning came important changes in the iconography of May Day. If May Day posters up to the mid-1950s can be seen more or less as copies of earlier models (Frank 1990, p. 108; Achten 1990, p. 240), the famous poster of 1956 (showing a small child with the caption 'on Saturday Daddy belongs to me') was a clear new beginning – and also an expression of a renewed (minor) social democratic 'ideology of hope'.[59] Notwithstanding the success of this and similar campaigns, however, the slowly growing number of trade union members remained far behind the strongly rising number of employees (Schuster 1991, p. 87).

Concerning Italy, the election results of 1948, disastrous for the left, have already been mentioned. In the following years the CGIL found itself encircled by the government, the employers and the 'free' unions (Renda 2009, p. 249). In the early 1950s it increasingly lost support within the factories, suffering a humiliating defeat in the elections for the internal commission at the Fiat car factory in 1954 (Renda 2009, p. 251). Membership plummeted, from the almost 5 million members in 1949 to the low point of 2,420,430 in 1967. These developments provoked a self-critical correction of union politics and a (reformist) re-elaboration of the significance and the role of May Day already under Giuseppe Di Vittorio, the historic leader of the CGIL (Renda 2009, p. 251ff.).

The undeniable successes of the trade unions in both countries in terms of salary increases and better working conditions did not prevent a decline in the number of participants in May Day events, which in the first half of the 1960s took on dramatic proportions. This was particularly the case in Germany, where the success of the 1958 anti-nuclear war campaign had masked a decline already in progress.[60] A similar development can be noted for Italy.[61] In both countries the bourgeois press commented on the decline, which also became the subject of cartoons.[62] Especially in Germany, within the trade unions an animated debate on the future of May Day celebrations developed, and in this context the mood of the members was also sounded.[63] Here and there, local union chapters proceeded to organize indoor celebrations, but in most cities they held on to the demonstration and outdoor rally, notwithstanding declining participation.[64] However, internal discussion led the unions to search for new formats for May Day events. Particularly in Germany, more festive elements were increasingly integrated into May Day events, while in Italy we can observe a stronger preservation of traditional event formats. In addition, the unions put pressure on other organizations to renounce their May Day events and more and more concentrated their own events in certain cities.[65]

'1968' and the Reappropriation of May Day

A part of the literature stresses the importance of the student movement for a revitalization of 1 May at the end of the 1960s (Korff 1989, p. 99f.). In Italy and Germany, however, at the beginning of the decade developments were already emerging within the workers' movement and its organizations that were of equal importance for a reappropriation of May Day. In Italy the harsh contrast between the CGIL and the CISL, said to have had the characteristics of a downright war (Renda 2009, p. 243), slowly abated. Since 1960 a growing on-the-ground collaboration between unionists of different confederations translated into May Day rallies that remained separate but increasingly operated in a united form (Renda 2009, p. 255ff.). In 1970 this led to the first joint May Day celebrations since 1948, and in 1972 the CGIL, CISL and UIL agreed on a common federative structure. Trade union unity had the side effect of significantly increasing the presence of May Day in the public media and the conservative press. For Germany developments in Frankfurt can be defined as characteristic: since 1962 the participation of 'guest workers' in the union rally and 'radical big talking' at the youth rally gained attention.[66] New participating groups, new topics and new event formats were increasingly integrated into the May Day activities.[67] In the reactions of the DGB, however, alongside integration efforts, paternalism and rejection are also discernible.[68]

Similar dynamics of integration but also of paternalism and rejection characterize the relationship of the trade unions in Germany and in Italy to the emerging new social movements since 1968. Particularly in Germany, parts of the media called on the unions to follow a course of strict dissociation (*Frankfurter Allgemeine Zeitung*, 4 May 1970). At the German May Day rallies in 1968, trade union speakers repeatedly spoke of solidarity with the students and underlined that many of their demands were also demands of the unions. At the same time, however, they criticized the methods of the student movement. The unions rejected the proposal to let representatives of the students speak at May Day rallies, consenting only to the reading out of written messages by union speakers. In the following years, the DGB forcefully opposed all attempts to disturb and particularly to take over its May Day events.[69] Contemporary witnesses underline the negative effect on mobilization of the attempts of new left groups to 'piggy-back' trade union May Day events (Achten 1990, p. 280). At least parts of the union, however, in the absence of physical violence seem to have remained critical of police intervention at their May Day demonstrations against groups of the new left.[70]

Developments in Italy were not dissimilar, but at least initially the CGIL in particular showed a more open attitude towards the new movements than the DGB. In fact, with the 'hot autumn' of 1969, the era of the new movements had found a far stronger resonance within the factories than in Germany. In 1968 the CGIL consented to students speaking at its May Day rallies, but it remained critical of certain positions of the student movement and rebuffed any attempt to condition its own politics or internal dynamics.[71] Initially a common front with the student movement existed against state repression, based on the Italian left's longstanding and deep mistrust of the police and on concrete experiences with police intervention during trade union activities in 1968–1969 (della Porta and Reiter 2003, p. 210ff.). At the CGIL May Day rally in Rome in 1968, a speaker denounced the 'marked hostility of the state apparatus and especially the police toward the trade union initiative of the workers' (*L'Unità*, 3 May 1968). The CGIL May Day manifesto of 1969 took up the traditional demand of the Italian left to disarm the police on public order duty.[72] In the course of the 1970s, however, this stand changed because of the fight against terrorism, because of the entrance of the PCI into the parliamentary majority of the governments of national solidarity and because of trade union support for the mobilization within the police for their demilitarization and unionization.[73] The collaboration among the three big trade union confederations further complicated the relationship of the CGIL with the new left. These groups in fact expressed their hostility towards moderate and Catholic groups also at May Day demonstrations and rallies (*L'Unità*, 3 May 1978; 3 May 1979). These mechanisms worked in both directions: at the 1977 May Day rally in Turin a representative of the feminist movement protested against the attempt of Catholic trade unionists to impede any reference to abortion (*L'Unità*, 3 May 1977).

For their own May Day narratives – and their polemic against the trade union events – the new left groups of the 1970s in both Germany and Italy borrowed heavily from the radical wings of the workers' movements of the earlier periods. In general, however, they participated in the trade union demonstrations and rallies – which, particularly in Italy, also led to clashes with union marshals and the police – holding their own events subsequently. The situation in West Berlin, where the extra-parliamentary opposition in 1968 organized its own May Day demonstration with (according to the police) 25,000 participants, remained an exception (Thamm 1990, p. 132ff.).

The most important influence of the 1968 movements seems to have been that they initiated a process of reappropriation of their own traditions within the old left that contributed to a revitalization of May Day. Such a process can be observed in particular in Germany, where it was also connected with the economic crisis since the mid-1970s (Steinkühler 1990). Both the number of participants and the number of May Day events in Germany rose again (Schuster 1991, p. 96; Rucht 2001, p. 159). In West Berlin, for instance, the biggest May Day demonstration in 20 years was organized in 1987 (Thamm 1990, p. 149). These mobilization successes, however, were no longer reached on pro-positive but on purely defensive platforms, particularly against unemployment. The 'ideology of hope', even in the form in which it had found expression in the DGB's 1956 May Day poster described above, increasingly seemed to be evaporating. At the same time, 1 May as the day of the workers' movement and the trade unions was increasingly marginalized in the public media, leading the *Frankfurter*

Rundschau (3 May 1988) to ask whether the world of labour was disappearing from the television screen.[74]

In Italy the revitalization of May Day connected with the efforts towards trade union unity showed signs of depletion already at the end of the 1970s. Particularly in certain cities, participation dropped significantly, in Rome reaching the 10,000 mark (*L'Unità*, 3 May 1979). In the early 1980s this trend was sharpened by increasing contrasts between the CGIL on the one side and the CISL and the UIL on the other, in particular on the 'scala mobile', the automatic adjustment of wages to inflation. In 1981 CISL leader Pierre Carniti was openly contested at the May Day rally in Rome (*L'Unità*, 3 May 1981), and in 1984 and 1985 the three trade union confederations again held separate celebrations.[75] As in the interwar period, disunity had a negative effect on participation. For its 1984 demonstration in Rome, the CGIL managed to mobilize only 4,000 participants (*L'Unità*, 3 May 1984). In the following year *L'Unità* (3 May 1985) lamented that the polemics had suffocated May Day and discouraged the participation of the workers. In 1986 unitarian May Day celebrations were re-established, but trade union unity remained precarious and did not have the same positive effect on participation as in the early 1970s. In addition, the inevitable compromises repeatedly provoked the discontent of the more left-wing trade unionists.

Competition and the Loss of Utopia

The May Day events of the traditional workers' movement were also faced with growing competition. In Italy, groups connected with the 'movement of 1977' began organizing a 'festa del non lavoro' that became a fixed feature in Rome from the early 1980s on. Increasingly, grassroots trade union organizations like the Cobas organized their own separate May Day events.[76] The Cobas also contributed to the success of the MayDay (later EuroMayDay) parades that, based on a platform in favour of precarious workers, since 2001 in Milan mobilized more participants than the traditional unions did.[77] The incomprehension of parts of the traditional left in front of these phenomena emerges from the presentation of the 2002 MayDay parade by *L'Unità* (1 May 2002) as an event organized by the established unions.

In Germany, particularly present in the media was the 'revolutionary First of May' organized by alternative and autonomous groups. The idea of a separate May Day demonstration independent from the DGB took hold in different cities for various reasons. In Dortmund it developed out of conflicts over the organization of the trade union event (Hilmer and Zaib 1997, p. 204ff.). In Berlin it emerged after incidents during the night of 1/2 May 1987, and was realized in 1988, favoured by the campaign against the International Monetary Fund summit (Lehmann and Meyerhöfer 2003). More fittingly defined as the day of struggle of the radical left than as the day of struggle of the working class, the 'revolutionary First of May' was also characterized by internal conflicts and discontinuity. Above all, criticism and resistance increasingly emerged against the riots that accompanied the event, particularly in Berlin, and that dominated coverage in the media (Blickhan and Teune 2003).

Right-wing groups also increasingly organized May Day events. The late 1990s in Germany saw a particular rise in media reports on these activities – and on the counter-demonstrations of unions and left-wing groups. Right-wing groups, however, not only sought to link to the 'day of national labour' of the national socialists, but continued a tradition reaching back to the 1960s.[78] In Italy, the extreme right to a far greater extent than in Germany succeeded in evolving into post-fascist organizations and in integrating into the political system since the 1990s. According to its own account the right-wing trade union UGL – successor organization of the CISNAL, closely connected with the neofascist party MSI in the post-war years – is now the third strongest Italian trade union in terms of number of members.[79]

Parallel to this growing competition, an equally growing distance between the dominant political parties and the trade unions of the traditional left can be observed on May Day. As mentioned above, the Social Democratic Party in Germany was less and less involved in May Day activities. Its own May Day events changed from celebrations organized for a city or a city quarter to celebrations of the district party organizations. At the DGB rallies fewer and fewer representatives of the SPD participated as speakers, in Frankfurt for instance disappearing completely in the mid-1980s. This growing distance became visible nationwide in 1988 with the controversy about Oskar Lafontaine as a May Day speaker because of his critical position on the union demand for a reduction in working hours with no loss of pay. In 2002 in Leipzig, open rejection greeted SPD chancellor Gerhard Schröder because of his reform policies (*Frankfurter Rundschau*, 2 May 2002). His appearance in 2003 was the last for several years of a leading social democratic politician at a central DGB May Day event.

As mentioned above, throughout the post-World War II period in Italy, the political parties of the left were less involved in the trade union May Day events than in Germany. Here, the growing distance between party and union closely mirrored changes in the Italian party system. After the fall of the Berlin Wall, the Communist Party evolved into the Democratic Party of the Left (in 1991), then the Democrats of the Left (in 1998) and in 2007 united with Christian democratic and liberal groups to form the Democratic Party.

An important phenomenon of the May Day celebrations of the last decades is therefore that 1 May 'belongs' less and less to the traditional workers' movement and its organizations. In the first post-war decade from 1946 to 1956, the DGB, SPD and KPD had organized 99 per cent of all May Day events reported by the *Frankfurter Rundschau*, but in the decade 1996 to 2006 they were responsible for only 56 per cent. For Italy, a parallel development can be observed: according to the local newspaper *Il Giorno*, in the decade 1996 to 2006, grassroots trade unions and autonomous groups organized 37 per cent of the May Day events in Milan.[80] At the same time, May Day events increasingly became purely trade union events, mirroring the success or failure of union initiatives.

Finally, contrary to the 'year of the movements' of 1968, the fall of the Berlin Wall seems to have had a negative impact on May Day. The centennial celebrations of 1990 indicated that if May Day might expect an upturn in third world and emerging countries, it faced a deep crisis precisely in countries where the traditional labour movement, regardless of whether in its social democratic or communist form, was particularly rooted. In 1990 1 May could be celebrated legally for the first time in South Africa, while in Moscow the secretary-general of the Soviet Communist Party, Mikhail Gorbachev, had to leave the tribune on the Red Square pestered by catcalls, and in England Margaret Thatcher called for the abolition of May Day as a national holiday. With 60,000 people, the first reunited Berlin May Day demonstration since 1946 mobilized only slightly more participants than the West Berlin demonstrations of 1987 and 1988. In the united Germany, participation figures in the following years remained below those in the Federal Republic of the 1980s. Confronted with the rise of neoliberal economic politics, trade unions appeared increasingly powerless, a fact that observers connected with the decline of May Day (*Frankfurter Rundschau*, 2 May 2000). In Italy the consequences of this aspect were sharpened by the different positions of the various trade union confederations towards the Berlusconi governments.

In both Italy and Germany the trade unions tried to counter the renewed decline in participation with new event formats of a more festive quality, geared in particular to attracting younger participants. In Germany the DGB experimented with a 'job parade' with techno music that in the early 2000s became the most successful event (*Frankfurter Rundschau*, 2 May 2002). In Italy by far the most successful event became the May Day rock concert organized by the CGI, CISL and UIL every year since 1990 in Rome. Particularly where the media are concerned, however, this event threatened to eclipse all other more political May Day events, even the central national demonstration organized since the early 1990s in a yearly changing city.

As always in the history of May Day, peaks in participation remained connected with concrete demands. However, whereas the pre-World War I peak emerged in a period of a general increase in participation and was connected with the pro-positive demand of equal voting rights, the post-1990 peaks were connected with defensive campaigns – in Italy against the new Berlusconi government (*L'Unità*, 3 May 1996) and in Germany against SPD chancellor Schröder's reform policies (*Frankfurter Rundschau*, 2 May 2003) – and emerged in a period of a general decline in participation. Particularly striking is the huge difference in participation between the peak years and the surrounding years: in 2003 about a million people are said to have demonstrated in Germany on May Day, whereas in the surrounding years participation reached only half that number.

Concluding Remarks

Comparing Germany and Italy, differences in the development of the workers' movement in the two countries – in Italy more plural, with weaker organizations, and with a stronger presence of radical positions – did reflect on the nascent May Day traditions. Italian May Day events and narratives were more contested within the workers' movement and also showed a higher conflict potential in relation to state authorities. However, conflicting moderate and radical May Day narratives also emerged as a feature of the German May Day. In addition, strong similarities existed, not only for the optimism surrounding May Day as the 'inaugural day of (the proletariat's) redemption', for the format of events and participation trends, but also for central demands beyond the eight-hour workday and workers' protection, in particular universal suffrage.

As far as the dominant socialist party is concerned, differences between Germany and Italy were already growing on the eve of World War I, leading to opposite positions on the war issue. In the immediate post-war years, the political lines of the main parties diverged further, with the Italian socialists advocating the immediate establishment of a socialist republic and the German social democrats a way to socialism through the acceptance of 'formal democracy'. Precisely these differences help to capture the common reasons for the growing crisis of May Day in the interwar period: the division of the workers' movement, its isolation in the resistance against reactionary and fascist counter-revolution, and above all the disenchantment of the high hopes connected with the revolutionary period 1918–1920, regardless of whether they were held by reformists or radicals, with a consequent erosion of utopian perspectives (see also Chapter 10).

The success of May Day in the immediate post-World War II period testified to the substantial failure of the fascist 'ideological transformation work' even in Germany. If the different position in the Cold War context led to greater integration of the workers' movement into the state in Germany, the substantial failure of the main political parties and trade unions of the traditional left in both countries to realize their aspirations for reconstruction forced them to parallel adjustments of their May Day narratives, concentrating on concrete reforms but also presenting a new version of the old 'ideology of hope'. These adjustments proved unable to completely offset the effects of the 'loss of 'proletarity'" – i.e. the slow disintegration of the working-class culture and milieu – but allowed the old left to initiate a process of reappropriation and revitalization of the May Day traditions in the wake of the 'year of the movements' in 1968. However, more and more thrown back on purely defensive positions, the new version of the old 'ideology of hope' also increasingly evaporated, leading to a crisis of the old left and its May Day particularly exposed after the fall of the Berlin Wall with the rise of neoliberalism (see Chapter 10). In addition, the May Day of the old left was increasingly faced with competition from new actors. 'Belonging' less and less to the traditional workers' movement, May Day also became less and less recognized and recognizable as heir to the old conception as the 'world holiday of the international proletariat' and its 'day of celebration and struggle'.

The punctual mobilization successes of the last years in Germany and Italy seem to indicate that, nevertheless, even after more than a hundred years, May Day conserves a mobilization potential that also echoes in the reports and editorials of the daily press.[81] In order to exploit this potential, a renewed reappropriation process seems necessary, for which signs are visible above all outside the established trade unions and the old left. However, as shown by the example of the EuroMayDay network – which also introduced a transnational element largely absent in the May Day activities of the established unions – groups sponsoring similar activities lack the consistency and endurance of the old left. Above all, it seems utterly unforeseeable whether and how to make up for the loss of utopia that affected the whole left, initially subtly and since 1990 openly (Eley 1995). In the last decades, this loss of utopia inevitably had a deep impact on a May Day that historically drew its strength in particular out of the connection of concrete demands with the socialist 'ideology of hope'. As Willy Brandt put it: social democracy without hope is like church without faith.

Notes

1 Boll 1992, p. 430. A comparative approach is also largely absent in volumes containing contributions on the history of 1 May in various countries (see Panaccione 1989; Marßolek 1990a).
2 Apart from the secondary literature, the following is mainly based on an analysis of the contemporary press, in particular (for the period from 1890 up to the fascist era) the main socialist daily newspapers in the two countries, i.e. *Vorwärts* and *L'Avanti!*; and (for the post-World War II period) West Germany's main centre-left newspaper, the *Frankfurter Rundschau*; and Italy's communist daily *L'Unità*. The obvious internal differences that exist in Germany and Italy, e.g. between May Day in industrial and rural areas, will not be discussed.
3 In 1913, the first Italian election with universal male suffrage, the socialist party drew 7.5 per cent of the vote and the recently split reformist socialists 2.6 per cent, while the German social democrats in the 1912 elections polled 34.8 per cent. On the eve of World War I the Italian party had *c.* 50,000 members, the German one more than 1 million. In 1908, the Italian socialist trade union confederation *Confederazione generale del lavoro* had 306,975 members of which 130,000 were agricultural workers (Renda 2009, p. 157). The German social democratic 'free' trade unions in 1913 had *c.* 2.5 million members.
4 See Chapter 2, p. 27 n.14, above; on the general response of the German social democrats to the Haymarket incident, see Sun 1986.
5 Antonioli 1988, pp. 39ff., 69. In a similar way Haymarket became an important element of Communist May Day traditions. Hobsbawm (1991, p. 112) has stressed the importance of May Day as a day for the commemoration of martyrs for anarchist movements.
6 Quoted in the liberal-democratic *Frankfurter Zeitung* (30 April 1890), which itself showed a more open attitude towards May Day.
7 Cf. the corresponding evaluation of SPD chairman August Bebel and of the Hamburg police from the year 1893 (Saul 1990, pp. 66, 76). An important factor in these developments was the economic crisis starting in 1890.

64   *Herbert Reiter*

8 According to *Vorwärts*, for the woodworkers of Berlin (the trade that in that city most massively suspended work on May Day (up to 20,000)), about one third of the May Day participants were hit by a lockout every year, usually for several days. The financial burden of having to support striking workers reinforced the reluctance of trade union leaders to commit resources to an event like May Day, perceived as having symbolic but little practical relevance (Vorstand des Deutschen Metallarbeiter-Verbandes 1907; Chapter 6, p. 139).

9 In Germany, in 1890 a petition was directed at the national parliament, and in 1891 a resolution was sent to the social democratic parliamentary group.

10 *La Stampa*, 2 May 1901. At least in some cities, this sort of action became increasingly controversial. In 1898 the Milanese trade unions decided not to present a petition to the mayor, as none of the demands raised in previous years had been addressed (*L'Avanti!*, 28 April 1898).

11 Initially, such action by local government was censured by the central government. In 1893, the city council of Imola was dissolved for that very reason. The promotion of May Day by local governments meant a significant step towards institutionalization: the 1893 manifesto of the Imola city council stressed that May Day was not a partisan manifestation (Antonioli 1988, p. 34f.; Arbizzani 1990, p. 46ff.).

12 The Prussian censorship was so thorough that only single verses of certain songs remained unscathed. For the year 1901 in Berlin, see Landesarchiv Berlin, A Pr. Br. Rep. 030, Nr. 8703, f. 20ff. In Italy as well, the confiscation or censoring of special May Day editions of newspapers, posters and leaflets was quite common and remained so in the early twentieth century.

13 The socialists consistently criticized Giolitti for refusing to accept responsibility for the restrictive measures taken by prefects. On parliamentary interrogations, see *L'Avanti!*, 4 May 1902; 1 May 1907.

14 In certain places the authorities tolerated informal mass walks through the city to an assembly point outside the city gates. In Leipzig in the 1890s, up to several tens of thousands are said to have participated in such walks (*Leipziger Volkszeitung*, 2 May 1898).

15 See for example the sentence of the Oberverwaltungsgericht, 23 December 1912, upholding the prohibition of the 1910 demonstration in Cologne (Geheimes Staatsarchiv Preußischer Kulturbesitz (GStAPK) Berlin, I. HA Rep. 77 CBS Nr. 753, vol. 1, ff. 437–441). Even if the court did not uphold the prohibition of the demonstration in single cases, it had been effectively impeded.

16 As an example, see *Hamburger Echo*, 8 February 1914, report on the joint assembly of party and trade union delegates for the preparation of May Day 1914. The trade union and party leadership had to admit that the impression of the event on the population was created not by the demonstration itself but by participants moving in loose groups through the city centre to the assembly point. The decision to organize a street demonstration in 1914 passed by only 429 to 421 votes.

17 In 1910 the Berlin police reported that participants in a part of the morning assemblies marched to or from the assembly hall in an ordered procession (GStAPK Berlin, I HA Rep 77 Tit. 2513 Nr. 2, vol. 7, f. 162). See also Lindenberger 1995, p. 304ff.

18 Here and in the following, examples for both countries refer to big cities. However, it has to be considered that probably up to the 1950s/1960s most May Day events took place in small and medium-sized cities.

19 See Renda 2009, pp. 109ff., 120ff., 130. The *Fasci Siciliani dei Lavoratori* (Sicilian Workers' Leagues) were a popular movement of democratic and socialist inspiration with which the socialist party broke in September 1894. The May Day events of the *Fasci* were joyous and festive celebrations of labour and of freedom.

20 With regard to gender equality, the Italian socialists lagged behind. In 1910 and 1911 their May Day manifesto called for male universal suffrage, to be extended to

women in an undefined future. Only the 1912 manifesto called for 'truly universal suffrage, extended to men and to women' (*L'Avanti!*, 1 May 1912).

21 See the editorial of party secretary Enrico Ferri on the general strike (*L'Avanti!*, 28 April 1906); Murtaugh 1991.

22 On Catholicism and May Day, see Robbiati 1990; Bertozzi 2009, p. 159ff. In Milan, a communiqué directed to all diocesan appointees invited them to celebrate 1 May, proclaiming that it was time that the day lost its subversive imprint and became a true and beautiful 'festa del lavoro' as it was in the times of the medieval Christian corporations (*L'Avanti!*, 30 April 1908).

23 The anarchist assembly in Berlin in 1895 saw only 250 participants (*Vorwärts*, 3 May 1895). Not infrequently, anarchists who attempted to agitate for their ideas at trade union or SPD events were thrown out of the hall (*Vorwärts*, 2 May 1893; 3 May 1894).

24 *Vorwärts*, 29 April 1906. On the mass strike debate and May Day in Germany, see Eichler 1992. In 1908, the revolutionary syndicalists were also expelled from the Italian socialist party.

25 Both the conservative and radical press ridiculed the events of the moderate trade unions as being attended above all by the unemployed (i.e. attendance was not an indication of being on strike) and pointed out the amount of alcohol reputedly consumed at socialist parties' celebrations.

26 Even in these closed meetings, the Leipzig police had insisted on excluding any relevant topics from the speeches or debates – including, among others, the 'Burgfrieden' (i.e. the war-time internal truce), war goals, peace goals or rising food prices. Faced with such restrictions, in 1916 the social democrats decided to cancel their scheduled gatherings (*Leipziger Volkszeitung*, 28 April 1916).

27 For reasons of space, in what follows the May Day activities of the smaller socialist, communist, anarchist and syndicalist groups cannot be discussed.

28 In the 1919 general election the socialists had emerged as Italy's strongest party with 32 per cent of the vote; with 24.5 per cent, the 1921 election brought a significant setback. In that election the newly formed communist party managed 4.6 per cent.

29 Under the title 'Democracy and democrats', the following year an editorial again defended the SPD's conviction that 'formal democracy' was an indispensable means for arriving at real democracy, for achieving socialist democracy and for overcoming capitalism. At the same time the editorial marked the differences with the bourgeois democratic party (*Vorwärts*, 29 April 1920).

30 The conservative press nevertheless polemicized against 1 May as a public holiday. According to the *Vorwärts* (3 May 1919), this 'reactionary Katzenmusik' was played under headlines such as 'The national day of lament', 'The day of repentance of the proletariat' or 'The dance party of the grave diggers of Germany'.

31 In the following years, May Day remained a public holiday in a continuously decreasing number of smaller federal states (Braun and Schwarz 1989, p. 26).

32 In the 1919 election for the constituent assembly, the SPD drew 37.9 per cent of the vote and the USPD 7.6 per cent. In the 1921 general election the SPD dropped to 21.6 per cent, the USPD secured 17.9 per cent and the KPD 2.1 per cent.

33 *L'Avanti!*, 1 May 1920. The same spirit prevailed in the manifesto of the *Confederazione generale del lavoro* (*L'Avanti!*, 1 May 1920). The May Day celebrations of 1920 were already characterized by considerable violence and increasing counterrevolutionary activity (*L'Avanti!*, 4 May 1920).

34 The socialist manifesto saw the declaration of 1 May as an official holiday as an attempt to strip May Day of its rebellious character (*L'Avanti!*, 1 May 1922). To justify its decision, the government complained that public employees had difficulty reaching their offices in the absence of public transport (*L'Avanti!*, 27 April 1922). For the internal and administrative character of the decision, see also Ricci 1990, p. 80.

35 At the rally in Rome, the protest against trials and persecutions of anarchists and social revolutionaries in Russia provoked the reaction of communists; at the rally in Turin the socialist speaker was interrupted by 'the inevitable small group of furious communists that seems to have the specific assignment to disturb the rallies where one of us is speaking' (*L'Avanti!*, 2 May 1922).

36 On the corresponding changes in May Day iconography, with images now tending towards programmatic statements and the aspect of agitation being pushed to the foreground, see Korff (1986, p. 54ff.; 1989, p. 91ff.).

37 The *Frankfurter Zeitung* repeatedly underlined police intervention against completely uninvolved citizens. An article published on 3 May 1929 contradicted the official version of the events in the Wedding district. According to police, officers had been fired at from an imposing barricade and from the windows and roofs of houses. For the *Frankfurter Zeitung*, in reality police had reacted to insults by drawing their weapons and ordering that all windows be closed, opening fire when this order was not followed. The barricade was erected only after the first death, with defensive intentions. The police continued to fire at all open windows and lighted windows even after they were closed, but had also machine-gunned houses without any particular target, proof being the bullet marks left behind.

38 See *Frankfurter Zeitung*, 2 May 1920. The Christian trade unions were opposed to May Day; on the position of the associations of white collar workers, see Kubik 1989.

39 See Lischber and Algermissen 1983, p. 46. According to the police, the SPD rally had 16,000 participants. Each party press gave significantly higher figures for its own respective rally.

40 As an example, see Gregor Strasser's editorial published by the *Völkischer Beobachter* (30 April 1931) under the title 'The German First of May'.

41 First signs of state repression against social democratic May Day events became visible in 1932 in the federal state of Braunschweig, where the NSDAP participated in the government. In 1931 Braunschweig had abolished 1 May as a public holiday.

42 The national socialists could celebrate 1 May 1933 without resistance from the trade unions. Not only the Christian trade unions and right-wing associations of white collar workers, but also the ADGB called upon their members to participate in the official events. The calls of the ADGB and the Christian trade unions can be found in Schuster (1991, p. 69ff.). On the ADGB's unparalleled misjudgement of the national socialist aims, especially as far as 1 May was concerned, see Ruck 1990, p. 177ff. This is all the more surprising as repression against the ADGB was already rampant before May Day 1933 (Wahlich and Willmer 1990, p. 102).

43 Of the 357 German speakers (an additional three were foreigners) mentioned, biographical data could be collected on 237; of these, 189 were still alive in 1933.

44 See Dyck and Joost-Krüger 1990, p. 229. The *Frankfurter Zeitung* (2 May 1932) had already underlined the strikingly strong presence of the bourgeois element in the national socialist May Day rally that year.

45 In 1923, the *Confederazione Generale del lavoro* called for abstention from work only in those places and professions where it was possible, avoiding in any case painful conflicts and further victims (*L'Avanti!*, 26 April 1923).

46 In the following, 'Germany' refers to the Federal Republic of Germany. On May Day in the East German Democratic Republic, see Oehlandt 1989; Sauer 1990; Protte 1997.

47 Also the temporal proximity of 25 April – the national holiday commemorating the liberation from Nazism/fascism – from early on led to a lesser involvement of

political parties in the preparation and organization of May Day celebrations in Italy than in Germany. In addition, the propaganda and fundraising for the socialist press – a common feature of both German and Italian pre-fascist May Days – in Italy was taken over by the newly instituted 'Festa dell'Unità' (Tonelli 2012).

48 In the 1950s, the by then centrally organized SPD event attracted more participants than the trade union rally. In addition, the youth organizations of the unions, the Social Democratic Party and collateral organizations organized a torchlight procession and rally on the evening before 1 May.

49 For one of these manifestos, see Kehm 1986, p. 102. Also at SPD events, however, the characteristic of May Day as a day of struggle was underlined (*Frankfurter Rundschau*, 4 May 1953).

50 For parallel developments in Sweden in the early 1940s see Chapter 4, pp. 91–91. On the impact of Cold War tensions on May Day celebrations see chapters 4 and 6.

51 Rucht 2001, pp. 154, 164f. In the social democratic camp, the format of the 'freedom rallies' did not pass without signs of internal opposition. In 1956 the youth organization 'Die Falken' protested with slogans like 'Neither Ulbricht nor Adenauer but German unity' (*Der Spiegel*, 9 May 1956).

52 At demonstrations and other events, communist party members showed their allegiance by wearing a red handkerchief around their neck. During the Cold War years, the wearing of such handkerchiefs was interpreted as a uniform and the prohibition on civilians wearing uniforms, directed against paramilitary militias, was applied (della Porta and Reiter 2003, p. 105).

53 See Boschini 1955, p. 10f. This pamphlet published by the ACLI also contained the accusation that 1 May had often been celebrated with immodesty and (too much) wine.

54 Among others, *L'Unità* reported incidents in Rome in 1953 and 1956, in Naples in 1951 and 1957 and in Piombino in 1954. On the evening before May Day 1950, serious clashes occurred in Celano. The police opened fire on the demonstrators; 2 people were killed and 11 wounded.

55 Needless to say, differently from similar campaigns of the DGB, the CGIL's peace and anti-nuclear weapons campaigns were part of concerted efforts of the Soviet bloc and the communist parties in the Western countries. However, the CGIL with its chairman Di Vittorio took an openly critical position on the invasion of Hungary in 1956.

56 In a 15-minute-long broadcast, the general secretaries of all trade union confederations (including the neo-fascist CISNAL) could direct a short address to the public. For protests against such programming, see *L'Unità* (1 May 1958; 1 May 1959).

57 Eric Hobsbawm (1991, p. 106) observed: 'Western official May Days were recognitions of the need to come to terms with the tradition of the unofficial May Days and to detach it from labour movements, class consciousness and class struggle.'

58 In a contribution to the *Frankfurter Allgemeine Zeitung* (30 April 1957), economics minister Ludwig Ehrhardt declared the end of class struggle. In a radio address, Chancellor Konrad Adenauer underlined that 1 May was no longer the demonstration of an oppressed class but a day of common pride in the achievements of a whole people (*Frankfurter Allgemeine Zeitung*, 3 May 1958). The radio address had been suggested in the cabinet meeting of 22 April 1958 by the interior minister, who had reported that according to surveys among workers a large part of them thought that they had enjoyed a better reputation after 1933 than in the Federal Republic (www.bundesarchiv.de/cocoon/barch/0000/k/k1958k/kap1_2/kap2_15/para3_8.html).

59 A reproduction of the poster can be found in the gallery of May Day posters on the DGB website (www.dgb.de/themen/++co++3d82150a-1294-11df-40df-00093d10fae2; accessed 25 August 2015). Albeit to a lesser extent, similar

developments can be observed in Italy. Stylistically and in terms of content, the title-page of the May Day 1963 issue of the CGIL journal *Rassegna Sindacale* shows little difference from the May Day posters of the DGB.

60   See *Der Spiegel*, 30 April 1958; 7 May 1958. On the development of the number of May Day participants in Berlin, Munich and Frankfurt, see Rucht 2001, pp. 156, 158; in Dortmund, see Hilmer and Zaib 1997, p. 184.

61   For the rally in Rome, up to 1956 *L'Unità* reported a participation of 100,000 and more people. For the following decade, no participation figures were provided. In 1968, a year for which the CGIL spoke of a significant increase in participation, according to *L'Unità* (3 May 1968) 50,000 people participated in the Rome rally.

62   For Germany, see *Frankfurter Allgemeine Zeitung*, 1 May 1961; 1 May 1966. These editorials underlined that for most workers 1 May was just another holiday. Some of the cartoons are reproduced in Achten (1990, pp. 245, 155f.). For *La Stampa* (1 May 1965), 1 May had become above all a spring holiday, emptied of revolutionary and even polemic charge. *Rassegna sindacale* discussed reports in the bourgeois press that May Day had become 'just a picnic', but substantially denied that this was the case (A.T. 1965).

63   In 1959 the metalworkers' union IG Metall asked its members whether 1 May was still in keeping with the times. The results show a sceptical affirmation of a domesticated rally style (Korff 1989, p. 99). Almost a decade later, according to a survey published by the DGB journal *Welt der Arbeit* (28 April 1967), 56 per cent of trade union members preferred May Day as a holiday and 36 per cent as a day of struggle; on average 12 to 14 per cent participated in May Day rallies and celebrations.

64   During the 1960s in certain Italian cities such as Naples, the unions also temporarily renounced organizing a street demonstration (Boldini 1967).

65   In Frankfurt, the SPD event was organized for the last time in 1968, the torchlight procession and rally of the youth organizations in 1971. In 1962 the trade unions in the DGB Frankfurt district (with at that time 190,000 members) had organized 58 May Day celebrations and rallies and 200 additional events; in 1965 there were 35 celebrations and rallies; in 1969, 29; and in 1973, there were 19 (*Frankfurter Allgemeine Zeitung*, 30 April 1962; 29 April 1965; 28 April 1969; 27 April 1973).

66   At the union rally a group of Spanish workers protested against the dictatorship in their country. The radical language at the youth rally was attributed to the pacifist Eastern marchers, but also to the 'Falken', a youth organization of the SPD (*Frankfurter Rundschau*, 30 April and 3 May 1962).

67   Around the Frankfurt youth rally, elements of the youth culture of the 1960s were increasingly taken up in the following years. At the trade union rally, solidarity with Spanish workers and their protest against the Franco dictatorship became important themes. In addition, it became consolidated practice not only to invite foreign workers to the rally with a leaflet in their own language, but also to organize specific events for them in the union building. Based on interviews in the Stuttgart area, Giacoia (1990) presents a picture of complete isolation of the foreign workers on May Day. However, also in that town in 1961, in addition to 70,000 May Day leaflets in German, the DGB printed 15,000 in Italian; welcoming addresses at the rally were given in German, Spanish, French and Italian (Frank 1990, p. 199ff.). As in France (Tartakowsky 2005, p. 192), parts of the press in Germany interpreted the strong participation of foreign workers and young people as a further sign of the decline of May Day. In Italy the participation of foreign workers became a topic only in the 1980s (*L'Unità*, 1 May and 3 May 1985).

68   The DGB, for instance, tried to persuade the Spanish demonstrators to use white instead of red banners and a more neutral language, allegedly to protect them from reprisals at home.

69   As an early example, see a declaration of the federal board of the DGB (*Frankfurter Rundschau*, 7 May 1969).

70 See *Frankfurter Rundschau*, 2–5 May 1977; according to Hilmer and Zaib (1997, p. 200), however, in Dortmund police had to convince the DGB to tolerate protests at their May Day events and not to call for police intervention.
71 In a declaration, the board of the CGIL condemned attempts to influence trade union positions and criticized the students for following extremist theses that the workers' movement had long overcome (*L'Unità*, 3 May 1968). On France, see Tartakowsky 2005, p. 182ff.
72 On this traditional demand also of the moderate Italian Left, see della Porta and Reiter 2003, pp. 122, 164ff. In 1968 in Avola and in 1969 in Battipaglia, four demonstrators were killed in clashes with the police (della Porta and Reiter 2003, p. 204ff).
73 See della Porta and Reiter 2003, p. 279f. The importance of trade union support in the fight for the demilitarization and unionization of the police was repeatedly stressed at the May Day rallies of the 1980s.
74 An example is provided by the television address of the DGB chairman on 1 May. Initially broadcast directly after the main evening news on the first channel, in 1978 it was moved before the news and subsequently pushed to the early evening and then to the afternoon. In 2003 the address was broadcast from 14.40 to 14.45.
75 In 1984, on the basis of an agreement between CISL, UIL and the industrialists, the Italian government led by socialist Bettino Craxi passed a law cutting four percentage points from the automatic adjustment to inflation. In 1985 an abrogative referendum promoted only by the communist party was defeated by 54.3 per cent of the voters.
76 When in the jubilee year 2000 the traditional trade unions agreed to renounce their May Day event and to celebrate a 'jubilee of the workers' presided over by the pope, the Cobas together with other left-wing groups as a counter-event organized the biggest May Day demonstration in Rome in more than 20 years, with 30,000 (according to the police 15,000–20,000) participants (*L'Unità*, 3 May 2000).
77 On the May Day parades coordinated by the EuroMayDay network that quickly spread to other Italian and European cities, see Chapter 10 and, among others, Mattoni 2012.
78 Casquete and Grastorf (2003, p. 125) quote a functionary of the national democratic party as saying that his party had been organizing May Day events for 38 years.
79 According to its own account, the UGL had 2,145,955 members in 2008. The television broadcast 'Report' (RAI 3, 26 October 2008) raised strong doubts about the accuracy of these figures. For its central May Day event in 2007 in Bologna, the UGL mobilized 20,000 people (*L'Unità*, 3 May 2007). The MSI evolved into *Alleanza Nazionale* and participated in the Berlusconi governments.
80 These data were collected in the course of the seed-money project 'The First of May between routine and contestation: A cross-national and historical comparison of Labour Day in Europe' financed by the European University Institute in 2005. The German data were analyzed by the author, the Italian data by Giulia Albanese.
81 *L'Unità* (1 May 2007) observed: 'As long as labour exists, we will not liberate ourselves from 1 May and its trade unions.' On 1 May 2009 the editorial of the *Frankfurter Allgemeine Zeitung* appeared under the title 'Day of counter-power' and an article published by FAZnet asked: 'Is 1 May experiencing a renaissance?'.

References

A.T. (1965). Solo un 'pic nic'? *Rassegna Sindacale*, 62, 2.
Achten, U. (Ed.). (1980). *Zum Lichte Empor: Mai-Festzeitungen der Sozialdemokratie 1891–1914*. Berlin and Bonn: Dietz Verlag.

Achten, U. (Ed.). (1990). *Wenn ihr nur einig seid: Texte, Bilder und Lieder zum 1. Mai.* Cologne: Bund Verlag.

Alto, G. (1990). *Hundert Jahre 1. Mai. Der Arbeiterkampf- und feiertag in München.* Munich: DGB-Bildungswerk Kreis München.

Andersen, A. (1990). 'Auf die Barrikaden, erstürme die Welt, du Arbeitervolk!' Der 1. Mai, die Kriegslinke und die KPD. In I. Marßolek (Ed.), *100 Jahre Zukunft. Zur Geschichte des 1. Mai* (pp. 121–143). Frankfurt a.M. and Vienna: Büchergilde Gutenberg.

Antonioli, M. (1988). *Vieni o maggio. Aspetti del Primo Maggio in Italia tra otto e novecento.* Milan: Angeli.

Arbizzani, L. (1990). *Di primo in Primo Maggio. Cento '1° Maggio' a Bologna e dintorni, 1890–1990.* Bologna: Grafis.

Bertozzi, D.A. (2009). *La festa dei lavoratori. Il Primo Maggio a Brescia dalle origini alla prima guerra mondiale.* Rome: Ediesse.

Blickhan, M., and Teune, S. (2003). 'Die Lust am Ausnahmezustand' – Der Berliner 1. Mai im Spiegel der Medien. In D. Rucht (Ed.), *Berlin, 1. Mai 2002. Politische Demonstrationsrituale* (pp. 185–220). Opladen: Leske + Budrich.

Boldini, S. (1967). Il Primo Maggio oggi: Rinnovamento nella tradizione. *Rassegna sindacale*, 111, 35–36.

Boll, F. (1992). *Arbeitskämpfe und Gewerkschaften in Deutschland, England und Frankreich. Ihre Entwicklung vom 19. zum 20. Jahrhundert.* Bonn: J.H.W. Dietz.

Bosch, H. (1980). Ideologische Transformationsarbeit in Hitlers Rede zum Ersten Mai 1933. In M. Behrens *et al.* (Eds), *Faschismus und Ideologie I, Projekt Ideologie-Theorie* (= Argument, Sonderband 60) (pp. 107–140). Berlin: Argument.

Boschini, A. (1955). *Primo Maggio Cristiano.* Rome: Edizioni ACLI.

Bouvier, B.W. (1993). Es wird kommen der Mai … Zur Ikonographie des Arbeitermai im Kaiserreich. *Archiv für Sozialgeschichte*, 33, 570–585.

Bowlby, C. (1986). Blutmai 1929: Police, parties and proletarians in a Berlin confrontation. *Historical Journal*, 29, 137–158.

Brackmann, P. (1990). Die Maikundgebungen in Osnabrück nach 1945. In U. Alberts *et al.*, *Vom Deutschen Metallarbeiterverband zur Industriegewerkschaft Metall. Texte und Dokumente aus der Geschichte der Metallarbeiter in Osnabrück* (pp. 136–146). Osnabrück: Rasch.

Braun, H.D., Reinhold, C., and Schwarz, H.-A. (1990). SchwarzRotGold (Anstelle einer Einleitung). In H.D. Braun, C. Reinhold and H.-A. Schwarz (Eds), *Vergangene Zukunft: Mutationen eines Feiertages* (pp. 9–15). Berlin: Transit.

Braun, H.D., and Schwarz, H.-A. (1989). Warum der Erste Mai am 1. Mai gefeiert wird. Überlegungen zur Zeitlichkeit eines Festtages. In Verein zum Studium sozialer Bewegungen (Ed.), *Hundert Jahre Erster Mai. Beiträge und Projekte zur Geschichte der Maifeiern in Deutschland. Ein Tagungsbericht* (pp. 11–36). Berlin: Selbstverlag.

Cahill, J.J. (1973). The NSDAP and May Day, 1923: Confrontation and aftermath, 1923–27. PhD thesis, University of Cincinnati.

Casali, L. (1990). Il Primo Maggio proibito 1923–1943. In G.C. Donno (Ed.), *Storie e immagini del 1° Maggio. Problemi della storiografia italiana ed internazionale* (pp. 113–136). Manduria, Bari and Rome: Lacaita.

Casquete, J., and Grastorf, I. (2003). 'Die Schlacht um die Straße': Die 1. Mai-Demonstration der NPD in der 'Reichshauptstadt'. In: D. Rucht (Ed.), *Berlin, 1. Mai 2002. Politische Demonstrationsrituale* (pp. 101–141). Opladen: Leske + Budrich.

della Porta, D. (2008). Eventful protest, global conflicts. *Distinktion: Scandinavian Journal of Social Theory*, 17, 27–56.

della Porta, D., and Reiter, H. (2003). *Polizia e protesta. L'ordine pubblico dalla liberazione ai 'no global'*. Bologna: Il Mulino.

Dyck, K., and Joost-Krüger, J. (1990). Unserer Zukunft eine Gasse! Eine Lokalgeschichte der Bremer Maifeiern. In I. Marßolek (Ed.), *100 Jahre Zukunft. Zur Geschichte des 1. Mai* (pp. 191–257). Frankfurt a.M. and Vienna: Büchergilde Gutenberg.

Eichler, J. (1992). *Von Köln nach Mannheim: die Debatten über Maifeier, Massenstreik und das Verhältnis der Freien Gewerkschaften zur deutschen Sozialdemokratie innerhalb der Arbeiterbewegung Deutschlands 1905/06. Zur Entstehung des Mannheimer Abkommens*. Münster: Lit.

Eley, G. (1995). What's left of utopia? Oder: Vom 'Neuen Jerusalem' zur 'Zeit der Wünsche'. *Werkstatt Geschichte*, 11, 5–18.

Eley, G. (2002). *Forging Democracy: The History of the Left in Europe, 1850–2000*. Oxford: Oxford University Press.

Elfferding, W. (1989). Der soldatische Mann und die 'weiße Frau der Revolution'. Faszination und Gewalt am Beispiel des 1. Mai. In Verein zum Studium sozialer Bewegungen (Ed.), *Hundert Jahre Erster Mai. Beiträge und Projekte zur Geschichte der Maifeiern in Deutschland. Ein Tagungsbericht* (pp. 56–73). Berlin: Selbstverlag.

Foner, P.S. (1986). *May Day: A Short History of the International Workers' Holiday 1886–1986*. New York: International Publishers.

Frank, S. (1990). *'Schon Vatis Opa war dabei …' Hundert Jahre Arbeiter-Maifeiern in Stuttgart*. Ed. DGB Kreis Stuttgart. Stuttgart: Silberburg Verlag.

Giacoia, G. (1990). Begegnung mit dem 1. Mai in der Emigration. Italienische Arbeiter in der Bundesrepublik. In I. Marßolek (Ed.), *100 Jahre Zukunft. Zur Geschichte des 1. Mai* (pp. 289–299). Frankfurt a.M. and Vienna: Büchergilde Gutenberg.

Giagnotti, F. (1988). May Day in Italy during World War I. In A. Panaccione (Ed.), *May Day Celebration* (pp. 131–190). Venice: Marsilio.

Hilmer, J., and Zaib, V. (1997). *Arbeiterbildung und Arbeiterkultur im östlichen Ruhrgebiet. Beiträge zur Arbeiterbildung, zur Maifeier und zum Leseverhalten* (Arbeiterkultur und Arbeiterbewegung 32). Münster: Lit.

Hobsbawm, E. (1991). Birth of a holiday: The first of May. In C. Wrigley and J. Shepherd (Eds), *On the Move: Essays in Labour and Transport History* (pp. 104–122). London and Rio Grande: Hambledon Press.

Hund, W.D. (1990). Der 1. Mai 1890. In Landeszentrale für politische Bildung (Ed.), *'Uns aus dem Elend zu erlösen können wir nur selber tun'. 100 Jahre 1. Mai: 100 Jahre Machtsicherung und Gegenoffensive in Hamburg* (pp. 23–41) (first published in J. Berlin (Ed.), *Das andere Hamburg. Freiheitliche Bestrebungen in der Hansestadt seit dem Spätmittelalter*. Cologne, 1981). Hamburg: Landeszentrale für politische Bildung.

Kehm, B. (1986). *Der 1. Mai im Spiegel der Bochumer Presse, 1927–1955*. Ed. Gemeinsamen Arbeitsstelle Ruhr-Universität Bochum/IG Metall and DGB-Kreis Bochum. Bochum: Institut zur Erforschung der europäischen Arbeiterbewegung.

Korff, G. (1986). Rote Fahnen und geballte Faust. Zur Symbolik der Arbeiterbewegung in der Weimarer Republik. In D. Petzina (Ed.), *Fahnen, Fäuste, Körper. Symbolik und Kultur der Arbeiterbewegung* (pp. 27–60). Essen: Klartext.

Korff, G. (1989). Bemerkungen zur Symbolgeschichte des 1. Mai. In Verein zum Studium sozialer Bewegungen (Ed.), *Hundert Jahre Erster Mai. Beiträge und*

72   *Herbert Reiter*

Projekte zur Geschichte der Maifeiern in Deutschland. Ein Tagungsbericht (pp. 85–103). Berlin: Selbstverlag.

Kubik, M. (1989). 'Roter Mai' und 'Weißer Kragen'. Die Stellung der Angestelltenbewegung zum Ersten Mai vom Kaiserreich bis zur Gegenwart. In Verein zum Studium sozialer Bewegungen (Ed.), *Hundert Jahre Erster Mai. Beiträge und Projekte zur Geschichte der Maifeiern in Deutschland. Ein Tagungsbericht* (pp. 104–116). Berlin: Selbstverlag.

Kurz, T. (1988). *'Blutmai': Sozialdemokraten und Kommunisten im Brennpunkt der Berliner Ereignisse von 1929*. Berlin and Bonn: Dietz.

Lehmann, F., and Meyerhöfer, N. (2003). 'Wünsche mir, dass es irgendwann so kracht wie früher' – Der Revolutionäre 1. Mai als linksradikales Ritual. In D. Rucht (Ed.), *Berlin, 1. Mai 2002. Politische Demonstrationsrituale* (pp. 55–99). Opladen: Leske + Budrich.

Lerch, E. (1988). Die Maifeiern der Arbeiter im Kaiserreich. In D. Düding, P. Friedemann and P. Münch (Eds), *Öffentliche Festkultur: Politische Feste in Deutschland von der Aufklärung bis zum Ersten Weltkrieg* (pp. 352–372). Reinbek bei Hamburg: Rowohlt.

Lindenberger, T. (1995). *Straßenpolitik. Zur Sozialgeschichte der öffentlichen Ordnung in Berlin 1900 bis 1914*. Bonn: J.H.W. Dietz.

Lischber, E., and Algermissen, G. (1983). *1. Mai – Hannover in der Weimarer Republik* (special issue of *Arbeitnehmer und Gesellschaft*. Ed. DGB-district Hanover). Hanover: DGB-Kreis Hannover.

Livi, A. (1964). 1° Maggio e opinione pubblica. *Rassegna Sindacale*, 35, 2, 4.

Mallmann, K.-M. (1996). *Kommunisten in der Weimarer Republik: Sozialgeschichte einer revolutionären Bewegung*. Darmstadt: Wissenschaftliche Buchgesellschaft.

Marßolek, I. (Ed.). (1990a). *100 Jahre Zukunft. Zur Geschichte des 1. Mai*. Frankfurt a.M. and Vienna: Büchergilde Gutenberg.

Marßolek, I. (1990b). Von Freiheitsgöttinnen, dem Riesen Proletariat und dem Aufzug der Massen: Der 1. Mai im Spiegel der sozialdemokratischen Maizeitungen 1891–1932. In I. Marßolek (Ed.), *100 Jahre Zukunft. Zur Geschichte des 1. Mai* (pp. 145–169). Frankfurt a.M. and Vienna: Büchergilde Gutenberg.

Marßolek, I. (1990c). 100 Jahre 1. Mai – (k)ein Grund zum Feier. *Journal Geschichte*, 5, 12–23.

Mattoni, A. (2012). *Media Practices and Protest Politics. How Precarious Workers Mobilize*. Farnham, UK and Burlington, VT: Ashgate.

Mooser, J. (1983). Abschied von der 'Proletarität'. Sozialstruktur und Lage der Arbeiterschaft in der Bundesrepublik in historischer Perspektive. In W. Conze and M. R. Lepsius (Eds), *Sozialgeschichte der Bundesrepublik Deutschland. Beiträge zum Kontinuitätsproblem* (pp. 143–186). Stuttgart: Klett-Cotta.

Müller, D.-H. (1990). Was soll am 1. Mai geschehen? In I. Marßolek (Ed.), *100 Jahre Zukunft. Zur Geschichte des 1. Mai* (pp. 77–101). Frankfurt a.M. and Vienna: Büchergilde Gutenberg.

Murtaugh, M. (1991). *Italian Labor in Protest, 1904–1914. Political General Strikes to Protest Eccidi*. New York and London: Garland.

Neri Serneri, S. (1990). Tradizione e opposizione. Il 1° Maggio in Italia durante il fascismo. In A. Riosa (Ed.), *Le metamorfosi del 1° Maggio. La festa del lavoro in Europa tra le due guerre* (pp. 29–71). Rome and Milan: Marsilio.

Oehlandt, T. (1989). Zur Geschichte des Ersten Mai in Berlin nach der Niederschlagung des Faschismus. In Verein zum Studium sozialer Bewegungen (Ed.), *100 Jahre*

Erster Mai. Beiträge und Projekte zur Geschichte der Maifeiern in Deutschland. Ein Tagungsbericht (pp. 74–84). Berlin: Selbstverlag.

Panaccione, A. (Ed.). (1989). *La memoria del Primo Maggio. Storia iconografica della festa dei lavoratori: gli inizi, il radicamento / The Memory of May Day. An Iconographic History of the Origins and Implanting of a Workers' Holiday*. Venice: Marsilio.

Panaccione, A. (1990). *Un giorno perché: Cent'anni di storia internazionale del 1° Maggio*. Rome: Ediesse.

Pepe, A. (1999). La scissione in Italia. In M. Antoniolo, M. Bergamaschi and F. Romero (Eds), *Le scissioni sindacali: Italia e Europa* (pp. 115–126). Pisa: Biblioteca Franco Serrantini.

Protte, K. (1997). Zum Beispiel ... der 1. Mai 1951 in Ost-Berlin: Agitation, staatliche Selbstdarstellung und Utopie. In D. Vorsteher (Ed.), *Parteiauftrag: ein neues Deutschland. Bilder, Rituale und Symbole der frühen DDR* (pp. 118–135). Munich: Koehler and Amelang.

Renda, F. (2009). *Storia del Primo Maggio dalle origini ai giorni nostri*. Rome: Ediesse.

Ricci, A.G. (1990). Fonti e iniziative dell'Archivio Centrale dello Stato per la storia del movimento operaio. In G.C. Donno (Ed.), *Storie e immagini del 1° Maggio. Problemi della storiografia italiana ed internazionale* (pp. 75–112). Manduria, Bari and Rome: Lacaita.

Riosa, A. (1990). Alcuni appunti per una storia della festa del lavoro durante il regime fascista. In A. Riosa (ed.), *Le metamorfosi del 1° Maggio. La festa del lavoro in Europa tra le due guerre* (pp. 73–89). Rome and Milan: Marsilio.

Robbiati, A. (1990). Garofani bianchi e garofani rossi. La Festa del Lavoro ed i cattolici italiani (1890–1915). In G.C. Donno (Ed.), *Storie e immagini del 1° Maggio. Problemi della storiografia italiana ed internazionale* (pp. 151–178). Manduria, Bari and Rome: Lacaita.

Rucht, D. (2001). Heraus zum Ersten Mai! Ein Ritual im Wandel, 1950–1999. In D. Rucht (Ed.), *Protest in der Bundesrepublik Deutschland. Strukturen und Entwicklungen* (pp. 143–172). Frankfurt a.M.: Campus.

Ruck, M. (1990). Vom Demonstrations- und Festtag der Arbeiterbewegung zum Nationalen Feiertag des Deutschen Volkes. Der 1. Mai im Dritten Reich und die Arbeiter. In I. Marßolek (Ed.), *100 Jahre Zukunft. Zur Geschichte des 1. Mai* (pp. 171–188). Frankfurt a.M. and Vienna: Büchergilde Gutenberg.

Sauer, B. (1990). 'Es lebe der Erste Mai in der DDR!' Die politische Inszenierung eines Staatsfeiertags. In H.D. Braun, C. Reinhold and H.-A. Schwarz (Eds), *Vergangene Zukunft: Mutationen eines Feiertages* (pp. 115–131). Berlin: Transit.

Saul, K. (1972). Der Staat und die 'Mächte des Umsturzes'. Ein Beitrag zu den Methoden antisozialistischer Repression und Agitation vom Scheitern des Sozialistengesetzes bis zur Jahrhundertwende. *Archiv für Sozialgeschichte*, 12, 293–350.

Saul, K. (1990). Machtsicherung und Gegenoffensive – Zur Entstehung des Arbeitgeber-Verbandes Hamburg-Altona 1888–1890. In: Landeszentrale für politische Bildung (Ed.), *Uns aus dem Elend zu erlösen können wir nur selber tun: 100 Jahre 1. Mai: 100 Jahre Machtsicherung und Gegenoffensive in Hamburg* (pp. 45–78) (first published in *Zeitschrift des Vereins für Hamburgische Geschichte*, 72, 1986). Hamburg: Landeszentrale für politische Bildung.

Schirmann, L. (1991). *Blutmai Berlin 1929. Dichtungen und Wahrheit*. Berlin: Dietz.

Schuster, D. (1991). *Zur Geschichte des 1. Mai in Deutschland*. Ed. DGB-Bundesvorstand, Abt. Medien-Kultur-Freizeit. Düsseldorf: DGB.

Schwarz, H.-A. (1990). 'Ich frage, Herr Polizeipräsident, wo ist die Verlustliste ihrer Beamten?' – Blutmai 1929. In H.D. Braun, C. Reinhold and H.-A. Schwarz (Eds), *Vergangene Zukunft: Mutationen eines Feiertages* (pp. 79–90). Berlin: Transit.

Seeger, C. (1995). Hannoversche Maifeiern und Gewerkschaftsfeste als Stimmungsbarometer im Kaiserreich. In H.-D. Schmid (Ed.), *Feste und Feiern in Hannover* (pp. 151–171). Bielefeld: Verlag für Regionalgeschichte.

Sobrero, P. (1990). Primo Maggio e fonti orali. Una ricerca nell'area pugliese. In G.C. Donno (Ed.), *Storie e immagini del 1° Maggio. Problemi della storiografia italiana ed internazionale* (pp. 293–324). Manduria, Bari and Rome: Lacaita.

Steinkühler, F. (1990). Die aktuelle Bedeutung der Maifeier für die gegenwärtigen Gewerkschaften. In I. Marßolek (Ed.), *100 Jahre Zukunft. Zur Geschichte des 1. Mai* (pp. 9–14). Frankfurt a.M. and Vienna: Büchergilde Gutenberg.

Sun, R.C. (1986). Misguided martyrdom: German Social Democratic response to the Haymarket incident, 1886–87. *International Journal of Labor and Working Class History*, 24, 53–67.

Tartakowsky, D. (2005). *La part du rêve. Histoire du 1ᵉʳ mai en France*. Paris: Hachette.

Thamm, L. (1990). Der Erste Mai einmal anders! Im Spannungsfeld zwischen neuen sozialen Bewegungen und Arbeiterbewegung. In H.D. Braun, C. Reinhold and H.-A. Schwarz (Eds), *Vergangene Zukunft: Mutationen eines Feiertages* (pp. 132–153). Berlin: Transit.

Tonelli, A. (2012). *Falce e tortello. Storia politica e sociale delle Feste dell'Unità (1945–2011)*. Rome and Bari: Laterza.

Ulrich, A. (1985). *Trotz alledem – der 1. Mai blieb rot. Zur Geschichte des 1. Mai in Wiesbaden während der Illegalität, 1933–45*. Ed. DGB-Kreis Wiesbaden-Rheingau/Taunus. Wiesbaden: DGB.

Vorstand des Deutschen Metallarbeiter-Verbandes. (1907). *Geschichtliches zur Maifeier in Deutschland*. Stuttgart: Schlicke.

Wahlich, U., and Willmer, W. (1990). Das Ende des Klassenkampfes? Thesen zum Umgang des 1. Mai während des Nationalsozialismus. In H.D. Braun, C. Reinhold and H.-A. Schwarz (Eds), *Vergangene Zukunft: Mutationen eines Feiertages* (pp. 97–102). Berlin: Transit.

4 The May Day Tradition in Finland and Sweden

Christer Thörnqvist, Tapio Bergholm and Margaretha Mellberg

Introduction

In international comparisons industrial relations systems and labour movements in the five Nordic countries are often lumped together in 'the Nordic model'. There are good reasons to do so: the historical and contemporary similarities are more compelling than the differences (Thörnqvist 2009). The Nordic labour movements, in particular the trade unions, have also had a strong and formalized cooperation ever since the formative period in the late nineteenth century, and all through the 1900s the Nordic unions joined forces in trade union internationals and other international bodies (Schiller *et al.* 1994; Misgeld 1997; Thörnqvist 2008). The first Scandinavian trade union congress was held in Gothenburg in 1886. Many Swedish workers' organizations were opposed to a Scandinavian congress, hence the location in Gothenburg instead of the capital Stockholm. At the time the struggle between supporters of socialist and non-socialist unions had reached a crucial stage, and the opponents of the congress were afraid that the both better-organized and more radical Danes would turn the scales in favour of socialism – which was also what happened (Lindbom 1938, pp. 95–101). Over the following decade and a half, the Scandinavian unions grew closer on ideological issues, such as shared socialist principles, and on practical ones, such as strike support (Lindbom 1938, pp. 371–384).

One could therefore expect that also labour movement rituals, as discussed and defined by Hobsbawm and others (see Chapter 1), would also look rather similar in the North. At this political cultural level, however, the differences between the countries become apparent. In his seminal work written already in 1922, Norwegian historian Edvard Bull argued that the most striking difference between the labour movements in the three Scandinavian countries was the relative strength of the left-wing socialists. In Sweden and Denmark the main labour movement stream early adopted a strongly reformist policy, while the radical fraction of the Norwegian Labour Party remained strong; in fact it even affiliated to the Comintern. The nation-level influence of the syndicalist union, SAC, and the Left Socialist Party on the Swedish labour movement was, according to Bull, already curbed in 1920, and Sweden had the most 'uniform' movement of the three countries (Bull 1922).[1] The leftist opposition was nonetheless strong enough to form a party of its own in May 1917, but with its strength mainly among the youth, its focus on fast gains instead of long-term planning and its very radical rhetoric, the New Left Party was according to social democratic rhetoric already doomed; it could never attract the necessary power for a take-over of government, most notably, to gain cooperation with the liberals in order to win universal suffrage (Nilsson 1959, pp. 587–591).

The Norwegian radicalism did not last much longer either; some ten years later its position was reduced to the same level as the Swedish and Danish leftists. Still, though, there was one country that was perceived as 'the Nordic exception'. Bull wrote about the 'three Scandinavian countries'. True, Iceland was still not independent of Denmark, but in the east Finland had announced its independence from the Russian empire in December 1917, officially acknowledged by Lenin on 4 January 1918. The country's path to an independent state was, however, covered with blood. Where class conflicts led to a general strike in Sweden (1909), Finland suffered a terrible civil war (1918) that left its mark on Finnish society for decades. The civil war deeply divided the labour movement, leaving a strong communist fraction in Finland. Nonetheless, despite the different points of departure, Finnish and Swedish labour market relations had more or less converged at the peak of the post-war boom in the 1960s. So despite the many similarities today, in this chapter we will examine whether the political rituals in the Finnish labour movement's culture have moved along the same path. The celebration of May Day had been more or less accepted in Sweden ever since the first demonstration in 1890. While the established society did not look kindly upon the socialist movement, the repression against socialist parties and trade unions was still comparatively limited in Sweden. In Finland, on the other hand, the labour movement emerged in a much more authoritarian context and developed in strong conflict with bourgeois society in combination with serious frictions within the movement.

This chapter discusses the differences and similarities in the labour movement's main political ritual, the May Day celebration, in Finland and Sweden, against this historical background from the onset in 1890 to the mid-1960s, with an emphasis on the periods before and between the wars.

The Formative Years: The Labour Movement and May Day Celebrations in Sweden and Finland before 1920

Organized Labour and the Formation of a Swedish Socialist Party

In historical perspective Sweden has turned out to be the most mainstream Scandinavian country. The first 'modern' trade union, in the sense that its purpose was to be a workers' collective organization in the struggle for higher wages and better working conditions, was formed in 1874 among tobacco workers in Malmö in southern Sweden. The initiative came from abroad. Danish tobacco workers saw Malmö as – in their own words – 'more or less a Copenhagen suburb' due to the short distance between the cities; therefore it was necessary to look to the Malmö workers' organization in order to avoid strikebreaking and low-wage competition across the borders. Also in Malmö, on 6 November 1881, the tailor August Palm, returning after years as a journeyman in Germany and Denmark where he had picked up socialist ideas, gave the first socialist speech in Sweden. The speech led to socialist agitation all over the country, both by Palm himself and his followers. In 1882 he launched the first social-democratic newspaper, *Folkviljan* (The People's Will) in Malmö, and in April 1884 the first social-democratic organization was founded in Gothenburg. The nation-wide socialist party *Socialdemokratiska Arbetarepartiet*, SAP, saw daylight in 1889 with Palm as its first chairman (Palm 1904). It was also the party that took the lead in the making of the May Day tradition, not the trade unions.

The First Swedish May Day Rallies

Although the Swedish labour movement does not have the same deep historical roots as its counterparts in Denmark, Germany or the United Kingdom, it managed to organize May Day demonstrations already from 1890 onwards, the year after the Second International introduced the tradition at its congress. Already in January 1889 there was an organized meeting by the not yet formalized, but rising social democratic movement in the Lill-Jans forest in the outskirts of the capital Stockholm. However, the target was the monarchy and not any matter of specific labour interest. On 14 July the same year there was another meeting in Lill-Jans organized by the social democrats in Stockholm. As hinted by the date, the meeting was largely in honour of the centenary of the storming of the Bastille, but the demand for universal suffrage was also made. Moreover in December 1889 an editorial in the social democratic newspaper *Social-Demokraten* stressed that 1 May the coming year should be a 'common day off' for all working people, so that they would be able to demonstrate for the demands raised by the Second International, most notably the eight-hour workday (Björklund 1966, pp. 63–64).

The first May Day rally was held in Stockholm at the former military drill-ground Gärdet, an open space in the heart of the capital that became the centre for labour movement demonstrations in the years to come. Reports of the number of participants vary. Some stated that there were 20,000 people; the organizers themselves said 30,000; while others claimed that there were 20,000 participants in the march, but no less than 50,000 listening to the speeches at Gärdet. Nonetheless the estimates are impressive considering that Stockholm only had approximately 250,000 inhabitants in 1890 (Engman 1999, p. 57). The speakers included, among several others, August Palm, the new party's leader. Palm had two years earlier managed to circumvent a ban on demonstrations. At Whitsun 1887 Palm announced in *Social-Demokraten* that he intended to take a 'Sunday morning walk' and looked for people willing to join him. The police had recently forbidden a protest rally against unemployment, but as Palm just 'took a walk', though followed by numbers of sympathizers and with a clear political agenda, the police could not object since it was in no way violent (J.-E. Olsson 1990, pp. 9–10; Engman 1999, p. 51). May Day mobilizations first emerged in judicial limbo, neither forbidden nor allowed. According to the Regulations for the Kingdom's Towns of 1868, giving a 'public talk' was on a par with 'plays, exhibition of animals and tightrope dancing', although the organizer was obliged to declare the purpose and nature of the arrangement (*Ordningsstadga för rikets städer af d. 24 mars 1868*, §13). While in the countryside there were no rules deriving this law, there were guidelines for when the police authorities should intervene or even disperse public gatherings (Bodin and Nycop 1980, pp. 28–29).

Among the speakers in addition to Palm at the 1890 rally in Stockholm we find Hjalmar Branting, who soon was to be the key protagonist of the party's reformist fraction and in 1920 become the first social democratic prime minister in Sweden. But there was also Branting's main antagonist, Hinke Bergegren. Bergegren was strongly influenced by anarchistic ideas and therefore expelled from the party in 1908, the year after Branting had been elected chairman.[2] The disagreements between Bergegren and the more strictly middle of the road social democrats were exposed the following year, which we shall return to below. In agreement with the international labour congress in Paris 1889 the organizers claimed that the May Day labour demonstration was part of a worldwide demonstration for the eight-hour workday. Although it was not the sole issue, for instance the demand for universal suffrage was present from the start, the eight-hour workday overshadowed other demands (Björklund 1966, pp. 63–67; Bodin and Nycop 1980, pp. 5–13; Engman 1999, pp. 53–60).

May Day demonstrations were organized in 20 more towns or municipalities. The largest took place in Gothenburg, with some 25,000 participants,[3] and Malmö with some 20,000 at the rally (Nerman 1956, p. 9; L. Olsson 2002, p. 27). These demonstrations, however, did not have such important speakers as appeared in Stockholm[4] and were thus not systematically subject to the same surveillance by the authorities. Among the smaller Swedish cities Norrköping, a city on the east coast with a large working-class population, had 20,000 participants at the concluding rally, while Hälsingborg in the south and Sundsvall in the north managed to attract 10,000 people each, according to the party's own records (Nerman 1956, p. 9). In Sundsvall the main standard proclaiming '8 hours of work, 8 hours of rest, 8 hours of recreation' against an all-white background, was carried by a young woman, Märta Nordén, who for the sake of a 'radical' impact wore a red veil, long red gloves and a red sash over her shoulder, all according to the local newspaper (J.-E. Olsson 1990, pp. 11–12). Not all rallies in the countryside passed unnoticed by the authorities. Several army regiments were held in military preparedness, thanks to rumours of rebellious uprisings circulating the days before the May

Day demonstrations (Bodin and Nycop 1980, pp. 10–12). However, despite these rumours the largest bourgeois newspapers, which while they generally found the demand for the eight-hour workday unrealistic, nonetheless were generally seemingly positive to the workers' demonstration in 1890 (Engman 1999, pp. 54–60).

The Ritual Tradition Settles

Throughout the 1890s the number of May Day participants remained about the same in Stockholm, the city with the most reliable estimates. In addition to speakers from the working class and the intellectuals associated with the labour movement, Knut Wicksell, one of the first academic economists in Sweden influenced by Marxism and a strong advocate of contraception to reduce poverty (Lönnroth 1985, pp. 46–47), gave a speech in 1893. Wicksell stressed that considering the high levels of unemployment at the time an eight-hour workday was not a realistic claim (Björklund 1966, p. 71). This was the first time an academic not directly affiliated with the labour movement was invited as a keynote speaker at a May Day demonstration.

The following year, 1894, the first international representative, Jules Margoux, was present, as well as the well-known author Ellen Key, who delivered one of the speeches, in her case on the topic: 'The woman and the standard working hour day' (Björklund 1966, pp. 71–72). The 1895 meeting at Gärdet has gone down in history for its legal consequences. Norway had since the 1814 war been affiliated to Sweden in a union which however was formed very much on Swedish terms. At the end of the century a Norwegian independence movement had begun to struggle for formal Norwegian sovereignty, a demand that important bourgeois and military circles in Sweden claimed should be met by military intervention. At the May Day meeting Hjalmar Branting brought the issue up in his speech, but in a way that could be interpreted as an exhortation to the listeners to prevent such a war by not obeying the authorities, or even respond with sabotage or murder (Grass 2010). Branting was sentenced to three months in prison, but the penalty was changed to a fine, and the whole trial became a catalyst for the mounting Swedish opinion against the right-wing warmongers (Björklund 1966, pp. 91–98; Haste 1988, p. 126; J.-E. Olsson 1990, p. 14).

In 1902 the May Day speeches and placards were influenced by the general strike for universal suffrage that was to be held two days later (Engman 1999, pp. 61–63). The strike was announced by two political parties, the social democrats supported by the liberals. Although it was not officially supported by trade unions, they were collectively affiliated with the Social Democratic Party, and the strike was considered successful by its organizers (Hamark and Thörnqvist 2013, pp. 5–6). As a prelude, however, the police had attacked a peaceful demonstration on 20 April in Stockholm with around 75,000 people rallying for universal suffrage; 72 people were arrested. Another pre-meeting arranged by the labour movement brought together some 25,000 workers in

Stockholm. Police and military forces also intervened against the May Day demonstrations in Jönköping and Eksjö, both in the region of Småland in southern Sweden (Bäckström 1977). Accordingly the May Day rallies included the issue of government repression.

Demands for the eight-hour workday, universal suffrage and an end to police repression dominated May Day demonstrations in the following years. The demands for universal suffrage were, however, not always clear-cut because of the debate within the party regarding women's right to vote. Many leading social democrats feared that if the income thresholds were not first eliminated, only women from wealthy families would be allowed to vote and that would only strengthen the right-wing parties (L.-E. Olsson 2002, pp. 37–38). The first woman to ever take the rostrum at a May Day rally, in Stockholm in 1891, was actually not a social democrat but the liberal Emilie Rathou, most remembered as the founder of Vita Bandet (the White Ribbon), the Swedish section of the World's Woman's Christian Temperance Union and a pioneer in the struggle for women's suffrage; women's suffrage was the main issue in her speech (Myrdal 1959, p. 341).[5] In 1911 social democratic activist Agda Östlund in her May Day speech at Gärdet argued that suffrage for women had values beyond class struggle. Bringing up the Australian example,[6] Östlund argued that with women voting there would no longer be any distressed children, which was crucial from 'a socialist and humanitarian viewpoint'. In addition to this pragmatic argument, Östlund repeatedly stressed the overarching argument: 'women are humans too' (*Morgonbris* 1911, p. 9). Ten years later when universal suffrage was achieved, Agda Östlund was one of the five first women to be elected to parliament (Flood 1954).

The conflicts over May Day emerged within the organized labour movement when the different ideological branches of the movement all realized the symbolic value of taking the lead in the organization of the May Day demonstrations and rallies. There had been internal tensions from the beginning of May Day demonstrations between social democracy and anarchism. In 1891 Hinke Bergegren was invited to speak in Gothenburg. On the day of the meeting the scheduled second keynote speaker, the tobacco worker Anders Sörensen, had 'fallen ill' and had to withdraw. A few days later the social democratic Malmö-based newspaper *Arbetet* clarified that Sörensen's real problem was that he did not want to speak on the same platform as Bergegren for political reasons. *Arbetet* argued that Bergegren's appearance was highly unsuitable as May Day manifested the struggle for both universal suffrage and statutory working hours, two things Bergegren and the anarchists 'hated' (Wistrand 1959, p. 214).

The struggle against anti-strike legislation, police repression in general and in particular the repression of workers' free right of association was, however, never internally controversial. Despite an anarchistic influence in the formative years there were never any calls for violence. Even so, police repression was always present. In 1908 the Young Socialists' standard with the slogan 'Overthrow the throne, the altar, and the money-bag'[7] was confiscated. The young painter who carried it was fined 300 Swedish kronor (Bodin and Nycop 1980, p. 23; Engman 1999, p. 74), a sum comparable to between one and two months' pay. The above-mentioned economics professor, Knut Wicksell, was sentenced to two months in prison for his speech on the issue (Björklund 1966, pp. 75–76). Banners with other slogans popular at the time such as 'Not a single man – not a penny to militarism', first employed by the Young Socialists in 1909, were also confiscated. Most confiscated or forbidden banners attacked the monarchy or the military, but the May Day context made otherwise harmless slogans provocative in the eyes of the police. Most notably in Oskarshamn (on Sweden's east coast) in 1909 the police forbade a banner with the fifth commandment (Lutheran and Catholic tradition): 'Thou shalt not kill'. On the other hand, we find examples of how demonstrators circumvented banned slogans. In 1911 one banner read 'The police have taken our banner' and in 1917 in Uppsala, someone had cut out the letters 're' with a knife in the slogan *Leve republiken*, that is, 'Long live the republic', which literally changed the meaning to 'Long live the audience', but left little doubt about the real meaning (J.-E. Olsson 1990, pp. 17–21[8]).

The Swedish labour movement's greatest defeat came in 1909. In response to several lockouts LO (the blue-collar labour confederation) called a general strike in August that year, which turned out to be one of the largest labour conflicts in European history, lasting a full month and at its peak with 300,000 workers involved. The strike was thus impressive, but it lacked power. The outcome was devastating as the trade unions lost more than a quarter of their members, a drop that continued for two more years before the trend was turned (Hamark and Thörnqvist 2013). Yet the strike had little impact on the May Day rallies. While it was a major defeat for Swedish trade unionism, the Social Democratic Party was not significantly affected. True, the party also lost members, but that was largely because former trade union members had been collectively affiliated to SAP. When they left the LO they therefore also left the party. And workers left the trade unions because they could no longer afford the fees after the conflict, not because they had lost their political sympathies. In Stockholm 35,000 people had joined the demonstrations in 1909, that is, before the strike, and the number was actually higher the year after with some 40,000 participants in the demonstration and 60,000 at the rally (Engman 1999, p. 66). Malmö also survived, yet the figures for Gothenburg, a city hit hard by the strike, show a decrease from 15,000 to 5,000 people (Björklund 1966, pp. 181–186).[9] The syndicalist association, SAC, was founded in 1910 as a reaction to LO's defeat in the 1909 general strike (Persson 1975, pp. 104–107).

The number of participants, at least in Stockholm, peaked the years before the war. In 1912, 60,000 people joined the meeting, which celebrated the British miners' strike that had won them the eight-hour workday (Björklund 1966, p. 77). One of the three speakers at the rally that day was Alexandra Kollontaj, or according to the police who monitored the rally, 'a Russian lady' (Bodin and Nycop 1980, p. 26). The year after there were 65,000 participants and the figure was even exceeded in 1914 with 70,000 people assembled at the rally. The number dropped during the war, with the exception of the revolutionary year 1917 when approximately 50,000 to 60,000 people took part in the demonstration and as many as 100,000 joined the rally at Gärdet. About 600,000 people joined the May Day demonstrations across the country. With the Russian February revolution in mind the authorities took no risks. The army patrolled the streets of Stockholm and the police were highly active in all major cities. Even the navy was in preparedness, ready to act in case there were street actions directed against the royal castle (Björklund 1966, pp. 120–121; J.-E. Olsson 1990, p. 22). That year was filled with demonstrations and actions for bread and potatoes, or in other words, the basics for survival under hard circumstances. The most prominent food rebellion in Stockholm, however, took place on 5 May, that is, after the May Day rally (Andrae 1998).

Even though the conservative newspapers had not been hostile towards the first May Day rally in 1890, already the first demonstrations spread a feeling of uneasiness among the upper classes. In an attempt to neutralize the socialist demonstrations, right-wing politicians organized alternative, highly nationalistic May Day rallies in the early years of the new century. The first one, at the heritage park Skansen in Stockholm in 1906, had a decidedly nationalistic theme in the aftermath of the dissolving of the political union with Norway the year before (Bodin and Nycop 1980, p. 52). In the aftershock of the 1909 strike the bourgeois press again made an attempt to promote the 'citizen festivals' on 1 May at Skansen, arguing that they had much more to offer than the socialist demonstrations. Although ostensibly moderately successful, the Skansen festival did not become a serious alternative to the meetings at Gärdet for the workers; it was rather a complement (Engman 1999, pp. 66–68). The social democrats' hegemony was never threatened by bourgeois attempts to appropriate the May Day celebrations.

So in conclusion, the May Day demonstrations in Sweden were relatively successful already from the start. They attracted a wide audience, many participants in the rallies, prominent speakers and much attention in the newspapers. It is further fair to say that they also became great manifestations of the labour movement's basic demands. Although always the object of surveillance by the police force, the demonstrations were able to give voice to 'subversive' ideas of universal suffrage and – even more subversive – against societal fundaments such as the monarchy, the church and the private ownership of big industries. As we shall see, the Finnish path was quite different.

The Origin of the Workers' Vappu in the Grand Duchy of Finland

Historically Finland used to be a part of Sweden, generally called 'the Eastern half'. In 1809 Sweden lost this territory to Russia. Finland then became a self-governed nation under the supremacy of the Russian empire, which had profound effects on the emergence of the Finnish labour movement and its May

Day traditions. In the 1880s some members of the educated classes founded the first workers' associations in Finland, the Helsinki Workers' Association. The founder and first chairman, the liberal aristocrat Victor Julius von Wright, in 1884 began to unite the activities of separate associations at the national level. This 'Wrightist' labour movement aimed to rectify the deprivations that plagued society as it became more industrialized and to avoid the exacerbation of social conflicts. The Workers' Party of Finland was founded in 1899 with the Swedish Social Democratic Party its role model. Later in 1903 the party changed its name to the Finnish Social Democratic Party (SDP), and adopted a socialist programme influenced by Karl Kautsky's interpretation of Marxism. However Finland's existence depended wholly on its eastern neighbour Russia. The constitution of Finland in the nineteenth century was old-fashioned, basically the same constitution as the late eighteenth century Swedish constitution. In 1906, due to Russia's war with Japan, followed by the internal turbulence, Finland was allowed by the tsar to abandon the constitution – by that time the oldest in Europe – and form the most modern European constitution with a one-chamber parliament and universal suffrage (Meinander 2012). The same year the SDP had in relative figures become the largest socialist party in the world (Norrena 1993, pp. 47–48).

In Finland the traditional May Day celebration – or Vappu – was shaped by students, the temperance movement, wars, the state and its repressive apparatus, as well as conflicts and cooperation within the labour movement. Beginning in the 1900s the traditional May Day event was a continuation of the Walpurgis Night festivities held to celebrate the advent of spring. In particular students continued their often copious consumption of alcohol at picnics in the Finnish capital of Helsinki. Due to the language struggle between native Finnish- and Swedish-speakers, each group with their own higher education establishments, students marched through the city to two different locations for their picnics. For both groups, though, student choral singing and alcohol were part of the picnic celebrating the defeat of winter. Walpurgis Night and May Day festivities were carnival-like events in the country and the celebrations were solidly entrenched within Finnish upper-class culture. From its inception organized labour's May Day found itself in conflict with the student picnic walks (Simola 1986, pp. 66–68; Lahtinen 1989, pp. 297–299; Ala-Jokimäki 2014, pp. 8–16).

Workers in the cities traditionally celebrated spring in the late 1890s not by demonstrating, but by taking 'walks' in parks, usually in early June and often jointly organized with the temperance movement. The first trade union to connect its activities to the national picnic tradition and the international workers' day was the printers' union by taking a boat trip to a picnic site at Korkeasaari, Helsinki in 1890. The union had requested the afternoon off and the majority of employers had agreed. The connection to the Second International was made, however weakly, as shorter working hours was the main point in union leader H.J. Forsström's speech. However, he reasoned that the international demand in favour of the eight-hour workday was impossible to achieve in one leap, Forsström pragmatically argued that a nine-and-a-half-hour workday was a more appropriate target for the printers in the near future (*Uutisia Helsingistä, Uusi Suometar,* 2 May 1890; *Kirjapainolehti,* no. 5, 31 May 1890; Nieminen 1977, pp. 60–62; Tuomisto 1984, p. 91). Thus from the beginning the first tentative steps taken by organized labour were orientated towards gradual reform. However, walks, boat trips and picnics were first and foremost leisure activities, not rallies for a socialist overthrow of society. It was not, as in the case with August Palm's Whitsun walk mentioned above or as the case was in Germany and Italy (see Chapter 3), a way to evade a demonstration ban.

The Politicization of Vappu

A socialist May Day was not celebrated by labour organizations for some years yet. Nor did the decision in 1891 by the Second International that May Day *had* to be celebrated on 1 May, not on the first Sunday in May or yet another date, make any impact in Finland. Notably in 1893 the printers again organized their Vappu picnic walk on Sunday 14 May (*Gutenberg Aikakauslehti/Tidskrift* 1893). The changed date was in part due to cold weather but also reflects the firm grip that the upper-class students had on May Day. Subsequently the Wrightist labour movement held its celebrations on later Sundays in May or early June. Two years later a more encompassing picnic walk for workers was held on 19 May 1895 in Helsinki. It was actually a full-scale demonstration procession with about 2,500 participants from nearly all of the local trade unions and other labour organizations. The procession marched through central Helsinki to the small island of Seurasaari, where nearly 6,000 people were gathered. The speakers were liberal bourgeoisie who in their speeches argued for a franchise reform limiting the number of votes to a maximum of ten per person no matter income or personal wealth, and including the demand for women's suffrage (*Työmies,* 25 May 1895).

The workers' picnic walks took root. Next year on 17 May there were processions in Helsinki, Tampere and Kotka (*Työmies,* 23 May 1896; Laaksonen 1963, p. 6) and later in Kymi, on 16 August (*Työmies,* 22 August 1896). These picnic walks did not follow the Vappu tradition of meeting spring, but they were part of the new workers' picnic movement. In 1897 the diffusion of celebration days was brought to an end when the Delegation of Workers' Associations recommended Whit Monday for workers' picnic walks. Walks were therefore organized on 7 June in nearly all of the major towns in Finland that year (*Työmies,* 1 May 1897 and 12 June 1897). There was also a minor ideological conflict in Helsinki. In the procession marshals from each participating organization wore sashes across their chests. The majority of marshals had patriotic blue and white ones but the marshals from the largest trade union locals had socialist red sashes (*Työmies* 19 June 1897).

Socialist activists furthermore had close connections with the temperance movement. In 1898 the two movements jointly organized a nationwide 'drinking strike' for a total prohibition of alcohol in Finland starting 1 May and thus an open challenge to the students' inebriated Vappu festivities. Even the university students' union decided to support the strike. Yet the call to join the demonstration received a cold response from the student choirs and the Swedish-language press. Members of the right-wing parties criticized the dominant role of the labour movement in the strike organization, but nevertheless the drinking strike received positive press from right-wing newspapers (*Työmies*, 30 April 1898; *Oulun ilmoituslehti*, 1 May 1898; *Uusi Suometar*, 30 April, 1 May and 3 May 1898; *Tampereen Sanomat*, 28, 29 and 30 April, 2, 3 and 4 May 1898). This also provided workers' associations and trade unions the opportunity to participate in two major demonstrations within the span of a month, as the marches organized by the Finnish Workers' Party were held on Whit Monday.

Gradually Vappu became more political when other political demands were introduced into the drinking strike and associated meetings. Still 1 May was not an important date in Finland. When Whit Monday came in May the Workers' Party instead recommended the first Sunday in June as the celebration day, as in 1901 (*Työmies*, 30 May, 6 June and 8 June 1901). In 1902 the Workers' Party began to sell demonstration badges before the workers' marches and events. On the 1902 demonstration's agenda were universal suffrage, the eight-hour workday and alcohol prohibition. It was the demand for the eight-hour workday that was highlighted on the badges. The printing was done in red on natural white cardboard (*Työmies*, 26 May, 30 May, 6 June and 19 June 1902). In Tampere some unions had been allowed to celebrate Vappu as a holiday as early as 1900. They celebrated International Socialist Workers' Day at the workers' hall. After the national general strike in 1905 workers in Tampere took the day off to have a proper socialist May Day demonstration and festivities. Factories were closed that day. Subsequently the Tampere Workers' Association decided not to organize a picnic walk in June, instead concentrating on May Day. Nonetheless this decision was overturned and a traditional workers' walk was organized in the beginning of June (Kirkko-Jaakkola 1987, pp. 28–31). In Helsinki the 1906 May Day theme was the franchise reform. The universal right to vote was the demand of the day. In many other cities too the traditional workers' walk on Whit Monday, 3 June 1906 became political demonstration rallies, as the Estates of Finland had just approved the establishment of a unicameral parliament to be elected by universal suffrage (*Työmies*, 31 May, 2 June, 5–9 June 1906).

Despite growing socialist influences there was still resistance to 1 May as *the* day of celebration. The Congress of the Finnish Workers' Party had discussed the matter in July 1901. The Congress decided, 38 votes to 9, to not move the demonstration walks and meetings to May Day. The main argument was the harsh weather conditions in early May. Despite this decision the same Congress decided to press for Vappu to be an official, general holiday (Soikkanen 1975, p. 50; Simola 1986, pp. 68–69.). A party congress in 1903 adopted a socialist agenda and changed the party's name to the Social

Democratic Party. And after the 1905 general strike the party congress in August 1906 rejected the Finnish summer walk tradition and unanimously decided to move demonstrations to the International Socialist Workers' 1 May (Suomen Sosialidemokraattisen Puolueen 1906, pp. 453–457). Yet bad weather meant that the demonstrations were often only partially or not at all concluded – even in Helsinki in the south of Finland. In 1909 the demonstration meeting was relocated from an open-air square to the workers' hall due to heavy rain and very cold weather. The same year sleet rain was so torrential that workers stayed indoors, for example in Kotka (*Työmies*, 3 May 1909).

The labour movement advanced rapidly in Finland between the 1905 general strike and the first general elections of a Finnish parliament in early spring 1907. The Social Democratic Party won 37 per cent of the votes and 80 of 200 seats in parliament. It was easy to believe in the forward march towards socialism in Finland when social democrats organized the first official May Day demonstrations on Wednesday 1 May 1907. Yet Russian authorities gradually took a firmer grip on the social movements in their own country as well as in the Grand Duchy of Finland after the revolutionary turmoil of 1905–1906. The SDP thus had to be careful with its Vappu demonstrations. Children were banned from demonstrations in 1912. All marches and meetings of the social democrats and trade unions during May Day were forbidden during World War I until the Russian revolution in March 1917 (Oinonen 2013, pp. 18–22).

Trade unions in Finland were in dire straits during World War I. The strike ban and wartime inflation gave employers the upper hand. However, in 1916 trade union and party membership started to grow. In the 1916 general elections, with a relatively low turnout of voters the social democrats gained an outright majority in the parliament with 103 of 200 seats. After the Russian February revolution the strike ban was lifted and there was a rush to the trade unions in spring 1917. The social democrats had a dominant position in the new government of the autonomous Grand Duchy of Finland after the first Russian revolution (Soikkanen 1975, pp. 191–207, 260–262; Bergholm 1988, pp. 255–262). Therefore revolutionary and optimistic aspirations were at the forefront in the May Day demonstrations, meetings and speeches in 1917. A record number of participants took to the streets on Vappu 1917 (Simola 1986, p. 69; Oinonen 2013, pp. 26–28).

Independence, Civil War and Vappu

In August 1917 the provisional Russian government dissolved the Finnish parliament, which with its left-wing majority had tried to detach the country from the authority of Russia. The leaders of the labour movement accused the bourgeois opposition of collusion with the Russians. The non-socialist parties achieved a majority in parliament in the October general elections. Suspicions grew and violent clashes increased. Parliament declared Finland independent on 6 December 1917. Yet the beginning for the new state was a grim one. A civil war between the White civil guards and the Red guards began in January. The Reds first took southern Finland, but they were already facing defeat when German troops landed on the south coast of Finland in support of the Whites and broke their resistance in April 1918. Only in some enclaves in White Finland could the labour movement celebrate May Day in 1918. The Reds knew their revolution was lost but held defiant demonstrations in Kymenlaakso, which the Whites had not yet conquered (Soikkanen 1975, pp. 207–308, 310; Bergholm 2003, pp. 14–15).

The victorious Whites aspired to crush the labour movement. Nearly all forms of activity by the workers' organizations were prohibited. During the war both sides committed murders and atrocities. After they had won the war the Whites executed not only members of the Red guards but also activists in the labour movement who had not participated in the war. The civil war and the prison camps took between 30,000 and 40,000 lives; most of them lost after the war was over. The labour movement suffered severe setbacks. Thousands of members had died, others had escaped to the communist regime in Russia and the property of the organizations had been destroyed. The pressure on the workers' organizations continued in a new Finland; the authorities and White civil guards harassed the leaders and the rank and file of the trade union movement. This pressure and repression served to consolidate the spirit of the labour movement, but at the same time it isolated the workers' organizations from the rest of society.

However some of the rights the workers' organizations had achieved were gradually restored. The social democrats were not successful in the March 1919 parliamentary elections but nonetheless gained 80 seats (Soikkanen 1975, pp. 309–358; Simola 1986, p. 70; Bergholm 2003, p. 16). The Social Democratic Party and the Finnish Federation of Trade Unions made a joint appeal to all labour organizations and workers to join the ranks of the red flags on Vappu to demand bread, justice, freedom and peace, the immediate release of Red prisoners and the end of the state of emergency. The repression was still obvious in April 1919 in the face of the recovery of the labour movement. In Tampere the party's Vappu-badges were confiscated on some technical legal pretext. The Helsinki police chief issued an ultimatum that the traditional route through the city centre was not possible. The rally had to go straight from the railway square to the traditional meeting place, Mäntymäki. On May Day the red flag was dragged down by authorities from the reconstructed Helsinki Workers' Hall. The police questioned the speakers at Mäntymäki and plans to prosecute them were deep-laid within the police force. Despite these troubles a new, bold trust in a bright future for the working classes reflected the mood among a surprisingly large number of demonstrators at the May Day rallies organized by the Finnish Social Democratic Party in 1919 (*Suomen Sosialidemokraatti*, 25, 29, 30 April, 2 and 12 May 1919).

This was, however, the last united labour movement May Day rally in Helsinki. The following year, 1920, the Left-Wing Socialists and the communists mobilized their own demonstrations. The year 1920 signalled the end of the Social Democratic Party's hegemony of the trade union movement and May Day to these competitors when a majority of the trade union locals decided to participate in the Left-Wing Socialist march (Laaksonen 1963, p. 7; Tapper 1995, pp. 66–71; Oinonen 2013, p. 42). However, the rift was not national. Both wings of the Finnish labour movement could cooperate in 1921, for example, in Hämeenlinna, Karkkila, Tampere and Viipuri. Nevertheless gradually separate demonstrations became the rule (Kirkko-Jaakkola 1987, pp. 43–45; Oinonen 2013, p. 35).

The Labour Movements and May Day Celebrations in Sweden and Finland from 1920 to the Radical Upsurge in the Late 1960s

May Day, Universal Suffrage and the Struggle for Parliamentary Power in Sweden

Universal suffrage had been on the May Day agenda more or less from the start. With growing parliamentary strength SAP had in coalition with the Liberals achieved suffrage in 1909 for men aged 25 and above, but only to one of two equally weighed chambers. Actually the 1909 reform was a conservative modification of a more radical liberal-socialist proposal. In 1901 Sweden had introduced compulsory military service for all young men. Universal military service rapidly became an argument for franchise extension under the slogan 'one man, one gun, one vote'. The rebellious upsurge in 1917 in the wake of the February revolution in Russia made clear that these guns could also be used against the domestic privileged classes, which removed the last serious resistance against universal suffrage. After a reform in 1918 the 1921 general election was the first ever with equal franchise rights for men and women, irrespective of income (Therborn 1977).

Already the year before, in 1920, Sweden had elected its first purely social democratic government – in fact the first in the world (Lönnroth 2014, p. 68). Hjalmar Branting became the prime minister of a cabinet consisting only of social democrats. But although the first Russian revolution had paved the way for universal suffrage and thus a social democratic rise to parliamentary power, the Social Democratic Party was also split by a left-wing secession in the aftermath of the February revolution (Schmidt 1996, pp. 142–156). The split had already led to the formation of a new party in May 1917, namely the Swedish Social Democratic Left Party (SSV), which was followed over the years by several more breakups, reorganizations and even mergers among the parties to the left of the social democrats (cf. Lönnroth 2014).

Some basic preconditions for the May Day demonstrations were now changed. Two of the main demands had after nearly 20 years been carried out. Universal suffrage was achieved, and in September 1919 a new law which guaranteed the eight-hour workday and the 48-hour working week was passed (Isidorsson 2001, pp. 53–54) partly as a result of strong extra-parliamentary pressures from both socialists and syndicalists (Persson 1970). While there were several exceptions, especially in female-dominated jobs in care work, retail and domestic labour, banners stressing the eight-hour day could no longer be at the forefront of the May Day demonstrations.

However, a new feature emerged after the split of SAP, as the May Day demonstrations became associated with party politics in a way they had not been previously. The social democrats were no longer in opposition to the government, but had to take responsibility for governmental policies and actions, and the challenges came as much from the political left as from the right. Moreover the 1920s was a decade dominated by weak governments and unstable parliamentary majorities, often with the SAP included in coalitions with the liberals. Hence the May Day rallies became demonstrations to support the Social Democratic Party, no matter if the party was in office or not (J.-E. Olsson 1990, pp. 23–24).

At first the tensions between the different labour movement organizations did not affect the May Day celebrations. At the local level, LO-affiliated trade unions were organized in so-called FCOs (central trade union associations). The FCOs began to emerge spontaneously in the early 1920s and were formalized in 1926 and gradually became more tightly associated with the LO's ideological ties to the Social Democratic Party over the following decade (Feurstein 2008, pp. 2–9). As the largest working-class organization in most towns and municipalities it was by tradition up to the FCOs to handle common arrangements, such as the May Day celebrations. Therefore throughout the 1920s and 1930s social democrats, syndicalists and communists frequently shared the same demonstration and rally. This was especially common in places where the FCO had a communist majority (Feurstein 2008, p. 55).

The communists at the time were largely members of the Swedish Communist Party, SKP, the new name after the SSV adopted the Comintern's 21 conditions in 1921, an ideological move that led to a return of many SAP members. The cooperation between SAP and SKP regarding demonstrations remained though, and became particularly manifest in 1928, when the two parties (and also the syndicalists) joined forces against new labour market legislation. A liberal minority government had put forth a government bill in February 1928 regarding two new laws, one to regulate collective agreements and the other the introduction of a special labour court. The proposal for the collective agreement act included severe restrictions on the right to strike, which was difficult for the labour organizations of all political factions to accept and led to massive protests across the country. Despite the protests the law was passed by parliament on 25 May the same year (Göransson 1988, pp. 207–220).

May Day Demonstrations and Party Politics

Neither social democrats nor communists, however, gave up their resistance to the legislation. At the SAP Congress in June 1928 it was unanimously decided to struggle against further anti-union legislation and to put the issue on the agenda in the upcoming general elections in autumn 1928 (Göransson 1988, p. 217). As a result the social democrats and the communists formed an electoral pact in order to 'prevent wasting votes'. In the elections in September, SAP and SKP therefore appeared under the joint ticket *Arbetarepartiet* (the Workers' Party). On the one hand, this was in line with the FCO trade union cooperation manifested in the joint May Day demonstrations. On the other hand, the electoral pact materialized at the worst possible moment from a social democratic point of view. In mid-July 1928 the Comintern at its 6th Congress in Moscow took a sharp turn towards its notorious ultra-left position arguing that social democrats and other more moderate left-wing organizations were 'social fascists', hardly better than outspoken fascists. Even though it did not significantly affect the electoral cooperation between the two parties it was a gift from above for the bourgeois parties. The Conservative Party in particular employed citations from Stalin arguing that the Comintern-affiliated SKP acted as his agent in Sweden. Hence the election was a devastating defeat for the *Arbetarepartiet*. Because of the conservatives' propaganda the election has gone down in Swedish history as the 'Cossack election', as conservative election posters showed pictures of Russian 'Cossacks' ready to take over Sweden (Lönnroth 2014, pp. 113–117).

Nevertheless the tradition of coordinated May Day demonstrations survived the ultra-left years until 1935, when the Comintern instead endorsed the so-called Popular Front in response to the Nazi take-over in Germany two years earlier. A separate SKP May Day demonstration was announced in Stockholm in 1929 but was cancelled because of 'bad weather'. The Finnish member of the Comintern's executive committee, Otto Wille Kuusinen, made ironic remarks about the Swedish communists' easy-goingness and the SKP was accused of right-wing deviance. The weather did not stop the social democratic demonstration, and the real reason for the discontinuation was rather growing tensions within the SKP, tensions that led to a new party split before the end of the year (J.-E. Olsson 1990, pp. 26–27). The strongest Swedish communist party after the split still showed unconditional obedience to Comintern directives. Despite the SKP's Comintern connections it was the social democrats that were most eager to turn the May Day demonstrations into an arena for party politics. A precondition for letting the FCOs handle the local demonstrations and rallies was that communists and syndicalists also accepted the LO as a 'neutral' organizer, despite the union confederation's strong connections to the Social Democratic Party. The FCOs could apply for experienced speakers directly from the LO in Stockholm, and these speakers were normally seen as 'standing above' party politics. However, beginning in 1931 the Social Democratic Party became more and more eager to ensure that the LO speakers were connected to the party and supported the party's official views. Organized communists were still allowed to join the rallies in the 1930s, but had to be prepared to have their banners checked by the social democrats, much like they had been checked by the police authorities at the turn of the century (Feurstein 2008, pp. 55–56).

Especially in the capital Stockholm the SAP refused to cooperate with the communists, despite several attempts from the SKP to arrange joint May Day rallies (Engman 1999 p. 75).

During the Spanish Civil War social democrats and communists cooperated in the support committee for the democratic government against the fascists. Under the impact from this cooperation they also had common May Day demonstrations. Often they began the marches in a joint rally but at the end of it the two parties went to separate meeting-grounds (J.-E. Olsson 1990, p. 28). However, in the longer run a split into separate May Day demonstrations was inevitable, at least in the larger towns and cities. The separation was, however, both delayed and complicated by the course of events in the 1930s and the outbreak of World War II. After the defeat in the 1928 election SAP had moved its policy in a less class-conflict-orientated direction, trying to form a 'people's party' rather than a 'workers' party'. In the 1932 election the party mobilized more than 40 per cent of the electorate and became by far the largest party. Supported by the Agrarian Party, SAP formed a government and remained in office until 1976 with only a short break in the summer of 1936. In 1938 the Swedish parliament declared May Day a public holiday according to law, the first secular holiday in Sweden.[10] On the one hand, this was a clear victory for the labour movement, but on the other hand, May Day no longer belonged to the workers; as a public holiday, it was a day now institutionalized and incorporated in society at large.[11] In a contemporary newsreel the social democratic prime minister Per-Albin Hansson declared that the workers' day had become the people's or folk day, and the workers' demonstration had grown to the citizens' demonstration. In 1939 the Social Democratic Party kept its grip on May Day by turning it into the day for the official celebration of the party's fiftieth anniversary. In the shadow of the dark clouds hovering over Europe, however, social democrats and communists put aside their disagreements and marched together in a 'unity demonstration' for national accord (Engman 1999, pp. 82–83).

The following year, 1940, the May Day celebrations became even more focused on national unity. In December 1939, and as a reaction to the Soviet invasion of Finland on 30 November, Prime Minister Hansson had formed a coalition government with ministers from all the bourgeois parties in parliament. The Swedish Communist Party was excluded for being too Soviet-friendly and was instead exposed to repression (J.-E. Olsson 1990, pp. 28–31). On 9 April 1940, German troops invaded Sweden's neighbouring countries Denmark and Norway. Subsequently, later in April 1940 Prime Minister Hansson declared that the May Day rallies would not be traditional workers' demonstrations but instead he invited the centre and right-wing parties to a joint 'civic procession' for national unity. Communist and national socialist parties were not invited. When the procession materialized the traditional red banners were not replaced but outnumbered by about 300 Swedish flags in Stockholm. The main speaker at the concluding rally was, however, Prime Minister Hansson, who was allowed twice as much time as the bourgeois party leaders. Hansson also walked at the head of the march, together with the Conservative leader Gösta Bagge. The rally attracted about 150,000 people according to contemporary newspaper sources (Engman 1999, pp. 85–95). The Communist Party, not allowed to join forces with the social democrats and the bourgeois parties, organized its own May Day rally in Vasaparken, Stockholm. According to the SKP's own records, the speech by the chairman Sven Linderoth was followed by 15,000 participants (Rothelius 2008).

Again in 1941, 1 May was dominated by a civic march jointly organized by the SAP and the centre and right-wing parties. However, in 1942 the May Day celebration was once again proclaimed 'the workers' day' by the social democratic leadership. The reason was that its symbolic value for the labour movement might otherwise become lost. Although organized solely by SAP and the FCOs, other 'democratic parties' were invited to join, that is, all parties but communists or national socialists. However, the bourgeois party voters in the May Day rallies seem to have been few. The communists held their own meetings, but this time so did the national socialists. The Socialist Party (*Socialistiska partiet*) had its roots in the communist/socialist party splits, but in the last years of the 1930s the party, strongly influenced by its leader Nils Flyg, moved closer and closer towards national socialism. In 1942 it was officially a National Socialist party (Lööw 1990, pp. 112–113). Despite diminishing membership and popularity among voters, Flyg managed to attract some 3,000 listeners at Medborgarplatsen in Stockholm on May Day 1942 (Engman 1999, p. 101).

On 1 May 1945 it was evident that the war was drawing to a close. Under the influence of the SKP's results in the general elections the year before, social democrats and communists once again mobilized a joint demonstration in Stockholm attracting some 50,000 at the rally (Olsson 1990, pp. 31–32). During the Cold War, however, the communists were once again marginalized by the social democrats. The SKP did not pick up the struggle over the May Day celebrations but rather in the mid-1950s instead discontinued most of its own rallies and urged its members to join the demonstrations organized by FCOs. Yet as the FCOs were becoming more and more dominated by social democrats, the SKP in practice left the hegemony over May Day to SAP. The social democrats also had problems. The 1950s saw a diminishing ideological interest and a dwindling number of participants in the demonstrations (J.-E. Olsson 1990, pp. 34–35). At the same time, the 1950s and 1960s were the social democratic harvest times, the heydays of the so-called Swedish Model, when both labour and capital gained from the post-war boom and industrial conflicts were sparse. Hence the lack of interest in demonstrations cannot be seen as a protest against social democracy or trade unions – they were the 'victors'.

A revival of the May Day demonstrations came with the growing interest in international issues in the 1960s, in particular the Vietnam War, but also apartheid in South Africa and the struggles for independence in the remaining

European colonies in Africa, as well as against the remaining European fascist regimes in Spain, Portugal and after 1967 Greece. This was also a rebirth of the May Day demonstrations on the left of the SAP (J.-E. Olsson 1990, pp. 38–45; Engman 1999, pp. 116–117). The rebellious upsurge in the late 1960s and early 1970s marked by demonstrations, strikes and new labour militancy was a highly international phenomenon that reached Sweden and Finland as well, and left its mark on May Day demonstrations in both countries.

Finland: May Day, Class and Conflict after the Civil War

Finland was a republic with a democratic constitution in 1919. The social democrats played an important role in the parliament, but their scope for action was restricted by the power awarded to the president.

After the civil war there was a schism within the Social Democratic Party. Three different groups can be distinguished. First, there was the largest group led by Väinö Tanner, which chose the path of political compromise with an eye on the Swedish social democrats (Lähteenmäki 1987). Second, there was an exiled communist party in Russia led by Otto Wille Kuusinen and formed by Red refugees from the civil war. Third there was the Socialist Workers' Party established in Finland, with close connections to the exiled communists. It was declared illegal in 1922, but emerged soon again under the name *Työnväen ja talonpoikien liitto* (Union of Workers and Smallholders). The latter party was active until 1930, when all communist actions became illegal by a special law (Saarela 2008, pp. 303–359).

The usual path for the rise of socialism has been poverty and an encompassing notion of injustice, leading to organized trade unions followed by an ideological awakening and the founding of political parties. This was, for example, the case in Sweden. In Finland the path towards socialism took another direction: political ideology came first (Kettunen 1987; Lahtinen 1987). This may explain the strong radical tradition within the Finnish trade unions. Finnish radical socialism in the 1920s was not inspired by Sweden, unlike the Finnish Social Democratic Party, which followed the Swedish Social Democratic Party's reformist course.

The radical tradition materialized in the May Day rallies. During the immediate post-World War I period May Day demonstrations were met with rather heavy repression, much as a consequence of the civil war. Red flags were banned, creating a cat-and-mouse game between police and demonstrators. On some occasions left-wing socialists ignored the restrictive regulations in order to provoke police repression. In Kemi activists dressed themselves with flags and carried flagpoles without flags in 1926. Social democrats put white board placards on poles with the names of organizations in Tampere 1931 (Kirkko-Jaakkola 1987, p. 44; Oinonen 2013, pp. 32–36).

The latter half of the 1920s also tells the story of influential Finnish fascist movements, the history of Finland thereby resembling more the situation in Germany, Italy (see Chapter 3) and Spain (see Chapter 5) than in Sweden. The labour movement was imperilled when the extreme right-wing Lapua movement began to operate in 1929. Its acts of terrorism directed against the leaders as well as the rank and file of the labour movement – coercion, muggings, forced deportations over the border into the Soviet Union and assassinations – paralyzed the labour movement in the summer of 1930. Between 1930 and 1932 Lapua appeared to be the winner in these political confrontations. The right-wing parties also won a clear victory in the 1930 general elections, which was characterized by open coercion of the voters and deleting names from the rolls of the enfranchised. The new parliament enacted legislation to allow the authorities to interfere in the activities of organizations branded as communist and in 1930 the authorities banned the activities of numerous trade unions and other left-wing socialist organizations (Soikkanen 1975, pp. 491–537; Bergholm 2003, pp. 26–27). However, Lapua's methods of terror directed towards individuals as well as groups spread umbrage even among those who were ideologically attracted to the movement. When the former president K.J. Ståhlberg and his wife became the object of a terrorist act – kidnapped and taken to the Soviet border – the fascists had gone too far (Karvonen and Lindström 1987, p. 159). The final blow was a failed *coup d'état* in Mäntsälä in 1932. The president, Svinhufvud, sympathizing with the ideology of the Lapua but not with its methods, simply sent the perpetrators home. The Lapua movement was declared illegal, but a fascist party, *Isänmaallinen kansanliike*, IKL (The People's Movement of the Fatherland), appeared in its place.

In these perilous times tensions between social democrats and communists ran deep; the hard-core tactics of the Third International which labelled social democrats as 'social fascists' fuelled conflicts. Communists organized May Day activities in Forssa, Tampere, Oulu and Viipuri in 1930 in protest against the demonstration ban. In Turku 1932 some communists attacked the police patrolling the social democrats' May Day meeting. Finnish communists were at the forefront of adopting Popular Front tactics in 1933, before the formal decision was reached by the Comintern in 1935. Thereafter many communists and their left-wing socialist comrades participated peacefully in social democratic Vappu demonstrations (*Suomen Sosialidemokraatti*, 3 and 4 May 1930; 2 and 3 May 1932 (editorials written by Sasu Punanen, pen-name of the editor, Yrjö Räisänen); Kirkko-Jaakkola 1987, p. 44; Bergholm 2003, pp. 25–29; Oinonen 2013, pp. 49–51). The struggle over flags and banners continued throughout most of the 1930s. The Party Committee of the Social Democratic Party decided in 1932 not to organize demonstrations at all because of the frequent and incoherent interventions of local police and the ministry of interior concerning flags and the right of assembly. The last straw from a social democratic perspective was an illegal directive to postpone all May Day events until after religious services and to include the official national flag in demonstrations and meetings if other flags were present. However, in Tampere the party section did not follow orders from the party office to ban the demonstrations, but held a demonstration with the Finnish blue and white flag in front of the red flags.

The Colour Red in the Interwar Period

On 27 April 1934 the so-called flag decree was passed in the Finnish parliament, banning red flags in May Day parades. Only national flags and board placards with slogans were allowed in Vappu rallies (Kirkko-Jaakkola 1987, pp. 44–46; Oinonen 2013, pp. 51–60). Right-wing politicians and authorities claimed that the 'poison of red revolution' should be kept away from Finnish children and school-age children were not allowed to participate in May Day demonstrations (Kirkko-Jaakkola 1987, p. 45; Ala-Jokimäki 2014). The colour red was considered rebellious, or as it was expressed at the time, offensive to good manners. In Jyväskyla people paraded with only the flagpoles, without the flags. It is indeed a classic among censorship protests to display the frame around what has been censored. Red pieces of cloth were also secretly put in places where these items would be noticed and nobody could miss the message. In 1932 in the town of Kotka the May Day demonstrators had some trouble hanging a red flag on the smokestack of a factory because people did not dare to purchase red cloth for fear of the secret police even though this was two years before the flag decree. Consequently white linen cloth was dyed red (Peltonen 1998).

At the women's prison in Hämeenlinna the political prisoners celebrated a memorable May Day in 1930. They all combed their hair, wore their scarves and tied their aprons in the same way and organized a march around the prison yard, walking in pairs and led by a woman carrying a child all dressed in red (the daughter of one of the prisoners) on her shoulders, the child thereby symbolizing the red flag. This incident became part of labour movement folklore during the following years. As late as 1963 a poem was written about the red flag, citing the women prisoners' parade with the little girl (Peltonen 1998).[12]

Finnish Working-Class Patriotism in World War II

The Soviet attack on neutral Finland in November 1939 united the people in the struggle to defend their country. The exile communist government in Terijoki, proclaimed the 'true government' by the Soviet Union, found little support among communists in Finland during the Winter War from November 1939 to March 1940 (Meinander 2012, pp. 122–179). During the Winter War national feelings ran high and overshadowed class struggle.

In a joint declaration in January 1940 the workers' and employers' central organizations announced that all barriers to negotiation ceased to exist and that in the future collective bargaining should be foremost. This so-called January Agreement recognized the right of workers to organize. The Party Committee of the SDP issued a statement in February 1940 affirming that there was no longer any impediment for social democratic members to join the civil guards, and the leaders of the Confederation of Finnish Trade Unions (SAK; from 1969, Central Organisation of Finnish Trade Unions) gave their support for this wartime truce with the civil guards (Bergholm 2003, pp. 30–31). Through participation in the war effort the labour movement gained recognition in the wider society. The ban on red flags was lifted with exceptional licence by the ministry of the interior before May Day 1940. Right-wing newspapers were pleased that social democrats were now willing to use the blue and white national flag at the May Day demonstrations and rallies. And social democrats (and communists) were proud citizens, who had earned with blood their right to again bear red flags (Tepora 2011, pp. 280–282; Ala-Jokimäki 2014, pp. 33–36). However the national consensus rapidly crumbled during the summer of 1940. The employers remained unyielding at the workplace, and some workers demanded a clear change of course in both foreign and domestic policy. The peace made with the civil guards was strongly criticized within both SAK and SDP (Bergholm 2003, p. 31).

After a short interlude Finland was again in war with the Soviet Union, this time as an ally of Nazi Germany. During the Continuation War 1941–1944, the Social Democratic Party took part in a wartime coalition government. During the war the Vappu meetings became more and more patriotic occasions including nationalist songs (Tepora 2011, pp. 284–285; Ala-Jokimäki 2014).

A majority of the SDP Party Committee gradually gave their support to the so-called Peace Opposition group in 1943–1944, but the party's strong man, Väinö Tanner, the minister of finance, and the majority of the social democratic members of parliament considered that concluding a separate peace too early would take Finland out of the frying pan into the fire. The deep mistrust between these groups that flared up during the war was to prevail for a long time (Bergholm 2003, pp. 32–33). The SDP social minister, K.-A. Fagerholm, who was close to the Peace Opposition, was forced to leave government in December 1943. He had publicly denounced brutal acts during the German occupation in Norway, thus the German ambassador gave the Finnish government an ultimatum. Fagerholm was replaced by Aleksi Aaltonen, also a social democrat and a loyal follower of Tanner. Hunger, casualties, war fatigue and growing knowledge of the coming defeat of Nazi Germany diminished the national unity to fight. In this situation Aaltonen brought before the parliament a motion to make May Day a public holiday. This was the ultimate symbolic recognition of the labour movement. Workers were honoured with their own holiday. The law was passed and the first bank holiday Vappu was celebrated on 1 May 1944 (Tepora 2011, p. 285; Ala-Jokimäki 2014, pp. 61–63; Bergholm 2014).

May Day after World War II

After the Finnish–Soviet armistice in 1944 it was still an open question whether Finland would be incorporated into the Soviet Union, as was the case in the Baltic states. This dilemma was settled by a treaty of friendship and non-aggression between the Soviet Union and Finland in 1948 (Nevakivi

1998, pp. 276–283; Meinander 2012, pp. 262–265). Finland was dependent on the Soviet Union in foreign policy matters and partly in economic affairs, but independent in domestic affairs. The roots of this political compromise can be traced back to the end of the Continuation War, when criticism of Finnish–German cooperation expressed by Finnish citizens appeared more openly (Mellberg 2004). There were however still traits that singled out Finland as different from the other Nordic countries; for example, the Communist Party, legalized in 1944, was among the three largest parliamentary parties. Strikes were not uncommon, peaking with the general strike in 1956 (Klockare 1971).

Initially the communists called the SAK leaders to account for the jingoistic statements they had made at the beginning of the Continuation War. The criticism was short-lived though, as SAK had adopted an anti-war stance in due course. The social democrats peacefully negotiated how the communists could increase their influence with trade union officers in SAK and its affiliated unions. In March 1945 the SAK tried to enhance cooperation between social democrats and communists by proposing united May Day demonstrations for both parties. This initiative was successful, even though many social democrats in particular had serious doubts about cooperation with communists. The participation in these first unified demonstrations was nearly as great as in 1917. At the same time there were tensions because the parties' organizers had divergent opinions about the political balance and ideological content of speeches, banners and slogans (Laaksonen 1963, p. 8; Bergholm 2003, pp. 33, 40–41; Bergholm 2005, p. 91; Tepora 2011, p. 285; Ala-Jokimäki 2014, pp. 71–77).

Joint rallies were also organized in 1946 and 1947. However, in Helsinki in 1946 the communists carried huge placards with Marx, Lenin and other figures in the history of international communism. For many social democrats it was humiliating to walk behind a large poster of Otto Wille Kuusinen, who had led the Soviet puppet government of Terijoki during the Winter War. Hence the local SDP in Helsinki protested strongly and urged the central SDP organization to cancel all cooperation with the communists in the coming year. The SDP Party Committee, however, turned down this demand based on an 'iconoclastic' conflict. Joint May Day demonstrations were still the rule in 1947, but there were no more unified slogans or banners. When the Control Commission of the Allied Forces left Finland in the end of 1947, the SDP changed its attitude, however. SAK again proposed in February 1948 unified Vappu meetings, but now the SDP categorically refused to continue cooperation with the communists.[13] Therefore the social democratic majority of the SAK executive board had to withdraw their decision. When SAK gave new directives in accordance with the social democratic party line to affiliated unions and local trade union branches in April that year, the communists voted against them. Trade unions should participate in joint demonstrations and meetings only where both parties could cooperate. In practice this gave veto power to the SDP and its local organizations. Local SAK branches dominated by the Communist Party refused to obey. They organized processions where trade union locals came with their flags. The conflict between social democrats and communists within the Finnish trade union movement grew progressively between 1946 and 1949. Communists in the Finnish trade unions found themselves in a problematic, intermediate position. On the one hand they should follow the even harder line of the Cominform against social democrats, portrayed as USA imperialist lackeys, and on the other, they should keep the Finnish trade union movement as unified as possible and secure that SAK remained an affiliated organization in the communist-dominated World Federation of Trade Unions (WFTU). In March 1950 the social democratic leadership of SAK took a harder stance in regards to May Day demonstrations. Local trade union branches that did not follow the official guidelines of SAK concerning Vappu activities would be expelled. National unions could also be expelled if they did not maintain control over their locals. The Communist Party protested strongly but at the end of the day surrendered. In this case the SAK's WFTU membership had a stronger influence on the Finnish Communist Party's decisions than the confrontational Cold War ideology of the Cominform and also – at the end of the day – the Soviet Communist Party preferred unity with the Finnish trade union movement (Bergholm 2005, pp. 90–100).

In addition to tensions between social democrats and communists the May Day demonstrations after the war also faced clashes with students, who opposed socialistic politics and regarded Vappu as an academic celebration. In 1947 some Swedish-speaking technology students joined a workers' rally with the intention of sabotaging the event, which they did by bellowing drinking songs. Their performance was stopped by the police. Later the May Day celebrations became fairly calm and well-organized demonstrations. Meanwhile the bourgeois festivities of Walpurgis Night on 30 April developed into a general celebration, instead of an academic tradition, as is the case in Sweden (YLE (Finnish Broadcasting Company), 1 May 2014).

In the late 1960s the Communist Party split into two factions, a revisionist majority and a Stalinist minority, which created new confrontational situations. Newspapers counted whether there were more red shirts (the majority faction) or blue shirts (the minority faction) at the May Day demonstrations (Oinonen 2013, p. 128). Communists and social democrats were at the time more or less equal, enjoying comparatively equal support within the electorate. The Social Democratic Party was usually slightly ahead, but the Communist Party was better at mobilizing their supporters for actions and rallies, especially for the May Day demonstrations. Nor did the Cold War end all joint May Day demonstrations. On the contrary, the radical 1960s made unified May Day demonstrations a more common feature in Finland despite hostility towards communists from many social democrats (Simola 1986, p. 73; Bergholm 2005, pp. 100–101). The joint demonstrations became more friendly and free from friction after the fall of the Soviet Union, but this is after our time period. It is still worth mentioning, though, that Vappu in general lost much of its reputation as a radical workers' day. In 1991 an opinion poll showed that 63 per cent of the Finnish population considered Vappu a celebration of the arrival of spring, about 18 per cent thought of it as the workers' day, and 12 per cent saw Vappu first and foremost as a party day for students (Karjalainen 1994, pp. 202–211). In the longer run the tradition of drunken university students has thus been stronger than workers' protests, protests that paradoxically once started with a drinking strike.

Conclusion

The May Day rituals in Sweden and Finland have followed very different historical trajectories. While Sweden in the formative years followed the Second International's May Day eight-hour workday edict, among other demands, and mobilized mass demonstrations and rallies, Finland followed a more cautious path organizing 'walks' and picnics later in May or early June. These early Finnish union events did not prioritize socialist politics but were rather leisure occasions. The Swedish May Day events, with the newly formed Swedish Social Democratic Party taking the lead and with the cooperation of the trade unions, on the other hand, were decidedly political demonstrations raising demands which challenged the social and political order. These differences in the early years can probably be explained by the political and cultural contexts in the respective countries. Sweden was a monarchy, but with a budding democratic political system taking shape and with a strong Liberal Party, which at the time was generally positive to the demands being raised by the organized labour movement. Finland in contrast was under the autocratic rule of tsarist Russia, which most certainly inhibited the development of a socialist labour movement. Furthermore, while there was a liberal influence in the country, Finland was marked by a highly conservative socio-political culture and deep-rooted class (and language) conflicts.

When tsarist Russia was thrown in turmoil its control over Finland suddenly weakened opening a window of opportunity in 1905 for a socialist labour movement. The labour movement was quick to seize this opportunity and in 1907 in the first elections with universal suffrage the Finnish SDP became in relative figures the largest socialist party in the world. Independence from Russia was proclaimed in 1917 and recognized by Lenin in January 1918. But this turn of fortunes only threw the country in a bloody civil war, which unlocked the door for Finland's conservative forces and not only weakened the Finnish labour movement but led to a divisive and long-standing split between more reformist-orientated social democrats and more revolutionary communists. These developments have left an indelible mark on the Finnish May Day tradition, which lives on today. The communists were forbidden and their May Day activities clandestine when fascist ideology in Finland was prominent in the 1930s and during World War II up to the armistice with the

Soviet Union in 1944. After World War II the social democrats held strong positions in parliament, as did the communists, but they never gained the same established position of power as the Swedish social democrats, not even after Finnish socialism had chosen the road of reformism. Due to the constitution of 1919 the powerful office of the president formed the government and thus a socialist parliament was effectively balanced by bourgeois presidents. This was especially the case during the presidency of Urho Kekkonen, who was in power for nearly two decades after 1956. In post-war Finland May Day demonstrations, while under specific historical situations demonstrations have been occasionally held jointly, have traditionally been mobilized separately – and after World War II by more or less equally electorally powerful parties. Subsequently the May Day rituals remained protest events, challenging the political order. However, the socialist May Day rituals were more or less overshadowed by the carnival festivities of the (bourgeois) students, continuing Walpurgis Night with their celebrations. The Finnish labour movement's events have, in short, not displaced the bourgeois students' Vappu festivities and May Day's general symbolic meaning as a celebration of the advent of spring.

In Sweden in stark contrast, the May Day tradition successively evolved with the reformist orientation of social democracy. While there were splits between social democrats and communists in Sweden as well, the Social Democratic Party retained its grip on May Day. Even in Sweden May Day demonstrators faced government repression, but not to the same degree as in Finland. Indeed, from periods in the 1920s and from 1934 onwards May Day became to all intents and purposes a day of celebration for the Social Democratic Party, in governmental power through much of the rest of the century. May Day rituals stressed solidarity within the Social Democratic Party as well as its history. The party maintained hegemony over May Day, out-manoeuvring the Swedish Communist Party, which was far weaker than their counter-part in Finland. Only in the early 1970s was the May Day tradition broadened to include protest, when the revisionist Swedish Left Party Communists (in 1990, the Swedish Left Party) began mobilizing major demonstrations. Today May Day in Sweden is still an entrenched political tradition and major event, widely covered by the media.

Notes

1 Bull himself belonged to the most radical stream of the Norwegian labour movement. He was also Norwegian foreign minister for a short period in 1928.
2 A liberal member of the Swedish parliament, Fridtjuv Berg, also took part in the rally and gave a speech in support of the eight-hour workday (Engman 1999, p. 57). Berg was a 'left-wing' liberal and there were no strong tensions between social democrats and liberals at the time. The anarchists were seen as a far greater source of annoyance, and it must be noted that the Second International recommended its members expel anarcho-syndicalists in 1908 (see Chapter 2). Therefore the personal conflicts between Branting and Bergegren cannot be said to be the sole reason for the latter's expulsion.

3 Wistrand (1959) states that there were only 4,000 people in the demonstration and 15,000 at the rally. The sources for his statement are, however, not transparent.

4 Fredrik Sterky, an important newspaper man during the 1890s who was elected first president of LO in 1898, spoke in Malmö (Bodin and Nycop 1980, p. 12), but at the time he was only 30 years old and his reputation as a key figure in the early labour movement had not yet formed.

5 The connection to the World's Woman's Christian Temperance Movement is not a coincidence. The organization was a path-breaker for women's political rights in many countries (Grimshaw 2004).

6 Australia introduced universal suffrage for 'white' women in 1902, the year after the Commonwealth of Australia received full dominion status (Grimshaw 2004).

7 In Swedish: 'Ned med tronen, altaret och penningpåsen'.

8 The main sources for police interventions against rallies and demonstrations do not emanate from either the labour movement or official police records, but from notes and paper clippings left by the chief of detectives in Stockholm during the first decades of the twentieth century, Gustaf Lidberg, now deposited at the Labour Movement Archives and Library (ARAB) in Stockholm. From 1908 onwards, Lidberg and his detectives collected all the information they could uncover about labour demonstrations including banners, slogans, charges, confiscations, etc. This information includes notices of the police authorities' considerations and decisions regarding whether slogans were acceptable or too offensive. After Lidberg's death in 1931 the files were sold at auction. In 1948, the collection was donated to ARAB by its last owner, Ture Nerman, a well-known publicist and during his lifetime a member of parliament for both the Social Democrats, the Left Socialists and the Communists.

9 The latter might, however, be partly a matter of different statistics; the numbers for 1909 cover the people at the rally, while the 1910 figures count only participants in the procession of demonstrators.

10 As in many European countries, 1 May represented the first day of spring and had thus been an ecclesiastical holiday in the Middle Ages, officially dedicated to the two apostles Philip and James, son of Alphaeus. In Sweden this medieval, very popular, May Day celebration survived the holiday abolition during the Reformation and was not discontinued until 1772 (Malmstedt 1994, pp. 33 and 165). In 2005 parliament declared Sweden's national day, 6 June, an official Swedish public holiday, replacing Whit Monday.

11 However, the May Day demonstrations and rallies in the countryside did not always take place on 1 May, but on the following Sunday in order to make it possible for all workers to join (J.-E. Olsson 1990, p. 54).

12 The poem was written by Taisto Summanen and is titled *Tarina punaisesta lipusta* (Story of the Red Flag).

13 There were similar tensions in Germany and Italy in 1948 (see Chapter 3).

References

Ala-Jokimäki, A.H. (2014). *Vapunvietto Helsingissä 1939–1945. Traditiota, politiikkaa ja karnevaalia suursodan varjossa*. Helsinki: Pro gradu-tutkielma, Helsingin yliopisto, Yleinen historia.

Andrae, C.G. (1998). *Revolt eller reform: Sverige inför revolutionerna i Europa 1917–1918*. Stockholm: Carlssons.

Bäckström, K. (1977). *Arbetarrörelsen i Sverige. 1. Den svenska arbetarrörelsens uppkomst och förening med socialismen*. Stockholm: Raben & Sjögren.

Bergholm, T. (1988). *Kovaa peliä kuljetusalalla I. Kuljetusalan ammattiyhdistystoiminta vuoteen 1924*. Joensuu: Auto-ja Kuljetusalan Työntekijäliitto AKT r.y.

Bergholm, T. (2003). *A Short History of SAK*. Helsinki: SAK.

Bergholm, T. (2005). Yhteisten vappujuhlien mahdottomuus ja ammattiyhdistysliikkeen yhtenäisyys. In M. Hannikainen (Ed.), *Työväestön rajat* (pp. 161–187) Saarijärvi: Työväen historian ja perinteen tutkimuksen seura, Väki voimakas 18.

Bergholm, T. (2014). 'Vappu vapaaksi 1.5.1944', SAK, homepage: www.sak.fi/ ajankohtaista/blogit/uusi-kulma/vappu-vapaaksi-151944-2014-04-25 (accessed 28 January 2014).

Björklund, C.J. (1966). *Första maj och förstamajdemonstrationerna*. Stockholm: Tiden.

Bodin, S., and Nycop, C-A. (1980). *Första maj 1890–1980*. Stockholm: Tiden.

Bull, E. (1922). Die Entwicklung der Arbeiterbewegung in den drei skandinavischen Ländern. *Archiv für die Geschichte des Sozialismus und der Arbeiterbewegung*, 10, 329–361.

Engman, J. (1999). *Rituell process, tradition och media: Socialdemokratisk första maj i Stockholm*. Stockholm: Etnologiska institutionen, Stockholms universitet.

Esping-Andersen, G. (1990). *The Three Worlds of Welfare Capitalism*. Cambridge: Polity Press.

Feurstein, T. (2008). FCO: De Fackliga Centralorganisationerna från opposition till instrument för Lokal kontroll 1925–1945. MA thesis, Uppsala universitet, Historiska institutionen.

Flood, H. (1954). *Agda Östlund: Pionjär i genombrottstid*. Stockholm: Kooperativa förbundets bokförlag.

Grass, M. (2010). *Hjalmar Brantings majtal 1890–1924 (1895)*. Arbetarrörelsens arkiv och bibliotek, www.arbark.se/2010/11/hjalmar-brantings-majtal-1890–1924/.

Göransson, H. (1988). *Kollektivavtalet som fredspliktsinstrument: De grundläggande förbuden mot stridsåtgärder i historisk och internationell belysning*. Stockholm: Juristförlaget.

Grimshaw, P. (2004). Settler anxieties, indigenous peoples and women's suffrage in the colonies of Australia, New Zealand and Hawaii, 1888 to 1902. In L. Edwards and M. Roces (Eds), *Women's Suffrage in Asia: Gender, Nationalism and Democracy* (pp. 220–239). London and New York: Routledge.

Gutenberg Aikakauslehti/ Tidskrift (1893). 2–3, Toukokuu, 55–59.

Hamark, J., and Thörnqvist, C. (2013). Docks and defeat: The 1909 general strike in Sweden and the role of port labour. *Historical Studies in Industrial Relations*, 34, 1–27.

Haste, H. (1988). *Det första seklet: Människor, händelser och idéer i svensk socialdemokrati, del I*. Stockholm: Tiden.

Hodgson, J.H. (1967). *Communism in Finland: A History and Interpretation*. Princeton, NJ: Princeton University Press.

Isidorsson, T. (2001). *Striden om tiden: Arbetstidens utveckling i Sverige under 100 år i ett internationellt perspektiv*. Gothenburg: Avhandlingar från Historiska institutionen i Göteborg, 30.

Karjalainen, S. (1994). *Juhlan aika: Suomalaisia vuotuisperinteitä*. Porvoo: WSOY.

Karvonen, L., and Lindström, U. (1987). Finlands fascism. In L. Karvonen and U. Lindström (Eds), *Finland, en politisk loggbok* (pp. 157–195). Stockholm: Almqvist & Wiksell International.

Kettunen, P. (1987). Missä mielessä vanha työväenliike oli poliittinen liike. In R. Alapuro et al. (Eds), *Kansa liikkeessä* (pp. 236–237). Helsinki: Kirjayhtymä.

Kirby, D. (1996). *Östersjöländernas historia 1772–1993*. Stockholm: Atlantis.

Kirjapainolehti [Finnish journal]. (1890). No. 5, 31 May.

The May Day Tradition in Finland and Sweden   103

Kirkko-Jaakkola, K. (1987). *Simaa, kuorolaulua ja punalippuja: Tamperelaisten vapunvietto 1860-luvulta vuoteen 1939*. Tampere: Tampereen kaupungin museot – Pirkanmaan maakuntamuseo.

Klockare, S. (1971). *Från generalstrejk till folkfront. Söndring och samling i Kekkonens tid*. Stockholm: Prisma.

Lähteenmäki, M. (1987). Orientering mot Norden. *Arbetarhistoria*, 11(42), 23–24.

Lahtinen, E. (1987). Finländarna i det nordiska samarbetet 1880–1918. *Arbetarhistoria*, 11(42), 20–22.

Lahtinen, E. (1989). Finland. In A. Panaccione (Ed.), *The Memory of May Day: An Iconographic History of the Origins and Implanting of a Workers' Holiday* (pp. 297–302). Venice: Marsiolio Editori.

Laaksonen, L. (1963). Turkulaisia julkisia vappuperinteitä vuosina 1919–1960. *Scripta Ethnologica*, 15, 3–21.

Lindbom, T. (1938). *Den svenska fackföreningsrörelsens uppkomst och tidigare historia 1872–1900*. Stockholm: Tidens förlag.

Linderborg, Å. (2001). *Socialdemokraterna skriver historia: Historieskrivning som ideologisk maktresurs 1892–2000*. Uppsala: Uppsala universitet.

Lönnroth, J. (1985). *Minervas uggla: Om ekonomerna som maktens predikanter*. Stockholm: Arbetarkultur.

Lönnroth, J. (2014). *Albin Ström och det frihetliga spåret i svensk arbetarrörelse*. Gothenburg: Korpen.

Lööw, H. (1990). *Hakkorset och vasakärven: En studie av nationalsocialismen i Sverige 1924–1950*. Gothenburg: Göteborg: Avhandlingar från Historiska institutionen i Göteborg, 2.

Malmstedt, G. (1994). *Helgdagsreduktionen: Övergången från ett medeltida till ett modernt år i Sverige 1500–1800*. Gothenburg: Avhandlingar från Historiska institutionen i Göteborg, 8.

Marjomäki, H. (1998). Translated communism: Remarks on 'politics translated' in the Finnish communist movement during the 1920s and 1930s. In T. Saarela and K. Rentala (Eds), *Communism: National and International* (pp. 259–272). Helsinki: SHS.

Meinander, H. (2012). *Republiken Finland igår och idag: Finlands historia från inbördeskriget till 2012*. Helsingfors: Schildts & Söderströms.

Mellberg, M. (2004). Bakgrunden till Paasikivi-Kekkonen-linjen i Finland. In R. Bohn, T. Wegener Friis and M.F. Scholz (Eds), *Östersjöområdet – från andra världskriget till det kalla kriget* (pp. 165–181). Odense: Friis.

Misgeld, K. (1997). *Den fackliga europavägen: LO, det internationella samarbetet och Europas enande 1945–1991*. Stockholm: Atlas.

Morgonbris [Newspaper of the Swedish Social Democratic Women's Association]. (1911). no. 6.

Myrdal, A. (1959). Kvinnorna bryter sig väg. In K. Nilsson (Ed.), *Arbetets söner: Text och bilder ur den svenska arbetarrörelsens saga: Del I Pioniärtiden* (pp. 337–356). Stockholm: Steinsvik.

Nerman, T. (1956). *Svensk arbetarrörelse i ord och bild 1881–1955*. Stockholm: Tidens förlag.

Nevakivi, J. (1998). Från fortsättningskriget till nutiden 1944–1998. In O. Jussila, S. Hentilä and J. Nevakivi (Eds), *Finlands politiska historia 1809–1998* (pp. 245–295). Esbo: Schildt.

104   Thörnqvist, Bergholm and Mellberg

Nieminen, M. (1977). *Suomen kirjatyöntekijäin Liiton historia 1: kirjatyöntekijäin ammatillisen järjestäytyminen ja ammattiyhdistyspolitiikka Suomessa vuoteen 1914*. Jyväskylä: Suomen kirjatyöntekijäin liitto.

Nilsson, K. (1959). Kommunismen i Sverige. In T. Lindfors (Ed.), *Arbetets söner: Text och bild ur den svenska arbetarrörelsens saga: Del IV Nydaningens tid* (pp. 585–615). Stockhom: Tiden.

Norrena, L. (1993). *Talonpoika, pohjalainen – ja punainen: Tutkimus Etelä-Pohjanmaan Järviseudun työväenliikkeestä vuoteen 1939*. Helsinki: Suomen Historiallinen Seura.

Oinonen, J. (2013). *Mielenosoituksia sanoin ja jaloin: Helsingin ja Oulun työväen järjestämä vapun vietto vuosina 1907–1982*. Oulo: Oulun yliopisto Historiatieteet pro gradu-tutkielma, 8.5.

Olsson, J.-E. (1990). 1 maj i Sverige 100 år. In *1 maj i Sverige 100 år: 1890–1990* (pp. 8–47). Stockholm: Kulturhuset.

Olsson, L. (2002). 'Det är ingen skam att vara socialist': Arbetarrörelsen före det politiska makttillträdet. In L. Olsson and L. Ekdahl (Eds), *Klass i rörelse: Arbetarrörelsen i svensk samhällsomvandling* (pp. 8–67). Stockholm: Arbetarrörelsens arkiv och bibliotek.

Ordningsstadga för rikets städer af d. 24 mars 1868. (1868). Stockholm: Norstedts.

Oulun ilmoituslehti [Finnish newspaper]. (1897). 1 May.

Palm, A. (1904). *Ur en agitators lif*. Stockholm: Björk & Börjesson.

Peltonen, U.M. (1998). Red memoirs from a 'black time' in Finland: Radical working reminiscences of the 1920s and 1930s. In T. Saarela and K. Rentala (Eds), *Communism: National and International* (pp. 273–298). Helsinki: SHS.

Persson, L.K. (1970). *Så fick vi 8-timmarsdag. Arbetarekalendern 1971* (pp. 121–139). Stockholm: Federativ.

Persson, L.K. (1975). *Syndikalismen i Sverige 1903–1922*. Stockholm: Federativ.

Roselius, A. (2007). *I bödlarnas fotspår. Massavrättningar och terror i finska inbördeskriget 1918*. Stockholm: Leopard förlag.

Rothelius, L. (2008). 1 maj-krönikan: 1 maj och enheten. *Proletären. 17*, www. proletaren.se/kronika/1-maj-kronikan-1-maj-och-enheten.

Saarela, T. (1998). International and national in the communist movement. In T. Saarela and K. Rentala (Eds), *Communism: National and International* (pp. 15–40). Helsinki: SHS.

Saarela, T. (2008). *Suomalainen kommunismi ja vallankumous 1923–1930*. Helsinki: Suomalisen kirjallisuuden seura, Historiallisia Tutkimuksia 239.

Schiller, B., Venneslan, K., Ågotnes, H., Bruun, N., Nielsen R., and Töllborg, D. (1994). *The Future of the Nordic Model of Labour Relations: Three Reports on Internationalization and Industrial Relations*. Copenhagen: Nordic Council of Ministers.

Schmidt, W. (1996). *Kommunismens rötter i första världskrigets historiska rum: En studie kring arbetarrörelsens historiska misslyckande*. Stockholm: Brutus Östlings Bokförlag Symposion.

Simola, M. (1986). Vappu. In U. Achten, M. Reichelt and R. Schultz (Eds), *Mein Vaterland ist International. Internationale illustrierte Geschichte des 1. Mai, 1886 bis heute* (pp. 66–73). Berlin: Asso Verlag.

Soikkanen, H. (1975). *Kohti kansanvaltaa 1. 1899–1937, Suomen Sosialidemokraattinen Puolue – Puoluetoimikunta*. Vaasa: Oy Kirjapaino Ab.

Suomen Sosialidemokraatti [Finnish newspaper]. (25, 29, 30 April, 2 and 12 May, 1919; 3 May and 4 May, 1930; 2 May and 3 May, 1932).

Suomen Sosialidemokraattisen Puolue. (1906). *Suomen Sosialidemokraattisen puolueen viidennen edustajakokouksen pöytäkirja. Kokous pidetty Oulussa 20–27 p:nä elokuuta 1906* (pp. 453–457). Tampere: Suomen Sosialidemokraattisen Puolue.

Tapper, M. (1995). *Valtiollis-poliittiset juhlapäivät Suomessa vuosina 1918–1939: Tutkimus suhtautumisesta vappuun, toukokuun kuudenteentoista ja itsenäisyyspäivään sekä niiden vietto.* Helsinki: Helsingin yliopisto, Historian laitos Pro gradu –tutkielma.

Tampereen Sanomat[Finnish newspaper]. (1898). 28 April, 29 April, 30 April, 2 May, 3 May, 4 May.

Tepora, T. (2011). *Sinun puolestas elää ja kuolla: Suomen liput, nationalismi ja veriuhri 1917–1945.* Juva: WSOY.

Therborn, G. (1977). The rule of capital and the rise of democracy. *New Left Review*, 103, 3–41.

Thörnqvist, C. (2008). Metall och världen. In L. Berggren et al. (Eds), *Det lyser en framtid: Svenska metallindustriarbetareförbundet 1957–1981* (pp. 909–1009). Stockholm: IF Metall.

Thörnqvist, C. (2009). The Nordic labour market model. *Revue d'Histoire Nordique/ Nordic Historical Review*, 9, 113–139.

Tuomisto, T. (1984). *Tienraivaajan osa: Sata vuotta Helsingin Työväenyhdistyksen historiaa 1884–1984.* Helsinki: Helsingin työväenyhdistys.

Työmies [Finnish newspaper]. (25 May 1895; 23 May 1896, 22 August 1896; 1 May, 12 June, 19 June 1897; 30 April 1898; 30 May, 6 June, 8 June 1901; 26 May, 30 May, 2 June, 19 June 1902; 31 May, 2 June, 5–9 June 1906; 3 May 1909).

Uutisia Helsingistä, Uusi Suometar [Finnish newspaper]. (1890). 2 May.

Uusi Suometar [Finnish newspaper]. (1898). 30 April, 1 May, 3 May.

Wistrand, H. (1959). Kamp år och genombrott i västra Sverige. In K. Nilsson (Ed.), *Arbetets söner: Text och bilder ur den svenska arbetarrörelsens saga: Del I Pioniärtiden*, 3rd edn (pp. 196–222). Stockholm: Steinsvik.

Ylikangas, H. (1995). *Vägen till Tammerfors: Striden mellan röda och vita i finska inbördeskriget 1918.* Stockholm: Atlantis.

5 May Day in Spain

Socialist and Anarchist Traditions

Eduardo Romanos and José Luis Ledesma

'[May Day is celebrated] year after year, without interruption', wrote the Spanish philosopher Miguel de Unamuno (1907), 'and this celebration seems to assume a ritual, a liturgical character. The value of these rituals is enormous, as long as their spirit is faithfully remembered' (p. 2). These words were written in 1907, before this annual festivity had been fully consolidated and at this time only referred to the socialist celebration; its anarchist counterpart was discreetly overlooked. In 1907, the meaning of May Day was still under construction. Other events to come, events that were to transform May Day and the whole of Spanish society – a civil war, a dictatorship that was to last 40 years and the restoration of liberal democracy from 1975 – could not even be imagined at this stage. Unamuno, however, had already perceived the ritual dimension of the celebration, which was repeated 'year after year'. It would appear that he had even understood the performative value of the rituals, which would be preserved 'as long as their spirit is faithfully remembered'. Over the last 125 years, this spirit has grown and has become more solid – it has changed, suffered from repression and re-emerged, only to vanish, or at the very least become hardly recognizable, in more recent times. In this chapter we aim to present a brief overview of the history of May Day in Spain, including its more significant milestones, personalities and meanings.

Early Days, Early Differences

In Spain, the so-called 'workers' festival' was created as an alternative to another celebration which fell very close in the calendar. The uprising of the people of Madrid against the French army, on 2 May 1808, which marked the beginning of the 'War of Independence' (known in English-speaking countries as the 'Peninsular War'), had been commemorated on this day for decades. The authorities attended ceremonies that aimed to increase the nation's patriotic sentiments, for example they attended mass and parades, and presented funeral offerings to honour the war dead. Later, this occasion became the subject of partisan controversies, and was to a large degree abandoned, but in the second half of the nineteenth century it was still one of the most important dates in the Spanish calendar (Guereña 1999–2000). After the creation of the *Federación Regional Española* (Spanish Regional Federation) of the AIT, in 1870, 2 May also became a day for protest, and the protests included calls to boycott the official celebrations, which were believed to run against the spirit of fraternity and solidarity which should inspire workers worldwide. In Spain, May Day was thus taken as an opportunity to transform these internationalist principles into a transgressive ritual, in which class, rather than national consciousness, was asserted (Pérez Ledesma 2007; Guereña 1986).

As was the case in other countries, the eight-hour day was another essential element of May Day and it was a demand that had already been on the internationalist agenda. It was one of the demands presented to the *Cortes* (parliament) in 1873, and it was repeatedly invoked in the strikes organized during the 1874–1881 'underground period'. The demand was reiterated once more before the *Comisión de Reformas Sociales* (Social Reform Committee), created in 1883 (Álvarez Junco 1976; De la Calle 1989). In fact, the impact of the American 'eight-hour campaign' gave a new boost to the activities of the First International in Spain, at a time when this organization had already disappeared in other countries (Álvarez Junco 1986). Spanish activists organized assemblies and rallies where the campaign was discussed and promoted, and funds were raised in support of the strikers. The activists also created a *Comisión interina de las ocho horas* (an Eight-Hour Interim Committee), which soon became 'the embryo of the *Federación de Resistencia al Capital* (Federation Against Capitalism)' (Álvarez Junco 1976, p. 549).[1]

The violent repression suffered by the American campaigners had a strong impact on Spain. The fate of the Haymarket martyrs filled the eight-hour claim with drama and, even more significantly, it 'represented a break from the hope of achieving people's political emancipation by means of the Republic' (Pérez Ledesma 2007, p. 36). From that point onwards, the anarchists adopted this demand as a symbol of open warfare between the working class and the state – even a democratic and federal one, as in the case of America – since it became clear that the state, regardless of the prevalent form of government, was irretrievably in the service of the bourgeoisie. The anarchist May Day celebration focused on mourning the anarchist heroes from Chicago, whose trial they saw as 'judicial murder'. According to the anarchist newspapers, the eight-hour day could only be attained by means of a general strike. 'We will not achieve the eight-hour day with peaceful demonstrations and useless, slavish petitions; we will succeed if we impose our will, and we shall impose our will by going on strike' (quoted in Álvarez Junco 1976, p. 552).

The quotation is from *El Productor* in 1890, and refers to the other May Day celebrations, those organized by the socialists. In Spain, May Day had, as in other countries, an integrative and mobilizing role, as it fuelled and forged the common identity, hopes and collective actions of the organized working class as a distinctive social and political actor (Pérez Ledesma 2007). That said, the Spanish case is characterized by what has been referred to as the 'dual origin' of May Day (Rivas 2010a), which actually exemplified the twofold nature of the Spanish organized labour movement. The anarchist and socialist celebrations were of a different character. While the anarchists tended to have their eyes set on Chicago, socialists looked to Paris, where in 1889 the founding congress of the Second International resolved to keep demonstrations peaceful and to present the workers' demands to authorities in an orderly fashion. It was hoped that the power of numbers could influence the authorities to legally reduce the working day to eight hours and to realize the additional measures in favour of workers voted by the Paris congress. For the Spanish socialists, the celebration had a joyful (in contrast to a mournful) meaning, which was far removed from the Chicago spirit (see Chapter 2).

These differences between the events organized by the two groups clearly featured in the first celebration of May Day in Spain, in 1890; these differences also had a territorial dimension. In Madrid, the celebration was moved to Sunday 4 May, on account of the pressure exerted by the socialists, who wanted to secure massive attendance for the different events; 2,000 workers gathered at a rally at the Liceo Rius and a huge demonstration (*El Socialista* reported 30,000 participants) concluded by submitting to the authorities a document with a series of demands aimed at relieving the plight of the working class. Things were different in Barcelona, where the socialists failed to convince workers' organizations to postpone the celebrations. The rally and the demonstrations which took place in the morning in the centre of the city were followed in the afternoon by more confrontational actions in other areas of the city. Hundreds of workers reached an agreement to go on strike in demand of the eight-hour day. The authorities declared a 'state of war' the following day. The conflict raged on for several days, and certain trades eventually obtained a total or partial reduction of working hours (Pérez Ledesma 1987, pp. 135–141; Herrerín 2010; Rivas 2010a). The mobilization had important consequences: this reduction of working hours drove important sectors of the working class closer to the anarchists, who brandished these concessions as a victory in the face of the fruitless moderation of the socialists, and, furthermore, the strong repressive measures implemented by the authorities confirmed the anarchist account of open confrontation between the working class and the state.

The typical response of the Spanish state to any challenge or protest was to regard them as a problem of public order leading to the adoption of a repressive policy. For example, in response to the action programme drafted by the workers' organizations for this first May Day, in 1890, the government replied by mustering troops in many cities (Lucea 2009, p. 131). This was, indeed, what the well-off classes expected of the government, both in the cities and the countryside. The well-off classes regarded the organization and public manifestations of the working classes with fear and hostility (Gil Andrés 2000, p. 57ff.). The 'state of war' was maintained in Barcelona for nearly two months. The following year, Cánovas, the conservative leader, who had replaced the liberal Sagasta in government, would not relinquish control of the streets. The government started issuing preventive surveillance orders to the military authorities in the weeks leading up to May, and thereafter they applied highly restrictive measures to demonstrations. Later, in the face of the incidents which took place in some cities on May Day, Cánovas declared by *Real Decreto* (Royal Decree) a 'state of war' in the country as a whole.

May Day incidents were repeated throughout the first years of the decade, especially in Barcelona, and the restrictive legislation remained in force even when Sagasta returned to power in 1893 (Rivas 1988; González Calleja 1998, pp. 66–68). In fact, these conflicts involved only a minority of the workers. More importantly, they were not part of a general and coherent strategy such as the general strike, which was ideally seen by the anarchists as the ultimate step of every collective action. At the Paris congress a resolution on the general strike was voted down, and in Spain it had no chance of leading to an insurrectional movement as, among other things, the anarchist movement was far from being widely established in the country at the time (González Calleja 1998, pp. 313–314). In any case, public demonstrations, including May Day rallies, were virtually forbidden up until the early twentieth century, and only gatherings behind closed doors were allowed. Furthermore, the state's repressive attitude towards this and other demonstrations (e.g. peasants' uprisings, strikes) helped justify the radicalization of some anarchist groups: these groups resorted to political violence, in the form of terrorist attacks on the authorities, throughout the 1890s (Núñez Florencio 1983; Herrerín 2008).

Tactical differences between anarchists and socialists regarding May Day widened in the 1890s. The socialists appealed to the 'good sense' of the workers, criticized the very idea of the general strike and placed their hopes in the growth of their associated trade union, the *Unión General de Trabajadores* (UGT), which had been created in 1888 (Pérez Ledesma 1987; Castillo 2008). For their part, Spanish anarchists promoted general strikes in order to extend the spirit of confrontation to other social sectors. In this regard, May Day could be regarded as the D-Day of social revolution. This was not about mere radicalization for its own sake, let alone irrational disorganization; in fact, as shown by the events that occurred in 1892, anarchist mobilization was 'made of opaque but sustained and coherent organization and planning' (Turcato 2011, p. 15). The anarchists were actually presenting May Day as a demonstration of the insurrectional power of the working class, via the symbolic representation of the revolutionary strike that would destroy bourgeois society (Tilly 1986, p. 439).

In conclusion, the modus operandi of socialists and anarchists was radically different: whereas socialists followed the logic of numbers, the anarchists followed the logic of damage (della Porta and Diani 2006, pp. 170–178), of threatening the stability of the state. In 1893, the anarchists formally withdrew from the celebrations and at the same time the demand for an eight-hour day was abandoned in favour of a revolutionary ideology with 'much more far-reaching' aspirations (Álvarez Junco 1976, pp. 552–553). The withdrawal of the anarchists and the more moderate strategy of the socialists were saluted with joy by the conservative media: what in 1890 threatened to become a 'terrible date for the struggle between different social sectors, has happily turned into a normal, peaceful day'.[2] In general, therefore, the evolution of the socialist and anarchist sectors was significantly different. Eventually, the violent radicalization of the actions carried out by a radical fringe of the anarchist movement led the state to apply repressive measures to the movement as a whole. The socialists, for their part, had an increasing presence among the working class, due to the expectations surrounding May Day and the participation of the *Partido Socialista Obrero Español* (Socialist Workers' Party of Spain – PSOE) in the general elections for the first time in 1891, two years after the founding of the party in Madrid (Castillo 1986). These were the first Spanish elections where universal male suffrage was applied. The most significant demands made during the labour day celebrations in the late nineteenth century generally included internationalist, political and social issues, such as international solidarity and world peace, the demand for political democratization, the eight-hour day and the regulation of child and female labour. In May 1898, the year of the Spanish-American War, the socialists also included additional political demands. The socialist newspaper *La República Social*, at Mataró, referred for example to the termination of the war, the reformation of compulsory military service (they asked for it to be extended also to the sons of well-to-do families) and the recognition of the 'right of the productive classes to participate in, and contribute to, the drafting of laws and public policies' (cited in Rodríguez 1998, p. 578).

The Consolidation and the Dual Nature of May Day (1900–1931)

The new century began with a change in the government's position: less repressive, more conciliatory attitudes were adopted and various measures were implemented in order to alleviate working conditions.[3] In 1902, permission was granted to carry out demonstrations on May Day; initially these were on the outskirts of cities and, later, in the centre. Permission was granted for these demonstrations in order to channel the political practices of the working class towards moderation (Herrerín 2010; Rivas 1987). This did not always happen, however, and there are reasons to believe that the second great wave of anarchist-led terrorism (1904–1909) was directly related to the failure of the eight-hour-day movement, to the government barriers to May Day celebrations and to the difficult economic situation which the textile and construction sectors were undergoing at the time (Núñez Florencio 1983, p. 50ff.). However, in the mid-term, even the anarchists changed their tactics in relation to May Day. Although they still thought that the socialist celebration was insufficient, some anarchist sectors soon came under the influence of French revolutionary syndicalism, the rituals of which were partially adopted (especially the rallies and strikes). In this case, these rituals were seen as a form of direct action that aimed to obtain the eight-hour day (Smith 2007, pp. 161–162; Rivas 2010b). In fact, the attitude of the *Confederación Nacional del Trabajo* (National Workers Confederation – CNT), a trade union, which would eventually become the umbrella organization for all forms of anarcho-syndicalism, was considerably more moderate in this regard. According to its founding agreement, which was reached at the organization's inaugural congress (1910), the eight-hour day was to be achieved through the strengthening of trade unionism and the slackening of other agitation activities (Bar 1981, pp. 210–211).

In the wake of the intense process of mobilization and organization of the working classes that occurred in the early decades of the twentieth century, May Day became consolidated as a mass ritual for the empowerment of workers' organizations. This was facilitated by the progressive strengthening of the major class-based trade unions (the UGT, socialist, and the CNT, anarcho-syndicalist) and by the relatively more permissive government policies regarding May Day celebrations from 1903 onwards, although this permissiveness was limited on the ground by provincial governors and local mayors to the point of abuse (Rivas 1988; Gil Andrés 2000, pp. 63–67).

In addition, the consolidation of May Day was part of a wider process of progressive substitution of the traditional protest repertoire with a 'new, more modern' one (Tilly 1978; Cruz 1998). In fact, in comparison with other countries, this process was relatively tardy in Spain. While in other parts of Europe the objectives were widening, and the national, rather than the local, sphere was being targeted, Spanish peasants and workers maintained parochial and patronage-related local protests for some time. The relative economic backwardness of the country, the inefficiency of the state, the limits of its democratic institutions and the brutality of the authorities in terms of the repression of protests are some of the reasons for the late adoption of the new repertoire (Castro 1989). As a result, local, nominally institutionalized and sometimes violent forms of collective action coexisted for decades with the emerging and more organized public meetings, rallies and demonstrations, trade union conflicts, nationwide campaigns and participation in politics via parliamentary channels. Riots, anticlerical episodes, invasions of rural estates and other kinds of public disturbances due to food shortages, taxation or conscription still took place in Spain until the 1930s. As a nationwide organized event, May Day was a symbolic and important driving force in this gradual change of repertoire.

During and after World War I trade unions became an increasingly influential agent in working-class-fuelled collective action. Thanks to Spain's neutrality in that conflict, the rising industrial demand coming from the belligerent countries generated a sudden and intense economic growth. Not surprisingly, CNT and UGT reached rates of affiliation never reached before and grew ever more organized and coordinated in their actions. Moreover, although their positions regarding the conflict and Spanish politics crucially diverged, both trade unions reached their first mobilizing alliances, such as the general strike of August 1917.[4] In addition, the Great War prompted the government to impose interventionist policies in relation to certain contentious issues, such as the supply of basic goods (Pérez Ledesma 1998). The combination of both trends contributed to the progressive elevation of the repertoire of action to the national level. More specifically, UGT leaders started organizing coordinated nationwide actions and intensifying the use of certain tactics and resources that had already been rehearsed during the preparation and celebration of May Day: rallies, demonstrations, petitions to the authorities, cultural programmes and symbolic actions. Gradually these types of actions took the place of other actions which up to that moment had been very common among workers and peasants such as urban and rural rallies, more or less paradigmatic of the former protest repertoire (González Calleja 1998, pp. 535–551; Cruz 2008, pp. 70–71).

At this stage, the celebration of May Day in Spain was following the patterns already at work in the rest of Europe, with regard to both its content and its form. Concerning the demands made during the celebrations, the eight-hour day had already been adopted by the government, in Spain as well as in other countries, in the aftermath of World War I. In Spain, this happened in 1919 after important labour-related conflicts, for example the *La Canadiense* strike via which the CNT managed to paralyse Barcelona for 44 days. Thereafter, issues such as the participation of trade unions in business management decisions and the socialization of productive assets took pride of place among labour-related legislative demands. Needless to say, the Russian revolution had a crucial influence on Spanish workers' demands and manifestos, which also included further demands in connection with the domestic agenda. The war in Morocco – one of the few remaining Spanish colonies – is worth stressing, especially after the incidents leading to the so-called 'Tragic Week' in Barcelona in 1909.[5] For several years, May Day manifestos always included calls for the cessation of hostilities, and they demanded that the policy which allowed conscripts to redeem their mobilization in exchange for a monetary fee be ended and also that those convicted for their participation in the Barcelona events be pardoned (Herrerín 2010; Lucea 2009).

The basis of the socialist ritual, in Spain as well as in other countries, included stoppages, political rallies and public demonstrations that ended with the presentation of a list of demands to the government. The demands were edited by the local unions leaders and presented to the workers for vote. Beyond their integrative and mobilizing nature, this ritual had also a practical dimension, as it included leisure activities and fundraising events. At these events, the workers attended theatrical shows and concerts, which were often organized in the framework of '*jiras campestres*' (picnics) in the city parks and the countryside, where funds were raised for the alleviation of the suffering of the poor and the workers who were on strike. In addition, Spanish socialists also organized more symbolic ceremonies, such as flower contests, the laying of the foundation stones of the '*casas del pueblo*' (the people's houses – a kind of social club for workers) and the naming of streets after Pablo Iglesias (PSOE's founder), especially after his death in 1925 (Rivas 1987, 2010b).

In other countries, as well as in Spain, flowers – which could be carnations, roses or poppies; the important thing was that they were red – symbolized the renovation, hope and joy that the socialists associated with May Day (Rivas 2010b). The *casas del pueblo* and the founder also had a strong symbolic value in socialist culture (Pérez Ledesma 1993). The *casas del pueblo* were the epi-centre of the PSOE's activities and a forum for the civil celebration of workers as the ascending social class; they became a sort of sacred place that socialists did not hesitate to define as a 'proletarian fortress', the 'unassailable bastion' of their group, and the 'workers' palace'. Finally, the mythologized figure of Pablo Iglesias, his doctrine and his example were a strong element of cohesion for Spanish socialism – one that went beyond any reference to an abstract pol-itical doctrine (Pérez Ledesma 1987).

Around May Day, socialist newspapers paid less attention to political events and turned instead to the promotion of international solidarity: effu-sive salutations to socialists in other countries were made, and didactic poems, short stories and illustrations were published for cultural promotion (Serrano 1986). The illustrations were inspired by a variety of topics, for example classical mythology (the worker being represented as the hero), the Enlightenment (with its exaltation of progress and its mockery of the clergy), Christianity and the revolution (with references to the union of nations and the caricature of the 'enemies of the people') (De Luis 1994). Much like other Catholic countries, the socialist May Day in Spain was filled with religious symbols – albeit symbols and metaphors instilled with a secular meaning (see chapters 2, 3 and 10). The Master, the Apostles, paradise, the Holy Family and the sower featured frequently in the celebrations. The redeeming nature associated with the celebration is, in this regard, no less important: it was believed that this celebration had the power to change society, by itself and without resorting to violence (Rivas 1990). In the words of a socialist in 1900, May Day was the 'prologue of the great work of universal redemption', which would be achieved 'without struggle, without spilling a single drop of blood'; it would 'grow more and more, until differences are erased and the human race becomes a single family' (Salazar 1900). In 1910, the main socialist news-paper defined May Day as 'the workers' Easter' (Núñez 1910). Three years later, this same newspaper alluded to May Day as the ritual of 'the new secu-lar religion of Love and Fraternity', the ritual with which the 'birth of that redeeming hope' and its 'continuous resurrection from persecution and cruci-fixion' were commemorated (De Répide 1913).

In reality, the socialist May Day was not just a naïve celebration of inter-class fraternity. The essentially festive, peaceful and ritualistic formal character of the socialists' May Day was compatible with the very idea that it was nothing less than a ritual celebration of the identity of the working class in contrast to, and to some extent in struggle with, the bourgeoisie. In addition, some socialists advocated for a more confrontational approach, for example, those who, in 1909, rejected May Day as what they considered a mere celebration of work, because for many workers work was 'nothing but pain and misery', and as a celebration of peace, because there was no peace or social justice to celebrate. From its birth, as a faction of the PSOE, in the early 1920s, the Communist Party (PCE) defended these more assertive positions. For the communists, May Day was not so much a day for leisure and vacation, but a date to advance the proletarian struggle. As they tried to create their own political space, the members of the PCE claimed that the target was not to unite the classes, imputing that idea to the socialists, but to stress what divided them (Rivas 1990, pp. 49 and 55–56). These arguments had, however, only limited support among socialists, while the PCE did not become politically significant until the beginning of the Spanish Civil War (1936–1939). In any case, the crucial point is not the communist alternative notion, but the anarchist one. The very existence in Spain of the solid libertarian May Day tradition and the very competition for representing the working class arguably brought the socialists to highlight and reinforce the distinctive elements of their own tradition. Thus, in contrast to the anarchists' stress on the confrontational nature of the May Day celebrations, the socialist discourse came to underline their peaceful and festive nature and what they implied regarding a long-term negotiating strategy of struggle for workers' rights and conditions.

Not surprisingly, the anarchists' criticisms against the socialist May Day were intense and surely distorted the actual meaning of the socialist May Day. Spain is unique in the sense that May Day remained dual for more decades and in a stronger manner than elsewhere. Before the communist emergence made the May Day dual in other countries, it already was so in Spain, with socialists on one hand and anarchists on the other, and it remained like this even after World War I. This, in turn, is a reflection of the exceptional role played by Spanish anarchism. In other countries, the anarchist movement either did not survive World War I, or it was not capable of adapting to the increasing access of the popular classes to institutional politics in the interwar years. Spain was the only country where a branch of anarchism remained strong within the labour movement in the aftermath of the Great War. As a result, the anarcho-syndicalist trade union CNT not only competed with the socialists but achieved hegemony in the labour movement in times of political openness (1917–1923 and 1931–1937)

But Spanish anarchism did not just consist of the CNT. On the one hand, before the foundation of the CNT, Spanish anarchism was a complex melting pot which included workers' societies and trade unions, but also social clubs, rationalist schools, defence committees, pro-convict committees, newspapers and printing presses, naturalist and vegetarian clubs, etc. On the other hand, the CNT was not purely anarchist. The majority of anarchists joined the CNT, but a significant number of the hundreds of thousands of CNT members did not join because they fully shared the anarchists' theoretical perspectives on libertarian communism, but because the anarchist approach to direct action and self-defence appeared to be the most efficient in labour-related conflicts. Even the leadership of the CNT remained divided between (at least) two major trends: a more individualist and 'maximalist' form of anarchism, which was aimed at instilling in the CNT a 'purely anarchist spirit', and a social anarchism – anarcho-syndicalism – which was aimed at reinforcing the idea that syndicalist structures were the basis of a future society. In any case, since 1917, if not before, and until the end of the Civil War (1939), the anarchists controlled the most powerful trade union in the country, something unparalleled elsewhere. The CNT was the most powerful libertarian organization in the world. Historians have long wondered about the reasons for this Spanish peculiarity. If presented as a form of 'primitive rebelliousness' (Hobsbawm 1959), anarchism can be attributed to socio-economic backwardness or to social and even religious factors. However, the supporters of this idea forget that the focal point of the movement – Barcelona and its environs – was the most industrialized region in the country. The success of the movement is explained by the fact that its ideas and practices were better adapted to confronting the inefficient and repressive Spanish state of the first third of the twentieth century.

As a result of all this, the dual nature of May Day persisted until the Civil War. The anarchists were against celebrating May Day in 'the socialist way'. By this, they meant the 'herd' walking 'before the eyes of those who would later shear them' 'in a burlesque, famished, docile procession' (Acín 1921). Accordingly, as expressed by the newspaper *Acción Libertaria* (Gijón) in 1911, they claimed that 'as long as the workers only bare their teeth to smile, the bosses will feel safe' (cited in Radcliff 2004, p. 250). Of course, we deal here with rhetorical and ideological elements used in a contentious debate for the representation of the workers, which also implied in the occasion the May Day, that the libertarians arguably inflated the contrast between the socialists' and their own celebrations. In short, they criticized the mystification of a day which had over time, according to them, turned into a harmless 'Holy Routine' with no impact on the bourgeois order or the state (Rivas 1990, pp. 52–53). By contrast, the anarchists, in line with the theories of Georges Sorel in France, understood stoppages as a recurrent opportunity to achieve their old objective of a revolutionary general strike, which explains the frequent clashes with the police.

Using the evidence collected by Rivas (1987) for the period 1900–1930, we can identify the evolution of organized political actions on May Day. Three major categories are distinguishable: (1) collective political mobilizations, including rallies and marches; (2) leisure or festive activities, including picnics and other cultural events such as balls, theatre plays, dinners, etc.; and (3) confrontational direct actions, essentially general or partial strikes (Figure 5.1).[6] As previously mentioned, most of the collective political mobilizations and festive activities were organized by the socialists, while the direct actions were generally promoted by the anarchists.

Collective political mobilizations generally followed a relatively stable pattern, with the exception of two periods. First, between 1907 and 1912 republicans and socialists joined forces in order to gain a larger share of parliamentary power, and for this reason institutional strategies were preferred

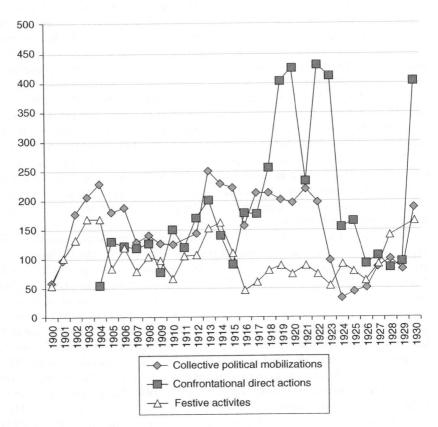

Figure 5.1 May Day contention, Spain, 1900–1930.
Source: Rivas (1987).

during these years. The second period, the dictatorship of Primo de Rivera (1923–1930), was a time when politically inspired actions were, to a large degree, prohibited. The frequency of political actions increased again in 1929, when the regime entered its final crisis.

Festive activities also followed a stable pattern: their frequency decreased over time in favour of more directly political and economic actions. They were, however, especially common during the final years of the dictatorship. The lack of data beyond 1930 makes it impossible to ascertain whether this was a response to the impossibility of mobilizing in any other way or whether it was simply a change of trend in favour of this sort of mobilization.

Finally, confrontational direct actions also grew continuously in intensity during this period, except for two short intervals. The first interval coincided with World War I. Until then, the growing trend had gone hand in hand with increasingly organized and larger trade unions. This trend changed in 1914 as a consequence of Spanish neutrality and the economic boost brought about by the demand for goods posed by the belligerent countries. The war years were a period of economic growth, high employment and relatively high salaries (especially in the most industrialized areas, like Catalonia, the Basque Country and Madrid, where, in addition, the level of unionization was higher). Everything changed with the end of the conflict: demand dropped dramatically, and industrial activity and the job market both shrank accordingly. The period 1918–1923 was very tough from an economic point of view; industrialists adopted very aggressive policies in order to maintain their profit margins, often at great cost to workers. It was no coincidence that these were the years of the 'gun law', especially in Catalonia: industrialists hired irregular security personnel, whose task was to shoot down problematic workers and trade union leaders. In response, the most radical factions within the CNT proposed that 'action groups' be created; these groups staged attacks against relevant industrial, political figures and the police (González Calleja 1999, pp. 105–253). During these years, the number of confrontational actions rose spectacularly. This new stage came to an end with the beginning of the dictatorship in 1923 and its associated repressive policies. The regime worked to dismantle the CNT while blocking the action of the UGT, which naturally resulted in a sharp drop in the number of confrontational actions. After the end of the dictatorship, the number of strikes increased again.

The geographical distribution of the different kinds of action is also of interest. It largely corresponds with the geographical distribution of the different ideologies at play, although this correspondence cannot be exact, especially when we examine it in detail. For example, it is possible to find celebrations of a festive nature and political rallies in Barcelona, but this was especially the case in cities where the socialists or the republicans were the predominant force (Rodríguez 1998). Similarly, although the northern regions were predominantly socialist, in the city of Gijón the weight of the CNT was such, and the hostility of these anarchists towards the 'inconsequential' celebrations of May Day pitched so high, that the celebrations never assumed this character of a 'proletarian festival'. According to Radcliff (2004, pp. 251–252), this stunted the evolution of proletarian culture as a whole in Gijón, since May Day provided the best opportunity for bringing all elements of this proletarian culture together. From the data it is clear that conventional and festive actions were concentrated in the areas where the socialists were predominant, that is, in the north (especially Asturias), León, Valencia, Andalusia and Madrid. Strikes were particularly common in Catalonia, most especially Barcelona, the most industrialized region of the country and a bastion of anarcho-syndicalism.[7]

These differences reflect the ideological and strategic differences between socialist and anarchist trade unions. The socialists, more or less in coordination with the political agenda of the PSOE, never missed the opportunity offered by May Day celebrations to consolidate the trade union's and the party's structures, their demands and identities. For their part, one of the marks of the anarchists' identity was their rejection of the state and this determined their strategy of 'direct action', i.e. outside of the institutional and political channels.

The geographical distribution of their impact also reflects their different organizational strategies. The UGT was a notably centralist organization from the time of its creation (Pérez Ledesma 1987, p. 200ff.), and, to a great degree, its actions were controlled by and directed from Madrid, especially on significant and symbolic occasions like May Day. The CNT was much more decentralized, which meant that local groups and cells had ample autonomy in terms of tactical and operational decisions. In addition, the often provisional nature of the CNT's central agencies, which were often routed by the police and persecuted by the courts, made central coordination difficult. The frequent incarceration of anarchist leaders forced the union's management cadres to be constantly renewed, and they often had to change regions as well. Under these circumstances, the chances of May Day actions being subordinated to broad 'political' considerations were slim, instead, these actions were directed at addressing specific, local labour and social conflicts.

Democracy and the Working Class in Movement: the Second Republic and the Civil War

The military coup staged by General Primo de Rivera, which was supported by King Alfonso XIII, and his dictatorial regime (1923–1930), were intended to solve the progressive crisis and ultimate breakdown of the restoration governments (1875–1931). The 1876 constitution and the normal activity of parliament were suspended, and May Day actions were also curtailed. In 1924, for the first time in 20 years, the authorities not only explicitly forbade public demonstrations but also used coercive methods, in cooperation with business owners, in order to limit strikes and force work in strategic sectors to continue. This strategy continued in use, with minor changes, over the duration of the dictatorship (Rivas 1988, pp. 98–106). Again, the socialist and anarchist positions were significantly different and so were the consequences which they suffered. The socialists, having found ways to collaborate with the regime, managed to consolidate the position of their trade unions, and generally they opted not to call for strikes and obeyed the prohibition against demonstrations.

The anarchists, on the other hand, openly opposed the regime and were subsequently repressed. Their organizations were, as a consequence, virtually dismantled (Barrio 1988, pp. 289–301). In accordance with the essentially heterogeneous nature of the anarchist movement, there was no single dominating trend within the movement. While some union leaders would have preferred to adopt a somewhat less aggressive position, others voiced their criticism of the passive attitude of the socialists, and their intended appropriation of May Day, unsparingly. Again, the accounts of the celebrations were in part at least the expression of ideological positions and were part of the discursive competition between socialists and anarchists – and between different branches of the libertarian movement – for representing the working class. In 1926, Manuel Buenacasa (1926), one of the most important leaders of the CNT in the 1910s, regretted the fact that, according to him, May Day was no longer about 'violent explosions, the people's anger against the tyranny of the privileged', as it had been in the second decade of the century. Now it was about strictly ordered, routine and innocuous demonstrations and 'binge drinking on the part of sheep-like leaders, and all this in front of a delighted bourgeoisie'. For CNT members like him, workers had to realize how their socialist leaders 'betray' them and they should never confuse the working-class tradition celebrations with 'the cold, solemn and official anniversaries of the ruling classes'.

The fall of the military dictatorship, the collapse of the monarchy and the proclamation of the Second Republic in 1931 were crucial turning points in Spanish contemporary political and social history. The Second Republic (1931–1936) significantly opened up the political space for collective action and rituals such as May Day. Not only did May Day then reach unprecedented levels of mobilization – most notably in 1936, it also underwent an intense process of politicization. During the Second Republic, May Day was an important annual milestone in the intense political and social mobilization agenda and, more specifically, in the reconstruction of the collective identities of the republican – and the anti-republican – political and social movements.

The republic was proclaimed shortly before May Day, on 14 April 1931; the king had left the country only two weeks before 1 May. The change of regime had occurred, according to eye-witnesses' testimonies, amidst a joyous atmosphere: people took to the streets waving flags and peacefully singing republican songs. Indeed, one of the defining elements of the republic was a change in the relationship between the state and civil society, which was now based on the generalization of social and political rights, including the right to demonstrate (Cruz 2014, p. 14). Two weeks later, when the first day of May arrived, the optimism had not yet subsided. Mobilization and a 'passionate exaltation' predominated in a succession of 'civil celebrations, popular rallies, and impressive parades' (Gaziel 1931). That year, therefore, was the first since 1923 in which workers could openly and legally demonstrate on May Day, and it also involved a huge 'magical' celebration. Following the customary ritual, demonstrators in many cities presented a document with their social and political demands to the authorities. But that year circumstances were special: some of the most prominent leaders of the workers' movement, such as the socialist leader Largo Caballero, as members of the government were the recipients of these demands (Juliá 1984, p. 17). Everything was new; as usual, May Day had been organized by the trade unions and the workers were on the streets, but this time the new authorities also included the Socialist Party and the republican regime was being celebrated by all. The day had not lost its character as a class celebration, but the traditional ritual was now seen as a form of 'joyous republican validation' (Cruz 2014, p. 131). The republic, identified in the preamble of the new constitution as a 'republic of workers of all classes', declared May Day a public holiday, thus associating the first day of May with the origins of the republican regime and the hopeful feeling that the republic had brought to the Spanish working classes.

The inclusive and massive nature of May Day remained constant during the republican period. 'Absolute general stoppage in Madrid' was the first entry of the day in the Prime Minister Manuel Azaña's diary (1978, vol. 1, p. 461), on 1 May 1932. Significantly there were no incidents, despite some fears of confrontations between the socialists and the anarcho-syndicalists following the conflicts between both trade unions which emerged in the previous weeks. 'General stoppage on occasion of the workers' day' was Azaña's entry the following year (p. 618). However, the celebrations gradually lost part of their connection with the new regime along the way. In 1932 and 1933, with Largo Caballero in office as minister of labour, May Day became, for the socialists, a ritual aimed at constructing and strengthening the socialist identity; it was no longer an occasion for them to present demands to the political authorities. However, for the anarcho-syndicalists it was about both identity and demands; the anarchists had never fully identified with the 'bourgeois' republic and were finding it increasingly difficult to operate due to government action, which logically favoured the UGT (Casanova 2005). Indeed, according to the most critical members of the CNT, the declaration of May Day as a republican public festivity annulled its proletarian nature. In the context of a huge discursive struggle between the anarchist and the socialist movements, in which the anarchists delegitimized the socialists for their involvement in bourgeois politics, according to the radical sectors of the former May Day had ultimately been turned into a secular Sunday celebration, with no religious service but many an official sermon (Radcliff 2004, p. 250). In 1934, under the government of a centre-right party, which was overturning the social measures that had been achieved in the previous two years, May Day regained its original character as a vehicle for the empowerment and the demands of the working classes. With their German and Austrian brethren repressed by fascist regimes, even the socialists claimed that that year, May Day recuperated its 'old flavor of protest and struggle' (quoted in Babiano 2006, p. 63). One year later, the political attitude hardened against the staging of massive demonstrations. This was part of the repressive measures imposed upon the labour movement in the wake of the revolutionary insurrection of October 1934. As a result of this hardening of attitude, even if workers' parades were generally peaceful (Bowers 1977, p. 152), rallies were forbidden in some cities, and tension with the security forces ensued in other places.

On 1 May 1936, the largest mobilizations to date occurred. The general elections held in February had seen the centre-right parties beaten by the 'Popular Front', a large coalition of left-bourgeoisie and working-class parties. Although this time the socialists did not enter the government, which was constituted only by the left republican parties, the new government offered a radical political opportunity for all sorts of mobilizations and collective claims in the context of both the political struggle and the social conflicts caused by the economic crisis and high unemployment levels (Ledesma 2013; Tarrow 1994, p. 84). There was a surge in activity, but the government held its own and did not give in to the demands. What the government could not do, however, was forbid the demonstrations outright, since that would have estranged it from its electoral base. Furthermore, the triumph of the Popular Front resulted in enormous expectations concerning the social reforms that popular protests were demanding –agrarian reform and the communal control of the commons, for example, which often featured among May Day demands (e.g. Majuelo 1989, pp. 289–290).

In this context, May Day served to channel many of these issues. There were some incidents and clashes, but very few indeed considering the hundreds of demonstrations and rallies that took place that day. The truly significant aspect was the high attendance and the symbolism given to the presence of the working class at what can be defined as a 'class festivity', the workers' occupation of the bourgeois cities at least for one day (Cruz 2006, pp. 145, 147). The workers' organizations were no longer identified with the Republic in the same way as they had been in 1931, and this was epitomized by the fact that this May Day seemed less a holy day than a day for struggle. In fact, workers did not have only one voice; for some, mainly in the socialist organizations, the day was a celebration of the unity of the workers' movement, while others, specially but not only in the libertarian organizations, saw it as a day for pushing forward in the context of the political struggle. In fact, in many cities, the CNT refused to join the celebrations, as some of its members saw them as ineffective in the struggle against the bourgeoisie and the state. However, regardless of the differences, everyone interpreted the events of the day as a demonstration of proletarian might and identity, as a demonstration of the power of a class which was on the streets to claim its dignity and its right to political participation and citizenship before a new government which had raised more hopes than its predecessors (Cruz 2006, pp. 145–148).

As is well known, the social and political groups who had the most to lose from these reforms brought them to an abrupt halt. In July 1936, a counter-revolutionary coalition, commanded by a sector of the army, staged a *coup d'état* against the republic. This putsch was only partially successful, and it led to armed conflict, which turned into a bloody civil war weeks later (1936–1939). Needless to say, May Day and all the myths, symbols and protests staged by the political left were eradicated in the areas controlled by Franco's side. May Day continued to be celebrated in the republican rear guard, and 1937 witnessed multiple events, rallies and speeches. But in the context of the Civil War, with all the material, political and symbolic resources at the service of the war effort, May Day was bound to lose its pre-eminence and visibility. In 1938 it was publically celebrated for what was to be the last time in many decades. In 1939, 1 May came one month after the end of the war. The country was under the dictatorship imposed by the victors and May Day was but a memory. Indeed, it was a bitter memory. The victors built their regime upon the punishment and repression of the vanquished. Throughout the country, informers reported on anyone with leftist ideas, and among the things they were reported for was their participation in May Day celebrations during the years of the republic. This, once more, demonstrates the importance of May Day for the definition of political and social identities in Spain in the 1930s.[8]

From Fascist Usurpation to Dissidence: Franco's Spain

While prohibiting all celebrations that were deemed to be subversive, Franco's regime promoted alternative formats that were aimed at justifying, praising and defending the new political, economic and social order. This tactic was applied to May Day: on the new official calendar it was replaced by *Fiesta de Exaltación del Trabajo* (Exaltation of Work Festival), the celebration of which coincided with the date of the *Glorioso Alzamiento* (Glorious Uprising) (18 July 1936). This celebration was established in 1938 with the publication of the *Fuero del Trabajo* (Labour Law), which formed the doctrinal basis for the new social national-syndicalist legislation (De la Calle 2003). The substitution of *Fiesta de Exaltación del Trabajo* for May Day sought to erase the memory of the workers' celebration as part of a broader plan which, among other things, involved the real and symbolic elimination of the rituals and identity-reproduction practices of the left and the trade unions (Richards 1998). Francoist national-syndicalism sought to replace class-based and internationalist trade unionism with a 'brotherhood of businessmen and workers'. The target was to suppress the sense of class struggle, and the people, in general, instead of just the 'working class', were to become the main protagonists of the celebrations. The government's propaganda apparatus strongly underlined the differences between the original labour celebration and the new Francoist festival. These contrasts are clearly expressed in a book edited by the 'Sección Femenina', the women's branch of the Falange (the regime's party), which thenceforth became officially incorporated into the institutional structure of the Francoist regime:

Nothing in this celebration will be reminiscent of May Day; no invidious Marxist parades walking across dead, not to say murdered, cities. That celebration, if we can call it that, promoted division among producers, gathered dispersed and amorphous masses, only joined by class hatred, for the purpose of rioting and of making demands of the government, demands which were often impossible to satisfy without grievously violating the body of the Nation. Our festival, in contrast, extols the brotherhood, the unity of all producers at the service of Spain ..., It will, therefore, be a celebration of a productive brotherhood, comprehensive, total and hierarchical, it will be a joyous and hopeful occasion, the commemoration of the resurgence of the nation, because work and production ... are subordinated to the Fatherland, and the Fatherland, its prosperity and greatness, are the ultimate aims and the only certainties of our destiny.[9]

The coincidence of the anniversary of the beginning of the war and the 'exaltation of work' was not casual. Thus, the celebration of the foundation of the new regime assumed a populist meaning, 'which worked as an extra factor of legitimacy for the regime in its national-syndicalist aspect' (Box 2008, p. 227). The target, which had already been achieved, of snatching the Fatherland from the claws of Marxism was linked in the Francoist imaginary to the ongoing reconstruction of the nation. This link was not something new. Fascist Italy had celebrated labour and the productive forces in general on 21 April, the anniversary of Rome's foundation. In fact, the Francoist *Fuero del Trabajo*, which sanctioned this union, was inspired by the fascist *Carta del Lavoro*, issued in 1927. In Spain, the celebrations were taken as an opportunity to legitimize the regime and bring together the forces on which it was based. Organized jointly by the civil, military and ecclesiastical authorities, the official ritual consisted of military parades, receptions, religious ceremonies and public events. The celebrations included highly symbolic events, which were appropriately disseminated by the propaganda apparatus: 'brotherhood meals', which were compulsory for company owners and employees; the handing out of donations to charities; raffles to award supporters of the regime from the working classes with trips, etc. (Box 2008, pp. 229–230).

However, May Day remained a significant date for many Spanish people who, after the earliest and bloodiest days of Franco's dictatorship, gradually resumed its celebration and turned it into an opportunity to express their dissidence. The best-known mobilizations were the general strikes of 1947, in Vizcaya, and 1951, in Catalonia (Lorenzo 1988; Molinero and Ysàs 1998; Vargas-Golarons 1990). In both cases the workers demanded better salaries and working conditions. These episodes had been preceded by minor work stoppages and strikes in the metallurgy sector in Vizcaya and also by a boycott of the tram system in the city of Barcelona. The regime acted with severity, but also conceded a small pay rise in 1951. These strikes demonstrated that the working class still had the ability to mobilize despite the harsh conditions imposed by the regime. In addition, by these actions the conditions of misery and repression suffered by the Spanish working classes became better known abroad.

May Day began to be officially celebrated once more in 1956, one year after Pope Pius XII gave a Christian meaning to the workers' celebration by consecrating the date to St Joseph, the patron saint of workers. While the fascist dictators had tried to erase the memory and tradition of the working-class ritual by usurping the socialist tradition – Hitler's Germany –, or by prohibiting it – Mussolini's Italy and post-war Spain (see Chapter 3), now, the Vatican tried to do the same by imposing another ritual, which was based on the Christian values of love, justice and spiritual evangelism (De la Calle 2003). The Francoist regime assumed the celebration in 'solidarity with the dispositions of the Holy See'.[10] In Spain the official ritual basically consisted of religious ceremonies and institutional speeches that praised the virtues of St Joseph, as well as official receptions where the authorities, including the labour minister and Franco himself, met the workers. For all practical purposes, the army disappeared from the celebrations. Now the organization of events fell to the church and the Falange, something which in itself gives an indication of the balance of power within the Franco's regime. The relationship between the church and the Falange (originally a fascist party) was never harmonious. These two pillars of the dictatorship competed for power, political influence and the ability to determine the regime's doctrinal basis. This competition extended to the ritual aspects of power and especially the attribution of meanings. Here, as well as in other areas, the church was triumphant in the symbolic struggle, as shown by the very language used to name the ritual, despite the initial advantage enjoyed by the Falange and the *Sindicatos Verticales* (state-controlled trade unions).

From 1958 onwards the *Sindicatos Verticales* started adding a performative element to the official celebrations, with the so-called *Demostraciones Sindicales* (trade union demonstrations): these were mass events that were celebrated in commemoration of the regime, and sporting, folkloric and cultural performances were included. They were held in the Santiago Bernabéu stadium, in Madrid, and, for many years, they followed the same ritual: Franco's triumphant entry into the stadium, the performance of the national anthem, a parade by the participants, a programme of sporting, folkloric and cultural events and the final climactic ovation of gratitude to the *caudillo*. These events sought to publicize the achievements of the regime and were part of a policy of 'legitimization by the exercise of power', which was to replace the legitimacy gained through victory in the Civil War (Aguilar 2008). The ritual appealed to the emotions of the audience, and it was a way of implanting the values of fascism: 'order, obedience, abnegation, strength, unity and greatness' (De la Calle 2003, pp. 103–104). The programme of celebrations started a few days before the beginning of May with the passing of new labour laws, notable among which was the *Ley de Convenios Colectivos* (Collective Agreements Act) (1958) and the inauguration of facilities aimed at improving the life of the working classes. The end of the celebrations did not halt the propaganda messages, which were mainly conveyed via the *Noticiarios y Documentales* (NO-DO) (News and Documentaries), newsreels which all cinemas were compelled to project before the main feature.

As usual propaganda failed to convince everyone. May Day was still seen by the working classes as an occasion to show their dissension. Gradually strikes began to enter the subversive ritual, especially after 1962, when the authorities were forced to declare a state of emergency in Asturias, Vizcaya and Guipúzcoa in response to labour conflicts. Later the regime started to try more subtle ways of demobilizing workers, for example by showing important football games and other sporting events on television, a practice 'that became routine in the [official] celebration' (De la Calle 2003, p. 107).

May Day also served to promote dissidence within institutions which were generally aligned with the regime. Religious services celebrating St Joseph, the only mass events allowed by the regime, progressively witnessed the emergence of a discourse critical to the dictatorship (Babiano 2006). While the higher echelons of the church celebrated the regime's victory over the workers' movement, activists of the *Hermandades Obreras de Acción Católica* (HOAC) (Catholic Action Workers' Brotherhoods) and *Juventudes Obreras Católicas* (JOC) (Catholic Worker Youth) promoted and disseminated the new social doctrine of the Catholic church set forth by the Second Vatican Council. Their publications expressed disapproval of the predicament of the working classes while demanding better salaries and more political freedom (De la Calle 2003). Members of these groups made contact with other sectors of the clandestine workers' movement, especially those with communist leanings. They also became involved with activists from the different groups within *Comisiones Obreras* (CCOO), a trade union which was declared illegal in 1967 but which continued to do important work and to oppose the *Sindicatos Verticales* (Ruiz 1993).

By the end of the 1960s, among increasing conflict, 'The day of St Joseph had changed from being an official festival controlled by the regime to being a clandestine celebration openly opposed to Francoism' (De la Calle 2003, p. 113). Local parishes continued to play an important role in the organization of dissidence. In response the regime resorted to force. Catholic activists suffered reprisals, their activities were prohibited and their publications were seized. At the same time it became common practice on May Day to gather in protest around the premises of the *Sindicatos Verticales*. As police action made such gatherings more and more difficult, small and well-organized groups of young people started organising *saltos* (literally, jumps), rapid and sporadic actions which mainly consisted of halting traffic in the centre of cities while chanting slogans and handing out anti-regime pamphlets. Thenceforth, and until the end of the dictatorship, these actions were combined with other small – but significant in the context of the heavy repression – subversive activities. These included brief stoppages, boycotts of transport networks and the staging of moments of silence in factory canteens (Babiano 2006; Herrerín 2010).

The Transition to Democracy, and Beyond

The first May Day after the death of the dictator did not differ much from the previous one. In May 1976 the political elites of the regime were still firmly in control, and opposition workers' organizations were still illegal; any activity that was considered subversive, public demonstrations of discontent for example, were completely banned. In Madrid the morning *saltos* were followed by a protest meeting in the afternoon at the Casa de Campo Park.

Around 5,000 people attended the call, made by *Comisiones Obreras* (Adell 1987; Babiano 2006). This attempt to revive part of the old ritual was crushed by a brutal operation by a unit of mounted police and the Guardia Civil. The statements published by the clandestine trade unions remembered their dead and wounded during the increasing number of strikes and protests. The economic crisis caused by rocketing oil prices came to aggravate the political crisis (Herrerín 2010). An important milestone in the repression was 3 March, when the clashes following a general strike in Vitoria left five dead and hundreds injured, many by police fire (Adell 1987; Sánchez-Cuenca and Aguilar 2009; Baby 2009). In 1976, the subversive celebrations of May Day mixed labour and political demands, calling for the end of the regime and its repressive policies.

The most conflict-ridden year of the period of transition to democracy, in terms of popular mobilization, was 1977 (Sánchez-Cuenca and Aguilar 2009). The progressive replacement of the political elites had not led to a significant decline in police brutality – brutality that resulted in the death of ten demonstrators (Baby 2009). In this general climate of violence, it is hardly surprising that the celebration of May Day ended in a fierce confrontation with the police. Despite the liberalization process set in motion by the new reformist government led by Adolfo Suárez – three days before 1 May, trade unions had finally been made legal – the ban on demonstrations was still in place. Other measures included the regulation and legalization of strike action (4 March) and the legalization of the Communist Party (9 April). The new conditions so created, in combination with the prospect of democratic elections, made this May Day a special occasion in terms of mobilization and an important milestone in the ongoing transformation of industrial relations.

Not all the trade unions found themselves in the same situation when the transition to democracy arrived. The CNT was very weak and to a great extent distant from the concerns and demands of a new generation of discontented workers. The UGT managed to adapt itself better to the new political context, among other reasons thanks to important international assistance (Herrerín 2004; Romanos 2011). Ahead of both, the *Comisiones Obreras* occupied a leading position with a very significant presence in the factories on the basis of its history of participation in the *Sindicato Vertical* elections. Although they differed about how to do it, the various workers' organizations all agreed on the demand to dismantle the old Francoist trade union structure, which finally happened in June 1977 (Herrerín 2010).

May Day 1978 was the first to be celebrated freely after nearly four decades of prohibition and repression. Hundreds of thousands of people took to the streets in the main cities amidst an atmosphere of great joy. The most representative unions – the CCOO and the UGT – held mass rallies in which important political leaders from the PCE (Communist Party) and the social-democratic PSOE (Socialist Party) participated (Babiano 2006). In fact, it was the politicians who made the closing speeches that day, clearly demonstrating the strong links that existed between the parties and the unions, more specifically, the CCOO with the PCE and the UGT with the PSOE. In some cities the CNT and other small unions, some of which were splinter groups of the major unions, held their own parallel demonstrations, a practice which was to be repeated in future years. Major and smaller unions also adopted a different stance with regard to the Moncloa Pacts, which had been signed in October 1977 by the government, the main parliamentary political parties, business associations and the CCOO, and ratified by parliament thereafter. These pacts aimed to achieve political stability and put an end to the economic crisis, and they are considered to be as crucial as the enactment of the Constitution of 1978 – and even its social and economic foundation – in the overall process of restoration of democracy via negotiation.[11] Eventually, the UGT followed in the wake of the PSOE and endorsed the pacts, but the CNT rejected them out of hand and continued to do so thereafter.

Political leaders played a less prominent role in the demonstrations organized by the major unions in following years. The UGT and CCOO operated in coordination until the victory of the PSOE in the 1982 general election. Thenceforth, for several years, the UGT closed ranks with the new government, while the CCOO distanced itself from both. The demands posed on May Day were still focused on unemployment, although other issues were also on the agenda, for example the end of terrorism. In 1985 and 1986 the CCOO campaigned against Spain's membership in NATO (it had been a member since 1982). The large unions joined forces again in 1988 for a general strike, followed by 90 per cent of the country's workforce. The strike was called after the growing estrangement of the UGT and PSOE, due to the social, labour and economic policies of Felipe Gonzalez's socialist government. The government measures included a reduction in old-age pensions, cheaper severance pay for firms and legislation in favour of the creation of low-quality jobs for young people. In the following year, the *Confederación General del Trabajo* (CGT), which had been created as an offshoot of the old anarcho-syndicalist CNT, joined in the celebrations organized by the large trade unions on May Day. The joint celebration continues to the present day.

Seen in perspective, participation in the 'workers' festival' has declined over the years. In the years of transition to democracy, after Franco's death, trade unions were capable of staging a million-strong demonstration. In the 1980s, attendance fell to hundreds of thousands, and in the 1990s and 2000s, to tens of thousands. The current demands are for more, and better, jobs, peace (both at home and abroad), the strengthening of international solidarity and, in more recent years, the construction of a social Europe, as opposed to a market-dominated Europe (Babiano 2006; Herrerín 2010).

With the consolidation of democracy, May Day in Spain progressively assumed the same role that it played in most Western societies, and it reflected a less mobilized society. The occasion is now a largely institutionalized celebration. However, the recent challenge to traditional trade unionism – and the concept of representation itself – launched by the so-called *indignados* movement (also known as the 15M movement) has added a new dimension to social mobilization. Traditionally, parties and trade unions transformed in response to cyclical waves of criticism from below, and this is often a reflection of the tensions between different notions of democracy (della Porta 2013, p. 53). The mobilization of the *indignados* may be regarded as a new stage within this sequence, as a challenge to the prevalent system of political representation and a demand for more internal democracy within the institutions that support it. Only time will tell whether the demands for more democracy and the adoption of the deliberative model by the *indignados* will have a lasting impact on the structure of trade unions, their strategies and forms of action.

Notes

1 The *Federación de Resistencia al Capital* was created in Barcelona in 1888 when several local groups merged. It replaced the previous Spanish branch of the First International.
2 Cited in Lucea 2009, p. 149. For this author, given the Socialists' moderate, 'ordered' and 'domesticated' attitude towards the celebrations, May Day was not a cause for concern during the early years of the twentieth century (pp. 156 and 166).
3 This included the passing of the *Ley de Accidentes del Trabajo* (Work Accidents Act) and the regulation of child and female labour in factories, both in 1900, the creation of the *Instituto de Reformas Sociales* (Institute for Social Reform) in 1903 and the passing of the *Ley de Descanso Dominical* (Sunday Rest Act) in 1904 (Herrerín 2010).
4 Although there was an anti-belligerent minority, the bulk of the Spanish socialist movement was pro-Triple Entente. As the left-wing bourgeois parties, socialists saw World War I as a 'war of ideals' between two radically different worlds: 'the old world of tradition, barbarity, hate, despotisms', in the Central Powers' case, and the modern world of 'civilization, equality, popular rights, freedom' as in the Allies' case (*El Socialista*, 12 September 1914, p. 1). While important controversies about this issue occurred across the heterogeneous anarchist movement, its main position remained anti-belligerent and pacifist (Meaker 1974; Forcadell 1978).
5 The 'Tragic Week' is what historians call the series of bloody confrontations which took place mainly in Barcelona, in late July 1909, between the Spanish army and the Catalan working classes backed by anarchists, republicans and socialists. The origins are found in the calling-up of reserve troops for the war in Morocco, and it resulted in an eruption of riots, strikes and burnings of convents. After a week of fighting, the army crushed the revolt, resulting in dozens of deaths.
6 Data come from the main newspapers between 1900 and 1930 and refer to the number and types of events organized on May Day (Rivas 1987, p. 183).
7 In the period 1900–1930 the number of strikes connected with May Day in Catalonia (1,257) and Barcelona (1,048) is more than double those launched, for example, in Castilla la Nueva (567) and Madrid (462).
8 See, for example, Archivo Histórico Provincial de Zaragoza, 'Responsabilidades Políticas', files 5621/2164, 5781/24, 5940/20, 5577/6, 5787/10, 5541/4, 5633/1, 5531/8, 5538/3 and 5563/12; Archivo del Juzgado Togado Militar n° 32, Procedimientos sumarísimos, files 454/4 and 1814/4.
9 FET-JONS, Sección Femenina de FET y de las JONS, Madrid, n.d., cited in Molinero 2005, p. 50, and Box 2008, p. 229.
10 *Boletín Oficial del Estado*, 27 April 1956.

11 Along with the approval of various civil and political rights which would be reinforced by the constitution of 1978 (assembly, expression and political and union
association, among others), the Pacts mainly implied a plan of economic stabilization and inflation control. It included measures such as the devaluation of the
peseta, a limit to wage increases on the basis of the predicted inflation rates and a
stricter monetary policy.

References

Acín, R. (1921). Otra procesión. *Lucha Social* (Lérida), 30 April, 2.
Adell, R. (1987). *La transición política en la calle: Manifestaciones políticas de grupos y masas, Madrid 1976–1987*, 2 vols. Madrid: Universidad Complutense.
Aguilar, P. (2008). *Políticas de la memoria y memorias de la política. El caso español en perspectiva comparada.* Madrid: Alianza.
Álvarez Junco, J. (1976). *La ideología política del anarquismo español (1868–1910).* Madrid: Siglo XXI.
Álvarez Junco, J. (1986). El anarquismo en la España contemporánea. *Anales de Historia Contemporánea*, 5, 189–200.
Azaña, M. (1978). *Memorias políticas y de guerra*, 2 vols. Barcelona: Crítica.
Babiano, J. (2006). *1 de Mayo: Historia y significado.* Albacete, Spain: Altabán.
Baby, S. (2009). Estado y violencia en la transición española. In S. Baby, O. Compagnon and E. González Calleja (Eds), *Violencia y transiciones políticas a finales del siglo XX* (pp. 179–198). Madrid: Casa de Velázquez.
Bar, A. (1981). *La CNT en los años rojo: Del sindicalismo revolucionario al anarcosindicalismo (1910–1926).* Madrid: Akal.
Barrio, Á. (1988). *Anarquismo y anarcosindicalismo en Asturias, 1890–1936.* Madrid: Siglo XXI.
Bowers, C. (1977). *Misión en España. En el umbral de la Segunda Guerra Mundial (1933–1939).* Barcelona: Grijalbo [*My Mission to Spain.* New York: Simon & Schuster, 1954].
Box, Z. (2008). La Fundación de un régimen. La construcción simbólica del franquismo. Unpublished PhD thesis, Universidad Complutense de Madrid.
Buenacasa, M. (1926). Respuesta [IV]. *La Protesta* (Buenos Aires), 240, 13 September, 13.
Casanova, J. (2005). *Anarchism, the Republic, and Civil War in Spain, 1931–1939.* London: Routledge.
Castillo, S. (1986). Organización y acción política del PSOE hasta 1900. In S. Juliá (Ed.), *El socialismo en España: Desde la fundación del PSOE hasta 1975.* Madrid: Editorial Pablo Iglesias, 9–34.
Castillo, S. (2008). *Historia de la UGT. 1: Un sindicalismo consciente, 1873–1914.* Madrid: Siglo XXI.
Castro, D. (1989). Agitación y orden en la Restauración. 'Fin del ciclo revolucionario'? *Historia Social*, 5, 37–49.
Cruz, R. (1998). El mitin y el motín. La acción colectiva y los movimientos sociales en la España del siglo XX. *Historia Social*, 31, 137–152.
Cruz, R. (2006). *En el nombre del pueblo. República, rebelión y guerra en la España de 1936.* Madrid: Siglo XXI.
Cruz, R. (2008). *Repertorios: La política del enfrentamiento en el siglo XX.* Madrid: CIS.
Cruz, R. (2014). *Una revolución elegante: España, 1931.* Madrid: Alianza.

De la Calle, Mª.D. (1989). *La Comisión de Reformas Sociales, 1883–1903. Política social y conflicto de intereses en la España de la Restauración.* Madrid: Ministerio de Trabajo y Seguridad Social.

De la Calle, Mª.D. (2003). El Primero de Mayo y su transformación en San José Artesano. *Ayer,* 51, 87–113.

De Luis, F. (1994). *Cincuenta años de cultura obrera en España, 1890–1940.* Madrid: Fundación Pablo Iglesias.

De Répide, P. (1913). La nueva pascua. *El Socialista* [Madrid], 1 May, 1.

della Porta, D. (2013). *Can Democracy Be Saved?.* Cambridge: Polity.

della Porta, D., and Diani, M. (2006). *Social Movements: An Introduction.* Malden, MA: Blackwell.

Forcadell, C. (1978). *Parlamentarismo y bolchevización. El movimiento obrero español, 1914–1918.* Barcelona: Crítica.

Gaziel (1931). El problema español por excelencia. *La Vanguardia* (Barcelona), 1 May, 5.

Gil Andrés, C. (2000). *Echarse a la calle. Amotinados, huelguistas y revolucionarios (La Rioja, 1890–1936).* Zaragoza: Prensas Universitarias de Zaragoza.

González Calleja, E. (1998). *La razón de la fuerza. Orden público, subversión y violencia política en la España de la Restauración (1875–1917).* Madrid: CSIC.

González Calleja, E. (1999). *El máuser y el sufragio. Orden público, subversión y violencia política en la España de la Restauración (1917–1931).* Madrid: CSIC.

Guereña, J-L. (1986). Del anti-dos de mayo al Primero de Mayo: Aspectos del internacionalismo en el movimiento obrero español. *Estudios de Historia Social,* 38–39, 91–104.

Guereña, J-L. (1999–2000). Les fêtes du 2 de mai ou la fondation d'une nation. *Bulletin d'Histoire Contemporaine d'Espagne,* 30–31, 31–47.

Herrerín, Á. (2004). *La CNT durante el franquismo: Clandestinidad y exilio.* Madrid: Siglo XXI.

Herrerín, Á. (2008). España: La propaganda por la represión, 1892–1900. In J. Aviles and A. Herrerín (Eds), *El nacimiento del terrorismo en Occidente: Anarquía, nihilismo y violencia revolucionaria* (pp. 103–140). Madrid: Siglo XX.

Herrerín, Á. (2010). De la lucha por la revolución a la defensa de los derechos: El 1º de Mayo en España a través de sus manifiestos. In L. Rivas (Ed.), *1890–2010. El 1º de Mayo en España: 120 aniversario* (pp. 69–94). Madrid: Fundación 1º de Mayo.

Hobsbawm, E. (1959). *Primitive Rebels: Studies in Archaic Forms of Social Movements in the 19th and 20th Centuries.* Manchester: Manchester University Press.

Juliá, S. (1984). *Madrid 1931–1934: De la fiesta popular a la lucha de clases.* Madrid: Siglo XXI.

Ledesma, J.L. (2013). La 'primavera trágica' de 1936 y la pendiente hacia la guerra civil. In F. Sánchez (Ed.), *Los mitos del 18 de julio* (pp. 313–339). Barcelona: Crítica.

Lorenzo, J.M. (1988). *Rebelión en la ría. Vizcaya, 1947: Obreros, empresarios y falangistas.* Bilbao: Universidad de Deusto.

Lucea, V. (2009). *El pueblo en movimiento. La protesta social en Aragón (1885–1917).* Zaragoza: Prensas Universitarias de Zaragoza.

Majuelo, E. (1989). *Lucha de clases en Navarra (1931–1936).* Pamplona: Gobierno de Navarra.

Meaker, G.H. (1974). *Revolutionary Left in Spain, 1914–1923.* Stanford, CA: Stanford University Press.

Molinero, C. (2005.) *La captación de las masas. Política social y propaganda en el régimen franquista.* Madrid: Cátedra.

Molinero, C., and Ysàs, P. (1998). *Productores disciplinados y minorías subversivas: Clase obrera y conflictividad laboral en la España franquista.* Madrid: Siglo XXI.

Núñez, F. (1910). La pascua obrera. *El Socialista* [Madrid], 1 May, 2.

Núñez Florencio, R. (1983). *El terrorismo anarquista (1888–1909).* Madrid: Siglo XXI.

Pérez Ledesma, M. (1987). *El obrero consciente.* Madrid: Alianza.

Pérez Ledesma, M. (1993). La cultura socialista en los años veinte. In J.L. García Delgado (Ed.), *Los orígenes de la II República* (pp. 182–192). Madrid: Siglo XXI.

Pérez Ledesma, M. (1998). El estado y la movilización social en el siglo XIX español. In S. Castillo and J.M. Ortiz de Orruño (Eds), *Estado, protesta y movimientos sociales* (pp. 215–231). Bilbao: Universidad del País Vasco.

Pérez Ledesma, M. (2007). The formation of the working class: A cultural creation. In J.A. Piqueras and V. Sanz Rozalén (Eds), *A Social History of Spanish Labour: New Perspectives on Class, Politics and Gender* (pp. 19–42). New York: Berghahn.

Radcliff, P.B. (2004). *De la movilización a la Guerra Civil. Historia política y social de Gijón (1900–1937).* Barcelona: Debate. [*From Mobilization to Civil War: The Politics of Polarization in the Spanish City of Gijón (1900–1937).* Cambridge: Cambridge University Press.]

Richards, M. (1998). *A Time of Silence: Civil War and the Culture of Repression in Franco's Spain, 1936–1945.* New York: Cambridge University Press.

Rivas, L. (1986). El Primero de Mayo, jornada obrera, 1890–1930. *Estudios de Historia Social,* 38–39, 271–337.

Rivas, L. (1987). *Historia del Primero de Mayo en España desde 1900 hasta la II República.* Madrid: UNED.

Rivas, L. (1988). Actitud del gobierno ante el Primero de Mayo, desde 1890 hasta la Segunda República. *Espacio, Tiempo y Forma. Serie V. Historia Contemporánea,* 1, 89–118.

Rivas, L. (1990). Ritualización socialista del 1º de Mayo: Fiesta, huelga, manifestación? *Historia Contemporánea,* 3, 45–57.

Rivas, L. (2010a). El doble origen del 1º de Mayo: La celebración del primer 1º de Mayo en España. In L. Rivas (Ed.), *1890–2010. El 1º de Mayo en España: 120 aniversario* (pp. 19–42). Madrid: Fundación 1º de Mayo.

Rivas, L. (2010b). Las organizaciones obreras, la celebración del 1º de Mayo y la configuración de un ritual: Análisis de las actividades del 1º de Mayo y su significado. In L. Rivas (Ed.), *1890–2010. El 1º de Mayo en España: 120 aniversario* (pp. 43–68). Madrid: Fundación 1º de Mayo.

Rodríguez Calleja, M. (1998). La celebración republicana, socialista y anarquista del Primero de Mayo. Tres casos concretos: Mataró, Barcelona, Manresa. In S. Castillo and J. Ortiz de Orruño (Eds), *Estado, protesta y movimientos sociales* (pp. 575–579). Bilbao: Universidad del País Vasco.

Romanos, E. (2011). Factionalism in transition: A comparison of ruptures in the Spanish anarchist movement. *Journal of Historical Sociology,* 24(3), 355–380.

Ruiz, D. (Ed.). (1993). *Historia de Comisiones Obreras (1958–1988).* Madrid: Siglo XXI.

Salazar, F. (1900). Entre las grandes solemnidades. *El Socialista* [Madrid], 1 May, 2.

Sánchez-Cuenca, I., and Aguilar, P. (2009). Violencia política y movilización social en la transición español. In S. Baby, O. Compagnon and E. González Calleja (Eds), *Violencia y transiciones políticas a finales del siglo XX* (pp. 95–111). Madrid: Casa de Velázquez.

Serrano, C. (1986). *El Socialista* ante el Primero de Mayo. *Estudios de Historia Social,* 38–39, 105–119.

Smith, A. (2007). *Anarchism, Revolution and Reaction: Catalan Labor and the Crisis of the Spanish State, 1898–1923*. New York: Berghahn.

Tarrow, S. (1994). *Power in Movement. Social Movements, Collective Action, and Politics.* Cambridge: Cambridge University Press.

Tilly, C. (1978). *From Mobilization to Revolution*. New York: McGraw-Hill.

Tilly, C. (1986). *La France conteste de 1600 à nos jours*. Paris: Fayard.

Turcato, D. (2011). Collective action, opacity, and the 'problem of irrationality': Anarchism and the first of May, 1890–1892. *Journal for the Study of Radicalism,* 5,1, 1–32.

Unamuno, M. (1907). 21 de abril–1° de Mayo. *El Socialista* [Madrid], 1 May, 2.

Vargas-Golarons, R. (1990). La huelga del Primero de Mayo de 1951 en Cataluña. In J. Tusell, A. Alted and A. Mateos (Eds), *La oposición al régimen de Franco* (pp. 22–42). Madrid: UNED.

6 May Day in Britain

Chris Wrigley

May Day demonstrations have been categorized by Eric Hobsbawm as an example of 'an invented tradition', one intended to validate and give some added authority to the growing labour movements around the world (see Chapter 1). But, as he also emphasized, labour movements have drawn on old traditions, especially of manual labour. Britain is notable for having long traditions of radical political movements which included the advanced views that surfaced during the civil war of the 1640s and the mass working-class politics of Chartism of the late 1830s and 1840s. The May Day demonstrations not surprisingly built on these traditions. The demonstrations also benefited from the liberal attitudes in Britain to peaceful demonstrations, a marked contrast to the repression in Austria, Germany and, above all, tsarist Russia. However, there were limits to tolerance. London police harried with vigour the many anarchists in a small demonstration held in London on 1 May 1890 (Wrigley 2015). However, in Britain anarchism had far less support than in Spain (see Chapter 5) and France, and it mostly troubled the authorities in London in the 1890s (Quail 1978).

The causes proclaimed by the British May Day demonstrators changed with changing political circumstances. But there was much more to the May Day demonstrations than the particular causes of the moment. In themselves, especially early on, the May Day events were powerful symbols of the burgeoning confidence and aspirations of a rising class. From the outset, Eric Hobsbawm has argued, the May Day commemorations became 'a highly charged festival and rite' and were 'perhaps the most ambitious of labour rituals'. He added that May Day 'was the ritual of class, community, struggle and union' (Hobsbawm and Ranger 1984, pp. 283–286; Hobsbawm 1984, pp. 69 and 76–80).

The May Day demonstrations not only advertised the May Day causes but also in effect invited those watching to support labour in its struggles. Moreover, as Pfaff and Yang have argued, when writing of rituals, 'Participation in politically alternative rituals may serve purposes of "re-identification"; helping to create and renew commitment, solidarity and identity among the movement's participants themselves.' They further commented of the May Day events that 'They evoke, generate and communicate the important sense of collective memory that sustains movement participation .... They help to marshal the past in support of present and future goals' (Pfaff and Yang 2001, pp. 554 and 579–580; cf. Chapter 1).

May Days before World War I

In the British early 1890s May Day demonstrations, the past that was mobilized for the present included both British and French radical memories. In the smaller 1890 London May Day demonstration held on 1 May the newspaper reports mentioned 'a flag party carrying red flags mounted with caps of liberty' and a 'band in uniform with red caps'. This band and those on the huge Sunday 4 May demonstration played the 'Marseillaise', as did a band which accompanied 6,000 May Day marchers in Leeds that year. The 'Marseillaise' continued to be played at some British May Days until at least 1905 (*Economist*, 3 May 1890; Wrigley 2009, pp. 77–93). Homage was also paid to the heroes and heroines of the Commune by having Louise Michel as a speaker at the 1892 and 1896 Hyde Park May Day demonstrations, while Leo Melliet, mayor of the 13th arrondissement during the Commune, spoke at the Glasgow May Day demonstration in 1895. Louise Michel spoke in French, her presence attracting many of the anarchists in the 1892 demonstration. Other prominent French speakers in London included in 1890 Paul Lafargue, Marx's son-in-law, and in 1896 Marcel Sembat, an independent socialist deputy (*Manchester Examiner and Times*, 2 May 1892; *Leicester Daily Mercury*, 2 May 1892).

There had been a long connection between radical and socialist French republicanism and advanced radical opinion in Britain due to French com-munities, including exiles who left France in 1848, 1849, 1851 and 1856, in London (and to a lesser extent Nottingham and Jersey) as well as an esti-mated 3,500 men, women and children from the Paris Commune who lived in England between 1871 and the amnesty of 1880 (Martinez 1981, pp. 54 and 73). The *Daily Mail* and other right-wingers of the British press liked to emphasize that foreigners were involved in demonstrations. At the time of the British anti-immigrant campaigns of the 1890s and early 1900s aimed particularly at poor Jewish people leaving tsarist Russia, which led to the Aliens Act, August 1905, the *Daily Mail* chose to emphasize 'aliens' at May Day events. Its 1901 list of foreigners at the London May Day celebration in Crystal Palace began with 'Groups of Jews and Jewesses' and its 1904 cover-age of the Hyde Park gathering was headed, 'Alien Labour in the Park' (*Daily Mail*, 2 May 1901 and 2 May 1904).

Internationalism was a key theme from 1 May 1890. Then, in London, there were banners with 'Workers of the World Unite' in English, French and German as well as 'Workers of the World We Hail You As Brothers', 'Those Who Do Not Celebrate This Day Are Slaves', 'No Master, High or Low' and 'Away with Authority and Monopoly! Free Access to the means of life' (*Commonwealth*, 10 May 1890; *Star*, 2 May 1890). The London demonstration on 1 May was notable for the presence of refugee anarchists, many of whom were linked to the Socialist League. The early mass Sunday May Days had an array of anarchist celebrities as speakers, including the French Michel, the Russians Kropotkin and Stepniak, the Italian Enrico Malatesta and the Dutch Domela Nieuwenhuis, all of whom were political refugees in London for varying lengths of time.

French revolutionary imagery, along with classical and much else, was used by Walter Crane in his May Day and other labour movement illustrations. Crane was the pre-eminent artist of the early May Days. Crane drew two major poster-size cartoons in honour of the Communards: 'Vive la Commune' (*Commonwealth*, March 1888) and 'In Memory of the Paris Commune' (*Black and White*, March 1891), as well as May Day cartoons for 1891, 1894 and 1895, all with Marianne figures each wearing a cap of liberty (Crane 1896, pp. 5, 7, 8, 9 and 11; Crane 1907). Crane's May Day designs were copied on labour movement banners and posters around the world (Panaccione 1989).

Places and Spaces

May Day demonstrations also drew on past radical associations with places. There was a powerful symbolism of place. In London the major May Day demonstrations between 1890 and 1906 (other than those of 1900 and 1901, held at Crystal Palace) were held in Hyde Park. Hyde Park had been the scene of parliamentary reform meetings in 1866–1867, and the socialist platforms in 1890 and after were erected beside the Reformers' Tree, burnt down in an 1866 demonstration. Hyde Park had also been the location of protest meetings against repression in Ireland, with 80,000 present at a meeting in June 1882. The Reformers' Tree was the location of regular Sunday meetings held by the Social Democratic Federation (Lee and Archbold 1933, p. 66). Similarly the May Day demonstrations in Glasgow, Edinburgh and Newcastle upon Tyne were arranged at favourite radical places (Glasgow Green and East Meadows, Edinburgh). In Sittingbourne, Kent, the 1891 May Day rally convened at the Rock estate, described in the local press as 'the favourite parade ground of trade unionists during the bargemen's strike and lockout of boilermakers twelve months ago' (*East Kent Gazette*, 2 and 9 May 1891). In Newcastle upon Tyne the large demonstration on the Sunday was in the Bigg Market (the barley market), a traditional place for radical demonstrations (*The Times*, 4 May 1891).

Linked to the choice of places with past radical connotations for the May Day rallies was the symbolism of marchers penetrating other classes' spaces. In London marchers gathered at traditional radical meeting points such as Clerkenwell Green in the East End, the Prince's Head, Battersea and Trafalgar Square in central London. They marched from working-class areas through the West End, something that made the London propertied classes nervous, especially after rioting in 'aristocratic' streets near Hyde Park in July 1855 and the damage to property in the Piccadilly, Hyde Park, Grosvenor Square area that had followed an unemployed demonstration in Trafalgar Square and jeers from young men in the Carlton Club in February 1886 (Maccoby 1938, pp. 46–47; Gilbert 1966, pp. 32–37). Rural labour made its presence felt by parading through the regional urban centres. In Britain this was so in Norwich on 3 May 1891, when large contingents of Norfolk labourers marched in triumph through the city centre (*Argus*, 5 May 1891).

Trade Union Presence

While May Day symbolism was strong in encouraging enthusiasm for May Day demonstrations, a crucial factor in large demonstrations was whether the demonstrations had trade union support. In London on 1 May 1890 socialist and anarchist purity failed to secure a mass mobilization, as William Morris and the Socialist League found out. While the anarchists were not as strong as in France and other parts of Europe, they had a notable presence in London, Walsall and a few other places in Britain in the 1890s (Quail 1978; Oliver 1983). In contrast the May Day demonstration on the Sunday was massive, at 200,000–300,000 people, perhaps the largest ever demonstration in London. Its size was due to Eleanor Marx and her associates securing the support of the primarily Lib-Lab London Trades Council (Thompson 1955; Kapp 1976; Quail 1978, p. 90). From the reports of the banners at the early British May Days it seems that the mass support came from the rapidly growing 'New Unions', and built on the enthusiasm generated by successful strikes in the London and other docks, the gas works and the match-stick makers. In London there was a series of huge May Day demonstrations on the first Sunday in May when these had the support of the London Trades Council. Similarly in Edinburgh in 1893 there were 5,000 people in the procession and big crowds along the route when the Edinburgh Trades Council backed May Day, but only 400–500 when it did not. In Northampton in 1890, 10,000 people joined the May Day demonstration when it was backed by Northampton Trades Council, but only 500 did so when the support was lacking. In the early 1890s Norwich, Chatham and Hull trades councils made a similar significant difference in support (*Edinburgh Evening News*, 5 May 1890; *Northampton Daily Reporter*, 5 May 1890; *Argus*, 4 May 1891; *Leicester Daily Post*, 2 May 1892; *The Times*, 5 May 1890, 4 May 1891, 8 May 1893 and 7 May 1894).

Support for May Days was further strengthened by people on strike. May Day demonstrations provided a public stage on which to air industrial griev-ances. The 1 May 1890 London demonstration included women on strike at the Clerkenwell envelope factory who collected money as they marched. In Norwich in 1891 shoemakers had just ended a strike and bricklayers were just beginning one. In general often those organizing May Day demonstrations did so by mobilizing workplaces, and for employers, support for May Day at their workplaces gave an indicator of worker dissatisfaction with their pay and/or working conditions.

Children

A feature of many British May Days was a large number of children present, quite often from Socialist Sunday Schools. For the children the May Day rallies provided a vivid experience of socialist solidarity with the older generations. For the other marchers, the children represented the socialist future, or at least the beneficiaries of it. The children also represented continuity, as in life generally; they were the older generation's replacements. They complemented the strong sense of continuity, with old Chartists present at the early May Days, and among the refugees in London demonstrations were men and women of 1848 as well as Communards of 1871.

Mass May Day Support

In the period 1890–1914 the most notable feature of the British May Days was the massive size of the first Sunday in May demonstrations in London in 1890–1894. Thereafter the London May Days fell back in size, at least until shortly before World War I. The figures for the crowds at Hyde Park depend on the newspapers' estimates and occasional police estimates. The sheer size of those in 1890, 1891, 1892, 1893 and 1894 made the numbers attending exceedingly difficult to estimate. The reporter from *The Times* in 1892 (7 May) wrote that the demonstrators in Hyde Park were 'in numbers which are beyond the reach of accurate estimate' and added that it was 'one of the largest, if not the very largest, which has ever been collected', while also commenting on the thousands and hundreds of thousands who had gathered on the Thames Embankment for the start of the processions. In 1890 the reporter from the *Manchester Guardian* observed, 'Nobody estimated the gathering ... at anything less than a quarter of a million, and if anybody guessed half a million, it would be impossible to say that he was wrong' (5 May 1890). Michael Davitt, one of the speakers, did assert that half a million people were present, while another speaker, John Burns, simply asserted that the demonstration was 'the greatest of modern times'.

The Sunday 4 May 1890 demonstration was somewhat smaller than that of 1892, but it surprised Europe that the largest May Day demonstration should be in Britain. In 1891 the Sunday demonstration was again vast, with a report stating that it took two hours for the procession to pass any point on its route. The *Manchester Guardian*'s report gave an estimate of 100,000 people in the procession and a further 100,000 in Hyde Park. Quite possibly the 1892 demonstration, when 1 May fell on a Sunday, was the largest of the five massive London demonstrations of 1890–1895. This time the author of the *Manchester Guardian* report (2 May) confessed, 'I have not the slightest idea how many people joined in the procession. The head of it arrived in Hyde Park shortly before three o'clock, and the extreme tail had not reached Buckingham Palace more than two hours later. Roughly speaking, the procession was about two miles long.' There was a large crowd in Hyde Park, many of whom 'showed by ribbons and badges that they were sympathisers'. The Sunday demonstrations of 1893 and 1894 were also large. In 1893 the procession arriving via Piccadilly entered Hyde Park from 2.30 p.m. until nearly 4 p.m. However, there were smaller crowds around the platforms.

Perhaps the surprise is not that the huge Sunday May Day rallies ended after 1894 but rather that the organizers succeeded in bringing together two groups whose views were essentially antagonistic. The very considerable size depended much on the London Trades Council's support, and this was secured in 1890 by Tom Mann, the radical trade unionist and a hero of the 1889 London dock strike, convincing the trades council to agree to the objective of the eight-hour workday and not to allow differences over the means of securing it (by collective bargaining or legislation) prevent participation. Even so, the London Trades Council's supporters marched separately to Hyde Park and listened to different speakers. In 1891 the Amalgamated Society of Carpenters and Joiners had their own May Day march on Saturday 2 May, stating that they 'repudiate socialist sympathies'. In 1893 both the Trades Council's supporters and the Eight Hour Working Day Committee's supporters still gathered at the Thames Embankment, but they followed different routes to Hyde Park and entered at different entrances (from Piccadilly and in by Marble Arch). The success of the early years also depended on the Socialist Democratic Federation being willing to organize for the first Sunday in May, thereby not requiring trade unionists to strike on May Day. However the second (Brussells, 1891) and third (Zurich, 1893) meetings of the Second International called on all countries to mark May Day on 1 May and called for strikes wherever possible (Labour Research Department 1929, pp. 5–6). The SDF followed this directive for May 1895.

The press reports give often reliable indications of the organizations involved in the major Sunday May Day demonstrations. The London Trades Council contingent in 1893 was in eight large sections: (1) shipping, (2) printing and paper, (3) leather, (4) metal, (5) general, (6) cabinet and fancy, (7) clothing and (8) building trades. In contrast the Legal Eight Hours Committee supporters were made up of large numbers of New Unionists, many from the various radical bodies (who were the left wing of the Gladstonian Liberal Party) and various socialists. In addition it was noted that there were a large number of French, German and Italian workers, and one platform was given to those speaking in foreign languages (*The Times*, 8 May 1893; Thorne 1925, p. 117).

The massive demonstrations in Britain were doomed when the socialists insisted that the demonstration should be on May Day, not on the first Sunday in May. At the time of the Sunday 1894 demonstration the SDF was emphatic that demonstrating on the first Sunday 'did not come within the meaning of the resolution passed at the International Socialist Congress at Zurich calling upon the ' "workers of the world" to demonstrate on the 1st of May', a point emphasized the following year (*The Times*, 2 May 1895). The outcome in 1895 was a small turnout on Wednesday 1

May, with women and children comprising a major portion of the marchers from the Thames Embankment to Hyde Park, with heavy rain soaking
them on the way and greatly diminishing the number of listeners for Tom
Mann, William Morris, Eleanor Marx Aveling, Henry Hyndman and other
socialist speakers. On Sunday 5 May, when there was no need for working
people to go on strike to be able to attend, there were larger audiences at
the nine platforms to hear the predominantly trade unionist speakers, but
the demonstration was judged to have been 'much reduced in comparison
with those of previous years'. This had been anticipated, with the platforms
placed in the shape of a horseshoe and so the crowds were confined in a
smaller space. In 1896 there were six platforms in Hyde Park, near Marble
Arch, each with 600–700 people listening to the array of SDF, anarchist
and New Union speakers (*The Times*, 2, 6 May 1895 and 2 May 1896). Of
the 1897 Hyde Park demonstration, the *Daily Mail* (3 May) commented,
'The police estimate the attendance at 8,000. The organisers of the meeting put it variously from 20,000 to 35,000.' The reporter thought that there
were fewer people present than usual as it was a Saturday, and the work-
men could not go home after a morning's work and return with their wives.
In 1899, the march to Hyde Park was made up of SDF supporters and
trade unionists, with a band leading marchers, 20 brakes (carriages) full
of men, women and children and some 20 bands from the Embankment
(*Daily Mail*, 2 May 1899).

The reduced numbers at May Day demonstrations from the mid-1890s
were also due to the decline in trade union membership in economically
adverse times. The economic boom in which unions had mushroomed ended
in late 1891. British trade union membership fell from 1,468,000 in 1892
to 1,388,000 in 1895, a drop of 5.4 per cent (Bain and Price 1980, p. 39).
However a feature of this fall was the collapse or near collapse of some of
the New Unions representing unskilled workers. The New Unions had been
among the most conspicuous groups at May Day rallies throughout Britain,
as well as supporting the Legal Eight Hours Committee's part in London
demonstrations. Figures for New Union affiliation to the Trades Union
Congress (TUC) suggest that by 1892 the New Unions had fallen to just
under 40 per cent of their 1890 size, and by 1896 they had fallen further to 25
per cent, before recovering to about a third of the 1890 figure by 1900 (Clegg,
Fox and Thompson 1964, p. 83).

There was also a feeling among the Lib-Lab trade unionists, who were the
more moderate of those marching to Hyde Park, that parliament was beginning to act. In 1893 it was noted by the *Manchester Guardian* (8 May) that
'The keynote of most speeches was that the battle was won.' Whereas 'the
principle of the Eight Hours Bill had been rejected by the late Parliament,
[it had been] affirmed by a considerable majority in the present Parliament'.
Gladstone had been returned to office in 1892, and in 1893 parliament
had passed a motion that supported the principle of an eight-hour day in
coalmines.

Cultural Celebrations

The London May Days broke away from being centred on the usual march across central London to Hyde Park after 1899. These events could be attended in the evening by those unwilling to go on strike. In 1900 and 1901 the London May Day celebrations were held on 1 May (weekdays) at the Crystal Palace. These moved the social element of May Days literally to centre stage. *The Times* judged the 1900 celebration to have been 'one of the most successful since the demonstrations started'. Nearly 150 bodies associated with the London Trades Council or the SDF were involved in the event. There was a day-long programme of high-quality entertainment, with George Bernard Shaw commenting very favourably on the performance of his three-act play *Widowers' Houses* (Lawrence 1972, pp. 165–166). Other diversions included comedians, dancing round a maypole, a ballad concert, cycling and athletics. In the afternoon there was an array of speakers on six platforms along the terrace. Two motions were moved. One expressed international fraternal greetings and the desirability of the cooperative commonwealth. The other motion contained both social and political demands, calling not only for the eight-hour day by legislation, the free maintenance of all children in the public sector of education (as opposed to fee-paying private education in the 'public schools'), the abolition of child labour, decent working-class housing and old-age pensions, but also demanding universal adult suffrage, the second ballot, wages for MPs and payment of MPs' election expenses. In the evening there were speeches by Henry Hyndman, James McDonald, Emile Vinek (Belgian Labour Party) and Julius Motteler (SPD). The day ended with a fireworks display which featured a set piece by Walter Crane that depicted the angel of liberty holding hands with representatives of labour (*Morning Post*, 2 May 1900; *The Times*, 2 May 1900).

At the Crystal Palace 1901 there were entertainments again, including a gymkhana, wrestling and roller-skating, but no maypole dancing. In the evening there was another high-quality play, Gerhardt Hauptmann's 1892 five-act drama, *The Weavers*, on the Silesian weavers' revolt against industrialization in 1844. There were also children singing on themes of liberty and labour. The afternoon and evening speakers included Henry Hyndman, leading New Unionists Tom Mann, Ben Tillett and Pete Curran, as well as G.N. Barnes, general-secretary of the Amalgamated Society of Engineers. Probably the entertainment proved too popular and the speakers attracted fewer people than in Hyde Park. For the more committed socialists the entertainment diluted the message of a day celebrating international socialism. There was a procession with banners in 1901, but it would not have been as inspiring as the marches from the Embankment to Hyde Park (*Daily Mail*, 2 May 1901). The Crystal Palace-style meetings were soon dropped for a return to the processions to Hyde Park.

The Pre-World War I Demonstrations

While the Edwardian London May Day demonstrations were no longer the massive events of those in Hyde Park in the early 1890s, they were still large. After the huge London May Day demonstrations of the early to mid-1890s, there are seldom estimates in the newspapers or other sources of the numbers present at May Days, other than comments on the crowds being larger or smaller than previous years. The 1904 demonstration was judged to be 'decidedly the largest for many years, because, doubtless, May Day this year fell on a Sunday' (*Daily Mail*, 2 May 1904). It was also helped by the magnificent weather. As well as the usual procession from the Embankment setting off at 3.30 p.m., contingents from Paddington, Willesden and Harlesden marched direct to Hyde Park. At 5.00 p.m., some 50 speeches were given from six platforms. The first platform had Socialist Sunday School Union children singing, followed by speakers well known for working with the Sunday schools. Four platforms had leading trade unionists such as Ben Tillett and Harry Orbell, three shop assistants' leaders and SDF speakers. The sixth platform was the International platform, with Friedrich Lessner and Herr Weingartz (in German), Wladyslaw Sikorski (Polish), C. Van Brussells (French), S. Elchtewyn (Yiddish) and C. Beck (Russian) (*Daily Mail*, 2 May 1904; *Programme of May Day Demonstration in Hyde Park on Sunday May 1st*, 1904). The next year the demonstration was smaller, more dependent on SDF support. At the rear of the procession there were brakes in which children sang. In Hyde Park there were seven platforms. One, on which there were children, had mostly women speaking. Two others had speeches mostly in Yiddish. At the international platform, speeches were made by representatives of the Polish Socialist Party and the Communist Club (*The Times*, 2 May 1905). Again in 1906 a feature of the march was the presence of Socialist Sunday School children. At Hyde Park there were 12 wagons from which speakers addressed a crowd estimated at 10,000 on such themes as 'the right to work', 'the emancipation of labour' and 'the nationalization of the means of production'. The 1908 May Day took place during a short recession and the Hyde Park demonstration was notable for the SDF stalwart Jack Williams leading a 500-strong group of unemployed men (*Daily Mail*, 2 May 1906 and 2 May 1908). The presence of children singing was popular and it attracted parents and other relatives. In 1909 1,500 Socialist Sunday School children arrived in brakes from various suburbs, while in 1910 over 80 wagonloads of children came and sang 'The Red Flag'. That year was notable for there being 300 Clarion cyclists wheeling bicycles decorated with red roses and for some 600 banners brought by trade unions and socialist societies, including one from a Japanese society, several in Yiddish and several from Clarion societies (*Daily Mail*, 3 May 1909 and 2 May 1910).

The renewed rapid expansion of trade unionism among unskilled workers in 1910–1914 was matched by a revival of huge Hyde Park rallies. The 1912 procession to Hyde Park was deemed to be 'probably the largest seen in the streets of London in connection with the labour movement'. In the park a very large crowd of many thousands listened to Keir Hardie and other speakers on seven platforms. After speaking in support of the tailors then on strike, Hardie said:

> At the present time there are some men in gaol for calling upon soldiers not to shoot strikers. I go a step further. I say not only don't shoot, but don't enlist. What business have you with soldiering? Remember this, that the crime of shooting a German workman, who is your comrade, is just as great as shooting a British workman here.

The pre-World War I London demonstrations continued to mark their international character by having speeches in several languages. In May 1914 speeches in Hyde Park were delivered in French, German, Russian and Lettish, as well as in English (*Nottingham Evening Post*, 2 May 1912 and 1 May 1914).

Summary: Before 1914

Dieter Rucht has emphasized the twofold nature of many May Days: the 'day of struggle' to further the workers' cause and the 'day of festivities' in which the participants enjoy themselves as if they were family (Rucht 2005). The May Days in Britain, especially during the first quarter of a century from 1890, were marked by social events as well as by the outdoor rallies. The SDF regularly held evening meetings in the East End after the Hyde Park open-air rallies. The link between the demonstrations and the festivities was well symbolized at the 1894 May Day rally in Nottingham when the ILP, with members of the Typographical Society, took a small printing machine on the march and 'printed en route a flaming announcement of our big social and dance' (Recchiuti 1981, p. 96). Yet, the outstanding feature of the early British May Days was the size of the demonstrations and the often huge crowds that listened to the speakers. In London the crowds were massive, especially from 1890 to 1894, and the speakers represented May Days as international events. May Days in Britain built on current trade union and socialist societies' strengths as well as on radical traditions. As a predominantly Protestant country, other than many Irish immigrants, these traditions were secular, unlike Catholic countries such as Spain, Italy, France and Ireland.

May Days 1915–1940

Between 1915 and 1940 the core of May Days remained international sentiments, but in some years strikes and lockouts or current politics came to the fore. In Britain the trade unions, the trades councils, the Labour Party and often the Communist Party (from 1920) were the key organizers and supporters of May Days, but the strong European presence through large numbers of political refugees was less evident in London than before World War I. The early 1890s divisions between socialists and anarchists had more or less disappeared, with the weakening of anarchism in Britain. Dividing lines between the wars were more between the Labour Party and trade unionists, on one side, and communists (and Trotskyists and the Independent Labour Party by the 1930s), on the other side, though this was often blurred at the local level through the left working together, not least for May Day demonstrations.

International sentiments continued to be expressed by the left during World War I, but in Britain May Day parades did not occur again in most places until late in the war. In the second half of the war there was growing war weariness and disillusion about war aims. Unlike Russia and Germany, for instance, in Britain there was not a challenge to the political system but there was further industrial unrest. On 1 May 1918 the Lanarkshire miners held a large May Day demonstration at Hamilton, with all production ceased in many pits, though a few 'patriotic miners' were working. The miners' agent denied that it was an anti-war demonstration, but said that the 'miners were not machines, and as they had been working at high pressure for full three years they needed occasional recreation and rest' (*Nottingham Evening Post*, 2 May 1918; Horne 1991, pp. 302–349). In Leicester a May Day meeting addressed by the local MP, Ramsay MacDonald, who was highly critical of the war, was marked by some violence by the pro-war British Workers' League (*Nottingham Evening Post*, 15 May 1918; Horne 1991, pp. 302–349). MacDonald and four other anti-war ILP Labour MPs all lost their seats in the 1918 general election, as did the anti-war Liberal MPs.

The Post-War Economic Boom

In 1919 and 1920 the post-war economic boom put labour in a strong position. The miners secured the seven-hour working day while the engineers secured the 47-hour week. Other industrial groups, railway workers and building workers all secured a 48-hour week or better (Clegg 1985, pp. 211, 253–255 and 267–271; Wrigley 1990, pp. 80–281).

In London, there was the traditional large Hyde Park May Day demonstration with Sylvia Pankhurst as one of the speakers. With 200 supporters she went on to Downing Street, and on being turned away, went to Westminster where she and Amelia O' Mahoney were arrested. In court Pankhurst made clear the special concerns of May Day 1919, denouncing the government's wars with Russia and Hungary 'to prevent the Soviet system from being established in Europe'. She also said that 'she had direct information that men in the London docks were being worked such as they never worked during the days of the great war, to ship munitions to Russia' (*The Times*, 3 May 1919; Romero 1987, p. 136). Outside of London the much strengthened Labour movement organized May Days. In Coventry a major wartime engineering centre, the trades council organized a major 'JOY-Day of May Day', which included a carnival at the football ground and an evening ball and whist drive (Nicholls 1986).

In 1920 May Day was marked by mass closures of factories, workshops and building sites in London and major urban areas. Backed by the TUC and the Labour Party some 8 million workers were estimated by the press to have taken part in marking May Day. At 2 p.m. there was a large procession from Charing Cross railway bridge to Hyde Park led by a band followed by some 500 members of the National Union of Ex-Service Men and an Irish contingent, some striking shop assistants, many bodies of trade unionists and co-operators. There were 12 platforms in Hyde Park. including one for a Socialist Sunday School choir and another as an international platform, with speeches in Yiddish, Russian, Polish, French and Esperanto, as well as in English. The resolutions moved at all the platforms covered social issues such as housing and food prices, maximum working hours (no more than a 44 hours a week), condemned proposals to impose income tax on the savings of industrial cooperative societies, called for the withdrawal of British troops from Ireland, hailed the Russian Soviet government and called for the Labour movement to force the British government to make peace with Russia on the basis of no annexation, no indemnities and no interference in Russian internal affairs (*The Times*, 1 May 1920; *Derby Daily Telegraph*, 1 May 1920; *Nottingham Evening Post*, 3 May 1920).

Economic Recession and After: Labour on the Defensive

Outside London, coal miners used May Day as an occasion to express their discontent. The mines had been state controlled in two stages in 1915 and 1916, with the owners given a guaranteed level of profits but with the state keeping the substantial additional profits coming from boom conditions. The miners demanded the nationalization of the coal industry as well as better pay and conditions. In 1920 the miners took May Day (a Saturday) as a holiday and held demonstrations. In coal towns such as Coalville in Leicestershire all the shops closed. On May Day 1921 the miners were in the midst of a bitter lockout which followed the owners' demands for wage cuts after coal prices dropped and the state withdrew early from the industry. At Nottingham, on a beautiful Sunday afternoon, several thousand people watched a pageant entitled 'Labour Unbound', representing workers achieving fuller lives. Led by bands and tableaux, some 1,500 miners marched through the market place. Speeches were made from two platforms, with George Spencer, a Nottinghamshire Miners' Association official and Labour MP for Broxtowe, declaring that the miners would continue to struggle against the owners' conditions until 'sheer starvation' forced them back to work (*Nottingham Evening Post*, 3 April 1920 and 2 May 1921). In 1922, the miners in South Wales stopped work on May Day, a Monday. At a May Day rally at Maesteg, South Wales, Vernon Hartshorn, MP and president of the South Wales Miners' Federation, spoke of the miners fighting back after the unfavourable settlement of 1921. However, in Durham the miners agreed with the owners to mark May Day on Saturday afternoon, 6 May, rather than on Monday 1 May, and this arrangement continued (*Aberdeen Journal*, 2 May 1922; *Sunderland Daily Echo and Shipping Gazette*, 29 April 1922; *Yorkshire Post and Leeds Advertiser*, 17 April 1925; *Gloucester Journal*, 25 April 1925).

After the miners' lockout of 1921 the next industrial group to be confronted by employers in the severe economic recession of 1921–1922 was the engineers. The great engineering lockout of 1922 featured in several May Day demonstrations in 1922. In Derby the Amalgamated Engineering Union Lock-Out Committee and the local Unemployed Committee were the organizers of the May Day march, led by the Imperial Veterans' Band, from the market place to a mass meeting in the Temperance Hall. This was a period when one strand of ex-servicemen was socialist (Englander and Osborne 1978; Englander 1987; Wrigley 1990, pp. 24–52). There, after speeches the resolution put to the meeting dealt with the engineering lockout as well as expressing greetings to the workers of the world and approving the pact between Russia and Germany. In Hull the 'larger than usual' procession, led by the new National Union of Railwaymen band and three large banners, ended at the Corporation field where 1,500–2,000 people heard speeches from three platforms. In Bristol a procession including several bands and banners made its way from Old Market Street to Greville Smyth Park in south Bristol, where crowds listened to speakers from three platforms. Charles Gill of the Miners' Federation warned that after the worsened conditions imposed on miners and engineers, other trades would be faced with substantial cuts in their working conditions (*Derby Daily Telegraph*, 1 May 1922; *Hull Daily Mail*, 8 May 1922; *Western Daily Press*, 8 May 1922).

The Unemployed, 1921–1940

There were high levels of unemployment in Britain from 1921 until 1940. This was reflected in many May Day demonstrations. One report of the large London demonstration of 1925 commented that 'it was discovered afterwards that the majority of those who kept the ranks were members of the unemployed, who were represented by nearly every trade union' (*Aberdeen Journal*, 2 May 1925). Some of the unemployed were active in the National Unemployed Workers' Movement (NUWM), which was organized by the Communist Party but its support went wider. Other active unemployed people supported trade union and Labour Party initiatives, including May Day demonstrations (Croucher 1987; Perry 2000; Ward 2013). In the 1930s May Day rallies often focused on the Labour Movement's vigorous opposition to the means tests (involving humiliating visitations by officials to ensure that those receiving benefits were destitute and without even minor luxuries), as in 1932 in County Durham (Ward 2013, p. 123).

Children

Children were the other group particularly commented on in newspaper coverage of 1920s British May Days. One report commented of the 1925 London demonstration that 'it was remarkable for the number of children who accompanied their parents or attended with Sunday school detachments'. On 1 May 1926 (a Saturday) in Dundee, it was reported that there were only about a hundred people in the May Day parade, 'the majority of whom were children', with more children in the two pipe and one silver bands that led the procession (*Western Daily Press*, 2 May 1925; *Dundee Courier*, 3 May 1926).

The General Strike

The General Strike of 3 to 13 May 1926 was a massive sympathy strike called by the TUC in support of the coal miners. It began in early May because the government's six-month subsidy to the industry ran out then, not because of May Day. However May Day demonstrations in mining areas were used to inform and rally miners for what proved to be a lengthy mining dispute. At Denbeath Bridge, Methil, Fife, there were two bands and several hundred people to hear Tom Kennedy, the local MP (for Kirkcaldy Burghs), and A. McTaggart, who chaired the Scottish Trades Union Congress.

After the calling off of the General Strike and the collapse of the miners' ability to resist work conditions worsened by the end of 1926, the Conservative government brought in legislation hostile to the trade union movement that became in July the Trade Disputes and Trades Union Act of 1927. Opposition to this bill was a focus of many British May Day demonstrations in 1927. In Nottingham in the large demonstration was a banner proclaiming, 'March 1834: men were transported for daring to be trade unionists'; May 1927: 'A Tory Government proposes to smash all trade unionists. Men and women defeat this. Join your trade union now'. In Mansfield Frank Varley, president of the Nottinghamshire Miners' Association and MP for Mansfield, told a large crowd that the bill was 'a blacklegs' charter'. In Stepney the Labour Council had red flags raised on five municipal buildings (though two were soon removed by opponents) (*Nottingham Evening Post*, 2 May 1927).

Fascism and Communism

In the interwar years May Days provided a major political platform for the Communist Party of Great Britain. The party could justly claim that its predecessors in the Marxist politics of London had been instrumental in organizing the huge early May Day demonstrations. Marxist pedigrees could hardly be outdone by Eleanor Marx with Friedrich Engels in support. Yet, in the 1920s and 1930s communist campaigns against moderate trade union leaders had ensured great hostility from most TUC and Labour Party leaders. This was reinforced by the Bolshevik and then Stalinist persecution of lighter shades of red in the Soviet Union. The May Day displays of military might in Red Square on May Days was felt to be menacing, not inspiring by many trade union members and Labour supporters. Yet at the local level communists frequently joined the rest of the labour movement at May Day demonstrations.

In contrast to much of continental Europe, in Britain there were no major clashes with fascists at the May Day demonstrations. One of the very few such clashes was in Glasgow in 1926, when 'a group of men said to be Fascisti' attacked some marchers resulting in several people being injured, but not badly. More common in Britain in the 1930s were clashes between crowds, often involving communists or Trotskyists. At the big London demonstration in Hyde Park of 1931 there were clashes between demonstrators and the police, with mounted and other police using their batons to disperse the crowd. Clashes between police and May Day demonstrators were relatively rare, unlike in Paris in the period 1890–1935.

The Labour Party and the Left

With the Independent Labour Party's disaffiliation from the Labour Party in July 1932 the ILP organized separate May Day meetings. The ILP moved further to the left, away from Labour preaching a democratic socialist purity in line with the aspirations (rather than the practice) of the early ILP pioneers. The Labour Party sought to reconnect with its working-class support, which in many industrial areas had been weakened in 1931, as shown by the collapse in parliamentary representation in that year's general election. The ILP, especially in Scotland, was often willing to hold May Day events with the Communist Party which approached the ILP in its efforts to construct a united front against fascism in March 1933, and this move attracted some on the left of the Labour Party.

The ILP, which weakened rapidly in most parts of the country, initially did well in London (Dowse 1966, p. 185). In 1935, on Wednesday 1 May thousands of Londoners marched from 25 meeting points to Hyde Park where from 5.30 p.m. left speakers including Tom Mann, Harry Pollitt (both Communist Party), Fenner Brockway (general-secretary of the ILP) and Dorothy Woodman (leader of the Union of Democratic Control). The resolution that year was, 'All present pledge themselves to redoubled energy in the great task of strengthening and extending the growing movement for working class unity which alone can defeat the war plans and Fascist aims of our class enemies.' This separate left May Day in London was repeated in 1936 with the same lead speakers, except that Aneurin Bevan MP replaced Fenner Brockway. Among those attending were several religious bodies and a contingent of Oxford and Cambridge University socialists. In the evening a communist May Day meeting in Shoreditch town hall marked Tom Mann's eightieth birthday 16 days earlier and then held a programme of singing, ballet, drama and vaudeville put on by the New Theatre League.

The Labour Party held May Day processions in Hyde Park, but on the first Sunday in May. On 5 May 1935 the London Labour Party organized the demonstration with its secretary, Herbert Morrison, as the main speaker. Morrison was heckled vigorously by communists over the London County Council (LCC) residential training centre, Belmont at Sutton, Surrey. A former orphanage (from 1853) and then workhouse (from 1908), the buildings were taken over by the LCC in 1930 as a residential training centre for unemployed men. Belmont, and similar centres at Hollesley Bay, Suffolk, and Denton, Essex, were denounced as 'slave colonies' by the communists as men were sent away from their families to grim buildings (London Labour Party 1935; Field 2013). On Sunday 3 May 1936 thousands of people marched from Victoria Embankment to Hyde Park on a demonstration organized by the Labour Party and TUC (All-London First of May Demonstration Committee, *May Day 1936: Souvenir Programme* (20-page pamphlet)); *The Times*, 6 May 1935 and 4 May 1936; *Taunton Courier and Western Gazette*, 6 May 1936).

In Britain the Labour Party and the TUC were careful to avoid anything that could be seen as a British version of the Front Populaire. In France in 1936 the Popular Front government of socialists and radicals was supported by the Communist Party (but without participating in the government). The Labour Party demonstrated as usual on the first Sunday of the month, while the Communist Party and its trade union supporters marked 1 May. The London Sunday May Day procession was four miles long, starting at the Thames Embankment and going to Hyde Park. Headed by striking bus workers, the marchers went under 'a forest of Red Flags, maypoles and banners'. The 1937 May Day demonstrations were marked by support for the democratic government in Spain as well as support for miners' unity in Nottinghamshire and the striking bus workers (Saville 1977, pp. 232–284; *The Times*, 3 January 1937).

In Glasgow that year there was left unity on May Day, marked by temporary cooperation between the ILP and the Communist Party following the ILP's disaffiliation from the Labour Party. As a result of this cooperation it was judged to have been the largest May Day demonstration there since World War I. Over 10,000 people took part in a procession with lorries, bands and banners from St George's Square to Glasgow Green, which was headed by the trade unions, the Labour Party, the ILP, the Co-operative movement and the Communist Party (*Aberdeen Journal*, 3 May 1937; Cohen 2007, p. 43). However, the left unity did not last long and ILP–CPGB relations deteriorated rapidly, in part over communist attitudes towards the Workers' Party of Marxist Unification (POUM) in Spain, which the ILP supported (Corthorn 2006, p. 189).

Coal Miners

Around Britain some of the best-attended May Day demonstrations were in coal-mining areas. The miners, who in most areas had been late joiners of the Labour Party (in 1909), were increasingly radical, with the major disputes of 1912, 1921 and 1926 and by the government's evasion of the nationalization of the mines in 1918–1920. The Kent miners celebrated May Days from the end of World War I and held large May Day demonstrations in Dover on the first Saturday in May from 1928. In 1936 the speakers were Jim Griffiths, president of the South Wales Miners and MP for Llanelli, and Ellis Smith, MP for Stoke. The Dover celebrations were pared down in 1939 and 1940, and the internationalism of the event evaporated in the face of the international crisis. In 1939 there were no processions or bands, just a meeting at 11 a.m. in the town hall on Saturday 6 May. At this John Elks, the secretary of the Kent Miners' Association, spoke of two burning issues: holidays with pay and conscription, due to affect some 400 miners on 1 July. The guest speaker was Aneurin Bevan MP, who denounced conscription and 'the old dodderer', Neville Chamberlain. He called for collective security through a triple alliance of Britain, France and Russia and 'a great charter of social progress'. The 1939 May Day format was repeated on Saturday 4 May 1940, when Josiah Wedgwood, MP for Newcastle under Lyme, was the speaker. The Kent Miners' Association president spoke of the pressures not to hold even that. but for miners to work on May Day (*Dover Express*, 24 April 1936, 28 April and 12 May 1939 and 10 May 1940).

As in the pre-war period, May Day organizers continued to marshal the past in support of present and future goals. In South Wales in 1939 the South Wales Miners' Federation, aided by the Labour Research Department, proudly looked back a hundred years to the Chartists, putting on a pageant. Large contingents marched behind 12 bands from Abertillery, Pontypool and West Wales to Pontypool Park, where 28 choirs sang and a two-part 'Pageant of South Wales' was performed, the first part dealing with John Frost and the Chartists, the second dealing with the succeeding hundred years, ending with an International Brigades and the bands playing 'The Internationale' (South Wales Miners' Federation, *May Day, May 1st 1939, Pageant of South Wales*).

The fiftieth anniversary of Red May Days was marked by the Bureau of the Labour and Socialist International releasing a manifesto for May Day. This included a call for 'the workers of the whole world' to react against aggression and to ensure that

> out of this torment a lasting peace should arise, built upon International Cooperation and on the Union of the peoples through Democracy, in order to maintain intact the possibility of realising Socialism, which alone will bring well-being and freedom to the World.

This May Day manifesto was supported by the Labour Party (The Labour Party, *Report of the Annual Conference, 1940*, p. 38). The British communists praised Stalin and avoided mention of Stalin's relations with Hitler prior to the Nazi invasion of the Soviet Union on 22 June 1941 (Mahon 1940). May Days were in abeyance during 1941–1945.

Summary: Between the Wars

In the interwar period the support for May Days waxed and waned, weakening often when labour was weak in the labour market, but vigorous in good times such as the post-war boom of 1919–1920. Support was also strong after major defensive industrial disputes such as that which occurred in the coal industry in 1926 or major international issues such as Franco's attack on the republican government in Spain. The defence of trade unionism and support for the Labour movement's anti-fascist struggles led to huge demonstrations, even if not as big as those in London in 1890–1894. However, even in economic booms, support for May Day demonstrations could be weak in some urban areas. For instance in Liverpool in 1920 only some 1,200 marched in heavy rain to Sheil Park and up to 2,000 listened to the speeches. When the May Day speakers vacated the platforms some Sinn Fein speakers took over addressing some 2,000 supporters who marched into the park when the May Day rally was part-way through (Davies 1996, pp. 17–18). In many conservative rural and southern counties many people still attended the traditional folk May Day celebrations of maypoles and country dancing. Even in 1940 there was traditional May Day dancing by children in Bath (*Bath Chronicle and Weekly Gazette*, 4 May 1940).

May Days from World War II

As in other countries, in Britain also May Days were affected by Cold War politics. In the late 1940s and 1950s there was often renewed conflict between the Labour Party and most trade union leaders and the Communist Party, with abhorrence of Stalinism in Russia and in the eastern European countries under Soviet control. May Day parades have continued to the present, but in many places the numbers participating dwindled, partly because of the substantial weakening of trade unionism after 1979, which fell by some 40 per cent by the end of the century (see Chapter 7). In many places the international message was muted, with May Days being used to promote the current concerns of the Labour Party or trade unions. In recent years, in particular in London, new social movement organizations increasingly participated in and sometimes helped to organize the May Day demonstrations.

In May Day demonstrations, the utilization of a radical past to press for a radical future observed for the 1890s and the interwar period remained prominent. For instance in Nottingham in 1948 the May Day march featured not only a banner marking the centenary of the great Chartist demonstration in London that accompanied the massive petition for reform of parliament but also several marchers in the clothing of the period of the Levellers.[1]

In Britain May Day processions and outdoor rallies continued in many urban areas but in other places these were often replaced by indoor meetings. In 1945 the London Trades Council organized a big rally in Hyde Park with contingents marching from St Pancras Arches, Stepney Green, Shepherds Bush Green, St George's Circus, the Prince of Wales on Harrow Road and the Latchmere Baths, Battersea (Mahon 1946). However, the Labour home secretary, Chuter Ede, banned political processions in London in 1948, 1949 and 1950, in response to Oswald Mosley's threats in 1948 to hold a fascist May Day march from the Victoria Embankment at the same time as that of the labour movement's procession. The ban did not extend to meetings in Trafalgar Square and in 1949 some 30,000 people attended the London Trades Council's rally in Trafalgar Square (*Aberdeen Journal*, 15 April 1949; London District of the Communist Party 1949; Mace 1976, pp. 224–227).

Decline of Mass Demonstrations

In Manchester in 1945 and 1946, Manchester Council of Labour (comprising Manchester and Salford Trades Council, Manchester City Labour Party and Manchester City Co-operative Party) organized large processions with bands and banners which marched from Albert Square to Platt Fields. In 1945 there they heard Harold Laski, Dorothy Elliott, Fred Lee, Hugh Scanlon and other speakers before the Unity Theatre performed *The Future Is Ours*. In 1946 the May Day programme emphasized 'Platform fitted with the latest sound equipment' (Manchester Council of Labour, 1945 and 1946). In 1946 in Bristol the Labour Party's decision to abandon the mass outdoor demonstrations and processions for an indoor meeting was described by the local press as 'a revolutionary decision'. It was explained as a response to heavy rain the previous year resulting in a loss of over £190. In Luton in 1954 the trades council voted for a meeting in the town hall rather than organize a procession (*Western Daily Press*, 11 January 1946; *Luton News and Bedfordshire Chronicle*, 22 April 1954).

By the 1960s fervour for processions with bands and banners was waning in many places. In Wigan the May Day demonstrations were abandoned in 1964. People had stood at their doors as the march went by, but in the market square few turned up to hear the speeches. In Mexborough after processions had been revived for some 11 years they were abandoned in 1966. Although 200 had marched on the day when Denis Healey spoke at the rally the numbers in the processions had usually been much smaller. On one blustery occasion only 30 people had joined the march. R. Cobb, the secretary of the Mexborough and District Trades Council, observed then that the bands at the back and front outnumbered the other marchers. He commented also that 'Some did not want to walk anymore and joined the procession when it was nearly over' (*Guardian*, 22 April 1966). In 1966 Birmingham Trades Council held a rally but abandoned its first Sunday in May procession. Describing the recent marches as 'a fiasco', Harry Baker, who had been the Trades Council secretary, said 'We only marched round empty office blocks' (*Guardian*, 22 April 1966). In Liverpool in 1966 instead of the procession and rally in the city centre Liverpool Trades Council and Labour Party opted for a gala at Kirby, a 'family day', with decorated floats and a parade going to Kirby stadium for a speech by Harold Wilson, the prime minister. Simon Fraser, secretary of Liverpool Trades Council, observed that it 'seemed natural nowadays that people would not support simply a walk through the streets and speeches' (*Guardian*, 22 April 1966).

Increasingly British May Day meetings focused on current politics, with less of the internationalism and aspirations to a much better socialist future of the kind suggested by the illustrations of Walter Crane. Crane's illustrations had been utopian, very much in line with the sentiments of William Morris's *News from Nowhere* (1890) yet in some ways precursors of the heroic proletarians of much Bolshevik and Soviet poster and other art. British May Days of the second half of the twentieth century had the colourful banners of the trade unions, minorities and pressure groups (such as CND, anti-apartheid and Amnesty International), but the demonstrations focused very much on the here and now.

Cultural Celebrations

In 1969 the Labour Party, trade unions and co-operators reverted to a cultural celebration, not very dissimilar to those of 1900 and 1901 at the Crystal Palace. At the Royal Festival Hall, actors and directors from the Royal Shakespeare Company put on 'The Merry Month of May: a narrative entertainment about May Day', drawing on various literary and historical sources. This was followed by speeches by Lord Beswick (Co-op), Alex Halliday (London Trades Council) and concluded by Harold Wilson. The programme wrote of the break with tradition, observing of the procession of past years that 'in spite of its brave show of banners and marchers [it] became more and more involved in traffic problems' and adding that each year 'the speeches at Hyde Park were heard less and less by the comrades coming in at the rear of the march' (London Joint May Day Committee 1969).

In 1970 in Britain the Labour Party was seeking a third successive electoral win and looking for the support of floating voters. Its May Day event, as in 1969, was a very clear attempt to distance itself from the international and socialist symbolism of May Days. The move away from the open-air tradition of the past to the Royal Festival Hall was portrayed by the organizers as 'an attempt to give it a modern setting and approach to a traditional event'. However, *The Times* journalist deemed 'the flavour yesterday' to be 'distinctly old fashioned' (*The Times*, 3 May 1970). The first half of the proceedings was a history of the nineteenth-century musical starring Labour-supporting actors Alfie Bass and Andrew Faulds (a Labour MP, 1966–1997). In addition the Musicians' Union and the Labour Party presented an annual May Day concert in the Royal Festival Hall. At 8 p.m. on Monday, 1 May 1972 the concert was performed by the Royal Liverpool Philharmonic Orchestra conducted by Charles Groves (Musicians' Union 1972). The sedentary Sunday May Days, 'in a new form and in a new setting ... a blending of the old with the new', failed to enthuse socialists and trade unionists in the way that the affirmation and camaraderie involved in the May Day processions and open-air meetings had done in the previous eight decades. Elsewhere in London and Britain traditional May Day rallies took place. These were larger when more people were attracted by issues such as nuclear disarmament, opposition to the Viet Nam war, support for the miners in their 1984–1985 dispute and opposition to the Conservative government's poll tax.

When the Labour Party and trade unions in London temporarily abandoned the outdoor march and rally the vacuum left was filled by a right-wing booking of Trafalgar Square for a 'May Day freedom' call by the Monday Club, a far-right pressure group within the Conservative Party. Six Conservative MPs spoke on 'law and liberty' and, against the background of the anti-apartheid campaign against the visiting South African rugby team, on 'keep politics out of sport'. They proclaimed that ordinary people 'are sick and tired of being preached at by weirdies, lefties, anarchists and progressives'. In preparing for the meeting the Monday Club had offered many rugby, cricket and other sports clubs banners inscribed: 'SOS Save our Sport'. However, most ignored this offer and the rally. Only some 500 people attended rally, outnumbered by about 1,000 communists and Young Socialists filing by them en route to another rally. Embarrassingly for the Monday Club the front row of the audience was made up of National Front members pleased to exercise freedom of expression in what *The Times* correspondent described as 'eye-catching banners, not entirely relevant to the subject of the rally' (*The Times*, 3 May 1970). The *Daily Mail*'s coverage on 3 May ignored the Royal Festival Hall event and the Monday Club's failure to secure an audience but instead made much of militant students' failure to mobilize more than some 200 for a march. This was in sharp contrast with the numbers of students involved in the British anti-Viet Nam war demonstrations or in West Berlin during the May Day demonstration in 1968. The attempt of the Labour Party and trade unions in London to dump May Day marches and rallies was a dismal failure there. May Day rallies continued in London and in several parts of Britain, often being especially strong in mining areas.

May Day as a National Holiday

With May Day becoming a national holiday in Britain from 1978, there were renewed endeavours to observe the holiday with celebrations. In Salford, for instance, there was a May Day gala in Buile Hill Park from 11.00 a.m. to 6.00 p.m. The emphasis was on community entertainment with sport at the fore but with a circus, a theatre and music strand of events as well as a children's arena with a range of entertainment for them. There were also many stalls with arts and crafts, real ale, Labour movement and a range of social groups participating. The red May Day message was there but very much second to bank holiday entertainment (Salford May Day Gala Committee 1978). However, with the bank holiday being on the first Monday in May part of the feeling of it being a special day was lost. Matthew Engel, in a newspaper article, complained that it had become 'a meaningless day off with a motif of cold rain, bored children, desperate parents and car boot sales' (*Guardian*, 2 May 1998).

In contrast, in Chesterfield May Day celebrations were strongly socialist and became very substantial annual events from 1978 to the present. The labour movement there was determined to establish support for the May Day bank holiday rather than let apathy allow the Conservatives to abolish it in favour of another date to mark the old Empire Day, or a Churchill or Thatcher Day. The Chesterfield labour movement was reinvigorated by the strong campaign which got Tony Benn elected as MP in March 1984. On the May Day bank holidays there were marches in the late morning from the town hall round the town and back to New Square or Rykneld Square, followed by speeches. The marches attracted leading trade unionists such as Rodney Bickerstaffe and Bob Crow and, after the miners' strike of 1984–1985, Anne Scargill and Betty Heathfield (Benn 2002, p. 173). The rest of the day was given over to a range of radical cultural events. Internationalism was always stressed, with, for example, in 1991 a trade union speaker from Namibia (who was presented with a motorbike to help trade union organization there) and speakers from Cuba, Pakistan, Venezuela and Portugal in 1992, 2013 and 2014 (Chesterfield and District Trades Union Council 1991, 1992, 1997, 2013 and 2014).

The TUC usually left the organizing of May Days to the London Trades Council and, from 1985, its successor body, the Greater London Association of Trade Union Councils (GLATUC). The 1998 May Day march (on Friday 1 May) from Highbury Corner to the traditional radical location of Clerkenwell Green to Trafalgar Square was the largest in London since 1979, with speakers representing British and international trade unions and exiled communities. In 1999 the march was bigger still, involving Black and Asian, Sri Lankan and Tamil representatives, as well as gay and lesbian groups. The rally was intended to be held at Trafalgar Square for the first time since 1951, with other marchers coming from Brixton and Soho, scenes of recent fascist bombings. However, the police blocked the GLATUC marchers from getting to the square, and also harassed an anti-capitalist demonstration, blocking its route at the edge of Trafalgar Square. In 2002 the May Day march went from Clerkenwell Green to Trafalgar Square, where the rally was not impeded, with some 16,000 present. In 2003 the TUC, which the previous year had held a May Day event in the Millennium Dome, nominated speakers for the rally in Trafalgar Square, which had a smaller attendance of some 10,000 (GLATUC, *Annual Report*, May 1999, May 2000, February 2002 and May 2003).

The May Days in London at the end of the twentieth and start of the twenty-first century had many features of those of the 1890s other than size; most notably internationalism in sentiment and in the presence of a wide range of nationalities and ethnicities. Probably the largest London May Day of these years was in 2005, a Sunday, when the organizers' estimate was 40,000 marching. The processions marched across central London but in these years made a point of setting off from a working-class area, Clerkenwell. Trade unionists were the larger part of the processions but trade unionism had shrunk from the 10,672,000 (density of 54.5 per cent) of 1980 to 7,295,000 (28.8 per cent) of 2001. The number fell further to 6,213,000 in 2012 (Labour Force Survey data in Department for Business, Innovation and Skills 2013, p. 22).

The May Day rallies still attracted and catered for strikers, but the numbers of strikers had dropped from 4,608,000 (and 29,474,000 days lost) in 1979 to 180,000 strikers (and 525,000 days lost) in 2001 (Wrigley 2002, pp. 19, 20 and 43). In the mid-1980s the May Day march went to Wapping to show solidarity with the print workers in their struggle with Rupert Murdoch. In 2000 and 2001 there was support for the Sky Chef and the Ford and Rover workers in their disputes. In 2006 representatives of the Vengest factory, Ryton, Coventry, joined the rally.

London May Days remained cosmopolitan. Much emphasis was placed on providing a platform for migrant workers and political refugees. In 2012 the march included Turkish, Kurdish, Chilean, Columbian, Peruvian, Portuguese, West Indian, Sri Lankan, Tamil, Cypriot, Iranian, Iraqi and Nigerian migrant workers or community representatives. The marches were marked by large numbers of banners and bands, such as the Big Red Band, playing a range of music from 'Guantanamera' (Cuban) to 'the Internationale' and 'The Red Flag'. At the evening May Day entertainment, Peruvian and other musicians performed. As in the early 1890s, when Eleanor Marx and Edward Aveling were the very efficient organizers, the early twenty-first-century May Days took considerable time to organize by the GLATUC's May Day Committee. Great care was taken to link the May Days with current international or industrial issues to bring new groups into the marches and rallies (GLATUC, *Annual Reports*, 1999–2013). The emphasis was on collaborating with a wide variety of groups, including Greens and gays, as well as various national and ethnic groups.

The May Days also gave opportunities for anti-globalization groups to make symbolic protests. In some ways such approaches to criticizing capitalism were descended from the concerns of agit-prop members in anti-Viet Nam demonstrations in 1967–1968. The Angry Arts film, *End of a Tactic*, on the 1968 demonstration outside the US Embassy in London questioned the effectiveness of such actions. Such concerns were reiterated by anti-globalization campaigners, including such small groups as the Wombles (White Overall Movement Building Libertarian Effective Struggles), the symbolic significance of whose activities at the London 2001 May Day demonstrations has been discussed by Justus Uitermark (Uitermark 2004).

Concluding Remarks

In the early 1890s socialism and independent labour politics were experiencing a renaissance in Britain after the relatively fallow years following the decline of Chartism. The May Day demonstrations provided an international focus for the burgeoning labour and socialist movements. The optimism, and even millennialism, of the early 1890s and beyond was expressed in much of the iconography of May Days, not least by Walter Crane's graphics and by many of the banners carried through the centre of London and other British cities and towns. The fervour of the unskilled workforce, male and female, who flexed their muscles in the industrial victories of 1888–1890 (and in many municipal elections of those years) was also displayed in celebrating May Day, whether on 1 May or the nearest Sunday. May Days represented the rebirth of hopes for better working conditions and, above all, better lives. 'Eight hours of work, eight hours of leisure and eight hours of sleep' was a powerful aspiration.

Between the wars UK trade unionism was initially very powerful. Membership had grown rapidly from 2,477,000 in 1910 to 8,348,000 in 1920. Although numbers fell with the 1921–1922 and 1931–1933 recessions, even at the lowest point in 1933 there were still 4,392,000 members. While trade union support had been crucial for the large May Days before 1914, the trade union input was even more important from 1918. Across Britain trades councils mobilized support for May Days with the TUC, as well as the London Trades Council, playing a substantial role in London and the Scottish TUC doing so with trades councils in various parts of Scotland. The Labour Party was the major political force but the Communist Party of Great Britain pressed hard in many industrial areas. Internationalism remained strong, especially in the face of the rise of fascism and the far right in parts of continental Europe. But something of the utopian optimism of the 1890s had partly evaporated. The calls for peace gave way to calls for action in support of the democratically elected republican government in Spain and for preparation for war.

Support for May Days emerged strong after World War II but it was soon affected by the Cold War and the annual parades of Soviet might in Red Square. In an age of television and consumerism there was less fervour in many areas for May Day parades, even before the decline of trade union strength from 1980. In many areas in the 1990s and 2000s a diminished labour and socialist movement maintained support for May Days in the aftermath of the Thatcher years and the 1984–1985 miners' strike. May Day was for the committed labour movement supporters, hoping to expand trade unionism and to defeat the Conservative Party, for national and ethnic groups who supported May Day aspirations and sought a forum in which to express their views and for those eager to promote particular issues and policies. In the early twenty-first century, May Days in Britain remained international days for labour, but lacked the mass support of earlier years.

Note

1 Photograph exhibited at the 'Secret Intelligence and Hidden Evidence' exhibition, Manuscripts and Special Collections, Weston Gallery, Nottingham University, 20 September 2013–5 January 2014.

References

Bain, G.S., and Price, R. (1980). *Profiles of Union Growth*. Oxford: Blackwell.

Benn, T. (2002). *Free at Last: Diaries 1991–2001*. London: Hutchinson.

Bryher, S., and Bale, S. (1929). *An Account of the Labour and Socialist Movement in Bristol*. Bristol: Bristol Labour Weekly.

Chesterfield and District Trades Union Council. (1991, 1992, 1997, 2013, 2014). *May Day Gala*. Chesterfield, UK: Chesterfield and District TUC.

Clegg, H.A. (1985). *A History of British Trade Unions since 1889*, vol. 2: *1910–1933*. Oxford: Clarendon Press.

Clegg, H.A., Fox, A., and Thompson, A.F. (1964). *A History of British Trade Unions since 1889*, vol. 1: *1889–1910*. Oxford: Clarendon Press.

Cohen, G. (2007). *The Failure of Dreams: The Independent Labour Party from Disaffiliation to World War 2*. London: I.B.Tauris.

Corthorn, P. (2006). *In the Shadow of Dictators: The British Left in the 1930s*. London: I.B.Tauris.

Crane, W. (1896). *Cartoons for the Cause: A Souvenir of the International Socialist Workers and Trade Union Congress, 1886–1896*. London: Twentieth Century Press.

Crane, W. (1907). *An Artist's Reminiscences*. London: Methuen.

Croucher, R. (1987). *We Refuse to Starve in Silence: A History of the National Unemployed Workers' Movement 1920–1946*. London: Lawrence & Wishart.

Davies, S. (1996). *Liverpool Labour: Social and Political Influences on the Development of the Labour Party in Liverpool, 1900–1939*. Keele, UK: Keele University Press.

Department for Business, Innovation and Skills. (2013). *Trade Union Membership, 2012*. London: The Stationery Office.

Dowse, R.E. (1966). *Left in the Centre*. London: Longman.

Englander, D. (1987). Troops and trade unions, 1919. *History Today*, 37(3), 8–13.

Englander, D., and Osborne, J. (1978). Jack, Tommy and Henry Dubb: The armed forces and the working class. *Historical Journal*, 21(3), 593–621.

Field, J. (2013). *Working Men's Bodies: Work Camps in Britain 1880–1940*. Manchester: Manchester University Press.

Foner, P.S. (1986). *May Day: A Short History of the International Workers' Holiday 1886–1986*. New York: International Publishers.

Gilbert, B.B. (1966). *The Evolution of National Insurance in Great Britain*. London: Michael Joseph.

Hobsbawm, E. (1984). *Worlds of Labour*. London: Weidenfeld & Nicolson.

Hobsbawm, E. (1991). Birth of a holiday: The first of May. In C. Wrigley and J. Shepherd (Eds), *On the Move: Essays in Labour and Transport History* (pp. 104–122). London and Rio Grande: Hambledon Press.

Hobsbawm, E., and Ranger, T. (Eds). (1984). *The Invention of Tradition*. London: Weidenfeld & Nicolson.

Horne, J. (1991). *Labour at War: France and Britain 1914–1918*. Oxford: Clarendon Press.

Kapp, Y. (1972, 1976). *Eleanor Marx*, 2 vols. London: Lawrence & Wishart.

Khramtsov, A. (1988). *May Day Traditions*. Moscow: Progress Publishers.

Labour Research Department. (April 1929). *The Meaning of May Day*. London: Labour Research Department.

Lawrence, Dan. H. (Ed.). (1972). *Bernard Shaw: Collected Letters 1898–1910*. New York: Dodd, Mead.

Lee, H.W., and Archbold, E. (1933). *Social Democracy in Britain*. London: SDF.

London District of the Communist Party. (1949). *Day of Struggle for Peace and Socialism: Souvenir of London's May Day 1949*. London: London District of the Communist Party.

London Joint May Day Committee. (1969). *May Day Festival of Labour: Sunday May 4th Royal Festival Hall*. London: London Joint May Day Committee.

London Labour Party. (1935). *'What about Belmont?' The Facts about Residential Training Centres under the Labour LCC*. London: London Labour Party.

Maccoby, S. (1938). *English Radicalism 1853–1886*. London: Allen & Unwin.

Mace, R. (1976). *Trafalgar Square: Emblem of Empire*. London: Lawrence & Wishart.

Mahon, J. (1937). *Report of Delegation to Paris on July 14th, 1937*. London: First of May Demonstration Committee.

Mahon, J. (1940). *May 1st 1940: The Meaning of May Day*. London: First of May Demonstration Committee.

Manchester Council of Labour. (1945). *May Day Demonstration*. Manchester: Manchester Council of Labour.

Manchester Council of Labour. (1946). *May Day Demonstration*. Manchester: Manchester Council of Labour.

Martinez, P.K. (1981). Paris Communard refugees in Britain. Unpublished PhD thesis, University of Sussex.

Musicians' Union. (1972). *May Day Concert*. London: Musicians' Union & the Labour Party.

Navosti Press Agency. (1990). *May Day: A Hundred Year History*. Moscow: Navosti Press Agency Publishing House.

Nicholls, D. (1986). *May Day 1886–1986*. Coventry: Coventry Trades Council.

Oliver, H. (1983). *The International Anarchist Movement in Late Victorian London*. London: Croom Helm.

Panaccione, A. (Ed.). (1989). *The Memory of May Day: An iconographic History of the Origins and Implanting of a Workers' Holiday*. Venice: Marsilio Editori.

Perry, M. (2000). *Bread and Work: The Experience of Unemployment, 1918–1939*. London: Pluto Press.

Peterson, A., Wahlström, M., Wennerhag, M., Christancho, C., and Sabucedo, J.-M. (2012). May Day demonstrations in five countries. *Mobilization: An International Quarterly*, 17(3), 281–300.

Pfaff, S., and Yang, G. (2001). Double-edged rituals and the symbolic resources of collective action: Political commemorations and the mobilisation of protest in 1989. *Theory and Society*, 30(4), 539–589.

Quail, J. (1978). *The Slow Burning Fuse: The Lost History of the British Anarchists*. London: Paladin.

Recchiuti, J.L. (1981). The Nottingham Independent Labour Party and the socialist revival 1880–1900. Unpublished MA thesis, University of Warwick.

Romero, P. (1987). *E. Sylvia Pankhurst*. New Haven, CT: Yale University Press.

Rucht, D. (2005). Threat and mobilisation: Comparing May Day protests in London and Berlin. *Mobilization: An International Journal*, 10(1), 163–182.

Salford May Day Gala Committee. (1978). *Salford May Day Gala*. Salford, UK: Salford May Day Gala Committee.

Sanders, W.S. (1927). *Early Socialist Days*. London: Hogarth Press.

Saville, J. (1977). May Day 1937. In A. Briggs and J. Saville (Eds), *Essays in Labour History*, vol. 3 (pp. 232–284). London: Croom Helm.

South Wales Miners' Federation. (1939). *May Day. May 1st 1939: Pageant of South Wales*. Cardiff: South Wales Miners' Federation.

Thompson, E.P. (1955). *William Morris: Romantic to Revolutionary*. London: Lawrence & Wishart.

Thorne, W. (1925). *My Life's Battles*. London: Newnes.

Uitermark, J. (2004). Looking forward by looking back: May Day protests in London and the strategic significance of the urban. *Antipode: A Radical Journal of Geography*, 36(4), 706–728.

Visser, J. (1989). *European Trade Unions in Figures*. Deventer, The Netherlands: Kluwer Law & Taxation Publications.

Viztelly, E.A. (1911). *The Anarchists: Their Faith and Their Record*. London: Bodley Head.

Ward, S. (2013). *Unemployment and the State in Britain*. Manchester: Manchester University Press.

Wrigley, C. (1990). *Lloyd George and the Challenge of Labour*. Brighton: Harvester-Wheatsheaf.

Wrigley, C. (2002). *British Trade Unions since 1933*. Cambridge: Cambridge University Press.

Wrigley, C. (2009). The European context: Aspects of British Labour and continental European socialism before 1920. In M. Worley (Ed.), *The Foundations of the Labour Party* (pp. 77–94). Farnham, UK: Ashgate.

Wrigley, C. (2015). Red May Days: Hopes and fears in Europe in the 1890s. In M. Davis (Ed.), *Crowd Actions in Britain and France from the Middle Ages to the Modern World* (pp. 208–223). Basingstoke, UK: Palgrave Macmillan.

7 The Context of Contemporary May Day Demonstrations in Six European Countries

Abby Peterson

In the remaining chapters the focus shifts to May Day rituals today and utilizes the demonstration survey data we collected in the European Science Foundation Euroscores Programme 'Caught in the Act of Protest: Contextualizing Contestation' (CCC), funded by FAS in 2009–2012 (principal investigator Professor Bert Klandermans, Free University of Amsterdam). This section is based on a set of cases of May Day demonstrations in six countries: Belgium, Britain, Italy, Spain, Sweden and Switzerland.

Against the background of the general context for European labour movements, in this chapter I will sketch the political contexts for May Day demonstrations during the period 2010 to 2012. To understand the political context of the May Day demonstrations in our study I pay particular attention to the institutionalized union strategies and the strength of the unions in the country in question, its industrial relations regimes, together with the strength of social democratic and/or socialist parties in the country. The industrial relations regimes signal the strength of organized labour in the countries included in our study. May Day rituals are performances of organized labour and the different industrial relations regimes set the perimeters for the staged events. Next, I will turn to the economic and political crisis and try to capture the impact that neoliberal monetarist policies, the so-called austerity measures, have had on the different countries in our sample. I find that in some countries, those most hit by neoliberal monetarist policies, austerity measures dominate the foreground scripts of today's May Day ritual performances. However, even in a country less impacted by austerity measures, the foreground script for the Swedish May Day performance of the Left Party centred on its opposition to the moderate-conservative government's neoliberal privatization of primary and secondary education and healthcare. Finally, I will account for how the organizers – trade unions and/or parties – have framed the demonstrations. Trade unions and in many countries social democratic and/or socialist parties are the partisan arms of the labour movement and hence to a large degree shape how May Day – the annual ritual of organized labour – is celebrated.

The General Socio-Economic Context for European Labour Movements

European May Day demonstrations are today staged within a specific socio-economic context – neoliberalism and its crisis. As della Porta (2014) points out this is not just an economic crisis, but also, and perhaps most importantly, a political crisis of responsibility.

> Neoliberal policies of deregulation, liberalization, and privatization reduce the capacity of political institutions to respond to citizens' expectations .... If neoliberalism had promised a separation of state and market ... instead political institutions are captured by giant corporations, as well as the growing collusion between business and politicians. The effects are then visible in a drastic increase of mistrust in institutions of representative democracy.
>
> (p. 24)

The current crisis has unleashed a wave of anti-austerity protests across Europe and May Day demonstrations are mobilizing labour movements within this climate of economic grievances and increase of mistrust in institutions of representative democracy – including (although to a lesser degree) a growing mistrust in their own traditional institutions, both unions and left parties. The crisis is to a large degree shaping how the rituals of May Day are being framed and enacted in the countries in our study. However, the impact of the current crisis is unevenly distributed among our country cases. Some of the countries have been hit harder than others, just as some groups of wage-earners within the national labour movements have been more affected by neoliberal monetarist policies – cutbacks in public spending, as well as deterioration of public services and related growth in inequality and poverty. The social justice theme typical of the 'old' labour movement, with its focus on the distribution of wealth, has again taken centre stage in the political debate (della Porta 2007, p. 21; Peterson, Wahlström and Wennerhag 2013, 2015). The question is whether what scholars have called the pacification or freezing of class conflict with the so-called mid-century compromise between labour and capital is beginning to thaw within the context of the current neoliberal crisis. Has class conflict re-emerged and is this reflected in today's May Day rituals?

May Day rituals developed in the early stages of industrial capitalism as an important manifestation of class struggle; the rituals were consolidated during the organized, state-regulated, Fordist, Keynesian, advanced stage of mature capitalism. In mature capitalism centralized and deep-rooted parties and unions structured institutionalized class conflict within the state. This latter stage was the heyday of Western European labour movements: the strength of the labour movement and its organizational bases, i.e. trade unions and in, many countries, social democratic/socialist parties, contributed to the development of a so-called mid-century compromise between labour and capital, with the growth of welfare states and citizens' and workers' rights. The Fordist compromise between labour and capital, however, led to the pacification of class struggle. At least during times of growth and prosperity class struggle was moderated through social reforms. Contemporary May Day rituals take place in a very different social formation of capitalism – unregulated financial markets and the meteoric rise of the financial class, together with the global expansion of capitalism, which is the hallmark of late neoliberalism.[1]

However, both the former Fordist Keynesian socio-economic regime and the current neoliberal regime have, according to Colin Crouch (2009, p. 22),

> had to manage an important contradiction, or at least tension: that between the insecurity and uncertainty created by the requirements of the market to adapt to shocks, and the need for democratic politics to respond to citizens' demands for security and predictability in their lives.

The crisis which has unfolded after 2008 reflects the contradiction between the requirements of the market and the demands upon representative democratic politics made by citizens. Hence the crisis is both economic and political.

The dynamics of economic and political globalization have generated a new set of 'winners' and 'losers' that to a degree supersedes traditional class cleavages from earlier stages of capitalism.

> The likely winners of globalization include entrepreneurs and qualified employees in sectors open to international competition, as well as cosmopolitan citizens. Losers of globalization, by contrast, include entrepreneurs and qualified employees in traditionally protected sectors, all unqualified employees, and citizens who strongly identify themselves with their national community.
>
> (Kriesi *et al.* 2008, p. 8)

This stage of capitalism then poses specific challenges to organized labour. With the erosion of the labour movement's traditional power base in industrial production in Europe, union membership is declining and the electoral basis of social democratic and socialist parties is undermined. The political space opened by neoliberalism opens as well an opposition to cosmopolitan liberalism often expressed as exclusivist and xenophobic nationalism (Kriesi *et al.* 2008). Parties on the far right are across Europe attracting many working-class voters who are disillusioned by social democratic and socialist parties and their capacity to offer them social protection.

In the countries in our study, the labour movements are meeting these challenges in different ways and with different degrees of (partial) success. Bartolini (2000, p. 22) argues that the institutional nature of the labour movement's organizations, both in relation to its social membership and its organizational form, is historically specific and country specific because it does not depend exclusively upon social class. The labour movements in our study have differently negotiated cross-class coalitions, as well as religious and language divides. What the labour movements appear to have in common is their lack of ability, or interest, in organizing those most affected by the crisis, what della Porta (2014) and Standing (2011) have called a new class – 'the social precariat' – young, often well educated, and unemployed or under-employed and with no social protection. The new class of the social precariat, together with many groups of unskilled labourers as well as migrants, are, to all intents and purposes, outside the realm of traditional organized labour movements. This situation poses a major challenge for Western European labour movements.

While scholars remind us that all of the stages of capitalism have had cyclical movements of growth and crisis, which were in turn moderated by compromises between free-market demands and demands for social protection, the economic and political crisis that the labour movements in our country sample are facing today is specific to neoliberalism. The austerity policies enacted to different degrees within these countries are bringing the language of class conflict back in movement mobilizations. But this is not only the industrial working-class language of the traditional basis of the labour movement. The neoliberal crisis today reflects 'the pauperization of the working class as well as the proletarianization of the middle classes' (della Porta 2014, p. 59). Peterson, Wahlström and Wennerhag (2015) found that in contemporary anti-austerity protests, particularly in trade union demonstrations, including May Day events, a significant number of participants reported a working-class identity despite an objective middle-class position. They conclude that the wave of anti-austerity protests in Europe is perhaps signalling a reawakening of what scholars have called the pacification of class conflict with the so-called Fordist-Keynesian compromise between labour and capital. However, as they point out, the new saliency of the class cleavage is now articulated in the context of neoliberalism.

Neoliberalism has the effects of exponentially increasing social inequalities, with a very small percentage of winners and a growing percentage of 'losers' (see e.g. Piketty 2014). The anti-austerity protests that have emerged have involved those affected by cuts in public spending and are subsequently cross-class coalitions, including a large component of people outside of the protected labour market, young, and often highly educated under- or unemployed precarious workers. May Day demonstrations today are to a large degree framed by the struggle against neoliberalism's monetarist policies and austerity measures and articulated within the country's industrial relations regime.

The Industrial Relations Regimes

The spread of globalization and its concomitant spread of neoliberalism are not universal moves on the part of capital or states. While many labour relations scholars hold that globalization pushes all countries towards neoliberalism and deregulation, thereby undermining the power of unions, another body of work argues that the impacts of globalization vary considerably – the so-called 'varieties of capitalism' thesis (e.g. Hall and Solskice 2001). Nationally specific contexts, and conflicts, provoke a reshuffling of the coalitions and identities on which the various union movements' political, economic and organizational strategies have long rested. Instead, for the purposes of our cursory review here, it is better to understand the recent trends in industrial relations in terms of the increasing divergence between the coordinated and liberal market economies (Thelen 2001; Iversen and Pontusson 1996). In liberal market economies we can observe a trend towards deregulation, including attempts to escape union regulation at all levels. The coordinated market economies, by contrast, appear to be seeking flexibility through 'controlled regulation (not deregulation but re-regulation of various issues at lower bargaining levels), but along with a continued commitment to coordination (especially of wage bargaining) at the multi-industrial level (though less and less at the confederal level)' (Thelen 2001, p. 13). To this duality of ideal types of political economies we can add a third – the 'mixed market economies' of southern Europe, or what Schmidt (2002, 2003) calls a kind of 'state-enhanced capitalism'. Like the coordinated market economies, the mixed market economies have historically been characterized by high levels of strategic coordination in the spheres of corporate governance and labour relations; however, unlike the coordinated market economies coordination has been largely secured by the actions of relatively interventionist states and not (or less so) by labour market institutions (Schmidt 2002). The global advance of neoliberalism is admittedly impacting even the so-called coordinated market economies and the mixed market economies, but not in the same ways in which neoliberalism is impacting the liberal market economies. Within the countries included in our study we can place Sweden and Belgium as classic coordinated market economies and Switzerland as a weakly coordinated market economy; Italy and Spain fall into the category of mixed market economies, which have retained state intervention in industrial relations but have turned to more corporatist, tripartite patterns of wage bargaining (Regini and Regalia 1997; Perez 2000). Among the six countries only Britain can be classified as a liberal market economy, which has a strong influence on their industrial relations regime. In the following I will account for the industrial relations regimes in each of the countries included in our study.

Sweden

In Sweden union density is high, with just under 70 per cent union membership among the employed in 2010 (Visser 2013). Even if union membership has steadily decreased from a high of 85 per cent in 1993, Sweden, Finland and Denmark are still world leading (Kjellberg 2009, p. 267). The Swedish trade union movement has historically been well integrated in the state and a key partner for the state's labour legislation, not least through the unions and in particular the Swedish trade union confederation (*Landsorganisationen*, LO), which brings together all blue-collar unions, and its close organic relations with the Social Democratic Party. Hence, the strength of trade unionism has relied heavily on its political channels rather than industrial action. The trade unions, upon the initiative of the Social Democratic government, established in the 1930s a 'basic agreement' with the employers' organizations, which encouraged a cooperative strategy by the unions resulting in almost uninterrupted industrial peace in exchange for social reforms and improved material conditions with which the foundations for the Swedish welfare state were laid (Kjellberg 2000; Hyman 2001, pp. 46–47). Subsequently, strike propensity in Sweden is low. The close historical interrelationship between LO and the Swedish Social Democratic Party, which governed for most of the twentieth century, encouraged a cooperative strategy by the unions and a 'social partnership' was forged – the integrative model of trade unionism. The same type of close official cooperation does not exist between the Social Democratic Party and the other two major trade union confederations, TCO (white-collar workers) and SACO (professionals), which never, officially as organizations, take part in May Day demonstrations.

However, the Swedish model of industrial relations is more than just a particular organizational configuration; what sets Sweden apart from most of the other advanced industrial societies is the 'unusually encompassing base of solidarity that unions were able to institutionalize and maintain' (Locke and Thelen 1995, p. 346). LO's solidaristic wage policy played a key role in this process. The moral economy of LO set the ideological terms of the labour unions' struggle. Egalitarianism and solidarity became the key underlying principles around which Swedish unions organized (Swenson 1989, pp. 68–69). While LO was forced to at least partially retreat from its solidaristic wage policy, egalitarianism and solidarity remain at the core of the identity of the labour movement in Sweden.

The stability of elite alignments provides a key to understanding the prevailing political culture in a country. In Sweden, the Social Democratic Party elites have more or less governed the country since the 1930s (apart from 17 years, after the mid-1970s); less since 2006 when a centre-right political coalition entered government. Since 2006 and during the entire period of our study (2010–2012) the Social Democrats had been in opposition, which makes a significant influence on how the rituals of May Day were framed by both the Social Democrats and the Left Party.

Belgium

While not reaching the level of membership density as in the Scandinavian countries, trade union coverage for wage earners is estimated at just over 50 per cent in Belgium, and the figure has remained relatively stable over the past 20 years (Visser 2013). Moreover, membership in the Belgian trade unions includes sizable contingents among the unemployed and (early) retired, which together account for around a third of their membership.

Historically, Belgian trade unionism has developed within a 'pillarized' context, with one trade union in each 'pillar'. Each pillar is affiliated with a political party and, subsequently, the Belgian trade union movement is split into three separate organizations – the socialist union confederation (ABVV/FGTB), the Catholic union confederation (ACV/CSC) and the smaller liberal union confederation (ACLVB/CGSLB). The 'pillarization' of Belgian trade unionism led to its stark institutionalization in the state apparatus. It is both within the state and to the state that the unions raise their demands (cf. Tilly 2004, p. 53). According to Van Gyes, De Witt and van der Hallen (2000, p. 106), 'in Belgium trade unions are clearly a fully-fledged "institution"'. However, these authors argue that while it may be the case that the trade unions are political institutions, they nevertheless try to play the role of a social movement with broad social interests, and see themselves as key players within Belgian civil society. They claim that there is some indication that the Belgian trade unions are repeatedly taking their distance, at least in their discourses if not in their formal structures, from their 'friendly' parties representing the same pillar, thus developing a 'mental' gap between themselves and party politics. Belgium is often grouped within the *social partnership regime* where the union density is relatively high and the political influence of the unions is high together with a high degree of autonomy to the state (Larsson 2013, p. 4). Belgium, where unions enjoy a good relationship with the state, will, nevertheless, and in contrast with the Scandinavian countries it is grouped with, mobilize members to mass actions on the streets. This radical potential for more unconventional strategies is reflected in Belgium's relatively high ranking in the European 'strike league table' (a list of European countries ranked by the days lost through strikes (DNW rates, i.e. 'Do Not Work' rates)) (Vandaele 2011).

In Belgium the party political system is linguistically divided between Flemish-speaking and French-speaking parties. There are no major national parties that bridge the language-divide. Following the general election held on 13 June 2010, a process of cabinet formation started in the country. The election produced a very fragmented political landscape, with 11 parties elected to the Chamber of Representatives, none of which won more than 20 per cent of the seats. The separatist New Flemish Alliance (N-VA), the largest party in Flanders and the country as a whole, has 27 of 150 seats in the lower chamber. The francophone Socialist Party (PS), the largest in Wallonia, holds 26 seats. Cabinet negotiations continued for a long time. On 1 June 2011, Belgium matched the record for time taken to form a new democratic government after an election, at 353 days. A socialist-led government coalition was named on 5 December 2011 and sworn in after a total of 541 days of negotiations and formation on 6 December 2011, and 589 days without an elected government. The instability of the party political landscape and the configuration of political elites have posed difficulties for the trade unions in

Belgium in forging more long-lasting alliances with governments in the country. Nevertheless, organized labour is a powerful influence in politics. Not simply a 'bread and butter' movement, much like the Swedish unions, Belgian labour unions take positions on education, public finance, defence spending, environmental protection, women's rights, abortion and other issues. They also provide a range of services, including the administration of unemployment benefits (Van Gyes, De Witt and van der Hallen 2000).

Switzerland

The major trade unions in Switzerland are historically allied with the Social Democratic Party and the party traditionally attracts most of its voters among blue-collar workers, and to a lesser degree among teachers and the elderly. The Swiss post-war model of labour relations is characterized by a weak form of corporatism and social peace (Kriesi *et al.* 1992; Kriesi 1995). Albeit in contrast with the Scandinavian countries the trade unions have consistently been the weaker party, with relatively low union density and coverage (17.1 per cent in 2010, Visser 2013), in combination with strong and well-coordinated employers' associations. Unions are also split between those with social democratic ties and those with Catholic bonds. Oesch (2010, p. 4) notes that '[in] Switzerland's culturally fragmented society, the strong salience of confessional and linguistic identities hampered the political articulation of the nascent class conflict from the beginning'. He further argues that the Swiss government has been promoting corporatism because of its relative weakness and its interest (also based on the national political tradition) in bridging the multiple potential conflict lines in Swiss society. The Swiss political system with its frequent popular referendums is furthermore an important instrument for trade unions to impose vetoes on unwanted reforms (Armingeon 1997). The referendum system moreover seems to lead to a greater stress on union strategies based on influencing public opinion compared to the Scandinavian model of corporatism, which is more focused on the negotiating table. Armingeon underscores that Swiss corporatism lacks integration with a Keynesian steering of the economy and welfare reforms to compensate for wage moderation. In sum, although Swiss unions work on a political level and although their strategies are not entirely unlike the 'social partnership' model of integrative unionism, we argue that in relation to our other cases, it is best characterized as 'business unionism' (cf. Hyman 2001), however, operating within a weakly coordinated market economy.

The Social Democrats have for decades been part of the 'grand coalition' (Social Democrats, Liberal Party, Christian Democratic Party and the Swiss People's Party), which governed Switzerland between 1959 and 2003. However, they have always had a minority share of the cabinet posts in the federal government. Also after the break-up of the 'grand coalition' in 2003, the Social Democratic Party has continued to be part of the federal government. In short, the stability of elite alignments is uncertain, with more fluctuating configurations of power since 2003. In addition a 'left' and a 'moderate' wing further divide the Social Democratic Party.

Spain

Trade unionism in Spain, disrupted during the long Franco regime, remerged from its underground existence in 1977. Since 1978, the largest confederations have been CCOO (*Comisiones Obreras*) and UGT (*Unión General de Trabajadores*), both representative of integrative unionism. Both confederations give priority to the action strategy of collective bargaining. In addition to these two major confederations on the national level, in Galicia, the Basque Country and Catalonia some unions are linked to independence parties with large popular support. These latter union organizations have some links with anarchist groups, especially when organizing demonstrations independently from the major union confederations.

Union membership in Spain is low compared to other OECD countries and the lowest in the six countries studied (Visser 2009). This can largely be explained by the fact that 90 per cent of the workforce is employed in small and medium-sized enterprises (Hamann and Lucio 2003). In spite of low affiliation levels, Spanish unions play a central role, for instance through representing the workforce in work councils and during negotiations, and in collective bargaining, which affects 90 per cent of wage earners in the private sector (Jiménez and Saurina 2005, pp. 7–8). These factors mitigate the low density of membership.

During the transition to democracy the two major union confederations, UGT and CCOO, were very close to the Social Democrats (PSOE) and the Communist Party (PC) respectively, re-enacting their historical roots. But this is no longer the case. During the 1980s, when the PSOE-led government advanced their pension and labour market policies, union opposition to the left parties was awakened and general strikes were called. Spanish trade unions have since the late 1980s retained a relatively high degree of autonomy with respect to political parties, which even allowed the unions to become involved in state agencies and administration during the conservative government of the Popular Party 1996–2004 (Hamann and Lucio 2003, p. 72). Trade unionism in Spain retains at least the potential for radical opposition, mobilizing class and regional interests in conflict with the state. Both Spain and Italy belong to what has been called a *polarized/state-centred regime* of industrial relations. Within this regime strikes and demonstrations 'are seen as an important means of political protest to influence the state to take action' (Larsson 2013, pp. 4–5). Both countries are usually in the lead of the 'strike league table', further indicating the radical potential of union movements in these countries (Vandaele 2011).

Although Spain has not witnessed the exceptional levels of strikes that swept the country during late Francoism and during the transition to democracy, levels remain high. In the last two decades, both CCOO and UGT have led general strikes in 1985, 1988, 1992, 1994, 2002 and 2010 (Gorodzeisky and Richards 2013; van der Meer 2000, p. 580). Nevertheless, the relative decrease in strikes and lockouts is probably a response to the involvement of unions and employers' organizations in the preparation, decision-making and implementation processes of the government's social and economic policy-making. The Spanish state has displayed a relative openness to trade union demands and influence and has since 1992 to a degree incorporated labour organizations in policy-making (Visser 2009; Beyeler and Rucht 2010). This explains high levels of protest activity with mostly moderate action repertoires. Political developments in conjunction with the economic crisis have, however, at least to a degree curbed this preference for moderate action strategies.

Between 1982 and 2014 social democrats (PSOE) have been in government for 21 years and the Popular Party for 11. In some of the legislatures the government had no majority but always found the support of minority groups, which were either the nationalist liberals who supported both left and right governments, or the left-wing parties that supported PSOE. These pacts have provided legislative stability in the past. This indicates the strength of left parties in Spain; however, after the 2011 elections a conservative majority governs the country. The ruling Popular Party has been shadowed by accusations of corruption and anti-austerity demonstrations have been accompanied by a strong mistrust of political parties and to a lesser degree the traditional unions (Peterson, Wahlström and Wennerhag 2013). While the level of mistrust of traditional unions is not as high as that of political parties, the level of mistrust is nevertheless relatively significant, posing a potential problem for the Spanish labour movement.

Italy

In Italy the trade union movement is dominated by three major politically aligned federations: CGIL (*Confederazione Italiana Generale del Lavoro*), CISL (*Confederazione Italiana Sindacati Lavoratori*) and UIL (*Unione Italiana del Lavoro*). After the collapse of the Italian party system in the 1980s direct ties with political parties have dissolved but they have retained their general political orientations. CGIL is more or less aligned with the social democratic Partito Democratico with a critical minority allied with the Communist Party's more left-wing successors. CISL's current leader supports the project of reuniting the Christian democrats who are presently dispersed among various parties (Namuth 2013, p. 1). UIL stresses its secular republican traditions. These three confederations claim roughly 12.5 million members, however almost 50 per cent are retired. According to Namuth, union density was about 35 per cent in 2013 (excluding pensioners). Operating within a coordinated market economy the industrial relations regime is polarized and state-centred and collective bargaining is conflict-orientated.

While at first blush the Italian labour movement, with its fragmented structure around ideological divides, would appear to be the precise opposite of the Swedish labour movement's highly centralized structure around occupational divides, Locke and Thelen (1995, p. 355ff.) point to a common ideological ground – the key role played by the ideas of egalitarianism within their union strategies. These authors write that 'stemming from the Hot Autumn struggles of the 1960s, egalitarianism became the ideological glue of the union movement, bringing together skilled and unskilled workers as well as cementing an alliance among the three competing confederations' (p. 355).

In 2009 an agreement reforming collective bargaining was forged with the Berlusconi government and the CISL, UIL and the right-wing union UGL, but the largest confederation, CGIL, did not sign. This agreement effectively divided the country's union movement. While CISL leader Raffaele Bonanni is a convinced proponent of round-table politics who believes that 'a good agreement counts for more than protest on the piazza' (Namuth 2013, p. 3), CGIL possesses the required strength for mass mobilizations in protest at the government's austerity measures. These mass demonstrations have collected additional support from (elements within) the moderate left Partito Democratico and the smaller left-wing parties.

Furthermore, since the 1990s new competing organizations have emerged in the private and public service sectors, autonomously operating rank-and-file unions and associations of the precariously employed, who feel unrepresented by the major unions and their strategy of concentrating on wage conflicts (Namuth 2013). CISAL and CONFSAL are both confederations of autonomous unions and Cobas is a federation of local rank-and-file committees, all which are of a significant size. The emergence of these new militant autonomous unions and committees has further divided the Italian labour movement between a left wing and a moderate and right wing. The radical left-wing unions and committees, reappropriating the traditional union language of egalitarianism as their own, also (but only to a degree) reflect the concerns of the growing army of precarious workers in Italy, estimated to be 17.5 per cent of the workforce, most under the age of 35 (Namuth 2013). According to della Porta and Mosca (2007, p. 6):

> [R]adical trade unions emerged in Italy during the 1990s from a series of labour mobilizations. In their forms of action, organizational formulas and discourses, they differ from the three traditional, confederate trade unions ... not only in their critique of neo-liberal reforms, but also in their emphasis on direct action, participative democracy and 'class identity'.

The spread of the autonomous trade unions marks a new labour militancy radicalized by the economic crisis and austerity measures, together with the deregulation of employment. But their growth also symbolizes the gap between precarious workers and traditional trade unions in mobilizations against precarity in Italy (Choi and Mattoni 2010, p. 226).

Britain

Britain is the sole country in our sample where trade unionism operates within a decidedly liberal market economy. Kathleen Thelen (2001, p. 39) argues that as in the United States, 'the trend in British industrial relations in the last twenty years has been in the direction of deregulation in the sense of sharply declining union influence at all levels'. Union density in Britain has steadily dwindled since its heydays in the 1960s and 1970s to 27 per cent in 2010 (Visser 2013). British trade unionism has been traditionally founded on what Richard Hyman (2001) calls the market-class axis and is based on a voluntaristic model with *de facto* rather than *de jure* rights. This implies that the state is more or less circumvented in its model of trade unionism – British unions, as 'industry's opposition', have historically conceived their role in primarily economic rather than political terms (Flanders 1970, p. 34ff.). According to Hyman (2001, p. 72):

> Even after they had helped create the Labour Party, at the turn of the century, they normally treated political action as very subsidiary to their main preoccupation with collective bargaining: and were very jealous of any attempt by governments – including Labour governments – to intervene uninvited in their terrain.

During the Thatcher regime the power of the unions fell dramatically: new legislation was enacted in their disfavour; the labour market was transformed and their traditional bastion of strength, the manufacturing industry, declined substantially; the level of unemployment rose significantly, particularly among manual workers; there was a sharp fall in trade union membership; and collective bargaining decreased in importance (Hyman 2001, pp. 103–106; Waddington 2000, p. 580ff.). These major setbacks during the Thatcher government led also to a dramatic weakening of trade unions' influence within the Labour Party, and the Conservative stand on industrial relations lived on during the New Labour government. What New Labour offered British trade unionism was a diluted understanding of 'partnership', which reinforced the legitimacy of the role of management as the protector of the common interests of workers and employers and which British trade union leaders have only reluctantly accepted (Hyman 2001, p. 111; see also Waddington 2000 and Howell 1999). However, this was an economic 'partnership', not a 'social partnership' with a given political role for unions, and deviates from the notion of 'social partnership' being forged elsewhere in Europe. With the return of a Conservative government in 2012 trade unions have again lost their albeit restricted power base in the state.

Occupying the terrain between market and class, British trade unions have traditionally displayed a militant, but sectional and defensive economism (Waddington 2000, p. 594; Phelps Brown 1990). However, the British trade unions' historical militancy has become a trait of the past. Since the

1990s British employers face a much more docile union movement, which now seldom implements its strike weapon (Thelen 2001). The UK is a typical example of a liberal pluralist regime of industrial relations, which implies that there is limited state intervention in industrial relations. Furthermore since the 1980s the UK union movement has had a decidedly limited role in transactions with the state. Facing the brunt of neoliberalism and deregulation within a liberal market economy, we can place British unionism today as containing elements of a highly suppressed form of radical-oppositional unionism and elements of a diluted and relatively unsuccessful form of business unionism (Hyman 2001).

The industrial relations regimes, together with the strength of social democratic/socialist parties in the countries in our sample, are influencing how and in what ways organized labour is meeting the challenges of the economic crisis and in many of the countries its concomitant austerity measures. It is important to keep in mind that the impact of the economic crisis has had an uneven impact across Europe and even in our country cases.

The Impact of the Crisis

From the early to mid-1990s the countries included in our sample all experienced to various degrees a period of economic growth; for some, particularly Spain and Britain, their economies boomed. What we now know is that this boom was built in large part on an unsustainable growth model. Underpinning much of that growth was a dramatic rise in household debt and/or public debt. The increase in household debt was driven by asset price inflation in housing and stock markets, as well as cheap goods from China and elsewhere in the Far East, which was fuelled by a global financial system that unleashed from regulation was developing ever more 'creative' ways of making money (partly by funding and encouraging the rising tide of household mortgage debt). According to Kitson, Martin and Tyler (2011, p. 289), 'the simple process was that consumers in many advanced economies could borrow cheaply to spend, and the resultant increase in consumer demand stimulated economic growth'. The economic 'good times', much of it driven by consumption, came to an abrupt end in 2008 with the global banking crisis. One of the consequences of the banking crisis and the recession it provoked has been sharp rises in levels of gross government debt in almost every Western economy (the notable exception in our sample is Switzerland and to a lesser degree Sweden). The common response has been the new politics of austerity. 'Governments almost everywhere have embarked, or are embarking on, programmes of major cuts and reductions in public spending on a scale not seen for decades' (p. 292).

As argued in the introduction, the global financial crisis has had different impacts on the countries in our study and has in addition impacted unevenly within the countries. Spain and Italy were the most dramatically hit by the crisis. In early 2008 the global crisis burst Spain's property bubble, leading to a weakening economy and soaring unemployment, which has since 2009 hovered around 26 per cent. The downside of the property bubble was a dramatic rise in the levels of personal debt. The average level of household debt tripled in less than a decade, putting pressure on lower to middle income groups to meet their mortgages and resulting in a wave of evictions across the country. While Spain's governmental debt was well below the EU average in 2009 and remains so, the country's financial problems stem from these high levels of private debt. The ratio of private to public debt is standing at 87 per cent to 13 per cent (Hadjimichalis 2011, p. 256; Lane 2012). The opposite was the case in Italy, which has relatively high levels of private savings and low levels of household indebtedness. However, in 2010 the Italian governmental gross debt stood at 116 per cent of the GDP and has risen steadily to a whopping 127 per cent in 2012, the second largest debt ratio after Greece (http://stats. oecd.org/OECDStat_Metadata/; see also Lane 2012). The real GDP growth rate volumes sank across the board in 2009 in all of the countries in our study; however, in Spain and Italy they have remained in minus figures. Their economic comebacks have been only marginal and in Italy the (significant) economic recovery has been geographically situated only in parts of northern Italy. As in Spain the European monetary fund put strong pressures on the government to cut their debt, resulting in severe austerity measures. While the unemployment rates have not rocketed as radically as in Spain, the levels are high, nearly 13 per cent in 2012. Again, unemployment has been geographically unevenly spread, with low levels in the industrial north and high levels in southern Italy and Sicily.

Belgium and Britain were also severely hit by the crisis, with sovereign debt/GDP ratios in Belgium just behind Italy at slightly over 100 per cent of GDP and in Britain slightly under (OECD; http://stats.oecd.org/OECDStat_ Metadata/). Both countries have had relatively weak economic recoveries after the 2009 recession measured by their real GDP growth rate-volumes (ibid.). In Britain the 'Conservative-Liberal coalition government announced the biggest cuts in state spending since World War II. The plan is to cut 490,000 public sector jobs' (Kitson, Martin and Tyler 2011, p. 294). While cuts in public spending have not been as spectacular as in Britain, Belgium has also launched a tough programme of austerity measures. Despite these policies, unemployment rates in both countries have remained during the period 2009 to 2012 at around roughly 7.5 to 8.5 per cent. In Britain the private sector has been able to pick up some of the slack after public sector lay-offs and in Belgium the unemployment rate increased less than in other European countries, reflecting widespread labour hoarding, in part through the extensive use of reduced work time schemes promoted by the labour unions (www.oecd. org/eco/surveys/Belgium2013_Overview_ENG%20(2).pdf).

Sweden and Switzerland are the two countries in our study which were least hit by the global financial crisis and the decrease in real growth rate volumes in 2009 were promptly in the black again in the period between 2010 and 2012 (http://stats.oecd.org/OECDStat_Metadata/). These are the only countries in our study in which the GDP per capita has steadily increased during the period 2009–2012. The unemployment rate in Switzerland is significantly low in relation to the other countries, remaining under 3 per cent during the period. Sweden on the other hand has a relatively high rate of unemployment, hovering around 8 per cent of the workforce. As in the other countries, the labour market does not function well for young people without upper-secondary education, for those with a non-EU migrant background or for the low-skilled in general. Anti-austerity measures in these countries also deviate from the other four countries in our study. Cutbacks in public spending have been relatively modest in Sweden under the conservative government coalition, which has instead accelerated the privatization trend in public services within healthcare and primary and secondary education. These latter neoliberal policies have awakened opposition in some elements in the labour movement, particularly the Left Party and its supporters. In Switzerland, with a liberal privatized welfare regime and a nominal public service sector, cutbacks in public spending do not pose the same threat as in the other countries in our study.

The economic crisis, and in some cases neoliberal monetarist policies, bear upon the foreground scripts for the performances of May Day, as does the underlying script which shapes the 'tradition' of May Day in the country – its conventional protagonists and their historical relationship with the labour movement.

The Performances of May Day Today

May Day rituals are still today the labour movement's annual trooping of the colour *and* a protest event for the claims on the movement's current agenda – currently within the context of neoliberalism and the present economic crisis. May Day ritual performances open for a variety of potential actors and directors, for example, trade unions, socialist/social democratic parties, communist parties, anarchist groups, new left parties, etc., together with scripts and props, for example, badges and buttons, flags, banners and placards, slogans and songs, which reinforce the sense of 'we'. In this section I will delve deeper into the country cases in our study, highlighting the foreground scripts of the ritual performances against the backdrop of the deep background scripts, which form the performances' underlying 'traditions'. The data for this section was collected by the CCC country teams and entered in the CCC database's supplementary files for each event.[2]

In *Sweden* May Day has been a national holiday since 1939. May Day marches in Sweden have historically been a ritual display of the labour movement's political community emphasizing, first, the historical links between the blue-collar trade unions and social democracy, and second and to a far lesser degree, the links between the working class and the Swedish Left Party (which until 1990 was the country's main communist party). Due to the historical division between the Social Democratic Party and the Left Party, May Day marches have usually been organized separately, with the LO unions solely co-organizing Social Democratic marches. Since the mid-1930s the May Day demonstrations have had a more or less official ritual character, and the demonstrations have been peaceful and above all predictable (Chapter 4). The development of the Left Party since the 1960s, from a party with its electoral base among blue-collar workers to principally attracting white-collar workers, professionals and highly educated radicals (Arter 1991, 2002), has also been mirrored in the social composition of the Left Party May Day marches (Peterson, Wahlström and Wennerhag 2011). The party and their May Day demonstrations customarily focus on so-called new social movement issues, i.e. feminism, LGBT rights, environmentalism, peace and human rights. Since the late 1990s the Left Party May Day marches in Sweden's major cities have been comparatively larger than those organized by the Social Democratic Party and LO (see Chapter 10).

We have studied May Day demonstrations in Stockholm in 2010, both the Social Democratic and LO demonstration (3,000 participants) and the Left Party demonstration (4,200 participants); the 2011 Social Democratic and LO demonstration (900 participants) and the 2011 Left Party demonstration in Malmö (2,000 participants); and the 2012 Social Democratic and LO demonstration (2,450 participants) and the 2012 Left Party demonstration (3,400 participants) in Gothenburg. From the placards, handouts and slogans during the demonstrations we interpreted the main issue of all of these demonstrations as addressing economic justice, with the goals for the demonstrations including reducing unemployment and stopping public sector cutbacks. The Social Democrats were in opposition and this was evident in the organizers' framing of the events in our sample. The reasons spokespersons for the organizers gave varied but we could discern a pattern with Social Democratic organizers more often emphasizing tradition – 'to celebrate the holiday of the Workers' Movement'. The following excerpt from an interview with a spokesperson from the 2010 Social Democratic May Day demonstration well summarizes the Social Democratic and LO stance on May Day.

To celebrate the red-letter day of the Workers' Movement, but also to focus the injustices we see in society; to create faith in the future and to channel the commitment of our members .... And it is also a unique opportunity, at least in our Swedish context, which brings us possibilities that almost no other political parties have to focus our viewpoints and to have an impact. For sure, there is a communicative purpose with this. May Day is an opportunity when the media really focuses on us. All media write about us on May Day, at least established media. Our opportunities are very good if one handles them in the right way. And for a political movement that wants to reach out with its message, this is an opportunity that it would be very stupid to miss.

Somewhat similarly, but emphasizing the range of 'new social movement' issues embraced by the Left Party, the spokesperson for the 2010 Stockholm Left Party march gave the following reasons for their annual May Day mobilizations.

> From the beginning to draw attention to the condition of the working class in Sweden. Since the 1940s we have increasingly focused on international issues such as imperialism, since the 1970s environmentalism and women's situation, and during the 1980s racism and discrimination of immigrants.

The spokesperson for the Left Party also emphasized the role that the May Day event has for mobilizing their supporters and as a display of strength as a socialist and feminist party.

The organizers from both the Social Democratic/LO union demonstrations and the Left Party demonstrations mention the importance of tradition, more so the former, but both also emphasize the importance of using the event to communicate their politics. In Sweden, May Day is a major media event and an opportunity to highlight their political messages (see Chapter 4 and Chapter 10).

The working classes in *Belgium* have celebrated May Day since the end of the nineteenth century and since 1947 May Day has been a legal holiday. During the 1950s struggles emerged between the leaderships of the Social Democrat Party, the Belgian Socialist Party (PSB/BSP) and the FGTB/ABVV trade union federation (Croes 2010). The struggles culminated in 1974 and as a result of multiple political factors, the union movement that was most closely related to the May Day event grew weaker. Subsequently, May Day lost much of its more militant oppositional character. Nowadays the May Day events are more or less peaceful marches with a relatively low turnout.

Our study includes the 2010 May Day demonstration in Antwerp organized by the main social democratic trade union ABVV and the Social Democratic Party with approximately 2,000 marchers. Like most of the May Day events in our study the main issue was economic and social justice and a defence of the public sector. The event organizers claim that:

> [G]iven the severe financial and economic crisis, the problem of austerity measures stands at the fore. In Antwerp the imminent closing of the Opel car factory is another major issue. Also with the elections next month, this May Day event is also very focused on that as well.

In relation to *Switzerland*'s May Day traditions, 1 May is a bank holiday in 14 cantons and May Day marches are staged in several cities. Yet even though the major May Day demonstrations are mostly peaceful, nearly every year there are street fights between young people from radical left-wing groups and the police, particularly in Zurich (Wessendorf 2008).

The main May Day demonstrations are organized collaboratively by the Social Democratic Party and those unions that are locally active. Size matters, however, and the manifestations are usually dominated by the largest leftist unions.

Two May Day demonstrations in Switzerland are included; first, the 2010 demonstration in Zurich with around 8,000 participants, which was organized by a May Day Committee including approximately 60 organizations. This coalition brought together small left-wing parties, parts of the Social Democratic Party, migrant organizations, foreign left parties and cultural organizations, together with Gewerkschaftsbund des Kanton Zurich, which is an umbrella organization for 13 Social Democratic trade unions in the canton. The demonstration focused on economic and social injustice and defended the public sector. Second, the 2011 demonstration in Geneva was considerably smaller and attracted around 1,000 participants. The event was, much like Zurich, organized by a coalition of the main trade unions and left political parties (the reformed communist party, Parti du Travail; Parti Socialiste; the Social Democratic Party; Solidarités, a local left-wing party; together with Les Verts, the Greens). The main issue addressed was wage inequalities and the demands were for the introduction of a minimum legal wage and equal pay for men and women.

The May Day tradition originated in 1890 in *Spain* and it was recognized as a national holiday in 1931 with the proclamation of the republic. From 1939 up to 1975 the celebration was forbidden, but since 1978 – after Franco's death in 1975 – it has been celebrated annually (Chapter 5). However, the first post-Franco May Day demonstrations were met with brutal repression from the police authorities, still sympathetic to Franco (Foner 1986). In the years during the democratic transition turnout was very high as May Day celebrations were vital for the construction of an open and democratic public space where people in general and workers in particular could symbolically take to the streets for at least a day. Furthermore, these May Day demonstrations staged during the years of the democratic transition allowed demonstrators the opportunity to appeal for the expected social democratic/socialist reforms. Once democratic life was firmly established, May Day turnout, not unexpectedly, diminished considerably (Chapter 5).

The May Day demonstrations in Spain included in the study were the 2010 march in Barcelona organized by CCOO and UGT with some 8,000 participants; and two 2011 demonstrations in Vigo, the largest metropolitan area of Galicia – one organized by the two main trade union confederations, CCOO and UGT, which attracted around 15,000 marchers and a smaller demonstration with *ca.* 2,000 participants organized by a radical left regional trade union, *Confederación Intersindical Galega* (Galician Union Confederacy). While invoking the 'tradition' of May Day as the celebration of the workers' movement, the main issue of the Barcelona event was economic and social justice and a defence of public services. According to an organizing spokesperson:

[I]t is the tradition each May Day to celebrate the workers' day in Spain, at least in the age of democracy. In this year we call on our members to mobilize because the government and economic elites are attacking our pension systems and they do not supply answers to the high level of unemployment.

The Vigo demonstrations were more specified as to their demands and both were organized in opposition to the labour reforms and welfare cutbacks. The large demonstration organized by the main trade union confederations also emphasized tradition *and* struggle.

We march because we celebrate Labour Day. Because this year we are in a context of continued financial stress resulting in increased job losses, a wage income decline, deterioration of working conditions, and significant cuts in social benefits and public services, we are calling for other policies which are more equitable.

The smaller Vigo demonstration targeted anti-austerity policies they perceived as coming from the capital. According to a demonstration spokesperson, under the theme 'employment not capital reforms, defend our rights', 'Galician trade unionism rejects the policy of social cuts taken by various governments following the guidelines of Madrid'.

In *Italy* the earliest May Day celebrations were met with severe restrictions and state repression, nonetheless prior to World War I the organized labour movement succeeded in consolidating the events, particularly in some northern industrial cities. The most popular format for these early May Day events, organized by the political parties, were festive garden parties beyond the city gates. And the most 'dignified' form of action for the socialist workers' movement was abstention from work (Chapter 3, p. 49). After the war May Day demonstrations and festivities were disrupted by fascist violence and between 1926 and 1945 May Day could only be clandestinely celebrated. In the immediate post-World War II years May Day demonstrations were massive and in contrast with the earlier demonstrations the trade unions now emerged as the main organizers of the celebrations. During this period the political parties on the left have become less and less involved in the May Day events (Chapter 3). According to Reiter, the May Day celebrations of the 'old left' are today increasingly faced with competition from new actors (Chapter 3, pp. 60–62).

In Italy the major trade unions organize two public events to celebrate May Day and address workers' rights: one relatively large national demonstration in an Italian city, which is changed annually, and a number of smaller demonstrations across the country, which often speak to more local concerns. According to Choi and Mattoni (2010, p. 229), these events are in stark contrast to the EuroMayDay Parade.

The EMP is not a traditional demonstration but a parade: a sort of carnival where various floats equipped with sound systems play different genres of music, from reggae to techno, followed by people dancing and parading at the same time, was novel with respect to traditional First of May demonstrations in Italy.

Choi and Mattoni maintain that from the start the organizers of EuroMayDay planned their event so that they would be perceived as different from the main trade union events. The EuroMayDay was first organized as a national event in 2001, but since 2004 the event is part of a transnational protest campaign (see Chapter 10).

The May Day demonstrations covered in Italy included a small event in Florence 2011 with around 500 participants organized by the three main trade union confederations: CGIL (post-communist), CISL (Catholic) and UIL (socialist). Workers' rights and social justice were the focus, but spokespersons emphasized more local concerns and stated that 'the target is the city government'. Where all of the other May Day events were organized as recurring annual events, the 2011 Florence march was the single May Day demonstration in our database where organizers claimed that the demonstration was a specific reaction to a specific event. The march was a response to the new ordinance initiated by the PD (Social Democratic) mayor of Florence[3] that shops would be kept open on May Day. 'Workers have only one holiday which is their holiday the whole year.' The 2011 May Day demonstration in Florence (on a Sunday) was a defence of May Day and its values. CGIL secretary-general Susanna Camusso declared: 'This date is our identity' (cited in della Porta and Reiter 2012, p. 14).

The 2011 Milan EuroMayDay brought together roughly 5,000 marchers and was organized by the San Precario Network, a radical left-wing activist network, and CUB, a radical left-wing trade union. Here the plight of precarious workers was the focus (see Chapter 10).

> Precarious and flexible working conditions have become the new working conditions and unions don't have a reply to solve this issue. Our goal is to solve the precarious condition with a universal income. Now we are also working towards a precarious workers' strike.

The tradition of May Day as a workers day in *Britain* is long; however, the day was first established as a bank holiday (national holiday) by the Labour government in 1978 and it has survived since then, albeit not without attempts by both Conservatives and some in the Labour Party to annul its status. Traditionally the marches are organized by trade unionists as a show of working-class unity, but the marches also gather a unique mix including workers from international communities, youth, students and other political organizations on the left. May Day celebrations in Britain are generally not a show of support for the Labour Party, but do garner backing from the left wing of the party.

In Britain the 2010 May Day demonstration in London brought together roughly 5,000 marchers and was organized by the London May Day

Organising Committee, which included various TUC trade unions and local and regional TUC chapters, immigrant organizations and various left-wing groups. Again the main issue was economic and social justice and a defence of the public sector. However, the spokesman for the organizing committee emphasized that their goal was

> to maintain the tradition of the international workers' day by reminding ordinary citizens of the tradition. May Day is important for international solidarity and to exchange messages with other capital cities around the world.

Discussion

Belgium and Sweden have deep-rooted May Day traditions celebrating the achievements of their powerful labour movements and supporting social democratic and/or socialist parties. In both countries May Day is a major media event. In Belgium, this had the effect of underlining traditions of the May Day ritual, but above all organizers emphasized their opposition to the government's austerity measures, the closing of the Opel plant and with the left in opposition the upcoming elections. In Sweden parallel demonstrations throughout the country are traditionally organized by the Left Party and the Social Democratic Party together with LO (the blue-collar union confederation). May Day in Sweden is a highly visible media event during which the Social Democratic and Left Party leadership give speeches across the country and state their goals – as in Belgium, May Day opens an 'official' arena for potential Social Democratic and Left Party opposition. In 2010, with elections pending in the autumn, the left was in opposition. May Day 2010 marked the kick-off for their bid to regain control of the government.

May Day in Spain, Italy and Switzerland does not have the same long-standing labour movement tradition as in Sweden and Belgium. The labour movements in both Italy and Spain experienced long periods of disruption during their respective dictatorships when its historical organizational bases, unions and socialist parties, had only underground, clandestine existences. In Switzerland May Day is recognized as a bank holiday in only some of its cantons: May Day is not a national holiday. Furthermore, support for the social democratic and/or socialist parties in Spain, Italy and Switzerland is more divided, with significant elements in the demonstrations with more militant agendas. In Switzerland, at the level of the demonstration context, the May Day event often attracts young radical left dissidents to the ranks of demonstrators, often leading to police–demonstrator confrontations (Wessendorf 2008). In Zurich 2010, rioting young people interrupted the May Day demonstration and over 400 were placed under arrest. The cultural tradition of May Day in Switzerland annually opens a potential space for dissent, which helps explain the high degree of contention in the 2010 ritual event in Zurich. With a relatively small radical milieu in Switzerland, the yearly May

Day ritual offers an opportunity for radical groups to 'piggy-back' the event and capture media attention (Peterson *et al.* 2012). Aside from the small fraction of militant youth in the Zurich demonstration, the May Day organizers for both of the Swiss demonstrations surveyed stressed social justice issues – the introduction of a minimum wage and equal pay for men and women. The organizers did not mention the history of May Day nor the celebration of past labour movement achievements.

In relation to Spain the tension between radical anarchist groups/unions with separatist regional interests and the major union confederations is inscribed in their model of labour relations, which is on the one hand polarized and on the other state-centred. Given this model of trade unionism, together with the strain of the economic crisis and widespread grievances following a 9.7 per cent growth in unemployment between 2007 and 2009, not unpredictably the events were framed by the organizers as contentious, which spokespersons substantiate. The major labour confederation organizers of the May Day events surveyed emphasized the celebration of the labour movement, its ritual content, but also underlined the necessity to protest the government's austerity policies. In contrast the organizers of the smaller event staged in Vigo by a radical Galician union stressed only their protest of labour reforms and austerity measures. Even the demonstrations in Italy reflected the tension or gap between the radical wing of the labour movement and the main trade unions. On the one hand the demonstration organized by the traditional unions in Florence focused on a local ordinance that local shops would be kept open on 1 May thereby undermining the tradition of May Day as a bank holiday. The organizers of EuroMayDay in Milan 2011, who distance themselves from the organized Italian labour movement, framed the event as a platform for precarious workers to voice their concerns, which they feel are not addressed by the major union confederations.

Britain is an anomaly among the countries in our study. Britain has the least entrenched May Day tradition and its status as a bank holiday remains threatened. May Day demonstrations find only weak support from the left wing of the Labour Party. May Day organizers in Britain are hence struggling to establish the event as a celebration of the achievements of the labour movement. What was fought for and won in the early twentieth century by the other countries in our comparison (given the disrupted May Day history of Spain under Franco rule and Italy under Mussolini) is still contended in Britain. The motives cited by the British May Day organizers are in the cultural context of British May Day 'contentious' – hence the paradox. Analysing the impact of the strain of the economic crisis measured by the short-term increase in the unemployment rate, Britain was again an anomaly. We would expect that the grievances generated by the growth in unemployment would have increased the salience of politically contentious motives, which was again not the case. Organizers underscored the need to protect the ritual of May Day as a celebration of the achievements of the labour movement. Furthermore, as Britain had the shortest time to elections and with the

Conservative Party leading in the polls, the strong effect of electoral proximity on traditional motives on the part of organizers rather than politically contentious motives seems counterintuitive.

In the countries in our study May Day demonstrations are attempting (to various degrees) to repair the bridges between the achievements of organized labour during the Keynesian, advanced stage of mature capitalism and the threats posed to these achievements in the contemporary stage of neoliberalism, accelerated during the economic crisis. Neoliberalism, with control of economic factors shifting from the public sector to the private sector, i.e. privatization and deregulation, together with fiscal austerity, tenders a new political context for May Day as the celebration of organized labour. The labour movements in our study are meeting this challenge in different ways and with different degrees of success. The achievements that had been, often bitterly, won through class struggle now have to be defended on different terms, in a new class structure. In the following chapters we will look more closely at the participants in contemporary May Day demonstrations. Who demonstrates? What are the demographic and socio-economic profiles of the participants? Has class, and class identity, re-entered the dynamics of May Day?

And perhaps most importantly, why do people demonstrate? Dieter Rucht (2003) has described the conventional May Day demonstrations of the 'red left' in London 2000 as a

> basically hollow ritual. Today, they only attract relatively small groups within the unionized workers. Participation is an obligation for those committed, and the speeches tend to lack inspiration and appeal. Instead of attending such a demonstration, nearly the entire working population has set other priorities for themselves: watching TV, washing their cars, going on a family outing.
>
> (p. 178)

May Day demonstrations are yearly political rituals in the six countries we studied and it is the organizers and most importantly the participants in these rituals who imbue the demonstrations with their meanings. May Day demonstrations are never 'hollow rituals', rather they are filled with meanings by participants. Our challenge is to understand why some participate and others choose to wash their cars and how those that do participate 'make sense' (Crossley 2002) of their participation.

Notes

1 Neoliberalism is an admittedly a 'fuzzy concept'. For this chapter I focus on a definition which emphasizes the contemporary trend where control of economic factors is shifted from the public sector to the private sector, i.e. privatization, fiscal austerity, deregulation and reductions in government spending in order to enhance the role of the private sector in the economy.

2 Unfortunately the supplementary data was unevenly collected by the country teams. In some countries interviews were conducted with demonstration organizers and the transcripts were entered in the database. For most of the countries the slogans and main placard texts were entered and for all of the countries a list of organizers and participating groups were entered. For most of the countries photo coverage of the demonstration was also entered.

3 At that time major Matteo Renzi, later prime minister of Italy and chairman of the PD.

References

Armingeon, K. (1997). Swiss corporatism in comparative perspective. *West European Politics*, 20(3), 164–179.

Arter, D. (1991). The Swedish Leftist Party: 'Eco-communism' or communist echo? *Parliamentary Affairs*, 44(1), 60–78.

Arter, D. (2002). 'Communists we are no longer, Social Democrats we can never be': The evolution of the leftist parties in Finland and Sweden. *Journal of Communist Studies and Transition Politics*, 18(1), 1–28.

Bartolini, S. (2000). *The Class Cleavage: The Mobilization of the European Left, 1860–1980*. Cambridge: Cambridge University Press.

Bekke, A.J.G.M., and Meer, F.M. (Eds). (2000). *Civil Service Systems in Western Europe*. Cheltenham: Edward Elgar Publishing.

Beyeler, M., and Rucht, D. (2010). Political opportunity structures and progressive movement sectors. In S. Walgrave and D. Rucht (Eds), *The World Says No to War: Demonstrations against the War on Iraq* (pp. 20–41). Minneapolis: University of Minnesota Press.

Choi, H.-L., and Mattoni, A. (2010). The contentious field of precarious work in Italy: Political actors, strategies and coalitions. *Journal of Labor and Society*, 13(3), 213–245.

Croes, N. (2010). Fifty years since 'strike of the century' in Belgium. Review of *La grève générale insurrectionnelle et révolutionnaire de l'hiver 1960/61* by Gustave Dache. June 2011, www.socialistworld.net/doc/4733.

Crossley, N. (2002). *Making Sense of Social Movements*. Buckingham: Open University Press.

Crouch, C. (2009). Privatised Keynesianism: An unacknowledged policy regime. *British Journal of Politics and International Relations*, 11(3), 382–399.

della Porta, D. (2014). *Social Movements in Times of Austerity. Bringing Capitalism Back in Protest Analysis*. Cambridge: Polity Press.

della Porta, D. (Ed.). (2007). *The Global Justice Movement: Cross-National and Transnational Perspectives*. Boulder, CO: Paradigm.

della Porta, D., and Mosca, L. (2007). *In movimento*: 'Contamination' in action and the Italian global justice movement. *Global Networks*, 7(1), 1–27.

della Porta, D., and Reiter, H. (with the collaboration of M. Andretta, S. Milan and F. Rossi). (2012). Desperately seeking politics: Political attitudes of participants in three demonstrations for worker's rights in Italy. *Mobilization: An International Quarterly*, 17(3), 349–361.

European Commission. (2009). *Industrial Relations in Europe 2008*. Luxembourg: Office for Official Publications of the European Communities.

Flanders, A. (1970). *Management and Unions*. London: Faber.

Foner, P.S. (1986). *May Day: A Short History of the International Workers' Holiday 1886–1986*. New York: International Publishers.

Gorodzeisky, A., and Richards, A. (2013). Trade unions and migrant workers in Western Europe. *European Journal of Industrial Relations*, 19(3), 239–254, doi: 10.1177/0959680113493694.

Hall, P.A., and Soskice, D. (Eds). (2001). *Varieties of Capitalism: The Institutional Foundations of Comparative Advantage*. New York: Oxford University Press.

Hadjimichalis, C. (2011). Uneven geographical development and socio-spatial justice and solidarity: European regions after the 2009 financial crisis. *European Urban and Regional Studies*, 18(3), 254–274.

Hall, P.A., and Thelen, K. (2007). Institutional change in varieties of capitalism. Manuscript. Minda de Gunzburg Center for European Studies, Harvard University.

Hamann, K., and Lucio, M.M. (2003). Strategies of union revitalivil.zation in Spain: Negotiating change and fragmentation. *European Journal of Industrial Relations*, 9(1), 61–78.

Hyman, R. (2001). *Understanding European Trade Unionism*. London: Sage.

Howell, C. (1999). Unforgiven: British trade unionism in crisis. In A. Martin and G. Ross (Eds), *The Brave New World of European Labor: European Trade Unions at the Millennium* (pp. 26–74). New York: Berghahn Press.

Jiménez, G., and Saurina, J. (2005). *Credit cycles, credit risk and prudential regulation* (No. 0531). Madrid: Banco de España.

Kitson, M., Martin, R., and Tyler, P. (2011). Geographies of austerity. *Cambridge Journal of Regions, Economy and Society*, 4(2), 289–302.

Kjellberg, A. (2009). Fackliga relationer och industriella relationer. In T. Berglund and S. Schedin (Eds), *Arbetslivet*. (pp. 241–283) Lund: Studentlitteratur.

Kjellberg, A. (2000). Sweden: The multitude of challenges facing Swedish trade unions. In J. Waddington and R. Hoffmann (Eds), *Trade Unions in Europe: Facing Challenges and Searching for Solutions* (pp. 529–574)Brussels: European Trade Union Institute.

Kriesi, H. (1995). The political opportunity structure of new social movements: Its impact on their mobilities. In J.C. Jenkins and B. Klandermans (Eds), *The Politics of Social Protest. Comparative Perspectives on States and Social Movements* (pp. 167–198). Minneapolis: University of Minnesota Press.

Kriesi, H., Grande, E., Lachat, R., Dolezal, M., and Frey, T. (2008). *West European Politics in the Age of Globalization*. Cambridge: Cambridge University Press.

Kriesi, H., Koopmans, R., Duyvendak, J.-W., and Giugni, M. (1992). New social movements and political opportunities in Western Europe. *European Journal of Political Research*, 22(2), 219–244.

Lane, Philip R. (2012). The European sovereign debt crisis. *Journal of Economic Perspectives*, 26(3), 49–68.

Larsson, B. (2013). Transnational trade union action in Europe. *European Societies*, doi: 10.1080/14616696.2013.813958.

Locke, R.M., and Thelen, K. (1995). Apples and oranges revisited: Contextualized comparisons and the study of comparative labor politics. *Politics and Society*, 23(3), 337–367.

Namuth, M. (2013). Trade unions in Italy. Report. Friedrich Ebert Stiftung, Berlin, http://library.fes.de/pdf-files/id-moe/09590.pdf.

Oesch, D. (2010). Trade unions and industrial relations in Switzerland. MPRA Paper 22059, http://mpra.ub.uni-muenchen.de/22059/.

Olsson, J.-E. (1990). 1 maj i Sverige 100 år. In *Första maj 100 år* (pp. 8–48). Stockholm: Kulturhuset.

Perez, S. (2000). From decentralisation to reorganisation: Explaining the return to national bargaining in Italy and Spain. *Comparative Politics*, 32, 437–458.

Peterson, A., Wahlström, M., and Wennerhag, M. (2011). Swedish trade unionism: A renewed social movement? *Economic and Industrial Democracy*, 33(4), 3–31.

Peterson, A., Wahlström, M., and Wennerhag, M. (2013). Is there new wine in the new bottles? Participants in European anti-austerity protests 2010–2012. Paper prepared for presentation at the ECPR General Conference in Bordeaux 2013.

Peterson, A., Wahlström, M., and Wennerhag, M. (2015). Beyond 'old' and 'new' social movements. Participants in European anti-austerity protests 2010–2012. *Acta Sociologica*, 33(4), 1–18.

Peterson, A., Wahlström, M., Wennerhag, M., Christancho, C., and Sabucedo, J.-M. (2012). May Day demonstrations in five European countries. *Mobilization: An International Quarterly*, 17(3), 281–300.

Phelps Brown, H. (1990). The counter-revolution of our time. *Industrial Relations*, 29(1), 1–14.

Piketty, T. (2014). *Capital in the Twenty-First Century*. Cambridge, MA: Belknap Press.

Pontusson, J., and Swenson, P. (1996) Labor markets, production strategies, and wage bargaining institutions: The Swedish employer offensive in comparative perspective. *Comparative Political Studies*, 29(2), 223–250.

Regini, M., and Regalia, I. (1997). Employers, unions and the state: The resurgence of concertation in Italy. *West European Politics*, 20, 210–230.

Rucht, D. (Ed.). (2003). *Berlin, 1, Mai 2002: Politische demonstrationsrituale*. Opladen: Leske + Budrich.

Schmidt, V. (2002). *The Futures of European Capitalism*. Oxford: Oxford University Press.

Schmidt, V. (2003). French capitalism transformed, yet still a third variety of capitalism. *Economy and Society*, 32(4), 526–554.

Standing, G. (2011). *The Precariat: The New Dangerous Class*. London: Bloomsbury Publishing.

Swenson, P. (1989). *Fair Shares: Unions, Pay, and Politics in Sweden and West Germany*. Ithaca, NY: Cornell University Press.

Thelen, K. (2001). Varieties of labor politics in the developed democracies. In P.A. Hall and D. Soskice (Eds), *Varieties of Capitalism: The Institutional Foundations of Comparative Advantage* (pp. 71–103). Oxford: Oxford University Press.

Thelen, K., and van Wijnbergen, C. (2003). The paradox of globalization: Labor relations in Germany and beyond. *Comparative Political Studies*, 36(8), 859–880.

Tilly, C. (2004). *Social Movements, 1768–2004*. Boulder, CO: Paradigm Publishers.

Uitermark, J. (2004). Looking forward by looking back: May Day protests in London and the strategic significance of the urban. *Antipode: A Radical Journal of Geography*, 36(4), 706–728.

Vandaele, K. (2011). *Sustaining or Abandoning 'Social Peace'? Strike Developments and Trends in Europe since the 1990s*. Brussels: European Trade Union Institute.

Van Gyes, G., De Witte, H., and van der Hallen, P. (2000). Belgium. Belgian trade unions in the 1990s: Does strong today mean strong tomorrow? In J. Waddington and R. Hoffman (Eds), *Trade Unions in Europe: Facing Challenges and Searching for Solutions* (pp. 105–142). Brussels: European Trade Union Institute.

Visser, J. (2013). Data base on institutional characteristics of trade unions, wage setting, state intervention and social pacts, 1960–2011 (ICTWSS), Version 4.0. Amsterdam Institute for Advanced Labour Studies, AIAS, University of Amsterdam.

Visser, J. (2009). Union membership statistics in 24 countries, http://digitalcommons. ilr.cornell.edu/key_workplace/273/.

Waddington, J. (2000). United Kingdom: Recovering from the neo-liberal assault? In J. Waddington and R. Hoffman (Eds), *Trade Unions in Europe: Facing Challenges and Searching for Solutions* (pp. 575–626). Brussels: European Trade Union Institute.

Wessendorf, S. (2008). Culturalist discourses on inclusion and exclusion: The Swiss citizenship debate. *Social Anthropology*, 16(2), 187–202.

8 Who Takes Part in May Day Marches?

Magnus Wennerhag

Introduction

Since their worldwide spread in 1890, May Day demonstrations have always been connected to a very specific social identity: social class. At the beginning, May Day demonstrations and rallies were thought to display the growing numbers of citizens belonging to the organized parts of the working class and reflect their claims for social and political rights. But what is the social composition of May Day marches more than a hundred years later? Is the annual street manifestation of the labour movement still dominated by workers – or are other social classes and groups also drawn to the streets when trade unions, socialist parties and organizations perform this yearly ritual?

In this chapter I examine which socio-demographic groups take part in contemporary May Day demonstrations in Western Europe. In particular I focus on social class, but also on other relevant social categories such as gender, age and ethnicity and whether they vary between specific types of demonstrations and between the countries in our sample. First, the chapter discusses the socio-demographic profiles of those taking part in such annual events. Are May Day participants more or less representative of the wider population? Do they differ from participants in other types of demonstrations? Second, I interrogate the composition and role of social class in May Day marches, both with regard to the individuals' objective positions in the labour market and their subjective class identifications, and analyse the factors that shape May Day marchers' class identity. Third, I analyse which social and political characteristics most strongly influence individuals' decisions to join a May Day parade.

This chapter's analysis is based on the survey data for individual demonstrators collected within the international research programme 'Caught in the Act of Protest: Contextualizing Contestation' (CCC). In this chapter I analyse the participants in 15 May Day demonstrations in six Western European countries surveyed during the period 2010–2012 (cf. Chapter 7). In order to determine whether participants in May Day demonstrations differ from participants in other types of street protests and marches, I also compare them with data from a sample of 23 additional demonstrations surveyed within the CCC project. In order to compare the social composition of the surveyed May Day demonstrations with the general population, I also use data from the European Social Survey and the Swedish SOM Institute's national survey.

The chapter begins with a short overview of the theories relating to the social composition of demonstrations that have become important for under-standing contemporary protest participation. This is followed by a discussion about how to conceptualize class at a theoretical level, and how social class is operationalized in the chapter's analysis. In the subsequent methods section, the different types of data and methods used in the analysis are briefly presented. In the following section, I analyse and discuss the chapter's three main topics: (1) the social groups that participate in May Day demonstrations and whether May Day demonstrators differ from participants in other types of demonstrations, (2) the May Day parades' class composition and (3) the social and political factors that influence decisions to join May Day demonstrations.

Earlier Research on Protestors' Social Class and Other Socio-Demographic Characteristics

The Social 'Normalization' of Protest Participation

Research on political participation has noted that since the 1960s citizens in Western democracies have become increasingly inclined to demonstrate in order to give voice to their opinions (see for instance Norris 2002; Norris, Walgrave and Van Aelst 2005). Street protests have become a 'normalized' way for citizens to express their grievances, opinions and political preferences (Van Aelst and Walgrave 2001), alongside their routine participation in general elections.

The research that first analysed the social profiles of demonstrators in a systematic way concluded that protesters were largely young, male and highly educated (March and Kaase 1979). However, surveys undertaken during the 1980s and 1990s showed that differences due to gender and age have decreased, while differences in the level of education persist (Van Aelst and Walgrave 2001, pp. 466–473; see also Verba, Schlozman and Brady 1995). This development has been described as a 'normalization of the protester', in the sense that those taking part in street demonstrations today are increasingly from a cross-section of the general population (Van Aelst and Walgrave 2001). Nevertheless, this research admits that the well-educated still dominate demonstrations.

May Day demonstrations attracted large numbers of citizens to the streets in the late nineteenth and the early twentieth century – decades prior to the post-war development described as a 'normalization' of street protest. Street protests were common during this period when democratic rights were fought for, introduced and consolidated in most Western European countries. Furthermore, these demonstrations were often – or were presumed to have been – dominated by individuals from the working class.[1] The social composition of the early May Day marches thus differs from that characterizing the street protests that became more common in the 1960s and which have instead been regarded as dominated by the highly educated middle class. In the analysis that follows the aim is to determine whether contemporary May Day demonstrations reflect the social composition of the general population to a higher or lesser degree than other types of demonstrations, in particular those staged by the presumably middle-class-dominated new social movements.

Earlier analyses of protest participation have typically used educational level as a proxy for social class. Even though the individual's level of education is an important determinant of her or his social class, in that it qualifies the individual for specific positions in a hierarchically structured labour market, analyses of protest participation have rarely studied participants' social class according to more refined class concepts. This lacuna exists for both the 'objective' side of class, i.e. the individual's position in the labour market, and the 'subjective' side of class, i.e. the individual's own sense of belonging to a specific (or no) social class.

Rare examples can be found of research on the class profile of the new social movements; movements that have often been associated with the increase in street protests since the 1960s. These movements have often been regarded as expressions of 'middle-class radicalism' (e.g. Eder 1995), although in Kriesi (1989) participation in new social movements is analysed with more refined class categories (on the basis of a Dutch general population survey). Kriesi's study shows that e.g. the environmental and women's movements attracted middle-class individuals to a greater degree than individuals from the working class (even though it was primarily specific parts of the middle class that became involved in these movements).

When comparing the labour movement's contemporary May Day demonstrations with the protests of the so-called new social movements, it is important to remember that since the 1960s the 'old' labour movements have been more or less influenced by, and sometimes even closely intertwined with, the 'new' movements. On the one hand, many of the smaller radical left-wing trade unions and activist networks that today stage or take part in May Day demonstrations have emerged from the 'new social movements' and the 1960s 'new left', as well as from more recent mobilization waves during the 1990s and 2000s (Andretta and Reiter 2009). Furthermore, the left-socialist/post-communist parties staging May Day parades are often connected with various new social movements, and in addition to more traditional workers' issues also include feminist, peace, environmental and LGBT matters on their agendas (e.g. March 2011, and Chapter 7). On the other hand, only in recent decades have the major social democratic, socialist and post-communist trade unions begun to seek allies among the 'new' movements, for instance during the mobilization of the global justice movement of the 2000s, and move cautiously in the direction of 'social movement unionism' (see e.g. Waterman 2001; Peterson, Wahlström and Wennerhag 2012).

Due to these different paths of development within the labour movement, the 15 May Day demonstrations included in the study are first analysed separately and then again in terms to belonging to three major groups.
The first group consists of the marches staged by the major trade union
confederations and/or a social democratic or socialist party. In the second
group the demonstrations have been organized by smaller radical left-wing
trade unions and/or radical left parties and activist networks. The third
group includes the few cases where a broader coalition consisting of major
trade unions and radical left organizations have mobilized the march. This
analytical division allows for a critical examination of whether the different paths of development within the labour movement imply that different
types of May Day demonstrations mobilize different socio-demographic
groups and classes.

Social Class and Political Action

How, then, can social class be measured in contemporary society? Many of
today's most influential methods for measuring social class draw inspiration
from Weber's class concept and focus on the individual's employment
situation. In contrast to Marx's more relational conceptualization of class
as the consequence of the conflict between the owners of the means of
production (*the capitalists*, i.e. the employers) and the owners of labour
power (*the proletariat*, i.e. the employed), Weber (1922/1978, p. 928) saw
class as a 'market situation'. For Weber, the common situation of specific
groups in the labour market brought different classes into existence. Weber
perceived education and other forms of merit as mechanisms that gave
access to, or created exclusion from, specific positions in the labour market,
and thereby also a range of social opportunities connected to these positions
(e.g. Crompton 2010; Wright 2009). In practice, this meant that when
studying class Weber understood the main dividing line to be between the
different working conditions and opportunities of the working and middle
classes. Subsequently, he subdivided the entire class of wage labourers that
Marx had seen as potentially united by their common interests vis-à-vis the
employers.

This Weberian class concept is the point of departure for Goldthorpe's class
scheme, which was first used empirically in the 1970s (and is often referred
to as the Eriksson–Goldthorpe–Portocarero, or EGP, scheme) (Crompton
2010). Here, class positions are defined on the basis of employment relations.
In the EGP scheme, a basic distinction between employers, self-employed and
employees is combined with a further distinction between different forms of
employment contracts. The category of employees – which comprises the
vast majority of people in developed countries – is subdivided into two ideal
contract types: the service contract and the labour contract. According to
Goldthorpe, the latter implies easily monitored work with a low degree of
required skills and expertise, while the opposite is true for the service contract
(Goldthorpe 2000, p. 208).

In Oesch's (2006a, 2006b) more recent and modified version of the EGP scheme, three contemporary labour market trends in developed countries are taken into account. These are the shift from production to service, women's increased participation in paid employment and rising educational levels (Oesch 2006a, p. 27). According to Oesch, the expanding middle class resulting from these trends cannot be properly dealt with by the EGP scheme, and he therefore introduces a horizontal distinction between different work logics (whereas EGP has only a single hierarchical dimension between the service and labour contract). Oesch identifies three work logics: the *organizational*, the *technical* and the *interpersonal*. The self-employed and employers are included in a fourth, *independent*, work logic (Oesch 2006a, p. 64). The resulting class scheme consists of 17 classes, which can be collapsed into an 8-class version.

In my analysis I have chosen to collapse the original 17 classes into a 9-class scheme (see Table 8.1; see also Hylmö and Wennerhag, 2015). Compared to Oesch's 8-class model, the two 'independent work logic' classes of large employers (with ten or more employees) and self-employed professionals are not collapsed into one combined class. This change is motivated by my analytical aims. As discussed by Peterson in Chapter 7, today's labour market is often described as characterized by growing insecurity. Under such conditions, self-employment increasingly becomes a necessary alternative to regular employment. The market position of, for example, freelance journalists differs significantly from that of large employers, which motivates separating the two classes in the analyses.

If class position is in principal perceived as a position in the occupational structure, how do categorizations of class then relate to political participation? For example, Oesch has used his class scheme to study participation in general elections and party preferences. His studies show that socio-cultural professionals, whose employment is structured by an interpersonal work logic (e.g. teachers, social workers, medical doctors), show a greater support for libertarian left parties than professionals subjected to a technical work logic (e.g. mechanical engineers, computer professionals, architects), who instead more often support conservative centre-right parties (Oesch 2008a, 2008b).

Other scholars have claimed that political preferences are primarily shaped by class identity, and not the individual's position in the labour market (Cigéhn and Johansson 1997). From this perspective, one's subjective sense of belonging to a specific class is not necessarily aligned with one's position in the labour market (Cigéhn, Johansson and Karlsson 2001; Crompton 2010). In this approach the 'subjective' aspect of social class is focused, but only the individual's recognition of different social classes and belonging to one of these, i.e. *class identity* (which is not to be confused with *class consciousness*, which implies a belief that one's own class has different and opposite interests vis-à-vis other classes).

For analyses of citizens' political preferences and voting behaviour, different approaches to social class have corroborated that both objective and subjective class have significance. Whether these two conceptualizations of class also contribute to our understanding of May Day participation will now be interrogated.

Table 8.1 Oesch class scheme, 9-class version

Employees				Self-employed
Interpersonal service work logic	**Technical work logic**	**Organizational work logic**		**Independent work logic**
				Large employers
Socio-cultural professionals and semi-professionals	Technical professionals and semi-professionals	Higher-grade and associate managers and administrators		*Business owners, department managers (10 or more employees)*
				Self-employed professionals
Medical doctors, social workers, teachers	*Computing professionals, architects, mechanical engineers*	*Financial managers, managers in small firms, public administrators*		Self-employed journalists, doctors and lawyers
Service workers	Production workers	Office clerks		Small business owners
Children's nurses, home helps, cooks, waiters, telephone salespersons	*Assemblers, carpenters, machinery mechanics, bus drivers*	*Bank tellers, mail sorting clerks, secretaries, fire fighters*		*Farmers, hairdressers, shopkeepers, lorry drivers (fewer than 9 or no employees)*

Methods and Data

The data used in this chapter primarily derives from 2,336 respondents to protest surveys from 15 May Day demonstrations in six Western European countries between 1 May 2010 and 1 May 2012. In order to compare May Day demonstrations with other types of demonstrations, 23 additional protests surveyed within the CCC project have also been included: ten trade union demonstrations, eight environmental protests and five Pride parades, where the two latter types of demonstration are regarded as 'new' social movement mobilizations. More information about the demonstrations surveyed within the CCC project and a more elaborate description of the project's standardized sampling procedure can be found in the Appendix.

In order to compare May Day participants with the general population I have used data for the relevant countries from the 2010 European Social Survey Round 5 (ESS5).[2] Since almost all the analysed demonstrations were staged in big cities, the ESS5 data is limited to those living in 'a big city' or 'the suburbs or outskirts of a big city'. To conduct a more limited analysis of the social and political factors that make May Day participation more or less probable I also used data from the Swedish SOM Institute's national population survey. The CCC, ESS and SOM data has been coded according to the Oesch class scheme.[3] In order to make it possible to identify the class position for those temporarily unemployed or retired, everyone has been included in the analysis. Furthermore, an extra tenth 'class' consisting of non-employed students has been added to the Oesch scheme. For more detailed information about this coding procedure and the ESS and SOM data, see Appendix.

Analysis

Who Takes Part in May Day Demonstrations?

With regard to the basic socio-economic features that are often analysed when political participation is discussed, we can see that the social profiles of the 15 CCC-surveyed May Day demonstrations display both similarities and differences. The variation is in part influenced by the profile of a specific demonstration – its main organizers and target constituency and how the May Day parade is framed. Furthermore, we can discern some systematic differences between the countries. This national variation should not of course be over-interpreted, because not all May Day marches can automatically be seen as representative of all possible May Day demonstrations in a specific country (especially in the countries where only one May Day parade was surveyed). Even so, the national variations can indicate significant differences that are due to specific national May Day cultures and more overall variations in national protest cultures.

As can be seen in Table 8.2, in general we find a higher percentage of men than women in the surveyed May Day demonstrations. However, the percentage of women varies both between and within countries. The highest percentage of

Table 8.2 Socio-demographic characteristics for participants in May Day demonstrations surveyed within the CCC project

Per cent (%)	Belgium	Italy		Spain			
	Antwerp	Florence	Milan – EuroMayDay	Barcelona	Vigo – CCOO and UGT	Vigo – CIG	Stockholm LO and Social Democratic Party
Age							
–29 years	7	3	36	11	3	13	13
30–49 years	27	23	50	36	53	55	22
50–64 years	41	50	9	39	35	28	34
65– years	24	20	2	12	9	4	31
Gender: female	34	47	53	32	42	38	49
Ethnicity: born abroad	3	2	1	6	2	6	9
University degree/study at university	27	73	73	52	33	38	58
Employment situation							
Work full-time	44	45	39	62	71	66	47
Work part-time	7	8	17	3	5	5	8
Freelance/ self-employed (without employed staff)	2	4	9	3	0	2	2
Self-employed with employed staff	1	1	4	0	2	1	1
Study full-time	4	2	13	6	3	8	9
Unemployed/ between jobs	2	3	5	7	14	16	2
Retired/pensioner	36	31	5	16	8	5	30
Housewife/ househusband	3	1	0	1	6	3	5
'Precarious conditions'	12	15	30	14	18	23	11
Cases (N)	**209–216**	**104–110**	**123–127**	**176–180**	**66**	**166–168**	**173–176**

Notes: Used measure of association between the variables is Cramer's V. * = 5%, ** = 1% and *** = 0.1% significance; *n.s.* = not significant.

women can be found in the EuroMayDay in Milan and the Swedish May Day demonstrations organized by the Left Party, the former organized by a radical left activist network and the latter by a left-socialist party.

Regarding age, most May Day demonstrations attract middle-aged and older people to a higher degree than young people. The highest percentage of young people (under 30) can be found in the May Day demonstrations in Milan, Zurich and the Swedish May Day demonstrations staged by the Left Party. The highest percentage of demonstrators aged 65 years or more was in Antwerp and in the

Sweden					Switzerland		United Kingdom	
Stockholm – Left Party	Malmö – LO and Social Democratic Party	Malmö – Left Party	Gothenburg – LO and Social Democratic Party	Gothenburg – Left Party	Zurich	Geneva	London	**Cramer's V**
25	20	38	18	35	33	12	15	.290***
29	29	38	29	33	39	28	34	.196***
37	25	18	29	24	20	47	31	.221***
9	25	5	23	8	7	13	15	.249***
60	44	50	53	58	44	47	34	.181***
17	13	9	11	10	15	31	26	.275***
79	51	79	45	83	62	59	79	.363***
45	48	38	48	44	21	38	39	.221***
14	7	18	6	22	45	29	11	.306***
10	4	11	2	9	15	9	11	.170***
2	2	0	0	1	1	1	1	n.s.
21	14	29	12	21	15	7	11	.222***
5	3	9	3	4	4	3	9	.169***
10	24	5	23	10	7	18	17	.271***
1	2	1	3	1	6	2	2	.104*
25	12	33	11	31	58	37	28	.289***
164–167	**95–97**	**139–141**	**155–160**	**202–209**	**130–135**	**202–206**	**164–178**	

Swedish May Day demonstrations organized by the trade union confederation LO and the Social Democratic Party. Also here, the general pattern is that May Day marches staged by radical left organizations and parties close to the 'new' social movements attract more young people and more women.

The percentage of May Day demonstrators born abroad (which can be seen as a proxy for ethnic minority status) does not follow a distinct pattern, but in comparison to the percentage of foreign-born among the general population, most May Day parades have a lower share of participants born in other countries.[4] Only in three cases – Geneva, London and the Left Party demonstration in Stockholm – is the percentage of foreign-born higher. The slightly higher degree of foreign-born in the London and Stockholm May Day parades (and the lower degree in Barcelona, Milan and Zurich) is consistent with Morales's (2011) analysis of the political participation of immigrant groups in European cities, which includes six of the cities in our study. However, whereas Morales's study shows that immigrant groups in Geneva have a lower degree of protest participation than native-born Swiss, our May Day data shows the opposite. Given that the country of birth varies significantly within the group of foreign-born in this May Day demonstration, this could be an effect of Geneva being a 'global city' with international institutions and organizations whose employees also take part in May Day parades.

The percentage of May Day demonstrators with university education varies significantly, primarily between countries but also between demonstrations. The proportion of May Day participants with university education is particularly high in Italy, the UK and in the Swedish May Day demonstrations organized by the Left Party. The lowest figures are found in Belgium. The general pattern is thus that May Day demonstrations staged by radical left organizations attract the highest percentage of university-educated participants.

In Table 8.3, the three analytical categories of May Day demonstrations are compared with other types of trade union demonstrations, environmental protests and Pride parades. When comparing different types of protests and parades, the social composition of May Day demonstrations staged by the radical left is similar to that of environmental protests and Pride parades, i.e. demonstrations staged by 'new' social movements. On the other hand, May Day demonstrations staged by the major trade unions and social democratic parties resemble other types of trade union demonstrations.

Table 8.3 also shows the ESS5 data for the general population in larger cities. Although we can find differences in educational levels between different types of May Day demonstrations, the percentage of university-educated people is higher in all types of May Day marches than among the general population.

Before turning to the question of whether specific patterns can be discerned in May Day participants' class positions, other aspects of the individual's employment situation need to be highlighted. In the lower parts of Tables 8.2 and 8.3, figures for some labour market-related aspects of the individual's situation are shown, for instance whether she or he works full- or part-time, is self-employed, unemployed, studies full-time or is retired.

Peterson (Chapter 7) discusses whether the European labour movements have managed to organize the groups often seen as being hardest struck by the 2008 economic crisis. More recently, this group has been labelled 'the precariat' (e.g. Standing 2011). This group primarily consists of young people who are under- or unemployed and experience low degrees of social protection, despite the fact that they are often highly educated. Indications for

Table 8.3 Socio-demographics: participants in May Day and other CCC-surveyed demonstrations and general population (ESS5 data)

Per cent (%)	May Day demonstrations			Other types of demonstrations			Cramer's V	National population in major cities ESS5 (2010)
	Traditional/major trade unions	Radical/minor trade unions and/or radical left org.	Broad May Day coalitions	Trade union	Environmental	Pride		
Age								
–29 years	8	27	18	13	24	35	.205***	22
30–49 years	30	46	34	41	34	46	.112***	35
50–64 years	39	21	32	37	30	15	.167***	24
65– years	20	4	12	7	11	3	.175***	20
Gender: female	42	49	39	44	54	52	.109***	52
Ethnicity: born abroad	5	6	25	8	11	16	.163***	18
University degree/study at university	48	63	69	50	69	70	.187***	37
Employment situation								
Work full-time	51	49	34	57	30	46	.228***	n/a
Work part-time	7	14	24	12	20	13	.141***	n/a
Freelance/self-employed (without employed staff)	3	7	11	4	13	10	.150***	n/a
Self-employed with employed staff	1	2	1	1	3	1	.051**	n/a
Study full-time	5	15	11	5	14	16	.145***	10
Unemployed/between jobs	5	9	6	5	7	7	.060***	6
Retired/pensioner	26	6	15	11	14	4	.187***	10
Housewife/househusband	3	1	3	0	4	1	.105***	20
'Precarious conditions'	13	27	38	20	37	27	.198***	n/a
Cases (N)	980–1,005	800–812	497–519	1,742–1,830	2,436–2,479	766–919		2,525

Notes: Used measure of association between the variables is Cramer's V. * = 5%, ** = 1% and *** = 0.1% significance; *n/a* = comparative data not available.

some of the relevant aspects of the precariat's social situation can be found in Tables 8.2 and 8.3. These mainly concern under- and unemployment, which are conditions that lead to lower degrees of social protection. The same can be said for self-employed individuals, who, like the under- and unemployed, are excluded from the 'standard employment relationship' that gives direct access to high degrees of social protection, an arrangement that typically today is reserved for the fully employed 'salariat' only (Standing 2011). In both the tables a variable for the percentage of under- or unemployed or self-employed (without employed staff) has been added in order to show the proportion of protesters living under potentially 'precarious conditions'.

The highest degree of May Day participants living under such potentially 'precarious conditions' can be found in the Swiss and British demonstrations, and among the May Day demonstrations staged by the radical left. In the demonstrations organized by major trade unions and social democratic parties, this proportion is much lower. However, roughly the same percentage of protestors living under potentially 'precarious conditions' found in radical left May Day marches can also be found in environmental protests and Pride parades. Some parts of the European labour movements, particularly those connected with the radical left and/or new social movements, thus seem to mobilize individuals living under the social conditions characterizing 'the precariat', while the more traditional major trade unions do not do this to the same degree.

The Class Composition of May Day Demonstrations

What is the social class composition of May Day demonstrations? As discussed earlier, class can be perceived as both a matter of the individual's 'objective' position in a hierarchically structured labour market and his or her 'subjective' sense of belonging to a social class, i.e. the individual's class identity.

Table 8.4 clarifies the class composition (according to the Oesch-9 class scheme) of the surveyed May Day demonstrations, and in Table 8.5 the corresponding ESS data for the general population of larger cities is shown. The traditional working class, which historically was mobilized in May Day demonstrations, is a group that in general is relatively weakly represented in all the surveyed demonstrations. The total percentage of individuals in the Oesch-9 classes belonging to this group – office clerks, production workers and service workers – at most adds up to 38 per cent (in two Swedish May Day parades arranged by LO and the Social Democratic Party), but on average oscillates around 23 per cent. Among the traditional working class it is primarily production workers who demonstrate on May Day. If we compare the May Day demonstrators with the general population (see Table 8.5), the proportion of individuals with working-class occupations in the May Day parades is more or less half that of the corresponding figure for the general population.

One explanation for this perhaps surprising pattern can found in one of the Oesch-9 classes belonging to the occupational middle class (i.e. employees and professionals), namely associate managers and administrators – a group that on average accounts for around 20 per cent of May Day demonstrators. Among the demonstrations organized by major trade unions, this proportion is even higher; in some cases just under 40 per cent. Due to the construction of the Oesch categories, this group also includes trade union officials and party functionaries. The relatively high proportion of associate managers and administrators could then be seen as an indirect result of the institutionaliza-tion and professionalization of the labour movement. From the perspective of occupational-based class categorizations, the car factory worker who goes from being a shop-floor union activist to a paid union official is transformed from a worker into a middle class employee.

Among the occupational middle classes we also find the Oesch-9 class, which has the largest proportion of May Day demonstrators: socio-cultural professionals and semi-professionals. In this class we find teachers (at all edu-cational levels), medical doctors and nurses, social work professionals, jour-nalists, etc. This class in particular dominates May Day demonstrations in Switzerland, the UK and the Swedish May Day demonstrations organized by the Left Party. These are also the May Day demonstrations in which we find a somewhat higher proportion of self-employed professionals, even though overall this group is quite small in the May Day marches. In this class we find people working in the media or as artists, authors, etc. However, if we com-pare the percentage of this Oesch class with the corresponding figure for the general population (see Table 8.5), most May Day marches mobilize a higher proportion of self-employed professionals than can be found in the general population. Table 8.5 also shows that the proportion of socio-cultural profes-sionals and semi-professionals is much higher in May Day demonstrations than among the general population.

In general, the trade unionists and other protestors who are mobi-lized in contemporary May Day demonstrations are more often from the occupational middle classes than from the occupations that tradition-ally constituted the working class. In comparison with the ESS data for the general population, the proportion of occupational middle class who take part in May Day marches is much greater. However, if we compare May Day marches with demonstrations staged by 'new' social movements (see Table 8.5), we still find that a higher proportion of individuals with working-class occupations take to the streets on May Day. Also, the May Day parades staged by major trade unions and social democratic parties attract the highest proportion of working class. In short, even though May Day parades do not mobilize as high a percentage of working-class indi-viduals as can be found in the general population, they nevertheless mobil-ize a higher share of this class than demonstrations staged by new social movements.

Table 8.4 Class composition (Oesch-9) in May Day demonstrations surveyed within the CCC project

Per cent (%)	Belgium	Italy		Spain			
	Antwerp	Florence	Milan – EuroMayDay	Barcelona	Vigo – CCOO and UGT	Vigo – CIG	Stockholm – LO and Social Democratic Party
Self-employed							
Large employers (10 or more employees)	0	1	2	1	0	0	2
Self-employed professionals	2	1	6	1	0	1	1
Small business owners	1	1	4	2	0	2	0
Employed: Professionals and employees							
Associate managers and administrators	37	37	17	30	33	29	35
Technical professionals and technicians	8	4	5	13	6	8	6
Socio-cultural professionals and semi-professionals	20	27	28	30	25	22	21
Employed: Workers							
Office clerks	7	6	4	1	2	3	5
Production workers	14	9	7	10	22	22	12
Service workers	7	10	14	5	10	5	10
Students not working	5	1	13	7	2	9	8
Cases (N)	**172**	**67**	**83**	**132**	**51**	**129**	**170**

Notes: Used measure of association between the variables is Cramer's V. * = 5%, ** = 1% and *** = 0.1% significance; *n.s.* = not significant.

With regard to the more 'subjective' side of class – class identity – other patterns can be identified (see Table 8.6), which depend more on the country in which the May Day demonstration is staged. On average, the percentage of demonstrators identifying themselves as (upper or lower) middle class is higher than that identifying as working class. The only countries where those identifying as working class dominate are Spain and the UK. This seems to indicate that class identification is more dependent on national discourses of class, the organizers of the May Day parade etc., than on individuals' positions in the labour market.

However, Table 8.7 illustrates that even though the proportion of May Day demonstrators identifying themselves as working class is on average lower than those identifying as middle class, the percentage of those who perceive themselves as working class is considerably higher among May Day demonstrators than

	Sweden					Switzerland		United Kingdom	
Stockholm – Left Party	Malmö – LO and Social Democratic Party	Malmö – Left Party	Gothenburg – LO and Social Democratic Party	Gothenburg – Left Party	Zurich	Geneva	London	**Cramer's V**
3	1	1	1	1	3	1	1	*n.s.*
6	2	8	1	6	13	6	8	.166***
2	2	3	1	2	2	3	3	*n.s.*
12	10	6	16	11	11	30	22	.258***
6	2	4	8	9	8	7	8	*n.s.*
40	27	37	23	40	39	37	36	.165***
2	7	4	4	4	2	2	4	*n.s.*
4	19	5	19	6	6	5	4	.200***
6	13	8	15	5	4	3	4	.133**
18	16	25	13	18	13	6	11	.191***
158	**86**	**132**	**142**	**197**	**112**	**174**	**160**	

among participants in protests and parades staged by new social movements. We can thus conclude that although May Day demonstrations to a certain extent mobilize more individuals identifying as middle class than individuals seeing themselves as working class, they still mobilize a higher share of people with a working-class identity than demonstrations staged by new social movements.

Having said this, the percentage of those identifying themselves as working class is on average almost double (40 per cent) the percentage of demonstrators with working-class occupations (23 per cent). This shows that 'objective' class does not necessarily coincide with 'subjective' class, and clearly indicates that the latter seems to be much more central for participation in May Day parades. The question is to what degree this difference between 'objective' class and class identity can be attributed to other factors, such as the above-mentioned cross-country difference.

Table 8.5 Class composition (Oesch-9): participants in May Day and other CCC-surveyed demonstrations and general population (ESS5 data)

Per cent (%)	May Day demonstrations			Other types of demonstrations			Cramer's V	National population in major cities ESS5 (2010)
	Traditional/ major trade unions	Radical/ minor trade unions and/or radical left org.	Broad May Day coalitions	Trade union	Environmental	Pride		
Self-employed								
Large employers (10 or more employees)	1	1	1	1	2	1	.044*	1
Self-employed professionals	1	5	8	3	8	6	.112***	2
Small business owners	1	3	3	1	5	4	.105***	8
Employed: Professionals and employees								
Associate managers and administrators	31	18	21	24	17	23	.117***	16
Technical professionals and technicians	7	6	8	6	7	6	n.s.	7
Socio-cultural professionals/ semi-professionals	24	30	37	37	35	28	.093***	13
Employed: Workers								
Office clerks	5	3	3	6	3	4	.058**	11
Production workers	14	11	5	9	3	2	.169***	17
Service workers	9	8	4	8	4	7	.083***	16
Students not working	6	15	10	5	16	18	.156***	10
Cases (N)	820	699	446	1,355	2,071	775		2,363

Notes: Used measure of association between the variables is Cramer's V. * = 5%, ** = 1% and *** = 0.1% significance; *n.s.* = not significant.

In order to test which social (and political) factors contribute most to May Day demonstrators' identification as either working or middle class, a binary logistic regression was conducted (see Table 8.8).[5] In the regression, control variables for age, gender and educational level were included, in addition to variables for the country of the demonstration, the individual's belonging to a specific Oesch-9 class, as well as political orientation on the left–right spectrum.

In general, the May Day demonstrators' class identity is affected most by the country in which the demonstration was held. For example, Spanish May Day demonstrators are more than eight times as likely to identify as working class as those participating in Swedish May Day demonstrations. Nevertheless, and not surprisingly, the individual's 'objective' class position is also an important determinant for class identity. For example, a working-class occupation makes it between three and six times as probable for an individual to identify with the working class (compared to those with other objective class positions).

Other factors that influence class identification are university education (the highly educated more often identify themselves with the middle class) and unemployment (the unemployed identify themselves more often with the working class), as well as the individual's placement on the left–right scale. Individuals who place themselves as decidedly left on the scale are much more prone to identify themselves as working class. Thus, class identity also seems to be a matter of political orientation.

What Kind of Social and Political Factors Influence an Individual's Decision to Join a May Day Parade?

What kind of social and political factors make May Day participation more probable at the individual level? Do socio-demographic factors such as class, age and gender play the most decisive role for joining a May Day demonstration, or do other factors, such as individuals' organizational belonging or their political attitudes, play a more important role?

In order to answer these questions I have 'pooled' data from the six CCC May Day surveys that were conducted in Sweden from 2010–2012 with similar data from the Swedish SOM Institute's national population survey for 2011 (see the Appendix for a more detailed discussion of this procedure). In this SOM Institute survey, respondents were asked whether they had participated in a May Day demonstration during the last 12 months. The analysis is limited to Sweden's three largest cities in which the CCC protest surveys were conducted. In this way, a comparison can be made between the individuals taking part in the main May Day marches in these cities and those who said they did not participate.

In Tables 8.9 and 8.10, the results of analyses of a set of different factors that contribute to May Day participation are shown. A binary logistic regression has been made for each model. In the first model (Table 8.9), the impact of socio-demographic standard variables is analysed. In the second model, the impact of occupational class according to Oesch is analysed separately

Table 8.6 Class identification among participants in May Day demonstrations surveyed within the CCC project

Per cent (%)	Belgium	Italy			Spain			
	Antwerp	Florence	Milan – EuroMayDay	Barcelona	Vigo – CCOO and UGT	Vigo – CIG	Stockholm – LO and Social Democratic Party
Upper class	0	0	0	0	0	1	0
Upper middle class	13	12	25	5	9	2	26
Lower middle class	41	58	49	17	14	11	42
Working class	35	24	14	77	73	84	29
Lower class	2	1	7	1	3	1	0
None	9	5	5	1	0	1	3
Cases (N)	**211**	**106**	**124**	**173**	**64**	**166**	**168**

Notes: Used measure of association between the variables is Cramer's V. * = 5%, ** = 1% and *** = 0.1% significance; *n.s.* = not significant.

and in the third model both occupational class and class identity are analysed in the same model. In the fourth model, all socio-demographic and class variables are analysed simultaneously.

In the two last models (Table 8.10), a row of other variables concerning organizational belonging and political attitudes are introduced: organizational affiliation, identification with specific political parties, left–right placement, political trust and satisfaction with democracy. This is done in two steps: first by introducing variables concerning political attitudes and ideology in the fifth model, and then by adding variables concerning organizational affiliation in the sixth model.

With regard to the socio-demographic standard variables analysed in Model 1, some factors are more important than others for explaining May Day participation. In particular, young people and those with a university education are more likely to take part in May Day marches. Even though Model 2 produces relatively minor differences for the factors that are statistically significant, it still shows that occupational class affects individuals' likelihood to join a May Day parade. Compared to production workers, socio-cultural professionals and semi-professionals are more inclined to demonstrate on May Day, although at the same time associate managers and administrators, office clerks and small business owners are less inclined to demonstrate than production workers. When class identity is introduced in Model 3, this shows that also when controlling for occupational class a working-class identity makes people more predisposed to participating in May Day demonstrations. When all the standard socio-demographic and class variables from previous models are analysed together in Model 4, most of the significant

Sweden						Switzerland		United Kingdom	
Stockholm – Left Party	Malmö – LO and Social Democratic Party	Malmö – Left Party	Gothenburg – LO and Social Democratic Party	Gothenburg – Left Party	Zurich	Geneva	London	**Cramer's V**
0	0	0	0	0	1	1	1	*n.s.*
20	13	17	17	15	20	41	11	.260***
53	38	49	35	55	41	35	20	.295***
20	43	30	44	27	23	17	57	.447***
1	1	1	1	1	4	0	1	.135***
6	5	2	3	2	11	6	9	.154***
162	**95**	**138**	**156**	**206**	**132**	**201**	**167**	

differences between the different factors remain. However, the significance for socio-cultural professionals and semi-professionals disappears, at the same time as the impact of university education becomes stronger. This shows that the likelihood of members of this occupational class taking part in May Day marches is closely correlated to a higher level of education. Models 1–4, all of which deal with socio-demographic predictors for May Day participation, only explain between 4 and 12 per cent of the variation (see Nagelkerke's pseudo-R^2 for the different models). It can thus be concluded that class and other socio-demographic factors influence individuals' decisions to demonstrate on May Day, although their forecasting potential is minor.

When the set of variables relating to political attitudes, ideology and organizational affiliation are introduced in Models 5–6 (Table 8.10), these models explain between 67 and 74 per cent of the variation (which is relatively rare when dealing with these types of survey-based social and attitudinal statistics) becomes clearer. Political and ideological factors, as well as organizational membership, play a more decisive role than socio-demographic factors in explaining why certain groups are more likely to join a May Day demonstration than other groups.

The single most determining factor is party membership, i.e. organizational affiliation. Party members are almost 16 times more likely to join a May Day demonstration than non-party members. Also, sympathies with certain political parties play an important role, which is perhaps less surprising. Left Party sympathizers are twice as likely to demonstrate on May Day than Social Democratic Party sympathizers. However, in comparison with Social Democratic Party sympathizers (and the quite small Feminist Party), those

Table 8.7 Class identification: participants in May Day and other CCC-surveyed demonstrations

Per cent (%)	May Day demonstrations		Other types of demonstrations				Cramer's V
	Traditional/major trade unions	Radical/minor trade unions and/or radical left org.	Broad May Day coalitions	Trade union	Environmental	Pride	
Upper class	0	0	1	0	1	1	.040*
Upper middle class	13	15	21	13	27	25	.156***
Lower middle class	38	38	29	38	46	46	.103***
Working class	43	42	38	40	11	16	.314***
Lower class	1	3	2	1	1	2	.041*
None	4	3	9	8	14	10	.135****
Cases (N)	**973**	**796**	**500**	**1763**	**2408**	**897**	

Notes: Used measure of association between the variables is Cramer's V. * = 5%, ** = 1% and *** = 0.1% significance.

Table 8.8 Binary logistic regression for determinants of working-class and middle-class identification (CCC data)

	Model 1			Model 2		
	Working-class identification			Middle-class identification		
	B	S.E.	Exp(B)	B	S.E.	Exp(B)
Control variables						
Age (29 years and younger = ref.)						
30–49 years	0.25	0.20	1.28	−0.03	0.18	0.97
50–64 years	0.13	0.21	1.14	0.17	0.19	1.18
65 years and older	0.41	0.24	1.51	−0.13	0.22	0.88
Gender: female	−0.38**	0.12	0.68	0.41***	0.12	1.51
Ethnicity: born abroad	0.45*	0.19	1.56	−0.56**	0.18	0.57
University degree/study at university	−1.13***	0.14	0.32	1.10***	0.14	3.01
Unemployed or between jobs	0.75**	0.28	2.12	−0.93**	0.29	0.40
Country of demonstration (Sweden = ref.)						
Belgium	−0.44*	0.22	0.64	0.05	0.21	1.05
Italy	−1.03***	0.26	0.36	0.51*	0.23	1.66
Spain	2.14***	0.18	8.53	−2.05***	0.18	0.13
Switzerland	−0.76***	0.20	0.47	0.42*	0.18	1.51
United Kingdom	1.53***	0.22	4.61	−1.61***	0.22	0.20
Class: Oesch-9 scheme (socio-cultural professionals and semi-professionals = ref.)						
Large employers (10 or more employees)	−0.24	0.68	0.79	−0.12	0.57	0.89
Self-employed professionals	−0.03	0.34	0.97	−0.43	0.29	0.65
Small business owners	0.14	0.43	1.15	−0.49	0.41	0.62
Associate managers and administrators	0.22	0.17	1.24	−0.01	0.16	0.99
Technical professionals and technicians	0.44	0.25	1.55	−0.40	0.23	0.67

Table 8.8 (cont.)

| | Model 1 | | | Model 2 | | |
| | Working-class identification | | | Middle-class identification | | |
	B	S.E.	Exp(B)	B	S.E.	Exp(B)
Office clerks	1.19***	0.31	3.28	−0.83**	0.30	0.44
Production workers	1.41***	0.24	4.08	−1.30	0.24	0.27
Service workers	1.77***	0.25	5.87	−1.45***	0.24	0.23
Students not working	0.25	0.25	1.29	−0.05	0.23	0.96
Left–right placement (far left, 0–1 = ref.)						
Left (2–3)	−0.72***	0.13	0.49	0.69***	0.12	1.99
Centre-left (4–5)	−0.65*	0.28	0.52	0.68*	0.26	1.97
Right (6–10)	−0.95	0.52	0.39	0.95	0.50	2.57
No left–right position	−0.53	0.51	0.59	0.56	0.49	1.75
Constant	−0.31	0.26	0.74	−0.18	0.24	0.83
Nagelkerke's pseudo-R^2	0.424			0.380		
Observations	**1,849**			**1,849**		

Notes: Columns show beta coefficient, standard error and odds ratio. Levels of significance: * = 5%, ** = 1% and *** = 0,1% significance.

sympathizing with the Green Party are only a quarter as likely to join a May Day demonstration, and the corresponding figure for the remaining parties (all of which are in principle right or centre-right orientated) is one tenth. As we might expect, those positioning themselves as 'right' on the left–right spectrum are also much less (less than one tenth, in terms of odds ratio) likely to demonstrate on May Day.

Another important factor is dissatisfaction with how democracy works at the national level. Those participants dissatisfied with Swedish democracy are almost twice as likely to demonstrate on May Day in comparison with those satisfied with Swedish democracy. This confirms the importance of the actual political situation for mobilizing people to May Day demonstrations. In the surveyed years 2010–2012, Sweden was led by a right-wing government, and dissatisfaction with its policies apparently influenced individuals' decisions to join the May Day marches staged by two of the main opposition parties.

It can thus be concluded that organizational affiliation with a political party is the single most important factor that influences individuals' decisions to demonstrate on May Day. However, party sympathies, general ideological orientation and dissatisfaction with democracy at the national level are also important factors. All these findings resonate well with previous research on which factors primarily influence individuals to participate in political protests. For example, social-psychological research stresses that the prime motives for individuals' political participation are social (that one knows other politically active people), ideological (that one shares the political values of a movement or an organization) and instrumental (that one believes that one's own participation can have an impact) (see e.g. Klandermans 2004 and Chapter 9 in this volume). While we can corroborate that ideological and social aspects are important for participation in May Day demonstrations, we cannot test the participants' instrumental motives due to the lack of compatible data.

Nevertheless, we can say that social class matters for May Day participation, even though it does not matter in the same way (or to the same degree) as organizational and political factors. In contrast to the dominant picture of May Day demonstrations as historically primarily mobilizing the working class – or at least the organized working class – the results are more ambivalent. On the one hand, individuals with certain types of working-class occupations (such as production or service workers) are as likely to demonstrate on May Day as individuals having certain types of middle class occupations are (for instance technical professionals and technicians). On the other hand, it is clear that the specific middle-class group of socio-cultural professionals and semi-professionals is mobilized to a much higher degree than all other occupational classes. From a historical perspective, this at least says something about how the types of wage-labourers mobilized by May Day parades have changed over time. Given the lack of similar data for the rest of our analysed countries, it is of course difficult to generalize for Western Europe as a whole. The large percentage of socio-cultural professionals and semi-professionals could be attributable to specific Swedish conditions, such as the country's

Table 8.9 Binary logistic regression: factors contributing to May Day participation (CCC and SOM institute data), part 1

	Model 1 Only control variables			Model 2 Only occupational class			Model 3 Only occupational class and class identity			Model 4 Control variables, occupational class and class identity		
	B	S.E.	Exp(B)	B	S.E.	Exp(B)	B	S.E.	Exp(B)	B	S.E.	Exp(B)
Control variables												
Age (29 years and younger = ref.)												
30–49 years	−0.68***	0.17	0.50							−0.62**	0.20	0.54
50–64 years	−0.28	0.18	0.76							−0.20	0.22	0.82
65 years and older	−0.56**	0.19	0.57							−0.30	0.24	0.74
Gender: female	−0.21†	0.12	0.81							−0.15	0.13	0.87
Ethnicity: born/grown up in another country	−0.02	0.18	0.98							0.14	0.21	1.15
University degree/study at university	0.54***	0.12	1.71							0.63***	0.16	1.87
Class: Oesch-9 scheme (production workers = ref.)												
Large employers (10 or more employees)				−0.21	0.51	0.81	0.35	0.56	1.41	−0.12	0.59	0.89
Self-employed professionals				0.35	0.38	1.41	0.61	0.41	1.84	0.13	0.43	1.14
Small business owners				−1.32***	0.40	0.27	−0.89*	0.42	0.41	−1.31**	0.46	0.27
Associate managers and administrators				−0.51*	0.23	0.60	−0.30	0.25	0.74	−0.58*	0.27	0.56
Technical professionals and technicians				−0.44	0.28	0.64	−0.26	0.29	0.77	−0.69**	0.32	0.50
Socio-cultural professionals/ semi-professionals				0.49*	0.23	1.64	0.70**	0.24	2.01	0.23	0.28	1.26
Office clerks				−0.83*	0.30	0.44	−0.74*	0.30	0.48	−0.93**	0.33	0.40
Service workers				−0.15	0.27	0.86	−0.10	0.27	0.90	−0.21	0.30	0.81
Students not working				0.40	0.26	1.50	0.63*	0.27	1.89	0.07	0.32	1.07
Class identity (working class = ref.)												
Middle class							−0.30†	0.15	0.74	−0.44**	0.17	0.65
Other class							−1.03***	0.30	0.36	−1.13***	0.31	0.32
Constant	−4.84***	0.17	2.55	−5.03***	0.19	2.12	−4.93***	0.20	2.34	−4.48***	0.28	3.68
Nagelkerke's pseudo-R²	0.040			0.073			0.086			0.115		
Observations	**1356**			**1329**			**1294**			**1250**		

Notes: Columns show beta coefficient, standard error and odds ratio. Levels of significance: † = 10%, * = 5%, ** = 1% and *** = 0.1% significance.

Table 8.10 Binary logistic regression: factors contributing to May Day participation (CCC and SOM institute data), part 2

	Model 5			Model 6		
	Including political and ideological variables			Including organizational variables		
	B	S.E.	Exp(B)	B	S.E.	Exp(B)
Control variables						
Age (29 years and younger = ref.)						
30–49 years	−0.26	0.31	0.77	−0.29	0.36	0.75
50–64 years	−0.16	0.33	0.86	−0.02	0.38	0.98
65 years and older	0.05	0.39	1.05	0.12	0.44	1.12
Gender: female	−0.38†	0.21	0.69	−0.34	0.24	0.71
Ethnicity: born/grown up in another country	0.62†	0.34	1.85	0.67†	0.39	1.96
University degree/study at university	0.80**	0.26	2.24	0.63*	0.29	1.88
Class: Oesch-9 scheme (production workers = ref.)						
Large employers (10 or more employees)	−0.16	1.03	0.86	−1.09	1.13	0.34
Self-employed professionals	0.95	0.68	2.58	0.97	0.73	2.64
Small business owners	−0.97	0.67	0.38	−1.14	0.71	0.32
Associate managers and administrators	−0.27	0.43	0.76	−0.95*	0.48	0.39
Technical professionals and technicians	0.03	0.50	1.03	−0.22	0.58	0.80
Socio-cultural professionals/semi-professionals	−0.04	0.43	0.96	−0.20	0.48	0.82
Office clerks	−0.58	0.51	0.56	−0.85	0.57	0.43
Service workers	0.10	0.45	1.11	−0.12	0.50	0.89
Students not working	0.30	0.48	1.35	0.21	0.54	1.24
Class identity (working class = ref.)						
Middle class	−0.08	0.25	0.93	0.05	0.27	1.05
Other class	0.18	0.55	1.20	0.35	0.59	1.42

Table 8.10 (cont.)

	Model 5 Including political and ideological variables			Model 6 Including organizational variables		
	B	S.E.	Exp(B)	B	S.E.	Exp(B)
Party sympathy (Social Democratic Party = ref.)						
Left Party	0.09	0.28	1.10	0.73*	0.31	2.07
Green Party	-2.08***	0.28	0.13	-1.35***	0.32	0.26
Feminist Party	-0.51	0.76	0.60	0.41	0.80	1.50
Other political party	-2.68***	0.42	0.07	-2.42***	0.49	0.09
Left–right placement (left = ref.)						
Right	-3.08***	0.47	0.05	-2.68***	0.55	0.07
Neither left nor right/no left–right position	-3.12***	0.35	0.04	-2.91***	0.42	0.05
Political trust and satisfaction with democracy						
Not satisfied with democracy in Sweden	0.61*	0.25	1.85	0.66*	0.27	1.94
Low trust in national government	0.03*	0.01	1.03	0.03†	0.02	1.03
Organizational affiliation						
Trade union				0.26	0.25	1.30
Political party				2.75***	0.33	15.59
Environmental organization				1.08**	0.35	2.95
Constant	-3.77***	0.44	7.42	-5.01	0.50	2.16
Nagelkerke's pseudo-R²	0.666			0.735		
Observations	**1,164**			**1,148**		

Notes: Columns show beta coefficient, standard error and odds ratio. Levels of significance: † = 10%, * = 5%, ** = 1% and *** = 0.1% significance.

high degree of unionization among middle-class occupations, although the same general class composition as in the Swedish case can be seen in most of the other surveyed May Day demonstrations presented earlier in the chapter.

Conclusion

Although the normalization of street politics has typically been attributed to demonstrations in Western democracies from the 1960s onwards, the history of May Day demonstrations goes back to the late nineteenth century. In this chapter I have examined which socio-demographic groups take part in contemporary May Day demonstrations in order to determine the degree to which the participants in these annual parades reflect the social composition of the general population, and thus confirm the thesis of the social normalization of the protester.

In comparison to the general population, May Day marches attract a larger proportion of the well-educated middle class and a smaller share of the working class. However, in comparison to demonstrations staged by new social movements, May Day parades display a much higher participation of citizens with working-class occupations and a smaller proportion of university-educated participants. Compared to these other types of demonstrations, May Day demonstrations thus stand out as having a social profile that is closer to the general population, even though it is still slanted towards individuals with middle-class occupations.

The more 'normal' or representative social composition is most evident in the May Day parades staged by the major trade union confederations and social democratic parties, while May Day demonstrations arranged by radical left organizations have greater similarities with protests staged by new social movements. On the other hand, with regard to the mobilization of other groups that today also experience a deterioration in social security, e.g. young people, the under- and unemployed, self-employed professionals, these are more present in the May Day demonstrations of the radical left, while the marches staged by the major trade unions and social democratic parties mobilize these groups to a lesser degree. It is thus important to stress that the different types of May Day parades that take place today also tend to mobilize different groups. In the context of austerity policies, a divide can be observed in how two groups that are both negatively affected by the economic crisis and its aftermath, namely the traditional working class and the group excluded from social security that is now often referred to as 'the precariat', are mobilized through different channels. This division also shows that it is important to acknowledge that contemporary May Day demonstrations fall back on different traditions within the labour movement and on different types of primary constituencies.

Class still matters for May Day participation, albeit in perhaps less predictable ways. Even though individuals with working-class occupations are more inclined to take part in May Day demonstrations than those from most other occupational classes, the group that is most predisposed to demonstrate on May Day belongs to the occupational middle class: socio-cultural professionals and semi-professionals. This indicates that among today's wage-labourers, it is not only individuals with traditional working-class occupations that take to the streets to protest against social injustices, but also other employees and professionals belonging to specific parts of the occupational middle classes (cf. Kriesi 1989). Apparently, May Day is not just a working-class affair, since today we can see other classes mobilized by the labour movement's calls for social justice. This seems to illustrate the changing conditions for political mobilizations in a Europe in which austerity policies of later years have not only undermined the social rights and opportunities of the working class but also for groups traditionally belonging to the middle class.

Despite the fact that my analysis has shown that class still matters for May Day participation, it has also revealed that other factors are even stronger predictors for individuals' participation in May Day marches, in particular their ideological convictions and political attitudes. These aspects are analysed in greater detail in the following chapter, which examines individuals' motives for participating in May Day demonstrations.

Notes

1 The question of who really took part in the first May Day parades is difficult to answer, because no protest surveys were conducted when these took place. Comparisons with today's situation are also difficult, given that the class composition of most European societies has changed drastically since the late nineteenth and early twentieth century, particularly with the expansion of the middle class. At the same time, it should be remembered also that during the first decades of the twentieth century social democratic parties in Europe drew extensive electoral support from the middle class (see e.g. Sperber 1997, p. 63ff.) and did not attract only working-class voters. It thus seems plausible that already early on the same parties attracted individuals from the middle class to the May Day parades.
2 The ESS5 covers the countries included in the CCC data used in this chapter, except for Italy, which did not take part in this round of the European Social Survey.
3 Here I would especially like to thank Anders Hylmö for manually classifying the occupation of all cases in the CCC dataset, as well as managing all the coding of the data into Oesch's class categories.
4 According to OECD (2013), in 2011 the percentages of foreign-born in the countries in our study were as follows: Belgium 15 per cent; Italy 9 per cent; Spain 15 per cent; Sweden 15 per cent; Switzerland 27 per cent; and the UK 12 per cent.
5 This type of regression plots so-called odds ratios for each factor (in the table labelled Exp(B)), i.e. a figure for how the probability of having a specific quality (here, identifying as working or middle class) is affected by other individual characteristics (e.g. gender) when the effects of many variables analysed simultaneously are considered.

References

Andretta, M., and Reiter, H. (2009). Parties, unions, and movements: The European left and the ESF. In D. della Porta (Ed.), *Another Europe: Conceptions and*

Practices of Democracy in the European Social Forums (pp. 173–203). London: Routledge.

Cigéhn, G., and Johansson, M. (1997). *Klassidentitet i upplösning? Om betydelsen av klass, politik och arbete i 90-talets Sverige.* Umeå: Umeå universitet.

Cigéhn, G., Johansson, M., and Karlsson, L. (2001). *Klassamhällets återkomst: Om klassidentitet, arbetsliv och fritid vid tröskeln till ett nytt sekel.* Umeå Studies in Sociology. Umeå: Umeå University.

Crompton, R. (2010). Class and employment. *Work, Employment and Society*, 24(1), 9–26.

Eder, K. (1995). Does social class matter in the study of social movements?: A theory of middle-class radicalism. In L. Maheu (Ed.), *Social Movements and Social Classes: The Future of Collective Action* (pp. 21–54). London: Sage.

Goldthorpe, J. (2000). *On Sociology: Numbers, Narratives, and the Integration of Research and Theory.* Oxford: Oxford University Press.

Hylmö, A., and Wennerhag, M. (2015). Does class matter in anti-austerity protests? Social class, attitudes towards inequality, and political trust in European demonstrations in a time of economic crisis. In M. Giugni and M. Grasso (Eds), *Austerity and Protest: Popular Contention in Times of Economic Crisis.* Farnham, UK: Ashgate.

Klandermans, B. (2004). The demand and supply of participation: Social-psychological correlates of participation in social movements. In D.A. Snow, S.A. Soule and H. Kriesi (Eds) *The Blackwell Companion to Social Movements* (pp. 360–379). Malden, MA: Blackwell.

Kriesi, H. (1989). New social movements and the new class in the Netherlands. *American Journal of Sociology*, 94(5), 1078–1116.

March, A., and Kaase, M. (1979). Background of political action. In S.H. Barnes, and M. Kaase (Eds), *Political Action: Mass Participation in Five Western Democracies* (pp. 97–136). London: Sage.

March, L. (2011). *Radical Left Parties in Europe.* London: Routledge.

Morales, L. (2011). Conceptualising and measuring migrants' political inclusion. In L. Morales, and M. Giugni (Eds) *Social Capital, Political Participation and Migration in Europe: Making Multicultural Democracy Work?* (pp. 19–42). Basingstoke, UK: Palgrave Macmillan.

Norris, P. (2002). *Democratic Phoenix: Reinventing Political Activism.* New York: Cambridge University Press.

Norris, P., Walgrave, S., and Van Aelst, P. (2005). Who demonstrates? Antistate rebels, conventional participants, or everyone? *Comparative Politics*, 37(2), 189–205.

OECD. (2013). *International Migration Outlook 2013.* Paris: Organisation for Economic Cooperation and Development.

Oesch, D. (2006a). *Redrawing the Class Map: Stratification and Institutions in Britain, Germany, Sweden, and Switzerland.* New York: Palgrave Macmillan.

Oesch, D. (2006b). Coming to grips with a changing class structure: An analysis of employment stratification in Britain, Germany, Sweden and Switzerland. *International Sociology*, 21(2), 263–288.

Oesch, D. (2008a). The changing shape of class voting. *European Societies*, 10(3), 329–355.

Oesch, D. (2008b). Explaining workers' support for right-wing populist parties in Western Europe: Evidence from Austria, Belgium, France, Norway, and Switzerland. *International Political Science Review*, 29(3), 349–373.

Peterson, A., Wahlström, M., and Wennerhag, M. (2012). Swedish trade unionism: A renewed social movement? *Economic and Industrial Democracy*, 33(4), 621–647.

Sperber, J. (1997). *The Kaiser's Voters: Electors and Elections in Imperial Germany*. Cambridge: Cambridge University Press.

Standing, G. (2011). *The Precariat: The New Dangerous Class*. London: Bloomsbury Academic.

Waterman, P. (2001). Trade union internationalism in the age of Seattle. *Antipode: A Radical Journal of Geography*, 3, 315–336.

Weber, M. (1922/1978). *Economy and Society: An Outline of Interpretive Sociology*, vol. 2. Berkeley: University of California Press.

Van Aelst, P., and Walgrave, S. (2001). Who is that (wo)man in the street? From the normalisation of protest to the normalisation of the protester. *European Journal of Political Research*, 39(4), 461–486.

Verba, S., Schlozman, K.L., and Brady, H.E. (1995). *Voice and Equality: Civic Voluntarism in American Politics*. Cambridge, MA: Harvard University Press.

Wright, E.O. (2009). Understanding class: Towards an integrated analytical approach. *New Left Review*, 60, 101–116.

9   Why Do People Demonstrate on May Day?

Mattias Wahlström

Marching on May Day is a long-lived ritual in Western European countries and it is a highly significant event for the organized labour movement. Although the importance of such marches has been taken for granted, the specific meaning of contemporary marches has not been well explored (for an exception, see Peterson *et al.* 2012b). As with other collective political events, they are also primarily understood in the light of the organizers' rhetoric and by how the mass media describe them. Nevertheless, the significance of May Day demonstrations and marches in Western Europe cannot be fully appreciated by simply using their organizers' accounts or media coverage. At least as important is the significance that May Day marches have for the people who take part in them. Do people consider May Day marches to be protests, or are they primarily social events or celebrations of past achievements? Moreover, do participants tend to confer different meanings on May Day marches in different national contexts? Do motives for participation vary systematically among different categories of marchers in a single event? These questions are relevant, and not just because understanding May Day rituals requires us to take into account the participants' understandings of their practice (cf. Roth 1995). With respect to research on protest mobilization in general, May Day marches provide a potentially deviant case in which the motives for participation may differ from participants' motives in reactive and less routinized protests.

In this chapter the meanings that participants confer on May Day demonstrations are examined through qualitative and quantitative analyses of responses to the survey question: 'Please tell us why you participated in this protest event.' This question was posed to participants in 15 May Day marches in six Western European countries: Belgium, Italy, Spain, Switzerland, Sweden and the UK. The responses, which admittedly were often very short and concise, were analysed and categorized according to types of motives. This categorization was the basis for coding the responses of all of the May Day demonstrators in the dataset. Apart from presenting an overview of the frequency of the types of motives in the different demonstrations, a number of hypotheses will be tested that provide a partial explanation for the variation in motives.

Theories of Protesters' Motives

There is a need for an initial word of caution regarding the object of study. There is no unequivocal causal relation between the decision to participate in a protest and the motives that people put forth when prompted to explain why they participated in a protest. In his discussion about 'vocabularies of motive', C. Wright Mills (1940) argues that the motives that people provide for their actions should be regarded as socially situated speech acts that do not necessarily reflect the underlying driving forces behind human actions.[1] Admittedly, even though it is a fair guess that the motives articulated in response to the questionnaire often have played a part in the process that led the respondent to be in the demonstration, they might be 'merely' retrospective constructions of what *ought* to have been the reason for participating. However, regardless of their causal force, first, the articulated motives reflect the types of legitimizations that are acceptable among participants in May Day demonstrations. Second, the significance that demonstrators construct around their participation is crucial for understanding their individual decisions to participate, even though it does not necessarily provide 'the whole story' in terms of explanation. Thus, although I wish to avoid a naïve causal understanding of the role of expressed motives for action, I shall nevertheless situate the motives stated by May Day participants in light of previous research and theories about individual motivation for protest participation. What does previous research tell us about what motivates people to participate in protests in general, and in May Day demonstrations in particular?

Motives for Protest in General

At the individual level, Klandermans (2004) distinguishes between three general types of motives (or perhaps motivations) for protest participation that have been identified in previous research: instrumentality, identity and ideology. Broadly speaking, *instrumental motives* are concerned with actually bringing about political change for the benefit of the individual participant or other disadvantaged groups. This perspective has strong proponents in resource mobilization theory (e.g. McCarthy and Zald 1977) and political process theory (e.g. McAdam 1999) and still dominates much theorizing on social movements and protest behaviour. However, today there is a broad consensus among scholars that other types of motivational factors also lie behind protest activities. One of these is *collective identity*, 'the shared definition of a group that derives from members' common interests, experiences, and solidarity' (Taylor and Whittier 1999, p. 170; cf. Melucci 1996). From an individual perspective, a requirement for participation is that the collective identity of a movement fits more or less with the individual identity of a potential movement participant – what Snow and McAdam (2000) term 'identity convergence'. Finally, motives for participation can be related to ideas and values. Klandermans (2004) conceptualizes this under the label of *ideological motives*, which are described as 'wanting to express one's views' (p. 365) and as linked 'to people's values and the assessment that these values have been violated' (van Stekelenburg and Klandermans 2010, p. 183). Thus, this category contains two elements: (1) wanting to express one's views (in order to be heard by others), and (2) acting in accordance with a moral principle (in principle, regardless of whether anyone notices). Several contemporary researchers also emphasize *emotions* as a distinct aspect of social movement participation (Flam and King 2005; Goodwin, Jasper and Polletta 2001). Van Stekelenburg, Klandermans and van Dijk (2011) argue that group-based emotions amplify the motivational importance of other paths to protest. The typical emotion mentioned in this context is anger (van Zomeren *et al.* 2004), but other emotions also appear to motivate people's protest participation, including a sense of fun (Wettergren 2009). Weber's (1978) classic typology of social action is seldom referred to in this context, but it is striking how instrumentality, ideology and group-based emotions closely resemble Weber's goal-rational, value-rational and affective action types, respectively. What is left is the traditional, or habitual, action, which I will return to below.

At the level of protest campaigns, Klandermans (1993) notes a distinction originally made by Turner and Killian (1987) between three action orientations: (1) value orientation, or an orientation toward the goals and the ideology of the movement; (2) power orientation, or an orientation toward acquiring and exerting influence; and (3) participation orientation, or an orientation toward the benefits of participation (Klandermans 1993, pp. 387–388).

As noted by van Stekelenburg and colleagues (2009), these action orientations of protest campaigns are not necessarily mutually exclusive. Instead, a single campaign may contain elements of all three orientations. These authors also link the power orientation to stronger instrumental motives among individual participants and the value orientation to stronger ideological motives. Presumably protest participants always have the urge to confirm their social identity to some extent (cf. Stryker, Owens and White 2000), but this urge should be particularly salient when the campaign has a strong participation orientation.

Whereas van Stekelenburg, Klandermans and van Dijk (2009) make a rare contribution to the relationship between the motives of protest participants and the character of the demonstration in which they take part, Ketelaars (2014) analyses how the degree of instrumental motivations of participants in anti-austerity protests varies depending on the wider political context. She found that a positive stance of the government in relation to the protest issue was positively correlated to the degree of instrumental motivation among participants. This is similar to the findings by Walgrave and colleagues (2011), who also analyse the variation of motives according to a classification of motives based on an intersection between instrumental and expressive motive types on the one hand and collective versus individual types of motives on the other hand. They find that protesters in the US are less likely than their

European counterparts to be motivated by the expectation that they could influence the politics of their government.

Participant Motives in May Day Marches

An analysis of participant motives in May Day demonstrations should not disregard the previous research on motives for protest participation. At the same time, there are good reasons to try to move beyond existing typologies and adopt an exploratory approach and develop an analysis that is sensitive to the specificities of May Day events. We can thereby better capture the experiences of participants and reduce the risk that central motivational dimensions are glossed over. For instance, it is not surprising that existing research on protest motives has emphasized the exceptional character of protest participation. From the perspective of the general population, this is indeed so; most people do not take part in any given protest and thus explanations must be found for why people participate. However, it can be easy to miss the fact that participation in some types of events may have a traditional (and even habitual) element for frequent protesters. Clearly, protesting can hardly become habitual in the strong sense of having an 'almost automatic reaction to habitual stimuli' (Weber 1978, p. 25). However, it can be habitual in the sense that some people participate simply because it is something they usually do. May Day marches form a category of protest events in which this type of motive coexists along with a broad range of other types of motives (as we shall see below) and is therefore not only interesting to explore in its own right, but also to increase our knowledge of protest motives in general.

Data

The analysis focuses on a selection of May Day demonstrations from the protest survey dataset constructed by the research programme 'Caught in the Act of Protest: Contextualizing Contestation' (hereafter CCC). It consists of responses to surveys that were distributed between 2009 and 2013 to participants in over 80 protests of different types. The surveys used a standardized methodology to ensure the reliability and comparability of the data. Fifteen of these protests were May Day demonstrations that took place in Western Europe: one in Belgium, two in Italy, three in Spain, six in Sweden, two in Switzerland and one in London. For an overview of these demonstrations, as well as a general description of the sampling and coding, see the Appendix.

A Typology of Motives

Participants in May Day demonstrations often express several different (and sometimes complementary) types of motives at the same time. To some extent, complementary meanings reflect the fact that various participants have different approaches to demonstrating on May Day, but to a large extent, these approaches overlap in complex patterns. The various types of motives were identified through a theoretically informed, yet largely inductive, analysis. First, a typology was constructed by examining the motives articulated in the 2010 May Day demonstrations. This typology was presented in a previous study (Peterson *et al.* 2012b). Next, based on the responses gathered at the 2011 and 2012 demonstrations, which included two events in Italy, the first version of the typology was revised to be more precise and nuanced. In what follows, I take the opportunity to elaborate on some of the details that were lost in the necessarily concise discussion by Peterson and colleagues (2012b). I comment on and exemplify each of the categories, and then make some general concluding remarks on local variation and on the typology as a whole, before we turn to a quantitative analysis of the motive types in Western European May Day demonstrations.

Celebrate Workers' Day

One of the most common responses to our question about motives was that the respondent was 'celebrating May Day'. In practice, this could mean that it was a great party that one enjoys coming to, but relatively often the respondents also specified some aspect of what the celebration was about. One Genevan demonstrator said, 'It's the holiday, the joy of gathering, of sharing preoccupations and hopes for justice.' Some primarily saw it as a commemoration of past generations of workers who had fought for the rights that they themselves now enjoyed: 'to honour the efforts of our parents and grandparents' as one marcher from Antwerp expressed it, or to 'show pride in my parents' as a marcher from Stockholm wrote. Others saw it as a special day for workers and those with leftist values. Echoing common statements about International Women's Day, a respondent from Stockholm noted, 'The left has one day per year, the right wing all the others.'

One respondent from Antwerp began her response to our question about why she participated in the demonstration by stating, 'This was not a demonstration!!!' Although other respondents explicitly referred to the event as a demonstration, she was not alone in pointing out that she did not consider the event to be a 'demonstration'. The respondents who followed this pattern variously labelled it a manifestation, a march, a feast, a celebration, a commemoration, a festival, a procession or a parade. One Florentine respondent wrote: 'I do not believe that the event of 1 May is a protest. It is a civic moment that bears witness to the importance of the human factor in work. Presently, the protest lies in the fact that this matter is always less considered.'

Some respondents also used religious language about the May Day celebration. A respondent from Gothenburg called it 'the holy day of the workers', and a Swiss respondent said, 'May Day is a holy day of obligation, like Easter for Christians.' An Italian marcher wrote, 'for a trade unionist ex-workman 1 May is "sacred"'. On the one hand, such statements appear to refer to the traditional aspect of May Day marches. It is a necessity by virtue of tradition. On the other hand, it communicates a strong symbolic meaning about the celebration that cannot be captured in anything other than religious metaphors. For these people, celebrating May Day is a ritual and an experience beyond the mundane realities of life.

Celebrate Political Accomplishments

Closely related to celebrating the workers' day was a celebration of not (only) the workers' struggle as such, but the accomplishments of previous generations. 'As a worker, I feel obligated to participate in our party. Not so long ago our actions were prohibited and persecuted, and for me it would be an insult to our ancestors who fought for this right not to go' (respondent from Vigo).

Another recurrent formulation was that participants demonstrated 'because it is a democratic right'. This is primarily interpreted as a way of honouring this right and maintaining it by using it. However, there is the possibility that when a Malmö respondent simply writes, 'my democratic right to express my opinion', this respondent is actually questioning the survey question itself, as if the respondent had replied, 'do not question my presence at this demonstration – it is my democratic right to be here'.

Tradition

> I have participated for 50 years in the social arrangements in Gothenburg, and of course, this year is no exception.
>
> (Respondent from Gothenburg)

Along with 'conviction' (see below), 'tradition' was the most common single-word response in the dataset. 'Tradition' in this context may refer to a personal habit, a concrete local tradition, the general tradition of May Day internationally, or some combination of all of these meanings. However, referring to a general tradition as a motive for participation also suggests that there is an element of personal tradition involved as well.

Therefore, in this category I also included responses that mentioned 'habit', or stated in various ways that this is something that one just does or has done for a long time. A significant number of (especially elderly) respondents made a point of stating that they had attended (almost) every May Day march since (year they started), or they indicated how many years they had taken part (the record among the respondents appears to be 60 years.)

These and other statements – that participation in May Day is somehow obvious, something one just does – are arguably related to what Crossley (2003) terms a 'radical habitus'. Bourdieu originally developed his concept of habitus to explain the reproduction of social structures, whereas Crossley argues that political activism may give rise to an activist habitus expressed in the appropriate 'taste', lifestyle preferences, and even as a somewhat oxymoronic habit of critical thinking. This habitus is most obviously expressed in the more unreflective 'I always participate' approach to May Day marching, but it is also evident in the acquired taste for demonstrating that may be necessary for experiencing the full enjoyment found among the social motives below.

Meet Family, Friends or Co-Members of an Organization

This category includes various forms of social motives. These can have an ostensibly coercive character, as was the case for one respondent from Gothenburg, who simply wrote, 'peer pressure'. For the most part, however, social motives have strikingly positive connotations. One respondent from Geneva wrote, 'reunion day: I meet with my "political family", and that encourages me'. This quote indicates both the close identification with other participants that is reaffirmed through this collective ritual and the sense of encouragement that one gets from meeting with like-minded people in a manifestation of power. This type of quotation shows that collective empowerment is not only an outcome of political protests (Drury and Reicher 2005, 2009); it is also recognized and even actively sought as a motive for coming to protest events. In a similar vein, a respondent from Gothenburg wrote, 'to "feel" the left-wing movement (to feel that we are many and strong)', and a respondent from Malmö explicitly stated, 'to consolidate my ideological opinion together with like-minded people'. However, such empowerment is not necessarily strictly political; it can also be very personal, as reflected in a quote from a Milanese demonstrator: 'nowadays participating in protest is the only thing that makes me feel alive'.

It is not only the purely 'political family' that participants mention in their motives; traditional types of family ties are also mentioned repeatedly. People come together to be with their children, siblings or parents and, presumably, to reinforce the social identity of the family. One demonstrator from Antwerp wrote, 'My mum and I always come because it is fun and my mum is a socialist', and a Malmö respondent wrote from a parental perspective (somewhat tongue-in-cheek), 'Because I care about the society that I live in and want to brainwash my children (!)' These quotations also give us a hint as to how the radical habitus, discussed above, can be reproduced across generations. Demonstrating on May Day functions as a form of socialization into a radical habitus.

Display Loyalty or Solidarity

A large number of respondents also considered their participation to be an expression of loyalty, identity or solidarity with a political group or category of people. I interpret this primarily as a display of collective identity (cf. Polletta and Jasper 2001, p. 291).

Included in this category are statements that one takes part simply as a consequence of one's identification with a group or a class. One respondent from Barcelona simply stated, 'because I consider myself a worker', and another respondent explicitly referred to 'class consciousness'. Altogether, about 4 per cent of the respondents (most of whom were from Vigo or Barcelona) cited class identity (in one way or another) as a motive for participation. Therefore, although the class base of May Day demonstrations is mixed nowadays (as seen in Chapter 8), some demonstrators nevertheless regard their working-class membership as an important element of their participation.

A specific case, which arguably should be included in this category, involves being motivated to participate by 'solidarity'. Roughly speaking, solidarity may encompass either (1) a collective to which one belongs or (2) a group or category of people to which one does not belong that is comparatively disadvantaged. In other words, this is the solidarity of what McCarthy and Zald (1977) call the 'conscience constituents' towards the 'potential beneficiaries' of the movement. The ambiguous meaning of 'solidarity' makes the responses that use this term difficult to interpret and classify, especially when the term is used on its own, as when a respondent simply stated 'out of solidarity'. It would not be appropriate to simply use a particular definition of solidarity from the literature, because we cannot know for sure whether respondents are using the term in the same way. However, the salience of the concept among May Day demonstrators is no doubt rooted in traditional Marxist uses of the concept.[2] Steinar Stjernø (2004) argues that the concept was initially used by Marxists to denote the borderless identification of common interests among the working class, a concept that would mobilize the working class in its struggle for a socialist society. However, it was subsequently broadened (particularly in a social democratic tradition) to encompass other classes and categories and, in some contexts, even the entire society. Stjernø demonstrates how this concept varies significantly between different socialist traditions (and Christian democrats), as well as between social democratic parties in different countries. In practice, the concept is still widely used, partly because its vagueness gives it a broad appeal. At the same time, it 'arouses connotations of collaboration and common efforts to establish public solutions in welfare and the social services, providing aid to poor nations and showing compassion to people in need' (Stjernø 2004, p. 257).

For the purpose of analysis, it is important to be aware of the tensions within the concept between more or less inclusive notions and more or less symmetrical relationships, including whether solidarity is regarded primarily as altruism or as mutual support. For instance, the question of asymmetry is clearly evident in union discussions about international solidarity (Peterson, Wahlström and Wennerhag 2012a; Waterman 1998). Among the respondents, approximately 13 per cent used this term to express their motives. Most used it in ways that – also based on the assumption that they were inspired by Marxist discourse about solidarity – implied identification with those with whom one feels solidarity. However, in some instances, it was used in ways that suggest the object of solidarity was an out-group: 'those who are exploited'. It is tempting to try to capture the distinction between in-group solidarity and out-group solidarity with different codes, as Peterson *et al.* (2012b) do. However, even though it is indeed a long way from identification with a class to supporting the weak in society (as motives for participation), there is arguably a common element of identification and recognition that different groups are, in a sense, in the same boat. As a respondent from Geneva wrote, 'I am sensitive to workers' lives and I am concerned for them, for all of us!' Identification can also be quite ambivalent, as is evident in the following quote: 'I grew up in a proletarian environment. Out of tradition. I felt connected to the working class, even if I'm not a worker in a sociological sense. Solidarity with the socially weak and excluded' (respondent from Zurich).

Conviction/Moral Duty

Although quite closely related to the previous category, there is a distinct type of motive that is linked to ideological or moral conviction, such that demonstrating is somehow a 'moral duty and obligation', as one Gothenburg participant wrote. Presumably, when someone refers to a conviction or a moral imperative, taking part in a demonstration is not done so much to make an impression upon others; it is done to be authentic and true to one's personal value identity (Gecas 2000). Van Zomeren and Spears similarly separate the motivation 'to protect "sacred" group values from "secular" encroachment' (2009, p. 670) from other motives focused on external impact. Klandermans (2004) distinguishes ideological motives for protesting from instrumental and identity motives, but in so doing he conflates two distinct types of action logics: value-rational and expressive. On the one hand, people may want to make their ideological and moral positions known to others, i.e. expressive actions. On the other hand, protesting can be the result of adhering to one's ideological principles, regardless of what others think about it. In the present analysis, conviction types of motives relate to the latter mode of logic, whereas the expression of personal positions is regarded as *taking a stand* or *protest government/politics* (see below).

In some cases, there is a blurred boundary between the *conviction/moral duty* and *loyalty/solidarity* codes, because it is not always clear whether responses are primarily concerned with collective identity or with principle. When someone writes, 'I am a socialist', the logic may be to demonstrate that one belongs to the group/party/category of socialist, or that one participates because of socialist ideological convictions. Of course, both aspects may be involved.

Support of One's Own Movement

A distinct type of motive concerns supporting one's own movement by participating. In many instances, this is closely related to displaying loyalty or identity to a group, but with the difference that this type of motive emphasizes concrete organizational or movement support rather than identification. This includes presenting oneself as an organizer, representing an organization in the march (such as a trade union or party), or simply stating one's position within the organization, e.g. 'union secretary' (Geneva). It also includes various formulations that use the term 'support', such as, it is 'important to show support' (Gothenburg).

Protest Government/Politics

> Because I hate the government.
>
> (Respondent from Malmö)

Perhaps the most prominent motive in the dataset was protesting against or expressing discontent with current policies or the state of the world in general. As a demonstrator from Zurich wrote, 'Take protest to the street. Make dissatisfaction visible. Show resistance to current politics.' People who say that they are there to protest do not necessarily expect their action to result in any direct political changes (although some certainly also have this expectation). The main reason is to make their dissatisfaction heard. A Malmö demonstrator wrote, 'I am angry and tired of Sweden's politically childish "give it to me" and "what is my gain in this" policies. Therefore, it feels good to shout out slogans.' Grievances that have not been acknowledged in other forums are brought to the streets, as was the case for this Genevan protester: 'After ringing on the door of the Rector's Council and the cantonal government, I got no answer. All we have left is to make the situation known to the public.' In some of the countries, the May Day celebration is actually regarded as a particularly good platform for voicing discontent (cf. Chapter 7), as this respondent from Stockholm said: '1 May is Labour Day. Then you should demonstrate against injustices in society and honour previous labour activists in all countries. 1 May receives publicity on TV and in newspapers. That doesn't occur with other demonstrations. They are silenced.'

In Florence, a very specific protest was held against policies that threatened May Day as such. A significant number of Florentine respondents cited a decision by the city mayor to keep the shops open in the inner city on 1 May as a major reason for demonstrating.

Finally, this category also includes more vague formulations about 'taking a stand' and expressing one's opinions. Peterson *et al.* (2012b) used a separate code for these, because it was not absolutely clear whether these opinions were actually oppositional. However, because official versus oppositional is not the main interest here, the two categories were judged to be too similar to be kept separate.

Accomplish or Prevent Change

Maybe some of those who lament the tired rituality of May Day celebrations will find it hard to believe, but a significant number of respondents appeared to ground their motivation for participating in a May Day march in a belief that the protest could actually make a difference to society. This can be formulated in terms of *bringing about change*, or *preventing change*, such as stopping further welfare cuts. This motive is closely related to the protest politics motive, but differs by implying that the protest is instrumental in bringing about social change – 'It is not to protest, it is to sustain society' (Milanese respondent) – or preventing it – 'Because there is still a slight chance for changing something' (another Milanese respondent). In practice, this includes expressions such as 'to defend X' or 'to fight for X'.

Especially in the 2010 Stockholm demonstration, several references were made to the upcoming election in September that year and to the fact that participation was a way to influence the election results.

Display Numbers

Some respondents emphasized the importance of making one's movement or social group visible as a motive for participating. This could also be expressed as displaying numbers or strength. One Zurich participant wrote, 'I find it important to show the public at least once a year that there is a strong (and not necessarily organized in parliament) workers' community which is also ready to fight.' Although this is related to the motive to protest against government/politics, showing strength is arguably distinguishable and may be related to notions of lowering the morale of political opponents.

Curiosity, Interest and Non-Political Motives

A small minority of the respondents (2 per cent) expressed motives such as 'interest', 'curiosity' or other incentives that neither seem concerned with the political struggle nor with identifying with the group carrying out the struggle. It should be noted that most of the respondents who cited curiosity or interest as a motive did so as a complement to other types of motives. Only about a dozen (0.5 per cent) of the respondents appeared to have attended merely out of curiosity, interest or other types of motives that did not imply identification with the political messages of the demonstration. Most of the curious participants probably did not take part in the actual march but were selected at those events where survey dissemination continued at the demonstration's end-point rally. For instance, quite a few of them were specifically curious about the speeches or, notably in Stockholm 2010 and Gothenburg 2012, to see the Social Democrats' party leader, who was the main speaker.

Some participants attended with a partner and made it clear that they did not otherwise sympathize with the demonstration's political message. A respondent from Milan wrote, 'I didn't want to go: I was in Milan at the house of a friend who "obliged" me to go. I am against this kind of protest.' This is distinct from the 'meeting friends' category, because it involves a clear dis-identification with the general collective. Others were musicians, dancers and photographers. 'I sing in a sociologist [*sic*] choir and came here today to sing with them.' One man (27 years old) claimed that he was there because he likes to, 'take a walk together with young girls'. Some said that they attended out of curiosity and to listen to speeches. Their curiosity occasionally was of professional interest: 'Interest for my degree, police studies with crime [psychology].'

A London demonstrator who actually may also have sympathized with the community noted, 'I was on my way home when I saw the procession outside Holborn Station. I stopped to look and when I found out it was terminating at Trafalgar I decided to join.' This is not unlike the ecological forms of mobilization that Zhao (1998) observed in the Chinese anti-regime protests of the late 1980s.

Broad Patterns and Local Contextual Variation

In several instances, the local and national contexts, as well as the timing of the demonstration, had a clear impact on the motives that the participants cited, in ways that are not immediately evident from a mere numeric count of the protest motives discussed above. In the 2010 Swedish demonstration, there was an upcoming election and a repeatedly cited motive was to have an impact on the outcome of this election. The centre–conservative alliance won the election, and it is notable how – especially in the Social Democratic May Day marches – criticism of the government was a particularly salient theme, which was also the case in the 2011 and 2012 demonstrations in Malmö and Gothenburg. The 2011 Florence May Day celebration came under attack in the form of a decision by the city mayor to keep the inner city shops open on 1 May, which led several respondents to cite the need to preserve the symbolic value and existence of May Day as motives. In the 2011 May Day demonstration in Geneva – less than two months after the nuclear disaster in Fukushima, Japan – a common motive was to protest against the local nuclear power plants.

In Vigo in 2011, many protesters mentioned the crisis and dissatisfaction with the government, thereby reflecting the contemporary wave of anti-austerity protests in Europe. A recurring theme in the protesters' statements was that May Day is indeed a tradition, but one that has become topical at present. Several respondents referred to May Day protests during the Franco dictatorship (cf. Chapter 5). In Vigo there was also a recurring micro-narrative about celebrating the political accomplishments of one's predecessors that are now threatened. 'Because it is a custom and for reasons of conscience, I think of all that is achieved and little by little we are losing, not giving value to people who in their time fought to get it' (respondent from Vigo).

At the EuroMayDay parade in Milan, precariousness was the most salient theme, along with migration and unemployment. However, the focus on precariousness (presumably) chiefly reflects the overall framing of EuroMayDay rather than the local context in Milan.

Further differences between locations and countries can be discerned more clearly if we turn to the quantitative analysis. However, to make such an analysis manageable, I propose a simplified coding scheme.

A Broader Typology

The identified categories are summarized in Table 9.1 and are grouped according to two classification schemes. One of these is Peterson and colleagues' (2012a) distinction between official rituals and oppositional aspects of May Day rituals. The ideal official ritual focuses on the past and tries to consolidate and manifest past achievements of the movement, even by reinforcing 'existing power structures', whereas an oppositional ritual is future-orientated and tries to challenge these power structures. The authors also identify a set of 'group-affirmative' motive types, as well as some motives that were ambiguous with respect to their official versus oppositional nature. The distinction between official and oppositional motives was based on the hypothesis that specific national conditions such as the system of labour relations and the position of social democracy would make some May Day rituals more oppositional, whereas others would focus on manifesting the prominent position of the labour movement in society.

The former classification is reconsidered and replaced for a number of reasons. First, and most importantly, this chapter is not primarily focused on the *rituality* of the demonstrations as such but on the compositions of individual motives. Second, it is not wholly satisfactory when a quarter of the codes are in a residual category because their official or oppositional connotations could not be definitely established. Third, a re-analysis of the responses for this chapter suggests that the official motive label might be less appropriate to use for most of the May Day demonstrations in our sample. Even in Sweden, where social democracy dominated the political arena for several decades during the twentieth century, the participants' motives turned out to be largely oppositional in the 2010 demonstrations because the Social Democrats were in opposition and many took part to criticize the incumbent right-wing government. As we saw in the above analysis of the concrete instances that were coded as expressing official rituality, many of them could hardly be regarded as official in a strict sense. Instead, references to tradition, for example, often implied traditional *militancy* in the family, and former successes of the labour movement were often celebrated with an edge towards them being threatened by contemporary austerity politics.

Instead, this chapter contributes with a more precise classification of the type of action logic that each code represents, and with a more general binary logic that includes all codes but one. Inspired by the classic Weberian (1978) discussions on rationalities of action and by the established categorizations of motives in the study of social movements discussed above, the dominant logic behind each motive type is stipulated.

The codes are also subsumed under two more general logics that I call an 'external influence' logic and a 'movement coherence' logic. The category of external influence includes all motives that concern influencing others for political purposes, including both instrumental concerns about influencing politics and expressive concerns about making an impression on others by demonstrating one's opinion or displaying movement strength in terms of numbers. In other words, the term 'influence' is used in a broad sense here, including what Habermas (1984) would term strategic, normatively regulated and dramaturgical rationalities, given that the action is focused on an external audience. Movement coherence includes motives linked to strengthening the demonstrating collective as such and/ or proving one's personal belonging to a collective identity. In contrast to the external influence motives, the movement coherence motives concern the 'internal' aspects of the demonstration and the demonstrating group. However, movement coherence motives are not automatically official, because they are likely to involve reinforcing a radical collective identity, displaying solidarity with oppressed groups in opposition to their oppressors, or showing support for a radical organization or group. Put somewhat differently, the external influence motives are concerned with furthering, or at least communicating, the movement's goals, whereas movement coherence motives involve the reproduction of the movement in various ways, thereby providing the necessary empowerment to continue struggling for the movement's cause. It is worth emphasizing that there is no hierarchy of importance between these broad categories; movement coherence is just as crucial as the possible external impact that a protest might have. However, because May Day demonstrations are normally considered to be rituals of a traditional and celebratory character, the following analysis will nevertheless emphasize the varying significance of external influence motives among the demonstrators.

Quantitative Variation in Motive Types

We will now turn to a quantitative analysis of the distribution of the participant motives in the studied demonstrations. The different motive types were not equally common nor evenly distributed across different protest events. To begin with, the pattern of motives can be studied for the different broader types of May Day demonstrations that we identified in our sample: demonstrations organized by traditional trade unions and social democratic parties, demonstrations organized by radical left organizations (post-communist parties and radical left-wing trade unions) and demonstrations organized by broad coalitions that mix elements of both of the former categories with no organizations clearly dominant (see Appendix). As noted in the Appendix, there is no obvious way to calculate averages for May Day demonstrators in our full sample. However, it is clear that the differing numbers of respondents in the sample of demonstrations

Table 9.1 Types of motives

General motive type	Action logic	Categorization by Peterson et al. (2012b)
Movement coherence		
Celebrate workers' day	Celebration/ commemoration	Official rituality
Celebrate political accomplishments	Celebration/ commemoration	Official rituality
Tradition	Habit	Official rituality
Support own movement	Instrumental (internal)	Group-affirmative rituality
Meet friends/co-members	Sociality/empowerment	Group-affirmative rituality
Conviction/moral duty	Value-rational (ideology)	Neutral/ambivalent
Display loyalty or solidarity	Value-rational (identity)	Group-affirmative rituality
External influence		
Accomplish or prevent change	Instrumental (external)	Oppositional rituality
Protest against government/ politics	Expressive	Oppositional rituality
Display numbers	Expressive (collective)	Neutral/ambivalent
Other motives		
To be informed/to listen/other	(Varies)	Neutral/ambivalent

must be addressed, and it is reasonable that the different countries are given equal weight in the sample. Here, demonstrations have been weighted proportional to their size relative to others in the same country within each demonstration category (see Table 9.2).

Although one must be careful in interpreting differences between categories, because they are not necessarily equally specific in meaning, it is notable that the predominant type of motive was to protest against the government or some particular political condition (between 36 and 47 per cent of the respondents), followed by showing *solidarity/loyalty* (around 23 per cent). Overall, *tradition* and *celebrate workers' day* also stood out as important, averaging slightly below 20 per cent for most demonstration categories. With respect to differences between demonstration types, participants in the radical left demonstrations stood out from the others as being somewhat more likely to express motives related to protest against the government or to accomplishing change, and less likely to refer to tradition or celebrating the day of the workers. Participants in the marches organized by dominant trade unions and social democratic parties appeared more likely to talk about supporting the movement or organization one belongs to and to refer to conviction or moral duty. Participants in the marches organized by mixed coalitions seemed

Table 9.2 Percentage within each category of demonstrations citing different types of motives, weighted according to relative demonstration size in country, within each demonstration category

Motive / Type Demonstration category	Protest government politics	Accomplish change	Display numbers	Support own movement	Tradition	Meet friends and co-members	Conviction/ moral duty	Celebrate workers' day	Celebrate political accomplishments	Become informed, to listen, other	Display loyalty or solidarity
Dominant trade union and Social Democrats	36	14	3	19	19	5	10	20	7	1	20
Mixed coalition	46	11	7	15	24	11	5	18	6	3	30
Radical left	46	17	4	7	11	7	7	16	8	2	23
Total	42	14	4	14	18	7	8	18	7	2	24

more likely than the others to refer to tradition or to express loyalty or solidarity. Because there were only two countries in the last category (Switzerland and the UK), their distinctness is perhaps more related to the context than the fact that it is a broad organizing coalition.

If we turn to the more comprehensive categories of *external influence* and *movement coherence* motive types, various comparisons can be made. For the sake of brevity, both motive types can be included in the same diagram. Because many respondents mentioned both motive types, I distinguish between those who exclusively mention one motive type and those who mention both types. The number of motive categories mentioned within each broader type is not considered. Figure 9.1 illustrates that there is indeed considerable variation between the different events in terms of broader patterns of motive types. Participants who exclusively had internal movement coherence motives were predominant in three demonstrations: Antwerp, London 2010 and Geneva 2011. In several other demonstrations, a large proportion of participants mentioned both motives types, or the distribution between internal and external motive types was relatively equal. The EuroMayDay protest in Milan was dominated by protesters who exclusively mentioned external influence motives. Again, it must be stressed that the broader motive types are aggregated from a different number of specific motive types, which means that any comparison of proportions expressing different types must take that into consideration.

No obvious differences between countries are immediately apparent in Figure 9.1, unless we are willing to extrapolate from the distinct predominance of movement coherence motives in Antwerp and London to Belgium and the UK, respectively. However, because we only have one case from each country, we must be careful with such conclusions.

Towards Explaining the Variation

Explanations for the individual variation in motives can presumably be found at the individual, demonstration and country levels. However, with relatively few demonstrations, and still fewer countries, any correlations at these levels are difficult to find and difficult to generalize. Therefore, the strategy employed in this chapter will be to analyse the data with multilevel logistic regression (Goldstein 2011) and to examine the extent to which any significant variation at the country or demonstration level can be explained by individual-level variables. In the next step, any remaining differences between countries and/or demonstrations will have to be interpreted in the light of the historical and contemporary context of each case.

As noted earlier, the focus will be on the external influence motives for protesting as a dependent variable. Somewhat simplified, participants who cited external influence motives clearly cared about the external May Day march audience as protesters; they did not only see the march as a ritual for the movement itself. Fifty-four per cent of the respondents cited at least one of

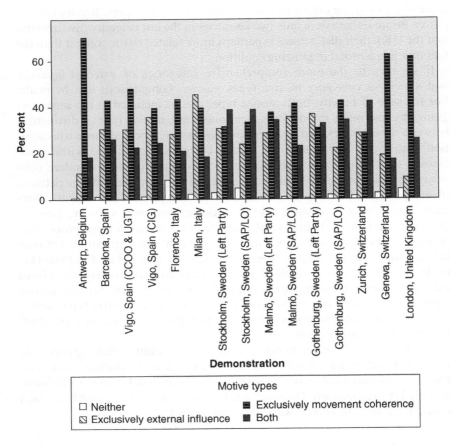

Figure 9.1 Percentage of participants citing broader motive types

the motive types categorized as *external influence*. It is a reasonable assumption that the proportion will vary significantly between demonstrations, and possibly between countries as well, depending upon different May Day traditions. The presence of domestic grievances and political opportunities is also a possible source of variation between demonstrations, but these factors are difficult to compare.

Individual-level hypotheses cannot be easily derived from previous research, because it was based on other classifications of motives, as demonstrated by the literature reviewed above. Nevertheless, this largely exploratory analysis will test a number of tentative hypotheses, based on the participants' general sense of institutional trust and efficacy, and on the participants' grievances and emotions about these grievances.

First, one plausible conjecture is that using a May Day protest as a platform to exert external influence suggests a sense of external efficacy; that is, it reflects the degree to which one feels able to influence politics, either through one's individual actions or as a part of an organized collective (cf. Acock, Clarke and Stewart 1985; Lane 1959). Ketelaars (2014) also found political efficacy to be positively related to instrumental motives. Even though external influence motives also have a non-instrumental, dramaturgical aspect, it is nevertheless likely that participants with a strong sense of external efficacy are also more prone to focus on the impression the protest makes on an external audience. Therefore, the first hypothesis is: *the higher the level of external efficacy, the more likely the protester is to be motivated by a wish to exert external influence.*

A related independent variable is trust in domestic political institutions, such as the government and the national parliament. May Day participants who have greater trust in these institutions can be expected to be less likely to want to use the march for exerting external political influence, because they have greater confidence in the established political institutions to address grievances without protest. This is related to William Gamson's (1968) assumption that a strong sense of efficacy combined with low trust in political institutions facilitates mobilization. A possible modification of the 'Gamson hypothesis' would be to say that it captures one mechanism for mobilization that involves external influence motives, whereas other combinations of trust and efficacy are associated with other motives (cf. van Stekelenburg and Klandermans 2014). In other words, *the greater the trust in domestic political institutions, the less likely a protester is to be motivated by a wish to exert external influence.*

Personally experienced grievances may also increase the likelihood of expressing external influence motives. If one experiences grievances directly, presumably there is a higher likelihood that one would want to use one's participation in a May Day demonstration primarily to protest against this grievance and influence others. Conscience constituents (McCarthy and Zald 1977) certainly may also express external influence motives, but they are perhaps more likely to focus on movement coherence and expressing solidarity with the potential beneficiaries of the movement. One proxy for personally experienced grievances related to the issues articulated by the May Day demonstrations is unemployment. Therefore, I hypothesize that, *personal unemployment increases the likelihood that a protester is motivated by a wish to exert external influence.*

Lastly, emotions have been shown to amplify the motivational strength of other motives (van Stekelenburg, Klandermans and van Dijk 2011). Perhaps emotions also mediate how grievances are translated into motives in the first place. Strong feelings of anger and frustration can be expected to increase external influence motives. Anger implies the moral blaming of an actor who can be held responsible for an action (Solomon 1984). Therefore, anger should be associated with motives related to the expression of such blame. This could possibly mediate some of the influence from grievance-related variables and from external efficacy. *Stronger feelings of anger and frustration increase the likelihood that a protester is motivated by a wish to exert external influence.*

As control variables I use age, gender and left–right political position. Age could affect the likelihood of expressing external influence motives in various ways, including a sense of disillusionment among older demonstrators regarding the effectiveness of demonstrations. In terms of left–right political position, one possibility is that respondents with a more left-leaning position might be more indignant about the centre-right politics currently dominating most European countries and therefore they might have a stronger focus on external influence. Gender is included only to control for possible response bias.

Operationalization of Independent Variables

As a measure of external efficacy, I used an index that was in the range of 2–10, constructed from two items in the questionnaire in which the respondents were asked to express the extent to which they agreed with the following statements: 'my participation can have an impact on public policy in this country' and 'organized groups of citizens can have a lot of impact on public policies in this country'. Cronbach's alpha for this scale was estimated to 0.69.

To measure trust in domestic political institutions, which are arguably the primary counterpart of the May Day demonstrations, an index (2–10) was constructed based on the self-reported trust in the national parliament and the national government (Cronbach's alpha: 0.79).

Similarly, to measure the emotions in relation to the issue of the demonstration, the following question was used: 'Thinking about [the demonstration issue] makes me feel …' The respondents were then asked to rate their emotions on five-point scales. An index in the range of 2–10 was constructed from the responses for anger and frustration. Because the distribution of answers was strongly skewed upwards (37 per cent received a score of 10 on the scale), Cronbach's alpha was rather low: 0.45. Thus, the effect of this variable should be interpreted with caution.

Unemployment was measured with a dummy variable from a question on employment situation. Age was calculated by subtracting the respondent's year of birth from the year of the demonstration.

Results and Analysis

To explore the variation at the country and demonstration levels, I initially constructed a three-level logistic regression model (see Model 1, Table 9.3). When I controlled for both the country- and demonstration-level variance, neither the country level nor the demonstration level displayed significant variation when taken as a whole. However, if we plot the demonstration-level residuals (Figure 9.2), we can see that two demonstrations deviate significantly from the mean; curiously it was the two Swiss demonstrations, with the

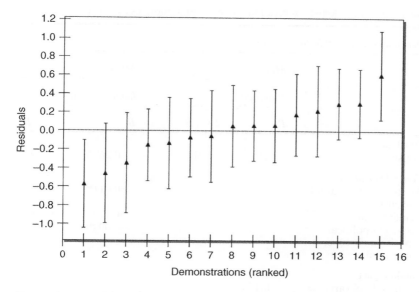

Figure 9.2 Demonstration residuals for external influence (controlling for country clustering).

Zurich demonstration at the high point and the Geneva demonstration at the low point. However, one should keep in mind that the variance estimates in a multilevel model are relatively conservative (compared with using dummies for countries or demonstrations). In addition, we have only six country cases, two of which contain only one demonstration. Thus, the extent to which we can safely disentangle country-level variance from demonstration-level variance is limited. Because of these problems, I decided to simplify the further regressions by bracketing the country level.

Model 2 introduced the control variables, and age and left–right position were significant. In this case, the odds ratio figures – 'exp(B)' in the table – can be interpreted as the predicted odds for citing external influence, provided that a specific independent variable increases one unit while the others are held constant. Table 9.3 reveals that the likelihood of citing external influence motives decreases with age. The beta coefficient is small, but one must keep in mind that it is the effect *per year*. The further towards the right that the respondents identify themselves politically, the less likely they are to express external influence motives. Gender made no significant difference in the model. When the country level was excluded from the model, variation at the demonstration level was significant. An examination of the demonstration-level residuals reveals that the demonstrators in Antwerp, London and Geneva were significantly below average in terms of external influence motives, whereas the demonstrators in the Left Party marches in Stockholm and Gothenburg, the

Table 9.3 Binary logistic regressions with external motives as dependent variable

Dependent: external influence motives

	Model 1		Model 2	
	Null model		Control variables	
	B	Exp(B)	B	Exp(B)
Fixed part				
Constant	0.069	1.071	0.269*	1.309
Control variables				
Age (centred on grand mean)			−0.011**	0.989
Gender: male			−0.119	0.888
Left–right political position (0–10, centred on grand mean)			−0.094**	0.910
Random part				
Country-level variance	0.175		–	
Demonstration-level variance	0.112		0.209	
Units: country	6			
Units: demonstration	15		15	
Units: individuals	2,254		2,156	

Notes: Levels of significance: * = 5% and ** = 1% significance.

Social Democratic march in Stockholm and the Zurich march were above average.

In Table 9.4, the independent variables are successively included in models 3–5. First, as hypothesized, Model 3 shows that a sense of external efficacy does indeed have a significant, positive effect on the likelihood of citing external influence motives. Also as expected, trust in domestic political institutions was negatively correlated with external influence motives.

As Model 4 shows, the effect of unemployment was not significant. However, when the measure of anger/frustration was included (Model 5), both it and the unemployment variable were significantly positively correlated with the likelihood of citing external influence motives, which is also in line with the hypotheses formulated above. This means that the effect of unemployment is only significant when the degree of anger/frustration is held constant.

Taken together, even if the independent variables all appear to have an impact, including them makes only a marginal difference for the unexplained variance at the demonstration level. Thus, the differences between demonstrations are not obviously reducible to the individual composition of protesters (at least not in terms of the variables included here). Because of the patterns found in the descriptive analysis, it would have been possible to suppose, for instance, that participants in demonstrations organized by the radical left would more frequently cite external influence motives. However, when this variable was included in the model (not presented here), no correlation was found between the category of organizer and this motive type.

Conclusion

The qualitative analysis of the motives formulated by May Day demonstrators for their participation shows that participants indeed employ a broad range of motive vocabularies. In particular, tradition (or habit) is a motive type that has been unexplored in the protest mobilization literature. The analysis also revealed that locally topical issues have a clear tendency to influence motives for participating in May Day marches. The demonstrations are used as a platform to address grievances that are currently salient for people living in a specific area, as well as to address national and international injustices. This chapter also presents a novel way of classifying motives articulated by protest participants. Even though some of these motives are specific to May Day demonstrations, other categorizations can be used as a starting point for comparisons between different types of protests. The distinction between external influence and movement coherence was derived from a central tension identified in the motives of May Day demonstration participants, but it should be possible to apply it to other types of protest events as well.

The descriptive quantitative analysis showed that May Day events (at least in the 2010s) are far from tired, routinized ritualistic acts. Instead, the largest category of motives was the protest category: people participated to express dissatisfaction with the current politics and state of society. This does not exclude the simultaneous importance of motives concerning social identity, solidarity and tradition. A first look at the patterns of the two broader motive types introduced in this chapter (external influence and movement coherence motives) shows considerable variation between protest events, which is probably attributable to different local protest cultures as well as contemporary local conditions. This should serve as an antidote to any simplified or reductionist narratives of what May Day marches are about.

The analysis of explanations for variations in motives at the individual level focused on external influence motives. The likelihood of citing such motives was positively correlated with a personal sense of external efficacy and negatively correlated with trust in domestic political institutions. Participants who feel relatively efficacious are more likely to regard participation in a May Day demonstration as a way to exert external influence. Conversely, greater political trust arguably makes demonstrators more likely to feel that there are other, more preferred ways to have a political impact. People who cited external influence motives also felt more angry and frustrated thinking about the demonstration issue. Personal grievances linked to the demonstration issue, operationalized as individual unemployment, also appeared to increase the

Table 9.4 Binary logistic regressions with external influence motives as dependent variable

Dependent: external influence motives

	Model 3		Model 4		Model 5	
	Null model		Control variables		Control variables	
	B	Exp(B)	B	Exp(B)	B	Exp(B)
Fixed part						
Constant	0.29*	1.336	0.27*	1.310	0.253*	1.288
Control variables						
Age (centred on grand mean)	−0.01**	0.990	−0.01**	0.990	−0.011*	0.989
Gender: male	−0.114	0.892	−0.117	0.890	−0.087	0.917
Left–right political position (0–10, centred on grand mean)	−0.068*	0.934	−0.068**	0.934	−0.057	0.945
Independent variables						
External efficacy (2–10, centred on grand mean)	0.092**	1.096	0.091**	1.095	0.092**	1.096
Domestic political trust (2–10, centred on grand mean)	−0.09**	0.914	−0.091**	0.913	−0.079**	0.924
Unemployed			0.399	1.490	0.508*	1.662
Anger/frustration (2–10, centred on grand mean)					0.075*	1.078
Random part						
Demonstration-level variance	0.233*		0.234*		0.219*	
Units: demonstration	15		15		15	
Units: individuals	2,085		2,085		1,803	

Notes: Levels of significance: * = 5% and ** = 1% significance.

likelihood that participants would cite external influence motives. Although these results do not directly address the classic controversy in social movement studies about the extent to which grievances lead to mobilization, they nevertheless indicate that the level of personal grievances (along with a sense of efficacy and trust in domestic political institutions) affects which motives people articulate when they protest.

A significant variation in motives could be discerned at the demonstration level, but there was no significant country-level pattern. The demonstrations where participants most frequently cited external influence motives were the march in Zurich in 2010, the marches in Stockholm the same year and the Left Party march in Gothenburg in 2012. This pattern did not disappear when age, left–right position, sense of external efficacy or trust in domestic political institutions were controlled for. The Stockholm marches took place during an election year, which helps to explain the pattern, in combination with a media tradition of covering May Day marches and the demands made in the marches (cf. Chapter 7). If one knows that the march will garner media attention and that therefore one has a real opportunity to influence others, then one is arguably more likely to be motivated by this. Both the Left Party marches and the Zurich march had a large number of different participating groups and organizations. It may be that a march with a broad range of participating groups implies a May Day event with a stronger emphasis on its external impact rather than an internal celebration of a more tightly knit community.

Conversely, there is no straightforward explanation for the comparatively low level of external influence motives among the demonstrators in Antwerp, Geneva and London. For instance, one might have expected a stronger external protest orientation among the Antwerp demonstrators, considering the contemporary closing of the nearby Opel factory (cf. Chapter 7). However, the London organizer's emphasis on maintaining a tradition (quoted in Chapter 7) might help us understand the relatively stronger emphasis on the movement coherence motives among the participants in this march.

In conclusion, although more work remains in the search for robust meso- and macro-level explanations for variation in motives for protesting (cf. Ketelaars 2014; Van Stekelenburg, Klandermans and van Dijk 2009), this chapter contributes to this effort by identifying some individual-level factors that explain variation in motives for participation in May Day marches. It also demonstrates that a partly inductive approach to studying such motives reveals a level of complexity and variation among protesters that tends to be lost in studies that rely exclusively on predetermined survey questions.

Notes

1 The distinction between the articulated reason for an action and the 'actual' underlying mental push towards an action is sometimes construed as that between motives and motivations (Franzese 2013). The specific meaning of these terms has

not been entirely consistent over time or across disciplines, but to minimize confusion, I refer to articulated reasons as 'motives' and to actual underlying reasons/drives, etc. for an action as 'motivations'. However, because not all researchers are equally keen on emphasizing this distinction, the term 'motive' may occasionally imply both meanings when used in the literature review. The reader should also note that the notion of 'vocabularies of motive' has been used in the literature on social movements to describe the *motivational framing* used by organizers to highlight the importance and urgency of participation by each individual participant (Benford 1993). However, these vocabularies of motive are prompted in the context of mobilizing others and maintaining engagement – what Einwohner (2002) terms 'fortifying strategies' – and not the type of vocabularies of motives elicited by a survey question about why one participated in a protest (as in this chapter).

2 The concept of solidarity also has a pre-Marxist tradition. In France, legal use of the term was made in the sixteenth century, and it is closely related to the concept of 'fraternity' used in the French Revolution. A distinct use of the term 'solidarity' was developed by the French sociologists August Comte and Emil Durkheim (see Stjernø 2004, pp. 25–36).

References

Acock, A., Clarke, H.D., and Stewart, M.C. (1985). A new model for old measures: A covariance structure analysis of political efficacy. *Journal of Politics*, 47(04), 1062–1084.

Benford, R.D. (1993). 'You could be the hundredth monkey': Collective action frames and vocabularies of motive within the nuclear disarmament movement. *Sociological Quarterly*, 34(2), 195–216.

Crossley, N. (2003). From reproduction to transformation: Social movement fields and the radical habitus. *Theory, Culture and Society*, 20(6), 43–68.

Drury, J., and Reicher, S. (2005). Explaining enduring empowerment: A comparative study of collective action and psychological outcomes. *European Journal of Social Psychology*, 35(1), 35–58.

Drury, J., and Reicher, S. (2009). Collective psychological empowerment as a model of social change: Researching crowds and power. *Journal of Social Issues*, 65(4), 707–725.

Einwohner, R.L. (2002). Motivational framing and efficacy maintenance: Animal rights activists' use of four fortifying strategies. *Sociological Quarterly*, 43(4), 509–526.

Flam, H., and King, D. (2005). *Emotions and Social Movements*. New York: Routledge.

Franzese, A.T. (2013). Motivation, motives, and individual agency. In J. DeLamater and A. Ward (Eds), *Handbook of Social Psychology* (pp. 281–318). New York: Springer.

Gamson, W.A. (1968). *Power and Discontent*. Homewood, IL: Dorsey Press.

Gecas, V. (2000). Value identities, self-motives, and social movements. In S. Stryker, T.J. Owens and R.W. White (Eds), *Self, Identity, and Social Movements* (pp. 93–109). Minneapolis: University of Minnesota Press.

Goldstein, H. (2011). *Multilevel Statistical Models*, 4th edn. Chichester, UK: Wiley.

Goodwin, J., Jasper, J.M., and Polletta, F. (2001). *Passionate Politics: Emotions and Social Movements*. Chicago: University of Chicago Press.

Habermas, J. (1984). *The theory of Communicative Action: Reason and the Rationalization of Society*. Cambridge: Polity Press.

Ketelaars, P. (2014). Bridging the protest macro-micro gap: Investigating the link between motivations, political efficacy and political context. M2P Working Papers, University of Antwerp.

Klandermans, B. (1993). A theoretical framework for comparisons of social movement participation. *Sociological Forum*, 8(3), 383–402.

Klandermans, B. (2004). The demand and supply of participation: Social-psychological correlates of participation in social movements. In D.A. Snow, S.A. Soule and H. Kriesi (Eds), *The Blackwell Companion to Social Movements* (pp. 360–379). Oxford: Blackwell Publishing.

Lane, R.E. (1959). *Political Life: Why People Get Involved in Politics*. New York: The Free Press.

McAdam, D. (1999). *Political process and the development of black insurgency, 1930–1970*, 2nd edn. Chicago: University of Chicago Press.

McCarthy, J.D., and Zald, M.N. (1977). Resource mobilization and social movements: A partial theory. *American Journal of Sociology*, 82(6), 1212–1241.

Melucci, A. (1996). *Challenging Codes: Collective Action in the Information Age*. Cambridge: Cambridge University Press.

Mills, C.W. (1940). Situated actions and vocabularies of motive. *American Sociological Review*, 5(6), 904–913, doi: 10.2307/2084524.

Peterson, A., Wahlström, M., and Wennerhag, M. (2012a). Swedish trade unionism: A renewed social movement? *Economic and Industrial Democracy*, 33(4), 621–647.

Peterson, A., Wahlström, M., Wennerhag, M., Christancho, C., and Sabucedo, J.-M. (2012b). May Day demonstrations in five European countries. *Mobilization: An International Quarterly*, 17(3), 281–300.

Polletta, F., and Jasper, J.M. (2001). Collective identity and social movements. *Annual Review of Sociology*, 27, 283–305.

Roth, A.L. (1995). 'Men wearing masks': Issues of description in the analysis of ritual. *Sociological Theory*, 13(3), 301–327.

Snow, D.A., and McAdam, D. (2000). Identity work processes in the context of social movements: Clarifying the identity/movement nexus. In S. Stryker, T.J. Owens and R.W. White (Eds), *Self, Identity, and Social Movements* (pp. 41–67). Minneapolis: University of Minnesota Press.

Solomon, R.C. (1984). Getting angry: The Jamesian theory of emotion in anthropology. In R.A. Schweder and R.A. LeVine (Eds), *Culture Theory: Essays on Mind, Self and Emotion* (pp. 238–254). Cambridge: Cambridge University Press.

Stjernø, S. (2004). *Solidarity in Europe: The History of an Idea*. Cambridge: Cambridge University Press.

Stryker, S., Owens, T.J., and White, R.W. (Eds). (2000). *Self, Identity, and Social Movements*. Minneapolis: University of Minnesota Press.

Taylor, V., and Whittier, N.E. (1999). Collective identity in social movement communities: Lesbian feminist mobilization. In J. Freeman and V. Johnson (Eds), *Waves of Protest: Social Movements since the Sixties* (pp. 169–194). Oxford: Rowman and Littlefield.

Turner, R.H., and Killian, L.M. (1987). *Collective Behavior*, 3rd edn. Englewood Cliffs, NJ: Prentice-Hall.

Van Stekelenburg, J., and Klandermans, B. (2010). Individuals in movements. In B. Klandermans, C. Roggeband and J. Stekelenburg (Eds), *Handbook of Social Movements across Disciplines* (pp. 157–204). New York: Springer.

van Stekelenburg, J., and Klandermans, B. (2014). In politics we trust ... or not? Anti-austerity demonstrators and their political elites. Unpublished manuscript.

Van Stekelenburg, J., Klandermans, B., and van Dijk, W. (2009). Context matters: Explaining how and why mobilizing context influences motivational dynamics. *Journal of Social Issues*, 65(4), 815–838.

Van Stekelenburg, J., Klandermans, B., and van Dijk, W. (2011). Combining motivations and emotion: The motivational dynamics of protest participation. *Revista de Psicología Social*, 26(1), 91–104.

Van Zomeren, M., and Spears, R. (2009). Metaphors of protest: A classification of motivations for collective action. *Journal of Social Issues*, 65(4), 661–679.

Van Zomeren, M., Spears, R., Fischer, A.H., and Leach, C.W. (2004). Put your money where your mouth is! Explaining collective action tendencies through group-based anger and group efficacy. *Journal of Personality and Social Psychology*, 87(5), 649–664.

Walgrave, S., Van Laer, J., Verhulst, J., and Wouters, R. (2011). Why do people protest? Comparing demonstrators' motives across issues and nations. Unpublished manuscript. M2P, University of Antwerp.

Waterman, P. (1998). *Globalization, Social Movements, and the New Internationalisms*. London: Mansell.

Weber, M. (1978). *Economy and Society: An Outline of Interpretive Sociology*, vol. 1. Berkeley: University of California Press.

Wettergren, Å. (2009). Fun and laughter: Culture jamming and the emotional regime of late capitalism. *Social Movement Studies*, 8(1), 1–15.

Zhao, D. (1998). Ecologies of social movements: Student mobilization during the 1989 prodemocracy movement in Beijing. *American Journal of Sociology*, 103(6), 1493–1529.

10 The Future of May Day

Abby Petersen and Herbert Reiter

As Eric Hobsbawm (1991, p. 118) emphasized, early May Day 'was about nothing but the future'. May Day was future-orientated in the labour movements' 'class demands of the proletariat' (e.g. the eight-hour workday), their general political claims (e.g. the struggle for and the defence of democratic rights) and the labour movements' underlying ideology. Early ritual May Day performances were less the expression of an ideology of revolutionary class struggle than of socialism as an 'ideology of hope'. The 'ideology of hope' found its expression in early May Day iconography that directly connected concrete demands with a vision of a future society, e.g. by depicting the eight-hour workday as the road leading to socialism symbolized by a rising sun. Since its beginnings May Day ritual performances were manifestations of the labour movements' collective identities *and* performances of their utopian visions of a future society. If the ritual performances were successful, in Alexander's (2004) terms 're-fused', then they 'moved' their participants and audiences emotionally, cognitively, morally and physically, and effectively manifested the labour movements' confident belief in a better future.

According to Ricoeur (1994, p. 132), 'utopia is the mode in which we radically rethink what family, consumption, government, religion, and so on are'. It is the *function* of utopias to challenge and explore the possible (cf. Mannheim 1979; Ricoeur 1986). The close connection between pragmatic social reform and utopian visions of a future society typical for early May Day in Western Europe survived repeated external and internal challenges since the outbreak of World War I. In the last decades, however, the future of May Day seems increasingly threatened by the mounting difficulties labour movements are facing in going beyond the defence of acquired positions, connecting concrete demands with perspectives that explore the possible and press for change in the prevailing order. In this chapter we will reflect upon this erosion of May Day's utopian dimension and the prospects for its resurrection.

Utopian Visions of the Future in the Past

Inge Marßolek (1990, pp. 363–364) imagines a Bremen worker from the 1890s, transported to the year 1990, watching the May Day demonstration in the city. Marßolek points out that the worker would inevitably be incredulous that the demand is for the 35-hour week; that people work five days a week; that the eight-hour workday has been a reality for decades; that the May Day demonstration passes through the city centre without police harassment, ending with a rally in front of the city hall; and that the Hanseatic city of Bremen for the last 40 years has been governed not by the rich merchants but by the Social Democratic Party.

Many of the concrete demands advocated at early May Day demonstrations were in fact realized (and in some sense perhaps exceeded) one hundred years later. On second thoughts, however, the worker imagined by Marßolek, after realizing that he found himself in the year 1990 probably would not be surprised that the eight-hour workday had become a reality. More than the realization of these demands by 1990, a late-nineteenth-century socialist activist would find it incredible that – even one hundred years after the first May Day and after decades of social democratic governments – workers still had to struggle, in a capitalist society, for better working and living conditions. Watching the 1990 May Day demonstration, in addition he may have been struck by a puzzling multitude of groups and voices and the lack of expressions of a unified and bonding vision of a future society.

As much as the concrete demands raised at early May Day events, in particular the eight-hour workday, were future-orientated and emotionally (and mythologically) charged, they in fact did not form May Day's utopian content. Socialist leaders like August Bebel (1893) were highly conscious of the vital importance that the pragmatic struggle for the betterment of the living conditions of the working classes had for the growth of the socialist movement. For Bebel and his fellow comrades, the May Day demands they voted upon at the Paris congress in 1889 were attainable in society as it existed at that time. However, for socialists the realization of demands like the eight-hour workday in the existing capitalist society would remain a mere palliative. The liberation of the working classes, the end of the exploitation of humans by humans, for them could come only with the collapse of capitalist society (expected sooner rather than later) and the construction of a socialist society. Against this background, as a Spanish socialist expressed it in the year 1900, May Day was the 'prologue of the great work of universal redemption', which would be achieved 'without struggle, without spilling a single drop of blood'; it would 'grow more and more, until differences are erased and the human race become a single family'.[1] The strength of the early May Day lay in connecting concrete demands with utopian visions, or (to stay within the party terminology at that time) connecting a minimalist programme of pragmatic social reform with a maximalist programme of a socialist society.

In fact, utopian visions – organized labour's efforts to stand 'outside' of reality and imagine other ways of living (Ricoeur 1994, p. 132) – have been a central element in May Day ritual performances. Marßolek (1990, pp. 364–367; abridged, our translation) quotes from a Vienna workers' newspaper an article published on 1 May 1910 that imagines the May Day celebration in the city in 1970:

Naturally May Day is a holiday, only the work necessary for the celebration of May Day is permitted. Vienna is a huge garden city and the cottages of the workers, all with a small garden, are decorated with red flags. Peonies and tulips from their gardens embellish their breakfast tables. In the morning the vehicles from the dairy cooperative and from the central food agency deliver milk, eggs, bacon or fish, fruit, vegetables, coffee, cigarettes, according to the order made the previous day, to the breakfast boxes of every house. In the morning 500 bands march through all the districts of the city, except the central districts that are dedicated exclusively to factories and workshops. The underground trains do not run as it is a holiday, but anyone who wants to can take a car (you find them on certain squares, everybody can take one, you only need to register in advance; usually one member in a family has a driver's licence). However, most people spend the day with friends in their district, as they moved into their neighbourhood because of elective affinity. May Day is celebrated on all the major squares throughout the city (800 tribunes), old songs of struggle from the past times of oppression are sung, youth choirs sing, etc. A young woman speaks, the article emphasizes her maidenly slenderness, in a long flowing dress through which the splendour of her noble body is chastely rendered. Her speech inspires thousands to excel in the service for the whole.

Comrades! Sisters! Brothers! ... Yes, we know that there was a time of possession mania. We know that once the spirit was shackled by the small devils of selfishness. We know it but we can hardly imagine it anymore. How was it possible that human beings crippled themselves, their bodies and their souls? How was it possible that thousands had to serve one person like slaves? How was it possible that instead of growing strong in freedom, in light and air, well groomed and well educated, people withered in contaminated air, in ugly homes, uneducated and hungry? In those times men knew only themselves and that made them small! We know that man and man, flower and animal, the grass in our gardens and the stone on which we step, are parts of *one* world, and only he who feels himself connected with all being [*Sein*], only he is worthy to be our brother. He who thinks of nothing but himself is and was wretched. He who rediscovers himself in the other, who has understood the great law of community, who does not trample down a blade of grass unnecessarily, who caresses every child with looks, who feels and knows what transpires inside his neighbour, he is rich. To the slave of the past society his possessions were his world, to us the whole world has become possession.

The article continues with its vision of the future and 'another way of living'.

In the afternoon everybody spends time with his or her families, some rest, some read (the central library provides everybody with the books they want, on loan or as a gift), and the children play in the large public playgrounds. In the evening people make music in their gardens (violin, flute, singing); and nobody staggers drunk through the quiet streets.

This utopian vision, merging the city with a rural past, was a poignant appeal in the struggle against modern industrialized society not uncommon in this period. Ulam (1965, p. 385) argues that 'socialism was born out of a nostalgia for an idealised past'. Early socialism's utopias were engendered by an agrarian society undergoing the birth pains of industrialization.

The early socialist 'futures from the past' did not construct their utopias as a blueprint of an ideal society with a detailed description of its functioning but as a projected wish, as a dream of what might be (Eley 1995, p. 7). The narrative presents a private and nostalgic image of a future May Day, against the background of an only vaguely sketched socialist society in which everybody is provided for according to his/her needs. We find descriptions of the conditions of consumption, prescriptions for leisure and a salutation of community, whereas the organization of work, of the economy, and of political life are strikingly absent. The author apparently could be certain that the readers could, on the basis of commonly shared beliefs, complete the picture and fill in any missing element.

Similarly, but with a greater confidence in the promise of science, Francesco Bonavita, in the Italian socialist daily *Avanti!* (1 May 1900; abridged, our translation), envisioned a utopian May Day future for the city of Paris in the year 2000, seen through the eyes of an old man from the past (finally arrived at the end of his great pilgrimage, contemplating with the eyes of a victor the land of his ideals) who is accompanied by a young man from the present.

The city has transformed Sacré-Coeur from the church, that as a symbol of faith dominated over the miseries of Paris, into a meteorological observatory: on the ruins of superstition now a temple of science rises that teaches the cult of mankind, the religion of humanity. Barracks, Catholic seminaries, hospices, have been changed into free schools, communal hospitals, public factories and magazines of production and consumption. As artistically important buildings the churches have been preserved but converted into museums and libraries; where once impenetrable mystery reigned, an immense wave of light had descended to bring the search of the good, the beautiful and the true. From houses and workplaces the cheerful songs of an army of emancipated workers can be heard.

In the cemetery Père Lachaise the old man from the past remains puzzled in front of two monuments: a small and modest statue representing sacrifice, dedicated to the fallen of the Paris Commune, and an immense monument, dedicated to the martyrs of work, with commemorative stones carrying the names of scientists, artists and workers, victims of their own works, crowned by the figures 'Glory' and 'Happiness'. The young man of the present explains: those died for the Commune, fighting – these for humankind, working. A new education teaches us new evaluations, unknown to you, about the value of the endeavour of those who kill and those who produce. Fighting for noble causes, those are the heroes of sacrifice, these are the pioneers of the happiness and of the glory of the world.

All means of locomotion serve those that are in a hurry and not those that have money. In front of the Louvre – intact as a museum and enriched with new pieces of art – the immense public storehouses of the city offer their abundant goods. People can take what they desire, only what every-body takes is recorded so that the city can keep track of the level of the individual and the collective demand. The vehicles of the public bakery bring the necessary bread into everybody's home; other vehicles bring meat, vegetables and fruit. Everything is recorded but nothing is paid; it is not the price that limits the needs but the quantity of production that limits the right to consumption. The celebration of May Day takes place in the place de la Concorde. The international exhibition organized for the occasion has become an international school of arts and crafts where the various nations demonstrate and teach the secrets of their indus-tries. The May Day paper is printed in eight or ten languages; the motto 'France to the French' has been changed into 'the world to humanity'.

The old man from the past, a sincere tear in his eye, solemnly takes his leave from the young man of the present, who watches him, touched: Never clip with profane thought the wing of the thought that proceeds towards the future. For these things that the present has accomplished, I, age of the past, have fought, have suffered, have despaired. If everybody were permitted, as I was today, to visit and examine the things of the future in the same way you can see in museums and study in books the things of the past, the men of conservative immobility would not be the torturers of the men of progressive conquest. I return to where I started from, you rest at your free celebration that has cost many tears of the distressed, a lot of blood of combatants, and pay tribute once also to that May Day that was one of the stations of a painful exodus towards the future and that today signs the glorious anniversary of a victory that cannot die.

Bonavita's utopian vision is markedly pre-October revolution. Except for echoes in the reminiscences of the old man from the past, references to class struggle or revolutionary masses are missing, and in the imagined Paris of the year 2000 only a small and modest statue is dedicated to the fallen of the Paris Commune. The immense monument rising next to it, dedicated to the martyrs of work, has a degree of resonance with the triumphant liberal utopian vision of the future, where wars, superstitions, diseases and poverty would be elimi-nated by the inevitable progress of science and education. As in liberal uto-pianism, some socialists, and particularly Marxist utopianists, placed their faith in the future in the hands of scientists and educators; however, in stark contrast to the liberal utopian vision these scientists and educators would be working in a socialist context for the benefit of all. In fact, the international exhibition imagined by Bonavita for the year 2000 is very different from the Paris world exhibition in 1889. It does not have the function of demonstrating the scientific or productive excellence of nation states but has become an international school of arts and crafts where the various nations demonstrate and share the secrets of their industries.

Bonavita's utopian vision also expresses anti-religious sentiments, anti-militarism and the internationalism of the Second International – 'the motto "France to the French" has been changed into "the world to humanity"'. For early May Day rituals across Europe a key utopian vision of the future centred on internationalism – 'Workers of the World Unite'. May Day was celebrated in the spirit of fraternity and solidarity to inspire workers worldwide. At the London May Day demonstration on Sunday 4 May 1890, banners with 'Workers of the World We Hail You as Brothers' were carried by the demonstrators in English, French and German (Chapter 6, p. 134). Eduardo Romanos and José Luis Ledesma claim that in Spain, 'May Day was thus taken as an opportunity to transform these internationalist principles into a transgressive ritual, in which class, rather than national consciousness, was asserted' (Chapter 5, p. 107).

While early socialists were fiercely anti-religious, particularly in Catholic countries socialist utopian visions were often provided an emotive force with the appropriation of religious symbols and metaphors giving them secular meanings (Hobsbawm 1991, pp. 115–116). According to Romanos and Ledesma, the Master, the Apostles, paradise, the Holy Family and the sower featured frequently in Spanish May Day ritual performances. A socialist newspaper in Spain 1913 alluded to May Day as the ritual of 'the new secular religion of Love and Fraternity', the ritual with which the 'birth of that redeeming hope' and its 'continuous resurrection from persecution and crucifixion' were commemorated (Chapter 5, p. 113). The Spanish socialist utopian vision in the early 1900s, Romanos and Ledesma argue, saw the redeeming nature of the May Day celebration in which the 'celebration had the power to change society, by itself and without resorting to violence' (ibid.).

The Erosion of Utopia

The labour movements' far reaching visions of a different 'way of living' remained unattainable, unrealistic 'wish-fulfilment' (Kumar 2010). As we have seen for the various countries covered in this volume, the sense of historical agency of the organized workers' movements with demands for a radically different future society started to erode with the disintegration of the Second International at the outbreak of World War I. In Western European countries during the interwar years, this process deepened through divisions within the workers' movements and with the apparent failure of both minimalist and maximalist strategies to realize societies foreshadowing a future as it had been imagined prior to 1914. This erosion of utopian perspectives also found its reflection in May Day iconography; images now tended towards mere agitation and programmatic statements (Korff 1986, p. 54ff.; Korff 1989, p. 91ff.).

Adam Ulam (1965, p. 383) proclaimed already fifty years ago that it had been the decline of utopian thinking that had seriously damaged the capacity of socialism to stir up the emotions of hope among its followers. As the examples of Germany and Italy show, in the immediate post-World War II years both the more radical and the more moderate wing of the workers' movement in Western Europe proved unable to organize a majority for their plans of reconstruction. Subsequently, both wings were forced to adapt their programmatic positions and their May Day conceptions. This adaption did not lead to the absence of utopian elements in the May Day celebrations in the countries covered in this volume. However, they were predominantly presented in the form of a more pragmatic and less bold 'ideology of hope', promising the realization of a better society through the gradual extension of a social democratic welfare state (see Chapter 3, pp. 56, 58, 62–63). In the final analysis, since the 1950s this proved to be increasingly the case also for communist parties and trade unions in Western Europe, notwithstanding a rhetoric that continued to stress May Day as a day of struggle and a positioning on the side of the Soviet bloc as far as international issues were concerned.

Labour movement scholars bemoaning the decline of trade unionism and social democracy across Western Europe after the 'golden age' during the 1960s are legion (e.g. Offe 1985; Merkel 1991; Pontusson 1995; Martin and Ross 1999; Ebbinghaus 2002; Bartolini 2000; Crouch 2011). Starting with the oil crisis in 1973, hopes for a better society became progressively threatened by the crisis of Keynesian economic policies. May Day demands turned more and more defensive, less future-orientated, and their connection with an envisioned 'just' society increasingly fragile. What lay at the very basis of social democracy – the belief in a slow but continuous advancement of the working classes through social reform – and its utopian vision of the future became more and more tarnished by repetition and by its failure to deliver upon its promises. Already by the time of the May Day centennial in 1990 this vision appears more as an invocation of, than a firm belief in, its continuing validity.

We will take an example from Sweden – a country profoundly shaped by decades of social democratic governments – to illustrate the increasing difficulties organized labour faced in projecting a vision of the future, and the corresponding impoverishment of the role of utopias in its May Day ritual performances. What follows is a segment of a discussion between the members of the Social Democratic Party's executive board, which includes the president of LO (the blue-collar labour confederation) about what slogans the party would promote on May Day 1985 (protocol Social Democratic Party; document registration no. 1889/F/8/6; Labour Movement Archives and Library, Stockholm; our translation).

> Olof Palme [then prime minister, assassinated in 1986]: 'Preserve', what do you think?

Anna Lindh [then leader of the Social Democratic Youth Association, later to be Sweden's foreign minister, assassinated in 2003]: Preserve is too passive, a little like 'yes to the Swedish model – no to system changes'. Can't we have 'develop the Swedish model – no to system changes'? Otherwise we will be met with a debate that we sound like we are altogether satisfied with how things are today.

Stig Malm [then leader of LO]: We have had a debate about what we stand for: we stand for to preserve, we stand for that which has been. The Conservative Party stands for changes, new fresh ideas, etc. Here it is a question about 'Responsibility, Preserve'. No, we should ask Anna what the young people think are important words that we should use, but we use different words .... We have to find some key words. A key word is an inserted clause in the phrase 'preserve – justice'. Justice, I think that most people would think that justice is reasonable. Justice is the opposite of egoism.

It is in the nature of utopia that it must promise not more of the same – i.e. preserve – 'but an entirely different and marvellous world' (Ulam 1965, p. 399). The social democratic leadership, planning the upcoming May Day ritual event were decidedly non-utopian. It is difficult to envision that the keywords in their May Day script, i.e. 'preserve – justice', would stir the hearts and imaginations of the May Day participants or its audiences. With elections pending in the autumn, Olof Palme concluded his May Day speech with the slogan of their ritual performance: 'for a society of freedom, justice and solidarity' (www. olofpalme.org/1985/05/01/forsta-maj-tal-i-sundbyberg-och-stockholm-6/; our translation). Reaffirming these fundamental social democratic values, however, Olof Palme was not painting the picture of a future better society, but calling for the preservation of the existing one.

The concern for the governing Social Democratic Party in Sweden at that time was in fact to preserve what they had achieved in the face of a burgeoning global fiscal crisis with their 'third way economic policy' based on reducing government debt (ibid.). The social democratic vision of the future presented in their May Day celebrations was far from utopian, 'perceived as representing a system essentially different from, if not antithetical to, the existing one' (Bauman 1976, p. 17). Rather we have May Day celebrations of a political party and its associated labour confederation governing the country and concerned with retaining its political power. May Day was perceived not as a performance of a utopian 'future' essentially different from the system that existed but as an electoral platform reminding their followers of their commitment to full employment and the welfare state. Even the pragmatic social democratic vision of a better future society, of a steady advancement of the working classes through continuous social reform, had given way to the conviction that a social democratic government could at best preserve the existing state of affairs. This was a dilemma faced by social democratic and socialist parties throughout Western Europe, whether in government or in opposition – to be forced into devising ways to protect the existing welfare state instead of projecting a better future society. This development marked if not the loss, the lack of faith in the pragmatic utopia which had flourished in the 1960s and early 1970s.

We will take another example from Sweden to illustrate the impoverishment of the role of utopias in organized labour's May Day celebrations. If the hope for a better future had turned into the preservation of the existing state of affairs, in the years to come it would develop into increasingly accepting cutbacks in order to preserve at least something. After the 1990 May Day march in Stockholm, Ingvar Carlsson, then Social Democratic prime minister, reminded the assembled supporters that it was the centenary of May Day celebrations in Sweden. He spoke about the 'atmosphere, sense of community and joy' that had characterized the history of the labour movement's May Day celebrations (document registration no. 1829/2/1/1/25/4; Labour Movement Archives and Library, Stockholm; our translation). He recapped for those gathered all of the achievements of the social democratic government during the 1980s. However, his main message was the threat posed by rising inflation to full employment and welfare. Carlsson warned that the government would continue its austerity measures and would continue to push promised reforms to the future. He recounted how Social Democratic governments in the past had to take unpopular decisions and quoted Per-Elvin Sköld, finance minister in the early 1950s Social Democratic government: 'If one has responsibility for the future one is forced to bear the discontent awakened by economic austerity measures taken in the present.' Carlsson emphasized that such measures were absolutely necessary if full employment and extended welfare policies were to be achieved in the future. 'A radical party has to have the courage to take unpopular decisions.' As the leader of what he called 'a radical party', Carlsson certainly did not offer those listening a radically desirable or longed-for near future. Carlsson concluded his May Day speech by fervently maintaining that 'Social Democracy is, and continues to be, the only political force that *can assume responsibility* for Sweden and the future of the country!' (emphasis in the commented original script). In short, if there remains a vague social democratic utopia, this can only come to pass in the far future with social democrats continuing to shoulder the burden of governing the country. There is a measure of hazard (cf. Bauman 1976) in assuming responsibility for the future – the social democrats are forced to take unpopular decisions. So while the (threatening) 'future' features in the message from Carlsson's speech marking the centenary of the Swedish social democratic and labour union May Day celebrations, utopian visions are pointedly absent. In their place we find a plea for renewed political power in order to save at least something of the welfare state in the future.

Karl Mannheim (1979), writing in 1929, observed that as utopian movements develop and enter the political arena, they inevitably lose their uncompromising opposition to the existing social order. As we have seen, the political parties and trade unions of the traditional workers' movement in

Western Europe moved from the far-reaching utopia of the pre-World War I period to the pragmatic utopian vision of a future society to be reached step by step through social reform in the post-World War II period. By the time of the May Day centennial in 1990, however, even this vision and with it the remaining utopian content of May Day rituals showed evident signs of crisis even in Sweden, the social democratic country *par excellence*. The following years of ascendant neoliberalism clearly raised the question: does utopia still have a place, or can utopia regain a place in the rituals of May Day?

May Day and Utopia in Times of Neoliberalism

Norberto Bobbio (1989, p. 39) posed the following rhetorical question on the eve of the dramatic events of 1989: 'Do people really think that the end of historical communism (I stress the word "historical") has put an end to poverty and the thirst for justice?' For Bobbio, for as long as poverty and the thirst for justice exists, the need for utopias will remain. This need for utopia seems particularly manifest for today's May Day rituals. What cannot be expected, however, is a return to the 'solid' epic socialist utopia of the late nineteenth and early twentieth centuries. If in the second half of the twentieth century we have seen the dominance of pragmatic or concrete utopias, in the 'liquid times' (Bauman 2013) of the new millennium the May Day ritual appears to call for a new 'kind' of utopia that can animate May Day ritual performances and unleash the imaginations of participants and audiences so as to visualize a better future. In 'liquid times' utopias are multifacetted, as multifacetted as May Day ritual performances have become; there is not one, but many, often competing, potential utopian orientations (cf. Alexander 2001).

As we have seen above, since the late 1970s the traditional workers' movement encountered increasing difficulties in providing a utopian dimension for 'the most ambitious of Labour rituals' (Hobsbawm 1984, p. 76). Geoff Eley (1995, p. 5) has observed that the end of communism and the fall of the Berlin Wall in 1989, marking a low point in the development of the socialist tradition, provoked a further acceleration of this process. Rather than bringing about the 'end of history', it brought the end of the time in which a possible future could be designed full of self-confidence; in which society as such could be changed and newly created; in which the unlimited possibilities of science, technology, nature and production could be mobilized for the creation of a 'good' society. Considering one generation as a necessary time span for a socialist new beginning, Eley assumes that the starting points for a renewal of utopia are most likely to be found at the lower levels of individual hopes and visions of the future. Can utopian visions and the fervour of utopian performances of May Day re-emerge in contemporary May Day celebrations?

Confirming the centrality of the May Day ritual for the traditional labour movement and its organizations, these actors continue to tenaciously hold on to the May Day tradition. Franz Steinkühler, the leader of the German metalworkers at the time of the May Day centennial, insisted on the 'timeless timeliness' (*Welt der Arbeit* 1990, p. 14) of demonstrations and May Day rituals; Susanna Camusso, leader of the Italian trade union confederation CGIL, underlined that 'this date is our identity' (*La Repubblica*, 30 April 2011). At least for the trade unions, a part of this May Day tradition persists as a day of protest. In times of rampant neoliberalism and financial crisis, this also leads to conflicts with governments led by social democrats and socialists. These tensions (which have led to party splits like the one provoked by Schröder's reform policy in Germany, or to the electoral near-annihilation of the socialist/social democratic party as in Greece) constitute an additional element contributing to the increasing difficulties of the traditional labour movement, both in raising future-orientated and not purely defensive concrete demands and in connecting their May Day demonstrations with a shared vision of the future that challenges the existing society. A shrinking and ageing organizational membership – and declining participation in May Day rituals – further underlines the seeming inability of the traditional labour movement to project a future able to speak to the younger generations, i.e. to those hardest hit by the contemporary fiscal and economic crisis (see Chapter 7). For Southern European countries like Italy and Spain, demonstration surveys have evidenced low and apparently shrinking levels of trust in political parties but also, to a somewhat lesser degree, in the trade unions of the old left, even at protest events mobilized by these very organizations (della Porta and Reiter 2012; Peterson, Wahlström and Wennerhag 2015).

However, the remaining potential within the traditional left for a revitalization of May Day and a reaffirmation of its utopian dimension emerges if we focus on the motives of participants in today's May Day demonstrations. Mattias Wahlström pointed out in Chapter 9 that May Day today is indeed meaningful for the rituals' participants. He found that the participants employed a broad range of motive vocabularies. 'The largest category of motives was the protest category: people participated to express dissatisfaction with the current politics and state of society' (p. 226). The annual rituals of May Day demonstrations are used as platforms to address local grievances, as well as to direct attention to national and international injustices – today as in the past. For their participants, May Day rituals persist as a day of protest. However, Wahlström could also confirm the simultaneous importance of motives concerning collective identity, solidarity and tradition, particularly, but not exclusively, in the May Day performances mobilized by traditional labour organizations. Contemporary May Day rituals are not only protest events but also celebrations of organized labour, its past achievements and its principle values (see also Chapter 7). These values continue to form a fundamental element in the utopian potentials of May Day rituals, and are being taken up also by new actors beyond the traditional workers' movement (Peterson, Wahlström and Wennerhag 2015; Andretta *et al.* 2013).

As we have seen, May Day 'belongs' less and less to the traditional labour movement, and it has become more and more appropriated by new political actors. Since the latter 1960s their appearance has both triggered revitalization processes of May Day performances within the traditional labour movement, as well as offering alternative ritual performances, 'piggy-backing' the space opened annually for protest on the left (Chapter 7). Vieira (2010) argues that for a brief period in the late 1960s and 1970s, linked to the 1968 student movements, a new moment of confidence appeared. 'During those few years, utopia was fed by the hope of change put forward by ecologist, feminist and New Left thinkers' (p. 18) offering 'critical utopias' presenting views of a better future, but by no means a perfect future.

The 'critical utopias' of this tradition continue to be present in today's May Days. For example, an old 'new' political actor in Sweden, the Swedish Left Party (formerly the Left Party Communists) has staged May Day demonstrations in the country's major cities that have for the last 25 years consistently been significantly larger than the traditional social democratic and labour movement events. Since the early 1970s, the party has gathered the issues and to a large degree the participants in Sweden's 'new' social movements: the feminist, environmental, peace, global justice, LGBT movements and so on (see chapters 7, 8 and 9). Hence their May Day demonstrations have more resembled a left-wing coalition of contemporary political challengers, brought together one day each year in their support of the party, but voicing their potpourri of particularized challenges to the existing society and performing a hotchpotch of more individualized 'critical' utopian visions.

Even exceeding the turnout of the Left Party demonstration in Gothenburg on May Day 2014 was the first May Day demonstration organized by the new Swedish political party, Feminist Initiative (F!), with over 4,000 participants. The demonstration was an exuberant performance of a feminist utopia staged on the traditional day of celebration of organized labour. The popular former Left Party leader, Gudrun Schyman, spoke to a buoyant and optimistic crowd about the party's utopian vision of active citizenship, of a possible future, which was in the hands of those gathered.

> I'll tell you, that what we are experiencing now is something that I think we can call a 'Feminist spring'. It blooms! And it blooms not only in the cherry trees, but the conversations between people. Joyous to finally be with, to participate. To finally be able to take on citizenship and be creative and participate in the construction of the society that we have and that which *we should have to come*. The longing that we all carry – to be part of something that is also larger than our own private little sphere. Getting the feeling that we are needed, that our experiences are important. That we are seen, that we shall be heard, that we can be who we are and that we create community .... This is to be a citizen, which allows us to achieve our full potential as humans. And it's powerful. You shall see, it is mighty, that we have a political will.
>
> (http://feministisktinitiativ.se; our translation, added emphasis)

While the concrete demands of F! focused on the six-hour workday, better anti-discrimination measures and wage equality, the utopian message in the speech above dealt with a notion of equality as active citizenship which involves being able to fully participate and feel reflected in the political, economic and cultural spheres – a programmatic plea for inclusion that also formed one part of early May Day utopian visions for a better future for the working classes. Active citizenship in this feminist May Day utopian vision is a strategy to achieve a better future.

The May Days of the Left Party, and even more so the May Day of the Feminist Party, are examples of the appropriation of the 'world holiday of the proletariat' by post-'1968' movements, of increasing attempts to connect May Day with contemporary struggles for societal change that are not always shared by the traditional workers' movement, and in particular by its organizations. The different groups mobilizing on May Day contribute not only their specific claims but also their specific utopian visions to today's May Day ritual performances. The connection of their utopian elaborations with the world of labour is perhaps often tenuous, but today's critical utopias and the vague guidelines they offer, according to Vieira (2010), must not be seen as a betrayal of the utopian visions of old times. The vaguer guidelines these critical utopian visions provide are certainly far removed, in this respect, from the origins of May Day, and the utopian elements in today's May Day ritual performances are far more multifaceted than in the immediate post-World War II period, or even the 1960s or 1970s. However, Peterson, Wahlström and Wennerhag (2015) found no indication that new actors in anti-austerity demonstrations, for instance, had abandoned the underlying principles of May Day's utopian vision – social justice and solidarity remain rallying calls in their motives for participating in anti-austerity protests.[2]

Neoliberal politics, privatization of public services, dramatically increased precarity and the fiscal crisis in fact led to renewed attempts by groups beyond the traditional workers' movement to reconnect May Day with the current problems of the world of labour. One of these attempts is represented by the Milan MayDay parades (which subsequently developed into the EuroMayDay network) and the symbolic representations developed by the organizers (see Chapters 3 and 7).[3] They show that a renewal of utopia may include a rejection of how the socialist tradition has developed in the last decades: 'We are the post-socialist generation, the post-cold war generation …. And we do not recognize ourselves in you, gloomy and tetragon layers of political classes already defeated in the twentieth century. We do not recognize ourselves in the Italian Left.'[4]

Probably the best-known element of the EuroMayDay symbolic representation is the image of San Precario, the patron saint of all precarious workers. This icon was invented as a conscious effort to construct a common imagery for precarious workers who could not recognize themselves in the older workers' categories at the centre of previous cycles of protest (Mattoni 2008). Its use quickly spread throughout Italy and to other countries, being taken up

258 Abby Peterson and Herbert Reiter

also by traditional workers' categories. San Precario is a fully developed iconography with his feast day – 29 February, symbolizing the intermittent character of precarious work – holy pictures, statues and a sanctuary (Tari and Vanni 2005).

The very image of the saint points to a promised land, but ironically and sceptically. The prayer to San Precario contains a list of the most pressing concrete demands of precarious workers, reminiscent of the demands for the protection of workers contained in the resolutions voted in at the Paris congress of 1889. Subsequently further demands were elaborated, spreading beyond the work-related sphere including housing rights, access to culture and so on. In particular the demand for a guaranteed minimum income (as a means for overcoming social and political exclusion) seems to echo the old socialist vision of a society where everybody is provided for according to his/her needs. These demands are based on the lower levels of individual hopes and visions of the future, but it is as yet unclear whether they can serve, as Eley (1995) hopes, as starting points for a renewal of utopia – in this case a renewal of the utopian content of May Day.

Today's potpourri of critical utopias appear less engaged with content and more engaged with the *means* of reaching a new, radically different, future. 'By imagining another reality, in a virtual present or in a hypothetical future' (Vieira 2010, p. 21), the critical utopian orientations potentially bring a creative dynamics to the ritual of May Day. However, these creative utopian attempts by new political actors at a new beginning have still to prove their robustness to revitalize the May Day ritual performances. While we find contemporary May Day celebrations far removed from the pre-1914 socialist utopia, and the post-World War II pragmatic 'small utopia' of social democracy has seemingly lost its vitality. Alexander (2001, p. 579) suggests that 'self-limiting, partial, and plural utopias inform' the political, economic, social and cultural struggles of contemporary life. So while the utopian content of May Day ritual performances has become increasingly multifaceted, there has not been an end to utopian thought and action. The challenge for both the traditional labour movement as well as for today's newcomers to the May Day ritual is whether they can re-fuse the ritual performance and its utopian visions so as to make possible cathexis between participants and their causes, and rouse empathy and identification in the ritual's audiences (Chapter 1, p. 9).

For now, the foreseeable future of May Day seems to remain between the poles of, on the one hand, clinging to its tradition as the day of protest and celebration of the traditional labour movement and, on the other hand, as yet tentative attempts for a new beginning. Regardless of this ambiguity, it is by itself remarkable that the protest day of a political movement became firmly established in the yearly calendar, albeit less and less recognized and recognizable as the 'world holiday of the proletariat'; and that even after more than 120 years it continues to aspire to be the occasion for eventful protest and for elaborating a utopian vision of a better society for the workers of the world.

Notes

1 See Chapter 5, p. 113. As repeatedly stressed in this volume, there were different May Day conceptions also in potential conflict with each other. Spanish anarchists presented May Day as a 'demonstration of the insurrectional power of the working class, via the symbolic representation of the revolutionary strike that would destroy bourgeois society' (Chapter 5, p. 109). In the following we will concentrate on the socialist May Day conception dominant in Western Europe.
2 The study based on the CCC database encompassed anti-austerity demonstrations, including May Day demonstrations, in Spain, Italy, Belgium and the UK; see also della Porta and Reiter 2012; Andretta *et al.* 2013.
3 Three political groups based in Milan created the parade that started in 2001 as a national protest event and spread to other European countries after 2004: a group of self-organized precarious workers, the Chainworkers Crew; a group of activists from a social centre; and a radical grassroots trade union, the *Confederazione Unitaria di Base* (Mattoni 2008). The self-managed social centres offer spaces for cultural, social and political activities in squatted buildings (for an example, see Membretti 2007).
4 Manifesto Bio/Pop del Precariato Metroradicale, written by supporters of Milan, Roman and Venetian social centres in April 2004, quoted in Tari and Vanni 2005. The same manifesto polemicizes against the rock concert organized every year on May Day by the traditional trade unions: 'San Giovanni [the piazza where the concert is held] has always been against San Precario. CGIL-CISL-UIL give as a gift a concert worth millions of euros because they want the kids to stay passive consumers instead of active precarious workers.'

References

Alexander, J.C. (2001). Robust utopias and civil repairs. *International Sociology*, 16(4), 579–591.
Alexander, J.C. (2004). Cultural pragmatics: Social performance between ritual and strategy. *Sociological Theory*, 22(4), 527–573.
Andretta, M., Bosi, L., della Porta, D., and Reiter, H. (2013). Protests and protestors in times of financial crisis in Italy. *Rassegna Italiana di Sociologia*, 54(4), 569–596.
Bartolini, S. (2000). *The Political Mobilization of the European Left, 1860–1980*. Cambridge and New York: Cambridge University Press.
Bauman, Z. (1976). *Socialism: The Active Utopia*. London: Allan and Unwin.
Bauman, Z. (2013). *Liquid Times: Living in an Age of Uncertainty*. London: John Wiley & Sons.
Bebel, A. (1893). *Zukunftsstaat und Sozialdemokratie. Eine Rede des Reichstagsabgeordneten August Bebel in der Sitzung des deutschen Reichstags vom 3. Februar 1893*. Berlin: Vorwärts.
Bobbio, N. (1989). The upturned utopia. *New Left Review*, 177, 37–39.
Bonavita, F. (1900). Una futura esposizione. 1° Maggio dell'anno 2000. *L'Avanti!*, 1 May.
Crouch, C. (2011). *The Strange Non-Death of Neo-Liberalism*. Cambridge: Polity Press.
della Porta, D. (2008). Eventful protests, global conflicts. *Distinktion: Scandinavian Journal of Social Theory*, 17, 27–56.
della Porta, D., and Reiter, H. (with the collaboration of M. Andretta, S. Milan and F. Rossi). (2012). Desperately seeking politics: Political attitudes of participants in three demonstrations for worker's rights in Italy. *Mobilization: An International Quarterly*, 17(3), 349–361.

Ebbinghaus, B. (2002). Trade unions' changing role: Membership erosion, organisational reform, and social partnership in Europe. *Industrial Relations Journal*, 33(5), 465–483.

Eley, G. (1995). What's left of utopia? Oder: Vom 'Neuen Jerusalem' zur Zeit der Wünsche. *Werkstatt Geschichte*, 11, 5–18.

Hobsbawm, E.J. (1984). The transformation of labour rituals. In *Worlds of Labour: Further Studies in the History of Labour* (pp. 66–82). London: Weidenfeld and Nicolson.

Hobsbawm, E. (1991). Birth of a holiday: The first of May. In C. Wrigley and J. Shepherd (Eds), *On the Move: Essays in Labour and Transport History* (pp. 104–122). London and Rio Grande: Hambledon Press.

Korff, G. (1986). "Rote Fahnen und geballte Faust: Zur Symbolik der Arbeiterbewegung in der Weimarer Republik." In D. Petzina (Ed.), *Fahnen, Fäuste, Körper. Symbolik und Kultur der Arbeiterbewegung* (pp. 27–60). Essen: Klartext.

Korff, G. (1989). Bemerkungen zur Symbolgeschichte des 1. Mai. In Verein zum Studium Sozialer Bewegungen (Ed.), *100 Jahre Erster Mai. Beiträge und Projekte zur Geschichte der Maifeiern in Deutschland. Ein Tagungsbericht* (pp. 85–103). Berlin: Selbstverlag.

Kumar, K. (2010). The ends of utopia. *New Literary History*, 41(3), 549–569.

Marßolek, I. (1990). Der 1. Mai im Jahre 2000: Hat die Utopie eine Zukunft? In I. Marßolek (Ed.), *100 Jahre Zukunft. Zur Geschichte des 1. Mai* (pp. 363–369). Frankfurt a.M. and Vienna: Büchergilde Gutenberg.

Mannheim, K. (1979)[1939]. *Ideology and Utopia*. London: Routledge and Kegan Paul.

Martin, A., and Ross, G. (1999). *The Brave New World of European Labor: European Trade Unions at the Millennium*. New York: Berghahn Books.

Mattoni, A. (2008). Serpica Naro and the others: The media sociali experience in Italian struggles against precarity. *PORTAL. Journal of Multidisciplinary International Studies*, 5 (2), doi: 0.5130/portal.v5i2.706.

Membretti, A. (2007). Centro Sociale Leoncavallo: Building citizenship as an innovative service. *European Urban and Regional Studies*, 14, 252–263.

Merkel, W. (1991). After the golden age: Is social democracy doomed to decline? In *Socialist Parties in Europe* (pp. 187–222). Barcelona: Institut d'Edicions de la Diputació de Barcelona.

Offe, C. (1985). *Disorganised Capitalism: Contemporary Transformation of Work and Capitalism*. Cambridge: Polity Press.

Peterson, A., Wahlström, M., and Wennerhag, M. (2015). Beyond 'old' and 'new' social movements? Participants in European anti-austerity protests 2010–2012. *Acta Sociologica*, 58(4), 293–310.

Pontusson, J. (1995). Explaining the decline of European social democracy: The role of structural economic change. *World Politics*, 47(04), 495–533.

Ricoeur, P. (1986). *Lectures on Ideology and Utopia*. New York: Columbia University Press.

Ricoeur, P. (1994). Rethinking imagination. In G. Robinson and J. Rundell (Eds), *Culture and Creativity* (pp. 118–136). London: Routledge.

Tari, M., and Vanni, I. (2005). On the life and deeds of San Precario, patron saint of precarious workers and lives. *Fibreculture Journal*, 5, http://five.fibreculturejournal.org/fcj-023-on-the-life-and-deeds-of-san-precario-patron-saint-of-precarious-workers-and-lives/.

Ulam, A. (1965). Socialism and utopia. *Daedalus*, 94(2), 382–400.
Vieira, F. (2010). The concept of utopia. In G. Claeys (Ed.), *The Cambridge Companion to Utopian Literature* (pp. 3–27). Cambridge: Cambridge University Press.

Appendix

Methods for Studying May Day Demonstrators

Sampling, Estimating Non-Response Bias and Pooling Data with General Population Surveys

Mattias Wahlström and Magnus Wennerhag

This chapter concerns some methodological aspects of protest surveys and data analysis. We start by providing an overview of the demonstrations we surveyed, describe the protest survey sampling method and proceed to an analysis of non-response bias. Thereafter we discuss how we combine the data from different demonstrations into averages, and we also discuss some of the more technical aspects of coding.

The demonstrations

In chapters 7–9, we used data collected within the research programme 'Caught in the Act of Protest: Contextualizing Contestation' (hereafter CCC) from a total of 15 May Day demonstrations which took place between 2010 and 2012 in Belgium, Italy, Spain, Sweden, Switzerland and the UK (see Table A.1). Additionally, in Chapter 8 another 23 demonstrations from these countries were used, in order to compare May Day parades with other demonstrations, staged by trade unions or 'new social movements' (more information about this is provided later in this chapter).

As can be seen in Table A.1, the demonstrations had slightly different types of organizers, which we chose to divide into three categories: (1) major trade union confederations (sometimes also including social democratic or socialist parties), (2) 'radical left' organizations (post-communist and radical left parties and radical left-wing trade unions) and (3) broad coalitions that mix elements of both of the former categories and where none is clearly dominant. These categories have been taken into account, in order not to lump apples and oranges when calculating mean scores in the dataset. In the first category, we include the Belgian demonstration in Antwerp, organized by the social democratic trade union confederation ABVV and the Flemish social democratic party Socialistische Partij Anders; the Italian demonstration in Florence, organized by Italy's three major trade union federations

(CGIL, CISL and UIL); the Spanish demonstrations in Barcelona and Vigo that were organized by the major trade union confederations CCOO and UGT; and the Swedish demonstrations in Gothenburg, Malmö and Stockholm that were organized by the Social Democratic Party and the main blue-collar trade union confederation LO. In the second category, we included the Italian EuroMayDay demonstration in Milan, the Spanish demonstration organized by the radical regional trade union Confederación Intersindical Galega that took place in Vigo, and the Swedish demonstrations organized by the Left Party, taking place in Gothenburg, Malmö and Stockholm. Finally, in the third category of broader coalitions, we included the Swiss demonstrations in Geneva and Zurich, as well as the UK demonstration in London. For more information on these mobilizations, see Chapter 7.

We regard the demonstrations as more or less representative of the trade union traditions in the countries in which they take part. For countries where the CCC research teams have sampled several demonstrations, they capture some of the diversity of May Day demonstrations in this country. Nevertheless we lack some types of May Day demonstrations that could have added somewhat to the complexity of our descriptions. In Italy we lack an example of the main annual May Day demonstration that gathers representatives from the major trade unions from all over the country. In Sweden we had a significant diversity since we sampled two demonstrations from each of the three major cities, yet on many locations there are other left-wing groups also demonstrating on May Day. These marches are typically quite small, except the anarcho-syndicalist marches, which currently appear to be steadily growing in some major cities. Finally, the London May Day march is perhaps not entirely representative of May Day parades found elsewhere in cities with higher union density and a traditionally more prominent industrial working-class population.

In Chapter 8, some additional demonstrations surveyed within the CCC research programme were included in the analysis, in order to compare the social composition of the May Day marches with other types of trade union demonstrations, as well as two categories of demonstrations often staged by new social movements: environmental protests and the Pride parades of the LGBT movement. In total, ten other trade union demonstrations, eight environmental protests and five Pride parades were included (for more detail, see Table A.2). All these 23 other demonstrations were surveyed in the same six countries as the May Day marches, and for each of the categories at least demonstrations in four countries were covered.

Sampling of survey respondents

The sampling method of the CCC programme has been described in detail by, for example, van Stekelenburg and colleagues (2012). Nevertheless, we will recapitulate the central aspects of the method here. These aspects are intended

Table A.1 Overview of surveyed demonstrations

Country	Belgium	Italy		Spain			Sweden
City	Antwerp	Florence	Milan – Euromayday	Barcelona	Vigo	Vigo	Stockholm
Year	2010	2011	2011	2010	2011	2011	2010
Most important organizers of demonstration	ABVV (Algemeen Belgisch Vakverbond) and sp.a (Socialistische Partij Anders)	CGIL (Confederazione Generale Italiana del Lavoro), CISL (Confederazione Italiana Sindacati Lavoratori) and UIL (Unione Italiana del Lavoro)	San Precario Network and CUB (Confederazione Unitaria di Base)	CCOO (Comisiones Obreras) and UGT (Unión General de Trabajadores)	CCOO (Comisiones Obreras) and UGT (Unión General de Trabajadores)	CIG (Confederación Intersindical Galega)	LO (Lands-organisationen) and Social Democratic Party
Main organiz-ers – spe-cification	Main Social Democratic trade union confederation and social democratic party	Main three trade un-ion confederations (post-communist, catholic and socialist/republican)	Radical left wing activist network and radical left wing trade union	Main two trade un-ion confederations (post-communist and socialist)	Main two trade union confederations (post-communist and socialist)	Radical left wing trade union	Main social democratic trade union confederation and social democratic party
May Day demon-stration type	1. Major trade union confederation	1. Major trade union confederation	2. Radical left organizations	1. Major trade union confederation	1. Major trade union confederation	2. Radical left organizations	1. Major trade union confederation
No. of dem-onstrators (accord-ing to CCC research teams)	2,000	500	5,000	8,000	15,000	2,000	3,000

to address two challenges when surveying participants in a demonstration: to ensure that each person participating in the demonstration has an (in principle) equal chance of being sampled and that potential response bias can be estimated.

To address the first challenge, the CCC teams used a structured sampling method (since a completely random sample of participants in a demonstration would be practically impossible). During each demonstration, two or more teams of researchers distributed questionnaires to one person in every Nth row, according to an algorithm that was calculated on the basis of the estimated size of the demonstration. For example, if the demonstration was estimated to consist of approximately 10,000 people, and was estimated to be roughly 10 persons broad, the teams would use a rule that would make sure that one person in each row would receive a questionnaire (i.e. in prac-tice every tenth person). The teams, distributing questionnaires from each side, would make sure that questionnaires were handed out to alternately the person on the edge of the march, the second person from the edge, the third person, etc. See Figure A.1.

If interviewers were allowed to hand out questionnaires on their own, there would nevertheless be a risk that they would not stick strictly to the rules set at the beginning of the march. It seems that interviewers are generally disin-clined to approach respondents that do not seem likely to accept a question-naire, and more prone to approach people that look friendly and are roughly

					Switzerland		United Kingdom
Stockholm	*Malmö*	*Malmö*	*Gothenburg*	*Gothenburg*	*Zurich*	*Geneva*	*London*
2010 Vänsterpartiet (Left Party)	2011 LO (Landsorganisationen) and Social Democratic Party	2011 Vänsterpartiet (Left Party)	2012 LO (Landsorganisationen) and Social Democratic Party	2012 Vänsterpartiet (Left Party)	2010 May Day Committee and Gewerkschaftsbund des Kanton Zurich	2011 CGAS (Confédération Genevoise d'Action Syndicale) and Parti du Travail (Swiss Party of Labour)	2010 LMDOC (London May Day Organising Committee)
Main radical left (democratic socialist) party	Main social democratic trade union confederation and social democratic party	Main radical left (democratic socialist) party	Main social democratic trade union confederation and social democratic party	Main radical left (democratic socialist) party	Coalition of left-wing groups, and main social democratic trade unions	Main trade unions and reformed communist party	Coalition between main social democratic trade unions and left-wing groups
2. Radical left organizations	1. Major trade union confederation	2. Radical left organizations	1. Major trade union confederation	2. Radical left organizations	3. Broad coalition	3. Broad coalition	3. Broad coalition
4,200	900	2,000	2,450	3,300	8,000	1,000	5,000

the same age as the interviewer (cf. Walgrave and Verhulst 2011). Therefore the interviewers were coordinated in teams by 'pointers' who counted the rows and persons and assigned interviewees to the interviewers. Since the pointers did not have to approach the presumptive respondents themselves, they were presumably less biased than the interviewers in terms of sampling.

In order to assure a reasonable response rate, the interviewers were instructed to provide the respondents with information about the project and the importance of filling in the survey. The questionnaires included a prepaid postal envelope, whereby the participants could fill in the survey at home. Nevertheless, since we had no opportunity to remind people, the response rates were low compared to many other population-based surveys. The response rates typically varied between 20 and 40 per cent (see Table A.2). There is therefore a risk of response bias. In order to address this second challenge of protest surveying, approximately every fifth participant also received a number of oral questions, which could be used as a reference point for the returned surveys.

Estimating Non-Response Bias

The method of posing face-to-face questions to every fifth respondent makes it possible to estimate possible non-response biases. This is based on the assumption that, with normally over 90 per cent response rate, those who

Table A.2 Surveyed demonstrations, distributed questionnaires and response rates

Demonstration type	Country	City/demonstration	Year	Oral interviews conducted	Mail-back questionnaires distributed	Questionnaires returned by mail	Response rate, mail-back questionnaire (%)
May Day	**Belgium**	Antwerp	2010	143	837	216	26
	Italy	Florence	2011	88	408	110	27
		Milan	2011	198	993	127	13
	Spain	Barcelona	2010	136	700	180	26
		Vigo – CCOO and UGT	2011	49	263	66	25
		Vigo – CIG	2011	124	340	168	49
	Sweden	Stockholm – LO and Social Democratic Party	2010	48	429	176	41
		Stockholm – Left Party	2010	53	430	167	39
		Malmö – LO and Social Democratic Party	2011	57	281	97	35
		Malmö – Left Party	2011	76	388	141	36
		Gothenburg – LO and Social Democratic Party	2012	66	454	160	35
		Gothenburg – Left Party	2012	87	521	209	40
	Switzerland	Zurich	2010	171	861	135	16
		Geneva	2011	151	747	206	28
	United Kingdom	London	2010	106	977	178	18
	Total: May Day			**1,553**	**8,629**	**2,336**	**27**
Trade union (other than May Day)	**Belgium**	Brussels – March for work	2010	122	466	129	28
		Brussels – No to austerity	2010	343	450	144	32
		Brussels – Non-profit demonstration	2011	132	634	197	31
		Brussels – We have alternatives	2011	145	767	169	22

Category	Country	Event	Year				
	Italy	Florence – General strike	2011	191	987	235	24
		Rome – No Monti day	2012	198	1,000	192	19
	Spain	Barcelona – Against capital, crisis and war	2010	96	300	77	26
		Santiago de Compostela – Against new labour law	2010	143	780	168	22
	United Kingdom	Madrid – Against labour law	2010	180	900	308	34
		London – TUC march for the alternative	2011	179	993	211	21
Total: Trade union				**1,729**	**7,277**	**1,830**	**25**
Environmental	Belgium	Brussels – Climate change	2009	143	777	334	43
		Brussels – Fukushima never again	2012	78	495	189	38
	Italy	Niscemi – No MUOS	2013	195	996	142	14
	Sweden	Stockholm – Anti-nuclear	2011	133	718	279	39
	Switzerland	Beznau – Anti-nuclear	2011	152	980	472	48
		Mühleberg – Anti-nuclear	2012	182	918	462	50
	United Kingdom	London – National climate march	2009	90	606	243	40
		London – National climate march	2010	152	966	359	37
Total: Environmental				**1,125**	**6,456**	**2,480**	**38**
Pride	Italy	Bologna	2012	188	1,000	216	22
	Sweden	Gothenburg	2012	80	445	162	36
	Switzerland	Geneva	2011	159	792	197	25
		Zurich	2012	94	478	150	31
	United Kingdom	London	2012	140	1,000	194	19
Total: Pride				**661**	**3,715**	**919**	**25**
Total				**5,068**	**26,077**	**7,565**	**29**

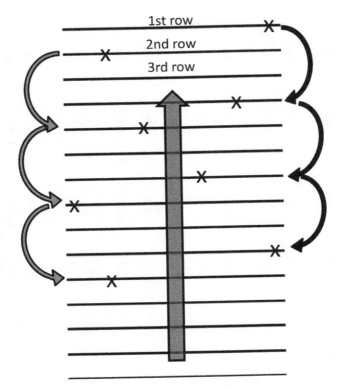

Figure A.1 Example of how an ideal-typical demonstration can be sampled. Image based on the CCC manual for data collection.

respond to the face-to-face questions better approximate the demonstrator population, compared to those who return their questionnaires.

There is no necessary connection between high non-response to a survey and non-response bias in the results. Those who respond to a mail-back questionnaire do not necessarily differ in any significant respects from those who choose not to respond (Leslie 1972). However, previous research has shown that specific socio-demographic and other individual characteristics can influence response rates (e.g. Rogelberg *et al.* 2003), subsequently these characteristics may be sources of non-response bias. For example, according to the leverage-salience theory of survey participation (Groves, Singer and Corning 2000) the saliency of a survey topic in combination with the respondent's general interest in this topic affects the respondent's general propensity to respond to a survey. This could mean that in a protest survey the least politically interested are also the least likely to respond. In an analysis of non-response bias in a survey of anti-Iraq war protesters in Glasgow in 2003, Rüdig (2010) found that women are more likely to answer questionnaires than men, the middle-aged more likely than young people and the well-educated more likely than those having a lower level of education. However, he found no significant correlations in relation to political opinions or interest in politics. Walgrave and Verhulst (2011) compared selection and non-response bias in a number of demonstrations on different issues, and when using the same sampling methodology used here they found no significant non-response biases except for age and position on the issue at stake in the protest. A set of questions measuring these basic socio-demographic and political characteristics has also been included in the CCC standard face-to-face questionnaire, which provides us with an opportunity to make our own estimations of non-response bias in May Day demonstration surveys.

The availability of data for both face-to-face interviews and returned postal questionnaires therefore allowed us to compare the group of individuals that did receive a postal questionnaire but did *not* return it (but still answered the face-to-face questions) with the respondents that sent in the postal questionnaire via mail. Our tests were conducted both on a general level, for all 15 May Day demonstrations, and for each demonstration separately. The tests focused on the characteristics that previously have been shown to influence response: male gender, young age and no higher education. We also included a measure of political interest because of its possible importance, despite Rüdig's results to the contrary. We hypothesized that those 'not at all interested' in politics would stand out among the non-respondents.

On the general level, the test shows statistically significant differences between the groups that sent in questionnaires and those that did not, regarding age, educational level and political interest (see Table A.3). We present only those individual demonstrations where statistically significant differences were found. First of all, only in one single demonstration did we find a significant difference between men and women, and there was no significant pattern on the general level. However, there is a significant overall tendency that non-respondents are more often young (27 per cent younger than 30 years vs 21 per cent among all respondents) and have no ongoing or completed university education (49 per cent vs 42 per cent among all respondents). Still, on the demonstration level, these differences are significant only in a minority of demonstrations in our sample.[1] Regarding political interest, our interpretation of these results is that this factor has only a marginal effect on the sample, given the fact that those not interested in politics are a very small group, both among the respondents of the mail questionnaire (1 per cent) and among the individuals that did not return the questionnaire (3 per cent).

The results of these non-response bias tests show that the descriptive data regarding in particular age and educational level must be interpreted with some caution. The descriptive data presented regarding the percentage of young people should be regarded as possibly slightly underestimated, while the percentage of university-educated may be slightly overestimated. It is, however, important to note that non-response bias has also been found in the surveys that we use to compare our CCC data (for more information about

Table A.3 Cases of significant non-response bias in the dataset

		Demonstrators sending in the questionnaire	Demonstrators not sending in the questionnaire	All surveyed demonstrators	Total (N)	Cramer's V
Gender: male (%)						
All demonstrations	**Total**	**55**	**58**	**56**	**3,356**	**n.s.**
Demonstrations with significant differences	Milan – EuroMayDay	47	59	54	278	.123*
Age: –29 years (%)						
All demonstrations	**Total**	**19**	**27**	**21**	**3,177**	**.084***
Demonstrations with significant differences	Antwerp	7	16	10	313	.152**
	Vigo – CCOO and UGT	3	16	7	97	.236*
	Gothenburg – LO and Social Democratic Party	18	38	22	194	.191**
	London	16	37	23	256	.238***
Education: No ongoing or completed university education (%)						
All demonstrations	**Total**	**40**	**49**	**42**	**3,142**	**.077***
Demonstrations with significant differences	Barcelona	48	62	53	276	.134*
	Gothenburg – Left Party	18	35	21	254	.172**
Political interest: Not at all interested in politics (%)						
All demonstrations	**Total**	**1**	**3**	**2**	**3,407**	**.087***
Demonstrations with significant differences	Milan – EuroMayDay	2	7	4	292	.121*
	Barcelona	1	4	2	277	.125*
	Stockholm – LO and Social Democratic Party	1	8	2	200	.197**

Notes: Levels of significance: * = 5%, ** = 1% and *** = 0.1% significance.

these surveys, see below). This is, for example, the case with the European Social Survey (ESS, which is made face-to-face and uses show cards), where non-response biases, in particular related to level of education, have been found, but also smaller differences regarding gender and age (Vehovar 2007). In the Swedish SOM Institute's national population survey (which is a postal survey), non-response biases have also been noted, where young people and men have been found to be less inclined to send in the questionnaire (Vernersdotter 2012).[2] In conclusion, since the surveys with which we compare our data also display similar types of non-response biases as our own CCC surveys, the comparative analyses should still be considered as sufficiently accurate.

Some researchers suggest various methods for weighting data to compensate for estimated non-response bias (e.g. Cobben and Bethlehem 2005). However, apart from the inherent problems of these methods, the fact that at most a few demonstrations for each variable display significant response biases creates difficult dilemmas. Should weights be applied only to those demonstrations where non-response biases are significant, or should overall weights be applied? In either case, there is an imminent risk that the sample is only further distorted. We therefore chose not to weight the data for these purposes. However, in the next section we will turn to another weighting-related issue, which is related to data aggregation.

Data Aggregation

First of all, considering the differences among the demonstration categories in our sample, we chose to compare averages across demonstrations within the three different categories of May Day demonstrations described above. The same procedure followed in Chapter 8 was used for the other types of demonstrations that were compared with the three categories of May Day marches. In order to calculate averages within these categories, there are three characteristics of the data that potentially need to be compensated by weighting. First, there are unequal numbers of respondents in the different demonstrations (e.g. the May Day marches range between 66 and 216 respondents). If this is not compensated for, the particular characteristics of demonstrations with fewer returned questionnaires than the average become under-represented in the sample. Second, within each category of demonstrations there are varying numbers of demonstrations from each country, not reflecting any real differences in numbers of May Day demonstrations in the country. If this is not compensated for, countries where the research team has surveyed more demonstrations weigh heavier in the data. Instead, the most reasonable position is to give each country equal weight within each category, which means reducing the weight of respondents in a demonstration proportionally to the number of demonstrations from the country within a category. Third, demonstrations are also of unequal size, but in this case it is less clear whether this should be compensated for when calculating an average. On the one hand, the size estimations that we use are at best rough, and the relative sizes of the demonstrations from a single country do not necessarily reflect the relative importance of these demonstrations in a national context. On the other hand, one might argue that it makes sense that participants in a smaller, and potentially more marginal, demonstration weigh lighter than those from a large and dominant demonstration. We could find no ideal solution to the latter dilemma, and therefore chose to calculate two different weights. The first weight compensates for the size of the sample from each demonstration and the number of demonstrations from each country in a single demonstration category, but within each country, it allows each demonstration to have equal weight regardless of their size. The second weight (the one used in the presented data, e.g. in Table 9.2) also compensates for sample size and number of demonstrations from a country, but also includes a weight that compensates for the size difference between the demonstrations within each country. These weights were applied when calculating averages but not in multilevel and other types of regressions, which compensates for differences in cluster sizes (Goldstein 2011).

Comparative Data

In order to make it possible to compare May Day participants with the general population in Chapter 8, socio-demographic data for the relevant countries from the 2010 European Social Survey Round 5 (ESS5) was used. The ESS5 covers the countries included in the CCC data used in this chapter, except for Italy, since the country did not take part in this round of European Social Survey. This ESS data allows for a comparison between the May Day participants (and protesters in other demonstrations surveyed within the CCC project) with the general population, and thus provides indications as to whether the social composition of the May Day demonstrations mirror the general population. Since almost all of the CCC surveyed demonstrations analysed in this book were staged in major cities (with more than 300,000 inhabitants), the data for the general population is, however, limited to those responding in the ESS survey that they live in 'a big city' or 'the suburbs or outskirts of a big city', assuming that this is the population that potentially could have been mobilized to the surveyed demonstrations. The ESS data shown in the tables is the mean values for all countries of our study.

Pooling Datasets

To analyse the social and political factors that make May Day participation more or less probable, data from the Swedish SOM Institute's national population survey were used in Chapter 8. In the 2011 SOM survey, a question was asked whether one had participated in a May Day demonstration during the last 12 months. This makes it possible to 'pool' the Swedish CCC May Day data with SOM Institute data for inhabitants in Sweden's three largest cities – Gothenburg, Malmö and Stockholm – in order to test the factors that most strongly contributed to people participating in May Day marches. Pooling data this way may appear controversial but has been justified by various authors under the labels 'endogenous stratified sampling', 'choice-based sampling' or 'case-control design' (e.g. King and Zeng 2001; Manski and McFadden 1981). It has been used in studies where the aim is to explain a characteristic that is very uncommon in the population at large, which makes the approach popular in epidemiology and studies of natural disasters.

The six May Day demonstrations that were surveyed in Sweden in 2010–2012 all took place in these three cities, and within roughly the same period when the SOM survey was conducted. The analysis is thus limited to Sweden's three largest cities. May Day participation in Sweden is still a geographically well-dispersed activity going on in most cities and towns in the country. We therefore assumed that all the individuals answering the CCC protest survey at a Swedish May Day demonstration were living in the area in which the demonstration took place. This makes our CCC data for six May Day demonstrations in Stockholm, Gothenburg and Malmö comparable with the SOM Institute's survey data for the general population living in the same areas. In this way, the individuals actually showing up at the main May Day marches in these cities can be compared with those in the same cities that explicitly say that they *did not* participate in a May Day demonstration. Through the analysis, we thereby compare those individuals that could have been mobilized to some specific demonstrations, but were not, with the individuals who were actually mobilized. When combining the SOM and CCC datasets we furthermore assumed that the respondents that in the SOM survey said that they had participated in a May Day march equal the respondents of our six CCC protest surveys. The very small group (N = 25) of SOM survey respondents that had taken part in a May Day demonstration ('ones'), were in the analysis substituted for the CCC respondents to the six May Day demonstrations, in order not to run the risk of counting any individuals twice in case they took part in both surveys. The major group of SOM survey respondents that did not take part in a May Day demonstration were in the analysis treated as 'zeroes' (King and Zeng 2001). Since most questions in the CCC and SOM questionnaire were identical or very similar, the two datasets were easily combined.[3]

According to King and Zeng (2001, p. 144), logistic regression on a pooled sample of 'zeroes' and 'ones' yields valid estimates of beta-coefficients, except for the constant that needs to be adjusted according to the formula:

$$\hat{\beta}_0 - \ln\left[\left(\frac{1-\tau}{\tau}\right)\left(\frac{\bar{y}}{1-\bar{y}}\right)\right]$$

in which $\hat{\beta}_0$ is the estimated constant in the model, τ is the fraction of 'ones' in the population (in our case, the fraction of May Day demonstrators in the SOM data) and $\bar{y}$ is the fraction of 'ones' in the pooled sample.

Table A.4 Survey question wordings and response alternatives

Variable	Survey question	Response alternatives
Age	In which year were you born? [Answer subtracted from year of the demonstration]	–
Education	What is the highest level of education that you completed? If you are a student, at what level are you studying?	None, did not complete primary education; Primary or first stage of basic; Lower secondary or second stage of basic; Upper secondary; Post-secondary, non-tertiary; First stage of tertiary (BA, university first degree); Second stage of tertiary (MA); Post-tertiary (PhD) [These were obtained from the alternatives in each national questionnaire, which had options reflecting the specific national school systems.]
Emotions	Thinking about [issue of the demonstration] makes me feel: [Angry, Frustrated]	Not at all; Not very much; Somewhat; Quite; Very much
Employment situation	What is your employment situation? (Check as many as apply)	I work full-time (including maternity leave or other temporary absence); I work part-time (including maternity leave or other temporary absence); I am freelance/self-employed (without employed staff); I am self-employed with employed staff; I study full-time; I am unemployed/between jobs; I am (early) retired; I am a housewife/househusband; Other. …
Ethnicity	In which country were you born? [Answer compared with the country where the demonstration was staged]	–
External efficacy	To what extent do you agree or disagree with the following statements? [My participation can have an impact on public policy in this country; Organized groups of citizens can have a lot of impact on public policies in this country]	Strongly disagree; Disagree; Neither; Agree; Strongly agree

Gender	Are you ...?	Male; Female.
Occupation	What is your occupation, or what was your last occupation?	–
Organizational affiliation	If you have been involved in any of the following types of organizations in the past 12 months, please indicate whether you are a passive member or an active member? If you are a member of several organizations of the same type, tick the highest or most 'active' category. [Trade union or professional association; Political party; Environmental organization]	Passive member/financial supporter; Active member
Party sympathy	With which party do you most closely identify right now?	–
Political interest	How interested are you in politics?	Not at all; Not very; Quite; Very
Political left–right identification	In politics people sometimes talk of 'left' and 'right'. Where would you place yourself on this scale, where 0 means the left and 10 means the right?	Left = 0; 1; 2; [...]; 8; 9; Right = 10; Do not know
Protest motives	Please tell us why you participated in this protest event.	–
Satisfaction with democracy	In general, how satisfied or dissatisfied are you with the functioning of democracy in your country?	Very dissatisfied = 0; 1; 2; [...]; 8; 9; Very satisfied = 10; Do not know
Subjective class	People sometimes describe themselves as belonging to the working class, the middle class or the upper or lower class. Would you describe yourself as belonging to the ...?	Upper class; Upper middle class; Lower middle class; Working class; Lower class; None
Supervisory position at work	In your main job, do/did you have any responsibility for supervising the work of other (or your own) employees?	No; Yes, for 1 to 9 persons; Yes, for 10 persons or more
Trust in political institutions	Below is a list of institutions. Please indicate, in general, how much you trust each of the following (types of) institutions. [National government; National parliament]	Not at all; Not very much; Somewhat; Quite; Very much

Variables and Survey Questions

Variables Derived from the CCC Questionnaire

The survey questions used to measure the variables used in chapters 8 and 9 are listed in Table A.4. As we have previously noted (Wahlström and Wennerhag 2014), because the questionnaire is filled in after protest participation some variables need to be interpreted with a degree of caution since they may be affected by participation. This should especially apply to variables such as sense of efficacy, trust, emotions and identification with other participants. Nevertheless, since the participants in a demonstration are arguably affected by their participation in a similar fashion, these variables can still be used in regressions as proxies for characteristics of the protesters prior to participation.

Coding Class

In Chapter 8, the class scheme constructed by Oesch (e.g. 2006a, 2006b) is used to analyse the class composition of May Day marches and other types of demonstrations, and to compare these with ESS and SOM survey data for the general population. In order to conduct this analysis, the data available in the CCC, ESS and SOM databases was coded according to the Oesch class scheme.[4]

In the Oesch class scheme class is coded based on information on individuals' (rather than households') employment status (employer, self-employed or employee), occupation and supervision status, in case of supervisory functions. In the CCC dataset, the Oesch class position was therefore derived from the variables 'employment situation', 'supervisory status', 'education level' and 'occupation' (for details of these variables and their alternatives, see Table A.4). The relevant data for the variable 'occupation' was obtained through a manual coding procedure, on the basis of the open-ended question in the CCC questionnaire about the respondent's current or former occupation. This manual coding was carried out according to the ISCO-88 standard.[5]

Since labour market position determines class position in the Oesch class scheme, a central concern was how to treat individuals not currently in employment. For instance, Oesch (2006a, p. 75) proposes a target population that covers only persons between the ages 20 and 65 currently working at least 20 hours per week, in order to derive class positions only for persons properly involved in the labour market. Full-time students, the retired and the unemployed are thus altogether left out of the original Oesch class scheme. In our analysis, however, we wished to extend the population coverage and make it possible to identify the class position for those temporarily unemployed or retired. Everyone, regardless of age or current employment status, was therefore included in the analysis. In order to make Oesch data comparable, this procedure was undertaken for all types of data that were analysed (CCC, ESS and SOM). The unemployed were coded according to their last paid employment. Furthermore, in order to analyse the relatively large group of full-time students, an extra tenth 'class' consisting of students was added to the Oesch scheme. The small share of respondents who are both full-time students and in paid employment were class coded according to their occupation, and do thus not appear as students in the tables presenting Oesch data.

Conclusion

To sum up, we argue that our quantitative data is based on the most reliable protest survey sampling method to date. There are nevertheless some indications of possible non-response bias related to age, higher education and political interest, which should be taken into account when evaluating the results. However, we have no reason to believe that any bias should be serious enough to jeopardize the main arguments in the preceding chapters.

We have also suggested methods for aggregating data from several surveyed demonstrations, which we believe can be applied to other studies based on this and similar datasets. We have finally argued that pooling protest survey data with data from general population surveys is a both legitimate and profitable approach to explaining protest participation. However, one must take care to define the reference population, which is not necessarily the same as the national population. In most cases, the sample from the protest population should ideally be pooled with a sample from the population living in the city or area where the protest took place, i.e. the area where one can identify those belonging to the mobilization potential of a specific protest.

Notes

1 In two of the Italian demonstrations, face-to-face data on age and level of education was missing in the dataset.
2 In the non-response analysis of the SOM Institute national survey, education level was not included.
3 When it comes to the variable 'ethnicity', the CCC survey asked in which country the respondent was born, whereas the SOM survey asked in which country the respondent 'grew up'. The question about 'class identity' in the SOM survey was phrased as which type of home the respondent lived in today, in terms of class. The questions about left–right political identification, satisfaction with democracy and trust in the national government had alternatives with different scales in the SOM and CCC surveys, which were converted into common scales.
4 We here especially wish to thank Anders Hylmö for manually classifying the occupation of all cases in the CCC dataset, as well as constructing SPSS syntaxes and managing all the coding of CCC data into Oesch's class categories. We also wish to thank Daniel Oesch for providing us with corresponding SPSS syntaxes for ESS data.
5 For a detailed description of the coding process and the variables used, see Appendix C in Hylmö and Wennerhag 2012.

278   *Mattias Wahlström and Magnus Wennerhag*

References

Cobben, F., and Bethlehem, J. (2005). *Adjusting Undercoverage and Nonresponse Bias in Telephone Surveys*. Voorberg, The Netherlands: CBS, Statistics Netherlands.

Goldstein, H. (2011). *Multilevel Statistical Models*, 4th edn. Chichester, UK: Wiley.

Groves, R.M., Singer, E., and Corning, A. (2000). Leverage-saliency theory of survey participation: Description and an illustration. *Public Opinion Quarterly*, 64(3), 299–308.

Hylmö, A., and Wennerhag, M. (2012). Does class matter in protests? Social class, attitudes towards inequality, and political trust in European demonstrations in a time of economic crisis. Working Paper, 'Caught in the Act of Protest: Contextualizing Contestation' project, www.protestsurvey.eu/index.php?page=publications&id=22.

King, G., and Zeng, L. (2001). Logistic regression in rare events data. *Political Analysis*, 9(2), 137–163.

Klandermans, B., Van Stekelenburg, J., Van Troost, D., Van Leeuwen, A., Walgrave, S., Verhulst, J., Van Laer, J., and Wouters, R. (2011). *Manual for Data Collection on Protest Demonstrations. Caught in the Act of Protest: Contextualizing Contestation (CCC Project). Version 3.0*. Amsterdam: VU-University of Amsterdam/Antwerp: University of Antwerp.

Leslie, L.L. (1972). Are high response rates essential to valid surveys? *Social Science Research*, 1(3), 323–334.

Manski, C.F., and McFadden, D. (1981). *Structural Analysis of Discrete Data with Econometric Applications*. Cambridge, MA: MIT Press.

Oesch, D. (2006a). *Redrawing the Class Map: Stratification and Institutions in Britain, Germany, Sweden, and Switzerland*. New York: Palgrave Macmillan.

Oesch, D. (2006b). Coming to grips with a changing class structure: An analysis of employment stratification in Britain, Germany, Sweden and Switzerland. *International Sociology*, 21(2), 263–288.

Rogelberg, S.G., Conway, J.M., Sederburg, M.E., Spitzmüller, C., Aziz, S., and Knight, W.E. (2003). Profiling active and passive nonrespondents to an organizational survey. *Journal of Applied Psychology*, 88(6), 1104–1114.

Rüdig, W. (2010). Assessing nonresponse bias in activist surveys. *Quality and Quantity*, 44(1), 173–180.

Van Stekelenburg, J., Walgrave, S., Klandermans, B., and Verhulst, J. (2012). Contextualizing contention: Framework, design, and data. *Mobilization: An International Quarterly*, 17(3), 249–262.

Vehovar, V. (2007). Non-response bias in the European Social Survey. In G. Loosveldt, M. Swyngedouw and B. Cambré (Eds), *Measuring Meaningful Data in Social Research* (pp. 335–356). Leuven: Acco.

Vernersdotter, F. (2012). Den nationella SOM-undersökningen 2011. In L. Weibull, H. Oscarsson and A. Bergström (Eds), *I framtidens skugga: Fyrtiotvå kapitel om politik, medier och samhälle: SOM-undersökningen 2011* (pp. 575–608). Gothenburg: SOM-institutet.

Wahlström, M., and Wennerhag, M. (2014). Alone in the crowd: Lone protesters in West European demonstrations. *International Sociology*, 29(6), 565–583.

Walgrave, S., and Verhulst, J. (2011). Selection and response bias in protest surveys. *Mobilization: An International Quarterly*, 16(2), 203–222.

Index

Aaltonen, Aleksi 96
abolition of May Day, as an event (Italy)
    49; (Spain) 121–2
Acción Libertaria (newspaper) 115
Adenauer, Konrad, 67n58
Alexander, Jeffrey 3, 4, 245, 258
Alfonso XIII, King (of Spain), 118
*Allgemeiner Deutscher
    Gewerkschaftsbund* (ADGB) 26, 45,
    47, 66n42
America: May Day tradition xiv–xv
American Federation of Labor (AFL)
    16, 17; eight hour working day,
    demands for 18
anarchists view of May Day 20, 26n11
Angriff (newspaper) 48
anti-austerity protests 9, 256; and May
    Day demonstrations (Europe) 161
Arbetet (newspaper) 80
Aveling, Edward and Eleanor 19, 136,
    139, 146, 155
Azaña, Manuel 120

Bagge, Gösta 92
Barnes, G.N. 140
Bebel, August 18, 19, 24, 27n15, 46,
    63n7, 246
Belgium: financial crisis (from 2008) 173;
    industrial relations regimes 165–7;
    linguistic and political differences
    166; May Day celebrations and
    demonstrations 176, 180; union
    influence and membership 165–7
Berg, Fridtjuv 100n2
Bergegren, Hinke 78, 80
Bergholm, Tapio x, 5, 6, 10
Berlin (Germany): assemblies 35–6,
    51–2; 'Blutmai' (1929) 24, 46–7;
    Resolution (1890) 23; Wall, fall of

and effect on May Day 61, 254;
    West Berlin 'freedom rallies' 52;
    woodworkers 64n8
Berlusconi, Silvio 61; Government of
    69n79, 170
Bernstein, Eduard 40, 42
Bevan, Aneurin 147, 149
Bobbio, Norberto 254
Bonanni, Raffaele 170
Bonavita, Francesco 248–9, 250
Bourdieu, Pierre 222
Brandt, Willy 54, 63
Branting, Hjalmar 78, 79, 88
Britain: anti-globalization protests
    (twenty-first century) 155;
    Chesterfield May Day 154; children,
    presence at May Day events 137, 141,
    146; cultural celebrations and May
    Day events 140, 152–3; date of May
    Day celebrations, changes to 138–9;
    decline of mass demonstration 151–2;
    economic recession (1920s) 144–5;
    eight-hour working day, demands
    for 138; engineering and engineering
    unions 145; fascism and communism
    146–7; financial crisis (from 2008)
    173; French republicanism, links
    to 134; general strikes (1920s) 146;
    Hyde Park (London), as a venue 135,
    141–2; Independent Labour Party
    (ILP) 147, 148; industrial relations
    regimes 171–2; internationalism,
    as a May Day theme 134–5, 155;
    inter-war period 150; Labour Party
    and the left 147–8; mass support for
    May Day events (pre-WWI) 137–9;
    May Day celebrations and traditions
    11, 133, 179–80, 181–2; miners
    and coal industry nationalization

144–5, 148–50; Monday Club 153;
participation levels, May Day events
139, 142, 144; political background
of 133; post-World War I and II
period 143–4, 150–51; pre-World
War I, demonstrations 134–5, 141–2;
public holiday, May Day, designation
of 153–6; trade union presence
136, 139; unemployment (inter-war
period) 145; union influence and
membership 171–2; World Wars I
and II 142–3
Brockway, Fenner 147
Budapest (Hungary), WWI xiii
Buenacasa, Manuel 119
Bull, Edvard 75, 76, 100n1

Caballero, Largo 119, 120
Camusso, Susanna 255
Cánovas, Antonio del Castillo 108–9
Carlsson, Ingvar 253
Carniti, Pierre 59
Catholic Worker's Association (ACLI),
Italy 53
Caught in the Act of Protest:
Contextualizing Contestation
(CCC) (Euroscores Programme)
160, 187–8, 193, 220, 262, 272–3;
class composition of demonstrations
*200–201, 202, 204–5, 206, 207–8,
210–12*; socio-demographics, profiles
of demonstrators *194–5*
Chicago, Haymarket massacre (1886) *see*
Haymarket massacre
Choi, H.-L. 178, 179
Christian Democratic Party (Italy) 52
coal mining areas (Britain), May Day
events 144–5, 148–50
Cobas (trade union organization,
Italy) 59
Cold War: Finland 98; Germany
50–52; Italy, tensions in 52–3; Soviet
Cold War May Day xiii; Sweden 92;
tension, post-World War II 50–51;
UK 150; USA xv
Comisiones Obreras (CCOO), Spain 125,
126, 127, 168, 177
communism: Berlin Wall, fall of 61, 254;
Britain 146–7; Finland 94, 97, 98;
Germany 45–6; Haymarket massacre
(1886), view of 24; Italy and Italian
Communist Party (PCI) 44; May Day,
view of 24, 45–6; Spain 114
Communist Party (Finland) 97, 98

Communist Party (Italy, PCI) 44, 50,
51, 58, 60
Communist Party (Sweden, SKP)
89, 90–91; separation of May Day
events 91–2
Communist Party of Germany (KPD)
45, 46, 51, 53
Communist Party of Great Britain 145,
146, 148
Communist Party of Spain (PCE) 114,
126, 127
Confederación General del Trabajo
(CGT) 127
Confederación Nacional del Trabajo
(CNT) 111, 114–15, 117, 118, 120,
121, 126, 127; Buenacasa, Manuel
(leader of) 119
*Confederazione Generale Italiana del
Lavoro* (CGIL) 52, 63n3, 169, 170,
179, 255; 1950s–60s 56, 57–8; state
intervention against 54
*Confederazione Italiana Sindacati
Lavoratori* (CISL) 52, 53, 57, 169,
170, 179
*Confederazione Italiana Sindacati
Nazionali dei Lavoratori* (CISNAL)
60, 67n56
Corriere della sera (newspaper) 55
Cossiga, Francesco 55
Crane, Walter 135, 140, 152, 155
Curran, Pete 140

Daily Mail (newspaper) 134, 139
Della Porta, Donatella 7, 161, 170
demonstrations *see* protests and
demonstrations
de Rivera, Primo 116, 118
Der Sozialdemokrat (newspaper) 19
DGB (*Deutscher Gewerkschaftsbund*)
union federation (Germany) 26;
and anti-communism 53; May Day,
view of 55, 58; trade union demands
(1950s) 56
Di Vittorio, Giuseppe 56, 67n55
Durkheim, Émile 3

Ede, Chuter 151
education levels of May Day event
participants 189, 196
Ehrhardt, Ludwig 67n58
eight-hour working day, demands for
16–17; American Federation of Labor
(AFL) role in 18; Britain 138; general
strikes in favour of 21–2; Spain

107–8; workers' movement 16–17, 78, 85, 107–8
Elks, John 149
Engel, Matthew 154
Engels, Friedrich 146
Eriksson-Goldthorpe-Portocarero (EGP) scheme 190–91
EuroMayDay Parade (Italy) 178–9, 181, 228, 233, 256; San Precario 257–8
European Science Foundation (Euroscores Programme), Caught in the Act of Protest: Contextualizing Contestation (CCC) 160, 187–8, 193, 220, 262, 272–3
European Social Survey Round 5 (ESS5) 193, 196, *197*, 199, *202*, 269–70, 272
'eventful protest', May Day as 2, 7–8, 23, 39, 258

Fagerholm, K.-A. 96
Falange, Sección Femenina 122, 124
fascism: Britain 146–7; Finland, development of 93–4; inter-war period 43–4, 48, 49–50; Germany 47–50; 60; Italy, violence and 43; labour day, designation of (Italy) 49–50; Spain 122–5
Federación Regional Española (Spanish Regional Federation) 107
Fédération Nationale des Syndicats 17
Feminist Initiative (F!), Sweden 256–7
festive May Day events 3, 22, 34–5, 40, 51, 56, 61, 113–14, 116–17, 140, 152
Fiesta de Exaltación del Trabajo, as replacement of May Day (Spain) 122
financial crisis (from 2008) 162; impact of 172–3
Finland 97–8; Civil War 76, 87; communism 94, 97, 98; date of May Day celebration, view of 85; divisions within labour movement 87–8; fascism 93–4; Finnish Social Democratic Party (SDP) 83; Finnish Workers' Party 85; Helsinki Workers' Association 83; historical and political background of 82–3; independence from Russia 86; *Isänmaallinen kansanliike* (IKL) 94; labour movement, growth of 86; Lapua movement 94; May Day celebrations (Vappu) 5, 10, 83, 98–9, 100; patriotism and national feeling (WWII) 95–6; 'picnic walk' tradition 83, 84; politicization of Vappu 84–6; post-World War II period 96–7;

prohibition and drinking strike 85; radical socialism, growth of 93; red, flags and use of colour 95; *Työnväen ja talonpoikien liitto* (Union of Workers and Smallholders) 93; Walpurgis Night festivities 83; workers' movement 83; World War I and II, impact of 86, 95–6; 'Wrightist' labour movement 83, 84
Finnish Workers' Party 85
First International (congress of) Geneva 17
Flyg, Nils 92
Folkviljan (newspaper) 77
Forsström, H.J. 83–4
Franco, Francisco, 4, 8, 11, 68n67, 122–4
Frankfurter Allgemeine Zeitung (newspaper) 46, 55
Frankfurter Rundschau (newspaper) 53, 55, 58–9, 60
future of May Day 245, 250–54, 258–9

Gamson, William 235
general strikes: Britain (1920s) 146; campaign for shorter working day 22; employers' measures against (Europe) 33; Germany, against Kapp-Putsch 43; LO (labour confederation), Sweden, call for 81; as May Day demonstration 21–2, 32, 34, 80; Spain (1940s–50s) 123; Sweden (for universal suffrage) 79–80
Germany: assemblies and demonstrations (early twentieth century) 35–6; 1968 movements 57–9; Berlin assemblies 35–6, 51–2; communist view of May Day 45–6; conflicting May Day narratives 62; DGB union federation 26, 55–6; Federal Republic 54; government intervention and May Day celebrations 33, 54; Hamburg demonstrations 35–6, 38; Independent Social Democratic Party of Germany (USPD) 42; inter-war period 41, 42, 44, 62; participation levels, May Day events 36–7, 44, 47, 48–9, 51, 56, 58, 61; police intervention in May Day events 66n37; political environment, early twentieth century 35; post-World War II period 50–52, 62; public holiday, May Day designation of 42–3, 48; radical groups, influence of 39–40; re-appropriation of May

Day (1960s) 57; 'revolutionary First of May' 59–60; right-wing groups, May Day events 60; rituals of May Day 32, 34–5; Second International (congress of), Paris, impact of 32; Social Democratic Party (SPD) 18, 20, 39, 40, 42, 45, 60; social movements (1960s–70s) 57, 68n67; workers' movement 31, 32, 42, 53–5; World War I, impact of 40–41
Gill, Charles 145
Giolitti, Antonio 35, 64n13
globalization, impact of 163–4
Goebbels, Joseph 48
Gompers, Samuel 16, 17
Gonzalez, Felipe 127
Greater London Association of Trade Union Councils (GLATUC) 154, 155
Great Soviet Encyclopaedia (3rd edition, 1979) 24–5
Griffiths, Jim 149

Hamburger Echo (newspaper) 8, 38
Hamburger Nachrichten (newspaper) 33
Hansson, Per-Albin 91, 92
Hardie, Keir 142
Haymarket massacre (1886) xiv, 6, 15–16; communist view of 24; Germany, effect of 32; influence of in Europe 19–20; Italy, effect of 32; Martyrs Monument 26, 26n17–18; Second International (congress of), Paris, links to 25–6; socialist view of 21; Spain, effect of 20, 107
Helsinki Workers' Association 83
Hobsbawm, Eric 1, 14, 133, 245; on origins of May Day 15
Hugenberg, Alfred 47
Hyde Park (London), as a May Day venue 135
Hyndman, Henry 139, 140

'ideology of hope' and utopian visions of May Day 38, 56, 58, 245–50
Iglesias, Pablo 112, 113
Il Giorno (newspaper) 60
Independent Labour Party (ILP), Britain 147, 148
Independent Social Democratic Party of Germany (USPD) 40, 42
industrial relations regimes 163–4; Belgium 165–7; Britain 171–2; Italy 169–70; Spain 168–9; Sweden 164–5; Switzerland 167–8

International Working People's Association 18
Isänmaallinen kansanliike (IKL), Finland 94
Italy: Catholic Worker's Association (ACLI) 53; Confederazione Generale Italiana del Lavoro (CGIL) 52, 54, 56, 63n3, 170, 179; *Confederazione Italiana Sindacati Lavoratori* (CISL) 169, 170, 179; conflict and street demonstrations 36; EuroMayDay Parade 178–9, 181, 228, 233, 256; fascist violence, inter-war period 43; financial crisis (from 2008) 173; government intervention and May Day celebrations 33, 49, 54; industrial relations regimes 169–70; inter-war period 41, 43–4, 62; Italian Communist Party (PCI) 44, 50, 51, 58, 60; Italian Socialist Party (PSI) 32n3, 38, 39, 41; massacres, protests against 38; May Day celebrations and demonstrations 178–9, 181; participation levels, May Day events 36–7, 51, 56, 59; *Partito Democratico* 60, 169; political environment, early twentieth century 35; post-World War II period 50, 52–3, 62; radical groups, influence of 39–40; re-appropriation of May Day (1960s) 57; right-wing groups, May Day events 60; rituals of May Day 32, 34–5; social movements (1960s–70s) 57–9; *Unione Italiana del Lavoro* (UIL) 169, 170, 179; union influence and membership 169–70; workers' movement 31, 32, 39, 54, 170; World War I, impact of 41

Kapp Putsch (1920) 43
Kautsky, Karl 83
Kekkonen, Urho 100
Key, Ellen 79
Klandermans, Bert 160, 218, 219, 225
Kollontaj, Alexandra 81
Kuusinen, Otto Willie 90, 93, 97

Labour Day (21 April), Italy 49
Lafargue, Paul 134
Lafontaine, Oskar 60
Lapua movement (Finland) 94
La República Social (newspaper) 110
La Stampa (newspaper) 33, 43, 49, 52, 53
L' Avanti (newspaper) 34, 37, 42, 43, 44, 49, 248–9; fascist violence against 41

Lavigne, Raymond 17, 19: campaign for shorter working day 22
Ledesma, José Luis x, 6, 10, 250
Liebknecht, Karl 40
Liebknecht, Wilhelm 18, 19
LO (blue-collar trade union confederation), Sweden 81, 90, 165, 175–6, 180, 251
London Trades Council 138, 140, 151, 154, 156
L' Unità (newspaper) 24, 44, 51, 52, 54, 59
Luxemberg, Rosa 23, 40

MacDonald, Ramsey 143
Maizeitung (1907) 38, 39
Manchester Guardian (newspaper) 137, 139
Mann, Tom 138, 139, 140, 147
Margoux, Jules 79
Marßolek, Inge 245, 246
Marx, Eleanor *see* Aveling, Edward and Eleanor
McCormick Reaper factory (Chicago) xiv–xv, 16
McGregor, Hugh 17
Mellberg, Margaretha x, 5, 6, 10
Melliet, Leo 134
Michel, Louise 134
Morales, L. 196
Morris, William 136, 139, 152
Morrison, Herbert 148
Mosely, Oswald 151
Most, Johann 18
Motteler, Julius 140
Mussolini, Benito 49

National Unemployed Workers' Movement (Britain) 145
Nazi Party (NSDAP), May Day rallies and challenges to socialists 47–8
neoliberalism, effect on May Day 161–3, 182, 182n1, 254–8
Nordén, Märta 78
'Nordic Model' 75–6
Norway, radicalism (early twentieth century) 76

Oesch, D. 167, 191; employment class scheme 191, *192*, 193, 198, 199, 276–7
O' Mahoney, Amelia 143
Östlund, Agda 80

Palm, August 77–8, 84
Palme, Olaf 251, 252

Pankhurst, Sylvia 143
Parsons, Albert 18
Partito Democratico (Italy) 60, 169
Pastore, Giulio 52, 53
Peterson, Abby x–xi, 9, 11, 225, 226, 229, 256
Pollitt, Harry 147
protests and demonstrations: 1890, first demonstration in Europe 1, 14, 76, 77, 78, 187; class composition of 198–203, *200–201*, *202*, *204–5*, *206*; classification and typology, of motivations 229–30, *231*, 276–7; collective identity, as motivation 218, 223–4; contextual variations, local and national 228–9; data aggregation, survey results 271–3; to effect change, as motivation 226–7; emotions, as a motivator 236; external influences, as motivation 233–41, *234*, *237*, *238*, *240*; Germany, assemblies and demonstrations 32, 35–6, 46, 51–2; government and politics, protest against 226; ideological motives 219; interest or curiosity, as motivation 227–8; Italy, celebrations and demonstrations 32, 178–9, 181; May Day marches 220–22; moral duty, as motivation 225; motivations behind 218–20; organizers of events, types of 262–3, *264*; post-World War II period 50–51, 96–7; research methods and analysis, into motivations 229–39, 262–77; social motives 223; solidarity, as motivation 224–5; in support of one's own movement 225–6; survey, demonstrations and respondents 263–71, *264–5*, *266–7*, **268**, *270*, *274–6*; as a tradition or habit 222–3; variations in types of motivation 230–36, *232*; view and interpretation of by participants 221–2; Workers' Day, celebration of 221–2
public holiday, May Day designation of 4: Britain 153–6; Finland 96; Germany 42–3, 48, 50; Italy 43, 50, 181; Spain 120; Sweden 91

Rathou, Emilie 80
reappropriation and revitalization of May Day 8, 57–9, 63, 93, 255
red, flags and use of colour 6, 16, 36, 50; Finland 95
Reiter, Herbert xi, 5, 6, 10, 178

right-wing groups, May Day events
(Europe) 60, 82
Rivas, Lucia 15, 115
Romanos, Eduardo xi, 6, 10, 250
Rote Fahne (newspaper) 24, 42,
45, 46, 47
Rucht, Dieter 142, 182
Russian Revolution (1905) 20

Sagasta, Práxedes Mateo 108, 109
SAK (Central Organization of Finnish
Trade Unions) 95, 97–8
San Precario 257–8
Scheidemann, Philipp 5, 42
Schröder, Gerhard 60, 61
Schyman, Gudrun 256
Second International (congress of)
Paris 6, 7, 8, 15, 16–17, 83, 108;
communism, connection to 24;
Germany, workers' movement and
impact of 32; Haymarket massacre
(1886), impact of 17–18, 25–6
Sembat, Marcel 134
Shaw, George Bernard 140
Sindicatos Verticales (trade unions,
Spain) 124, 125, 126
Sköld, Per-Elvin 253
Smith, Ellis 149
sobriety, and May Day
celebrations 5–6
Social Democratic Party (Finland,
SDP) 83, 85–6; divisions within 93;
post-World War II period 97–8
Social Democratic Party of Germany
(SPD) 18, 20, 39, 40, 42, 45, 60;
May Day events organized by
47, 51; public holiday, May Day
designation of 42
Social Democratic Party (Sweden, SAP)
88, 90–91, 165, 175–6, 251, 252
Social-Demokraten (newspaper) 77
Socialist Democratic Federation
(Britain) 138, 140, 142
Socialist Party (Italy, PSI) 32n3,
38, 39, 41
Socialist Party (Spain, PSOE) 110, 127,
168, 169
Socialist Workers' Party (Finland) 93
socialists, impact of May Day on
20–21, 22–3
socio-demographics, profiles of
demonstrators *194–5*; age variations
194–5; class composition and
identification 198–203, *200–201, 202,*
204–5, 206, 207–8; education levels
189, 196; employment class schemes
191, *192*; foreign-born participants
195–6; gender variations 193–4;
labour market trends 191; May Day
events 187–8, 189; non-May Day
events, comparisons with 196, *197*;
'normalization of the protester' 188–9;
party membership 205–9; 'precarious
conditions' of protesters 198; research
methods and analysis 188–90,
193–8; social and political influences
203–13, *210–12*; social class 190;
'social precariat' 163, 196–8; street
protesters 189
Sorel, Georges 115
Sörensen, Anders 80
Sozialistische Einheitspartei Deutschlands
(SED) 51
Soviet May Day, representation of xiii
Spain: anarchism 114–15, 118; Civil
War 121–2; *Comisiones Obreras*
(CCOO), Spain 125, 126, 127, 168,
177; communism and the Communist
Party (PCE) 114, 168; democracy,
transition to 125–7; dictatorship,
impact of 117; dissidence, against
Franco's regime 124–5; dual
nature of May Day 108, 114, 115;
eight-hour working day, demands
for 107–8; *Fiesta de Exaltación del
Trabajo* 122; financial crisis (from
2008) 173; Franco, Francisco 122–4;
geographical variations 117–18;
government intervention and May
Day celebrations 108–9; Haymarket
massacre (1886), impact of 20,
107; industrial relations regimes
168–9; May Day celebrations and
demonstrations 6, 10–11, 108, 112,
115–16, 116, 119–21, 125–7, 177–8,
181; organized political actions, May
Day events 115–17; participation
levels, May Day events 177; *Partido
Socialista Obrero Español* (PSOE)
110, 127, 168, 169; Peninsular War,
commemoration of 106–7; political
differences and May Day event
tactics 109–10, 118–19, 120; religious
symbols and May Day 113; Second
Republic (1931) 119–20; *Sindicatos
Verticales* (trade unions) 124, 125, 126;
socialists' May Day, 113–14; 'Tragic
Week' 112, 128n5; *Unión General de*

Trabajadores (UGT) 109, 111, 112, 117, 118, 120, 126, 127, 168, 177; union influence and membership 168–9; workers' movement 107; World Wars I and II, impact of on May Day events 117
Spencer, George 144
Spies, August 18, 19
Ståhlberg, K.J. 94
Steinkühler, Franz 254
Sterky, Fredrik 101n4
St Joseph's Day 4, 53, 123–4, 125
Suárez, Adolfo 126
Sweden: Cold War, impact of 92; FCOs (central trade union associations) 89, 90, 92; Feminist Initiative (F!), Sweden 256–7; financial crisis (from 2008) 173–4; first demonstrations in, May Day events 77–9; general strike for universal suffrage 79–80; industrial relations regimes 164–5; labour movement (early twentieth century) 75–9, 81; Lill-Jans forest 77; LO (blue-collar trade union confederation) 90, 165, 175–6, 180, 251; Malmö, May Day demonstrations in 77, 78; May Day demonstrations in 2, 10, 76, 90–91, 100, 174–6, 180, 203, 209, 251–2, 253, 273; national unity and May Day events 91; participation levels, May Day events 79, 81–2, 175–6; party politics and May Day events 89, 90–91; police intervention in May Day events 80–81, 101n8; revival of May Day demonstrations (1960s) 92–3; right-wing groups, May Day events 82; Social Democratic Party 88, 90–91, 165, 175–6, 251, 252; Stockholm, May Day demonstrations in 4, 78; Swedish Communist Party (SKP) 89, 90–91, 92; Swedish Left Party 175–6, 180, 256; Swedish Social Democratic Left Party (SSV) 88; Swedish Social Democratic Party (SAP) 77, 88, 89–90, 91; Swedish SOM Institute 193, 203; union influence and membership 164–5; universal suffrage and May Day demonstrations 88; World War II, impact of 91; Young Socialists 80, 81
Swedish Left Party 175–6, 180, 256

Swedish Social Democratic Left Party (SSV) 88
Swedish SOM Institute 193, 203; population survey 271, 272
Switzerland: financial crisis (from 2008) 173–4; industrial relations regimes 167–8; May Day celebrations and demonstrations 176–7, 180–81; union influence and membership 167–8

Taft-Hartley Act xv
Tanner, Väinö 93, 96
Tartakowski, Danielle 19
Thörnqvist, Christer xi, 5, 6, 10
Tillett, Ben 140, 141
Times (newspaper) 137, 140, 152
Togliatti, Palmiro 52
Trades Union Congress (TUC), Britain 148, 154, 180; union membership 156
Turati, Filippo 34, 44
Työnväen ja talonpoikien liitto (Union of Workers and Smallholders), Finland 93

Unamuno, Miguel 106
Unione generale del lavoro (UGL) 60, 69n79, 170
Unione Italiana del Lavoro (UIL) 52, 53, 57, 169, 170, 179
Unión General de Trabajadores (UGT) 109, 111, 112, 117, 118, 120, 126, 127, 168, 177
universal suffrage and May Day demonstrations: Sweden 88; women's right to vote 79–80

Vienna (Austria), May Day 1970 247–8
Vinek, Emile 140
Völkischer Beobachter (newspaper) 47
Volks-Zeitung (newspaper) 33
Vorwärts (newspaper) 1, 17, 22, 23, 34, 37, 38, 42, 43, 47, 48

Wahlström, Mattias xi, 1, 3, 12, 224, 255–6
Walpurgis Night festivities (Finland) 83
Weber, M. 190, 219
Weimar Republic: May Day events under 42–3, 44–7
Wennerhag, Magnus xi, 4, 11, 224, 256
Wicksell, Knut 79, 81
Williams, Jack 141
Wilson, Charles E. xv

Wilson, Harold 151, 152
Woodman, Dorothy 147
workers' movement 66n37; Catholics
    in Italy (post-war) 53; divisions
    within (Germany and Italy) 42,
    43–5, 47; eight-hour working day
    16–17, 78, 85, 107–8; Finland 76,
    83, 83–4, 87; Germany 31, 32, 38,
    42, 48; industrial relations, effect on
    163–4; inter-war period (Europe)
    42, 48; Italy, 31, 32, 38, 39, 49, 53,
    54, 170; May Day, significance of
    15–16, 23, 217; National Unemployed
    Workers' Movement (Britain) 145;
    neoliberalism, effect on 161–3; 'Nordic
    Model' 75; 'picnic walk' tradition
    (Finland), effect on 84; political
    environment, impact of (Europe) 35;
    post-World War II period (Germany
    and Italy) 51; 'social precariat' 163,
    196–8; socio-demographics profiles, of
    demonstrators 190; Spain 107–8, 112;
    state integration (Germany and Italy)
    53–5; Sweden 75–6, 77, 80, 81; union
    influence and membership, decline of
    162; Unitarian rallies (Germany and
    Italy), 1920s 44; violent oppression of
    (Germany) 48; Weimar Republic 47;
    woodworkers (Berlin) 64n8; 'Wrightist'
    labour movement (Finland) 83
Workers' Party of Finland 83
working classes: 'demonstrations' and
    social representations xii–xiii, 3; May
    Day 'rituals' xii
World Federation of Trade Unions 98
World Wars I and II: Britain, impact
    of 142–3; Finland, impact of
    86; Germany, impact of (WWI)
    40–41; inter-war period 41, 150;
    Italy, impact of (WWI) 41; May
    Day demonstrations relating to 8;
    participation levels, May Day events
    (Germany) 49; Spain, impact of 117;
    Sweden, impact of 91
Wright, Victor Julius von 83, 84
Wrigley, Chris xi, 6, 11

For Product Safety Concerns and Information please contact our EU
representative GPSR@taylorandfrancis.com Taylor & Francis Verlag GmbH,
Kaufingerstraße 24, 80331 München, Germany

Printed and bound by CPI Group (UK) Ltd, Croydon, CR0 4YY
08/06/2025
01896991-0013